ANTHROPOLOGY
The Cultural Perspective

ANTHROPOLOGY
The Cultural Perspective

SECOND EDITION

JAMES P. SPRADLEY
late of Macalester College

DAVID W. McCURDY
Macalester College

WAVELAND
PRESS, INC.
Prospect Heights, Illinois

For information about this book, write or call:

    Waveland Press, Inc.
    P.O. Box 400
    Prospect Heights, Illinois 60070
    (708) 634-0081

ISBN 0-88133-442-1

Printed in the United States of America

10 9 8 7 6 5

PREFACE

When work on the first edition of this text began over seven years ago, we believed that cultural anthropology possessed a unique perspective. More important, we felt that the book helped students to see people of other cultures in their own terms. An ethnographic approach stressed the discovery of what others know and do. Ethnological inquiry, including cross-cultural comparison and explanation, highlighted cultural differences, explaining them as reasonable responses in the context of daily life. We called this anthropological approach the *cultural perspective*.

We are still convinced that the cultural perspective is a valuable tool for those trying to make their way in complex modern society. This is clearly true for individuals who must interact with people from societies with very different cultures from theirs as well as appropriate to social intercourse inside their own country. Although we usually assume that fellow citizens share our assumptions and rules for doing things, there are many cultural differences among the countless groups surrounding us. By taking a cultural perspective, we feel that cross-cultural misunderstandings can be avoided or at least handled amicably.

In the first edition we adopted several design strategies that worked best to teach a cultural perspective; we have retained them in this book.

1. We discuss anthropological concepts and theory *in the context of detailed concrete ethnographic situations*. Most chapters use a single case to develop a particular topic. For example, we offer a framework for understanding social structure in the context of Kwakiutl society, and kinship systems are treated in the context of Bhil society. Where extended cases are not feasible to explain a concept, we introduce shorter examples, thus creating more cross-cultural variety.

2. We use *an inductive, problem-solving approach*. We do not simply present concepts and theory in isolation, illustrating each as it is defined; instead, read-

ers are placed in puzzling situations that can be unraveled by using particular concepts. For example, in the context of a Highland New Guinea society, we present the details of everyday life as encountered by an anthropologist in the field. People are caring for pigs, building houses, weeding gardens, and making sacrifices to ancestral ghosts. The problem emerges: How does one discover the way this array of seemingly unrelated customs is interconnected? The concepts of world view and values help make sense of the problem.

3. We focus on *the traditional concepts and assumptions of cultural anthropology*. We feel that the usual concepts most adequately reflect the cultural perspective and are most easily taught by instructors.

4. *We use data and examples from our own society*. We believe that the cultural perspective involves a theory of behavior that applies to people in every group, even anthropologists. To demonstrate the usefulness of the cultural perspective in our own lives, we include several extended cases and numerous examples from our own society. In Chapter 1 we look at the culture of tramps and American prisoners of war in Vietnam. In the chapter on politics we discuss the organization and activities of an antinuclear power group. We use a description of the Jehovah's Witnesses side by side with one of Azande witchcraft in a later chapter on religion.

We have also made several changes based on reader suggestions received during the past four years. By eliminating three chapters, deleting some boxed material, and shortening some examples, we have *reduced the length of the book*. The two chapters on language and communication are now *one* simpler chapter. The two original chapters on fieldwork have been simplified and condensed into one, as have the two chapters on territorial groups and associations.

Even though we have reduced overall length, we have *added some important material*, too. A new chapter on marriage and family structure is included as well as an appendix detailing the appropriate steps for a student ethnographic project. Additional material on primates is discussed in Chapter 4. The chapters on culture, kinship, ecological systems, and economic systems have been substantially revised, and many other chapters incorporate smaller changes for easier reading and clarity. We have also included some theory from cultural evolution, although a functional approach to explanation still prevails.

The information here has more or less been covered in the second paragraph (insert) on pg. 3. Perhaps a final paragraph such as the following one might be appropriate.

Finally, we anticipate that the revised layout of the text will increase readability and that the new material will make the book a more valuable aid to both the instructor and the students.

James P. Spradley
David W. McCurdy

ACKNOWLEDGMENTS

We thank the many people whose assistance and counsel made this edition of *Anthropology: The Cultural Perspective* possible. Among them are Irving Cooper, acquisitions editor, who gave valuable advice and encouragement, Elaine Honig, who edited the manuscript, and Kathy Bendo, who secured new photographs. Several anthropologists provided us with ethnographic data and critical comments, and we are grateful to them. Laura Nader advised us about the anthropology of law and the Zapotec. Mervyn Meggitt contributed both data and interpretation in regard to Mae Enga culture. Rada and Neville Dyson-Hudson provided extensive ethnographic data and comments about the Karimojong. We also thank Paul A. Dahlquist for reading and revised manuscript for the second edition and giving comments and advice. Mary Lou Burket, Elizabeth Throop, and Jean Huff have contributed invaluable assistance in the preparation of the book. Finally, we could not have completed this work without the support and encouragement of Barbara Spradley, Carolyn McCurdy, and our children. We appreciate their patience and their understanding of a project that intruded into family life.

J.P.S.
D.W.M.

CONTENTS

CHAPTER ONE

Culture

Anthropology is the study of human beings. Forty years ago this science was a mystery to most people. It brought to mind exotic places and strange customs, explorers in khaki shorts and pith helmets, stones and bones, the missing link, and digging up the past. In recent years the mystery has faded and some anthropologists have even become an attraction on the late-night talk shows. Still, many people have only vague and outdated ideas about anthropology. This book concerns only the largest subfield, cultural anthropology, which narrows the focus of research to the thousands of cultures human beings have created. While some cultural anthropologists continue to study remote nonliterate peoples, others are investigating the ways people behave in New York subways, urban high schools, and neighborhood taverns. From aborigine encampments in Australia to courtrooms of North American cities, anthropologists are at work describing cultures. They listen to children, judges, grandmothers, clan chiefs, and corporate executives. They record tribal initiation rites and college graduation ceremonies; they study the ways of native curers in Mexican villages and psychotherapists in U.S. cities. Their investigations share a common goal: to discover cultural similarities and differences wherever they occur.

Even a casual glance at what people do from one society to another reveals striking differences. When a Toda woman from south India reaches physical maturity, she marries a group of brothers. A Bunyoro man from Africa first marries when he is about 35 years old and thereafter acquires as many more wives as he can afford. In the recent past the Jalé of Highland New Guinea ate the enemies they killed in combat; American soldiers in Vietnam piled them up and counted them. On Taiwan, Chinese farmers teach their children that there is no justification for hitting another person; in the United States parents encourage their sons to fight back when attacked. Many young American couples employ chemical, mechanical, and surgical means to limit family size; in rural India a man and his wife remember the gods faithfully to ensure the birth of many healthy offspring. A president of the United States buries the family dog in a carefully manicured cemetery plot complete with headstone and sentimental epitaph; a Bontok Igolot from the Philippines divides his canine with the members of his family at dinner. Such differences in behavior occur because people have learned different cultures.

THE NATURE OF CULTURE

In this book we will define <u>culture</u> as *the acquired knowledge that people use to interpret experience and to generate behavior.* This cultural knowledge is like a set of tools for getting along in life. All of us make use of what we know to make sense out of what happens (to interpret experience) and to act appropriately (to generate behavior)—we make continual use of our culture for these purposes (see Figure 1-1). It is impossible, for instance, to drive a car without knowing the cultural rules for interpreting red and green lights, the purpose of ignition keys and accelerator pedals, and the intentions of other drivers. In order to drive a car in appropriate ways you need to stay on the right side of the street, stop at red lights, yield to oncoming cars when turning left, and a host of other things. Driving automobiles is only one cultural activity. In a typical day you might also use your culture to buy food, shop for clothes, write thank you notes, enroll in college, work in a factory, and buy a birthday present for your father.

Both uses of culture—to interpret experience and to generate behavior—occur together in actual situations. We are constantly making interpretations and using them to guide our actions. Although they occur simultaneously, we want to consider them separately for purposes of clarity.

Interpreting Experience

Imagine that you were to visit an Ibo village in Nigeria and to stay in the hut of Unoka, a man described by Chinua Achebe in his novel *Things Fall Apart.* You might record the following scene:

One day a neighbor called Okoye came in to see him. He was reclining on a mud bed in his hut playing on the flute. He immediately rose and shook hands with Okoye, who then unrolled the goatskin which he carried under his arm, and

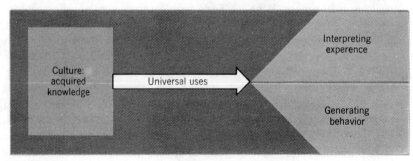

FIGURE 1-1
The culture concept.

sat down. Unoka went into an inner room and soon returned with a small wooden disc containing a kola nut, some alligator pepper and a lump of white chalk.

"I have kola," he announced when he sat down, and passed the disc over to his guest.

"Thank you. He who brings kola brings life. But I think you ought to break it," replied Okoye, passing back the disc.

"No, it is for you, I think," and they argued like this for a few moments before Unoka accepted the honor of breaking the kola. Okoye, meanwhile, took the lump of chalk, drew some lines on the floor, and then painted his big toe.[1]

In this brief encounter between Okoye and Unoka, many things have occurred. Certain forms of social behavior took place such as calling on a neighbor, talking, playing a flute, shaking hands, breaking a kola nut, and unrolling a goatskin. The encounter has been a brief event in the normal course of life for two Ibo men. Objects were present such as the kola nut, the lump of chalk, the mud bed, the hut, and the alligator pepper. If you stayed among the Ibo for many days, you would see similar kinds of encounters.[2]

While these actions are part of Ibo experience, *they are not part of Ibo culture.* Even the recurrent patterns of behavior like shaking hands, playing the flute, offering a kola nut, and arguing over who should break the kola are not part of Ibo culture. Our definition rules out the people, the objects, the place itself as features of this culture. Culture refers only to the knowledge that people use to interpret actions, objects, and events. For Okoye and Unoka, their culture consists of all the things they must know in order to understand life and act appropriately as adult Ibo men. It includes their beliefs about how neighbors should treat one another, their rules for visiting and showing hospitality, their standards for evaluating kola nuts, their ideas about how to feel toward each other, and many other important conceptions. To paraphrase Ward Goodenough's classic definition of culture, "Ibo culture is not a material phenomenon; it does not consist of things like mud beds and kola nuts, people like neighbors, behavior like playing the flute, or emotions that people feel when they break kola nuts together. It is rather an organization of these things. It is the forms of things that the Ibo have in mind, their models for perceiving, relating, and otherwise interpreting them."[3]

Because the Ibo experience is unfamiliar to us, we easily recognize that it has special cultural meaning to men like Unoka and Okoye. Within our own society, however, we seldom distinguish between the events and objects of experience and

[1]Chinua Achebe is the most prominent African novelist, and his works provide an excellent introduction to Ibo life and culture. Achebe was born a member of the Ibo tribe in 1930 and has written numerous books and short stories. The preceding selection is from his best known, *Things Fall Apart.* London: William Heinemann, Ltd., 1958, pp. 9–10. Three other books dealing with changes in the Ibo culture are *No Longer at Ease,* Greenwich: Fawcett, 1960; *Arrow of God,* New York: John Day, 1964; and *A Man of the People,* Garden City, N.Y.: Doubleday, 1966.

[2]See Victor C. Uchendu, *The Igbo of Southeast Nigeria,* New York: Holt, Rinehart and Winston, 1965, for an anthropological study of a group of people closely related to those dealt with in Achebe's novels.

[3]Ward H. Goodenough, "Cultural Anthropology and Linguistics," Georgetown University Monograph Series on Language and Linguistics, No. 9, 1957, p. 167.

the cultural knowledge for interpreting that experience. Most people take it for granted that reality is present in pretty much the same form to everyone. This outlook is called *naïve realism*, a view that carries with it the security of certain knowledge.

Skid Row: U.S.A.[4]

We can clarify the distinction between culture and experience if we look at some people who live on skid row in most large cities in the United States. Imagine that you were to visit the older, deteriorating sections of a city such as Chicago, Seattle, Boston, or Minneapolis. You set out to make some observations one morning about 11 o'clock. A lone man moves slowly along the sidewalk toward you. Everything about him seems to announce to the world that he is down and out. Ill-fitting clothes cover a hollow chest and sagging muscles. The lines in his face, half hidden beneath the shadow of a faded hat, suggest that he is old before his time. His shoes are cracked with age and exposure to the weather. An overcoat, pocket bulging from a half-empty bottle, covers a sports jacket that long ago found its way to a secondhand clothing store. His course is unsteady, his face unshaven, and as he passes, you are assaulted by the odor of cheap wine. He stops at the end of the street and leans against the brick wall of an old building; here he will stay for an hour or more. You wonder, "Who is this man and what is he doing?"

A black and white police car cruises slowly down the street, and the uniformed men inside look at you and the man leaning against the building. Across the street another man, younger and slightly better dressed, enters a liquor store. Several minutes later he appears with a small package cradled in his arm and turns up a side street. When the light changes you follow him, observing that he has entered an alley half a block away. You slow down at the entrance to the alley to peer after the man; then you stop to see what he will do. He joins three or four other men, some sitting on a loading dock, others standing, and they form a close group. A bottle passes from one man to the other; each person raises it to his lips for a quick drink. You wonder how these men met and what they are doing.

By chance you look across the street and up the long alley in the other direction. It is dark and cavernous, lined with tall buildings, and bordered here and there with cans of trash and garbage. An older man, his white hair nearly shoulder length, makes his way in your direction while pushing what appears to be an old baby carriage. He stops before a dark outcropping of debris and picks something up and throws it into the carriage. As he approaches, you can see bottles, wire, and other objects that cover the bottom of the carriage. He passes you without a word and moves off in the direction of the group of men. When he arrives where they have congregated he stops; you can see that someone hands him the bottle for a quick gulp.

You decide to circle the block and return to this alley later in the afternoon. In front of some doorways you have read signs such as "Cliff's Bar" and "Vera's Bar and Grille"; neon lights announce various brands of beer through dark and dirty windows. You pass another bar and a man approaches you with a package of

[4]James P. Spradley, *You Owe Yourself a Drunk: An Ethnography of Urban Nomads*, Boston: Little, Brown, 1970.

screwdrivers and wrenches and asks, "Would you like to buy some good tools for $2? They're worth $5." You decline this offer and then watch as others are stopped and asked the same question. Finally, you see the tools change hands and the man pockets the money he received and walks into the bar. At a convenient place you stop and observe some people on the other side of the street. A man enters a small storefront with a sign over the door, "Ace Blood Bank"; within 5 minutes he appears again and heads up the street. About an hour later you will see him enter the Ace Blood Bank again, this time to remain inside for more than 30 minutes. You wonder what he is doing and why he returned for this second visit.

Tramp Culture

What you have seen, heard, and experienced are all subject to cultural interpretations. If you talked to the men you observed and found out how they defined life on skid row, things would appear differently (see Figure 1-2). The first man you saw walking down the street was not a down-and-outer or a vagrant loitering on the street. Like the others, he was one kind of "tramp" engaged in carrying out a complex plan for "making it." More specifically, he was a "mission stiff" trying to "meet a live one." From one perspective, each of the men you saw were doing the same thing, "trying to make it." In order to satisfy a number of basic wants, including food, clothing, a place to sleep, something to drink, and money for travel,

The original name for the older, deteriorating sections of town was skid road, *a term that originated in Seattle to describe the road down which logs were skidded to the sawmill. Bars, flophouses, gambling houses, and other places common to the lives of tramps were prevalent along this road. The name became* skid row *as it was adopted throughout the country. This mission stands on a corner near the heart of Seattle's skid row. "Making the mission" is a strategy for making it that many tramps use for a variety of purposes. They may go for a single meal, for sleeping a single night, to find a job, to get clothing to "peddle," or they may get on the program. The mission stiff travels from mission to mission.*

tramps have learned cultural rules for getting along. This mission stiff had selected a corner, not merely to stand idly or to rest, but with an eye to meeting a live one, some individual who would spontaneously offer him money, a job, or something to drink. The uniformed policemen who drove by were, from a tramp's perspective, two "bulls," a cultural category that includes several kinds of bulls. A tramp's very survival can sometimes depend on knowing how to identify each kind of bull and how to anticipate their behavior.

The man you saw come out of the liquor store was also a tramp, one his peers would call a "home guard tramp" because he rarely traveled beyond this city. He was not simply buying a bottle but was "making a run," a particular strategy for making it if you have no money. Before you saw him he had joined the group in the alley as they collectively engaged in a way to make it called "pooling," each contributing a small amount to purchase a single item. Because this home guard tramp had no money to add to the combined capital of the group, he offered another resource; he would go to the store to purchase the bottle and thereby establish his rights to share in its contents.

The man with the baby carriage was another home guard tramp who was trying to make it by "junking," collecting bottles, copper wire, and other things that could be sold to a nearby junk company. For him, and others who have learned this culture, the carriage was actually a "junky cart." For tramps, a junky cart has many meanings that an outsider could never discover by observation. One man joined with a partner in Chicago and secured a large cart. As he pushed it from one place to another, the second tramp slept peacefully, hidden beneath an old coat and an odd assortment of junk they had collected. From time to time they traded places. When the old man you saw junking joined the tramps drinking in the alley, he employed still another way to make it, "cutting in on a jug."

It was a "box car tramp" who approached you trying to sell tools; his efforts took the form of "taking a rake-off." While in a bar, he met a man who had

FIGURE 1-2

Kinds of tramps. Tramps recognize many different attributes for distinguishing among these various types. For example, a ding *is a professional panhandler or beggar; a* bindle stiff *and an* airedale *are men who carry all belongings in a bedroll and travel from town to town along the railroad tracks, the* airedale *walking, the* bindle stiff *riding. Rubber tramps travel from place to place in old cars; mission stiffs survive by going to skid row missions, where they must take a* nose dive, *a reference to bowing the head in prayer.*

Tramp		
	Rubber tramp	
	Mission stiff	Professional nose diver
		Nose diver
	Home guard tramp	
	Airedale	
	Working stiff	Sea tramp
		Construction tramp
		Fruit tramp
		Tramp miner
		Harvest tramp
	Bindle stiff	
	Box car tramp	
	Ding	

"boosted" the tools from a department store, a specialized kind of stealing. This man did not want to sell the tools on the street himself. An informal contract with the box car tramp guaranteed both men a part of the profits from the sale. The second man acted as salesman and took a "rakeoff." When he finally accomplished his task, he joined the other man inside the bar to conclude their brief economic partnership. While you saw bars with names of current or former owners, tramps saw different kinds of bars like "working bars," "bull-dagon bars," and "hangouts," each with special cultural meaning. Some were places to "perform"; others were places to find employment. Even the alleys and doorways are culturally defined as places to drink or sleep; trash cans and large boxes can quickly become a concealed bed for a tramp who is "trying to make a flop." The man you saw entering the Ace Blood Bank was "peddling blood," or "making the blood bank," in order to earn money for his personal wants.

These terms are not simply colorful names for kinds of people, actions, places, and objects that are apparent to any observer. They convey special meanings to tramps that would be impossible to discover by observation alone. Tramps have acquired a complex culture, one that enables them to interpret these things in a particular way. And they also use this cultural knowledge to act in ways they consider appropriate: making a jug, avoiding the bulls, meeting a live one, making a run, junking, pooling, peddling, making a flop, and hundreds of other complex behavior patterns. If instead of visiting skid row in some large city, you were observing people in an isolated forest homestead in Ecuador, it would be even more difficult to grasp the meaning of their experience. But whether one lives on skid row, in the Equadorian forest, or in a university dormitory, cultural knowledge provides us with the means for interpreting experience.

Generating Behavior

A fundamental requirement for all social life is the ability to read the actions of other people correctly and to anticipate what they are going to do. Often, in order to act, we must interpret other aspects of our experience as well: the time of day, where we are located in space, and the meaning of objects in the environment. Interpreting experience and generating behavior are, thus, closely interwoven in the course of life. The relationship between culture and behavior is complex, but we can begin by considering some artifacts, objects that some would say are part of a culture.

When an anthropologist sets out to study another culture, the most obvious features of life are human behavior and the artifacts in use. One sees people hunting and building fires and making spears. They eat, talk, plant crops, treat the sick, build houses, and do hundreds of other things. Although some behavior is unique to individuals, the vast majority of activities are generated by cultural knowledge shared by members of the society. The anthropologist observes behavior and artifacts with an eye to discovering the cultural knowledge that underlies them. Cultural knowledge is like a recipe for producing behavior and artifacts. Consider the following example.

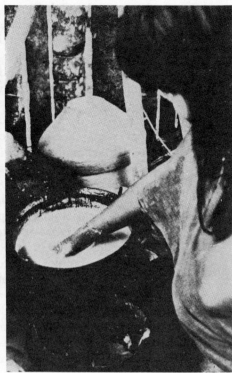

Left, a Jívaro woman stirring boiled sweet manioc mash in conjunction with mastication to prepare it for fermentation. Right, another Jívaro woman dipping out fermented manioc beer to serve to guests.

At the foot of the Andes, in the forests of eastern Ecuador, lives a fierce group of Indians known as the Jivaro.[5] Scattered over nearly 2000 square miles of forest are some 245 houses where the Jivaro live. Individual families, composed of a man, his wives, and children, occupy single oval houses isolated deep in the forest. A large garden that surrounds each house contains crops such as sweet manioc, peanuts, maize, yams, pineapple, and onions. The men hunt with poison darts and blow guns. They use special poison to kill fish in the nearby streams and rivers. The Jivaro have learned a complex culture, developed over many generations, for surviving in this dense forest.

If you visited these isolated homesteads, as Michael Harner did in 1956, you would observe many activities associated with the main crop, sweet manioc. Men clear the land for gardens; women plant, weed, and harvest the manioc. The women have learned cultural recipes for making beer from the manioc and nearly

[5]Michael J. Harner, *The Jivaro: People of the Sacred Waterfalls*, Garden City, N.Y.: Anchor Press/Doubleday, 1973.

everyone drinks beer each day. Men will consume an average of three or four gallons apiece each day and women must prepare beer for their husband and his frequent guests. Women drink one or two gallons daily and even 10-year-old children drink half a gallon each day. The women harvest the manioc early in the morning, cut it in pieces, boil it, then make a mash, which they chew and spit back into the pot. The liquid is separated from the manioc fibers, mixed with water, and allowed to ferment.

These cultural recipes for making manioc beer consist of instructions for putting things together in a meaningful way. They specify the necessary equipment, the proper sequence of steps involved, and even the required time intervals. They identify things to do that are appropriate such as chewing the manioc mash and returning the masticated material to the pot. Their recipes rule out a vast number of inappropriate acts such as allowing men to harvest the manioc or chew the mash.

But the cultural recipes of the Jivaro cover more than preparing food and drinks. Culture consists of instructions for generating the whole range of appropriate behavior. For example, the Jivaro believe that Nunui, a supernatural or class of supernaturals, cause the manioc to grow by pushing the plants up from underneath the ground. Nunui comes out at night seeking cleared places to dance. The Jivaro provide these by clearing the forest for manioc gardens. The women carefully weed the gardens to keep them clear for Nunui's dancing; otherwise Nunui would go deep underground and the plants would suffer accordingly. Nunui causes the manioc to grow at night; they decrease in size during the day. This leads the women to harvest the tubers early in the morning before their size decreases. The women also sing songs to Nunui as they approach the garden in order to appease her. They also believe that manioc plants can suck human blood from those who pass unprotected through the garden. For this reason, adults warn children to stay clear of the gardens. Visitors who must walk through the garden to approach the house will wear a manioc plant in their belts as protection. Jivaro culture, then, provides individuals with recipes for how to behave in many different situations. Thus they use their culture to generate appropriate behavior.

UNIVERSAL CHARACTERISTICS OF CULTURE

Every culture is used by people to interpret experience and to generate behavior. And every culture is a complex system of meaning. This is equally true of the culture used by the Jivaro in the Equadorian forest and the members of the Stock Exchange in New York City. We can better understand the concept of culture by examining those characteristics that are present in every human culture.

Culture is Composed of Categories

Every system of cultural knowledge is made up of categories. A category is any group of objects, persons, activities, or events that people treat as if they were equivalent. We have already seen how tramps use categories for their own identities, for different kinds of police officers, and for actions like "making a run." The

Jivaro categorize the various crops grown in their gardens and activities aimed at appeasing supernatural beings. Cultural categories are such a permanent feature of our lives that we often overlook their importance.

Let us look at a common category in American football. At various times during any football game players will throw the ball through the air in the direction of other players who usually try to catch it. These efforts at throwing and catching the ball take an infinite variety of forms. Sometimes the ball goes long distances; other times it travels only a few feet. Some balls travel toward the end of a playing field, others toward the sideline or even off the playing field. Sometimes a single person attempts to catch the ball, other times a whole group of players scramble to catch it. As the ball travels through the air it may wobble, spiral, turn end-over-end, or move in some other pattern. If you watched every football game played in the United States during any season you would never see one of those "throwing and catching" activities exactly like any other. Each one would be unique. However, players, referees, and those who know the culture of American football group all these distinct activities together into a single cultural category: *the forward pass.* For purposes of playing football, all these different activities are treated as forward passes.

In a similar fashion, cultural categories classify and organize every aspect of human experience. In the mountainous interior of Zamboanga Peninsula on the island of Mindanao in the Philippines, lives a group of people called the Subanun.[6] Their culture contains hundreds of thousands of categories. An important category with many subcategories is one called "persons" (*getaw*). If you observed a ritual offering in process it would be easy to see some of the persons involved. Several women prepare a cereal food and serve it with a side dish of meat and some rice wine. Someone lights incense and strikes a resonant porcelain bowl in rhythmic fashion. Several people work together to construct a small platform or altar; many people eat the food after it is offered to unseen persons recognized by the Subanun. As an outsider it would be impossible to immediately grasp how individuals classify the various persons involved. Only through patient inquiry could you discover the different cultural categories employed by the Subanun (see Figure 1-3).

The Subanun have terms for the various categories of participants at their ceremonial offerings. Everyone present is a getaw, or person. Subcategories of getaw include "souls," "demons," "assistants," "mediums," "raw-food-eating gods," and many more. In order to understand the activities connected with offerings, you would first need to distinguish among the various categories of participants in the way that the Subanun do. The "raw-food-eating gods," for example, are persons who periodically go up the streams of Subanun country and then send disasters on the people—disease epidemics or rats and locusts, the "pets" of these gods, that destroy crops.

Categories enable human beings to escape from the confusion of a world where everything is different and unique. Once a person is classified as an "assistant,"

[6]Charles O. Frake, "A Structural Description of Subanun 'Religious Behavior,' " in Ward Goodenough, ed., *Explorations in Cultural Anthropology*, Chicago: Aldine, 1964.

Persons	Supernaturals	Souls	
		Spirits	
		Demons	
		Gods	Sky gods
			Raw-food-eating gods
			Sunrise gods
			Underworld gods
	Mortals	Functionaries	
		Assistants	
		Beneficiaries	
		Audience	

FIGURE 1-3
Participants in Subanum offerings. (Source. Adapted from Table 1, p. 118 in Charles O. Frake, "A Structural Description of Subanum 'Religious Behavior,'" in Ward Goodenough, editor, Explorations in Cultural Anthropology, 1964.)

"medium," or "sky god," the Subanun know what to expect from such a person in the context of offerings. The person may not always behave appropriately, but at least knowing how to categorize others gives some degree of security in a complex world.

Culture is a Symbolic Code

Every culture has the characteristics of a code. Codes involve symbolic meanings assigned to things; people learn these meanings and use them to order their lives. Let us consider an actual code, which will help us understand this characteristic of all cultures.[7]

During the Vietnam War many American servicemen became prisoners of war. Beginning as early as 1965 some were kept in isolated cells at the famous "Hanoi Hilton." Complete separation from other POWs was part of the Vietcong strategy for reeducating these men. Although placed in adjacent cells, the POWs had no visual contact with each other and if they called to one another severe punishment followed. Under these circumstances a code came into use that allowed communication by tapping on the walls between cells. The POWs literally learned to "talk through the walls" by means of a simple "tap code." Use of this code allowed them to maintain organization and higher morale, and enhanced their chances for survival. Men with years of imprisonment learned recent news from new prisoners; recent arrivals learned what to expect from more experienced POWs.

[7]Philip Butler, "The Tap Code: Ascribed Meanings in Prisoner of War Communications," *Urban Life: A Journal of Ethnographic Research*, 5, 1977, pp. 399–416.

During the Vietnam War, U.S. prisoners were incarcerated in isolation cells that precluded verbal communication. In this prison, dubbed the "Hanoi Hilton" by the Americans, the prisoners developed the tap code.

The "tap code" used the letters of the alphabet (minus the letter K) arranged in rows and columns like this:

		Columns				
		1	2	3	4	5
Rows	1	A	B	C	D	E
	2	F	G	H	I	J
	3	L	M	N	O	P
	4	Q	R	S	T	U
	5	V	W	X	Y	Z

The number of taps for each letter followed this arrangement. A POW first tapped the number of the row, then, after a brief pause, tapped out the number of the column. Thus the letter "C" became one tap (row 1) followed by three taps (column 3). For the POW, whether tapping or listening through the cell wall, this series of taps symbolized the letter "C."

The POWs assigned meaning to the tapping sounds and their system for doing this became a *code*. The tapping sounds were transformed into *symbols*, which carried meaning. Every culture assigns symbolic meaning to patterns of sound, movement, objects, places, people, and many other things. Consider the color and style of hair in our own society. Afro hairstyles, bouffant hairstyles, pigtails, long hair, short hair, bald heads, bleached hair, dyed hair—all have their symbolic meaning. All have coded information attached to them that we "read" and understand without hesitation. Or take the cultural codes associated with our eyes. Staring, rolling your eyes, winking, fluttering the eyelids, piercing gazes, staring vacantly, squinting—all these different eye movements have meanings associated with them.

Cultural codes can be usefully compared with the genetic code. A genetic code is used to store information chemically. You acquired a large amount of biological information from your parents about the color of your eyes, the number of teeth and fingers you have, the size of your ears, and much more. Until recently, it was known that this information was stored within the sex cells, but no one knew the rules for decoding it. Now the genetic code is rapidly being deciphered. The chromosomes within the nucleus of each living cell contain millions of molecules of a chemical substance called DNA (Deoxyribonucleic Acid). The molecular structure of DNA is not unlike a spiral staircase with a limited number of different stairs that can be arranged into a larger number of patterns. The particular way in which these stairs are arranged codes the information necessary to assemble amino acids into proteins. While there are less than 35 amino acids, these, in turn, code hundreds of millions of proteins that account for the variety of all living things. The genetic code allows for an enormous amount of information to be reduced to microscopic size and then passed from one generation to the next.

Cultural information is not coded chemically, but symbolically. Instead of being limited to a material such as DNA, cultural codes involve symbols that can be arranged into an infinite number of combinations. It is this feature of culture that is at the root of human variation.

Culture Is an Arbitrary System

Every culture assigns meaning to things in an arbitrary fashion. As anthropologists have studied cultures all over the world, one fact has become clear: a particular culture does not result from a discovery of the natural groupings of objects in the environment. Not even scientists discover the way things "really are." The categories of a culture are not given *carte blanche*: they are invented by people to classify and organize experience. We all divide up our worlds, but the categories we use are not god-given. This means that the culture of the anthropologist, as well as those of tramps and the Subanun, is an arbitrary system.

The POWs in Vietnam could have arranged the alphabet in a different manner to create a different system of taps. They could have assigned a number to each letter in the alphabet and tapped numbers to represent letters. Like all cultural systems, the one they selected and used was arbitrary. At the same time, once the

POWs had agreed on following the "tap code" with five rows and five columns of letters, they used it consistently. Individuals did not decide to change the code each day. Changes did occur, but they did not alter the entire system. For example, two more columns were added for the numbers one to ten. Once this new addition was agreed to, it became part of the code and was used in a consistent fashion.

In the same way, all cultural codes, although arbitrary, are not used in a random fashion. Assigned meanings tend to remain consistent over time. A tramp who survives by going from one religious mission on skid row to another is called a mission stiff. If he continues to act in this symbolic way tomorrow, next week, next month, he will continue to be seen as a mission stiff. Other tramps will not call him a mission stiff today, a bull next week, and an anthropologist next month. The agreed-on meanings of a culture can and do change, but not in a random or capricious manner. When changes occur, a process we will examine carefully in Chapter 17, new symbols with consistently assigned meanings emerge.

Culture Is Learned

Another universal characteristic of culture is that human beings acquire it through learning. Consider the experience of the POWs who had to *learn* the "tap code." When new prisoners arrived at the Hanoi Hilton, they were immediately placed in isolated cells. Unfamiliar with the "tap code," they found themselves without any means of communicating with other POWs. Then one day would come a series of taps on the wall of their cell. What did it mean? Who was on the other side? The first message worked out to help newcomers learn the code involved eight taps followed by nine taps. This meant "HI" in a code that merely used the place of each letter in the alphabet (ABCDEFG*H*, ABCDEFGH*I*). When a new POW had deciphered this meaning, he would respond with the same number and sequence to say "HI" in return. Then began a long and repetitious process during which the veteran POW would attempt to teach the "tap code" to the newcomer using only taps. It usually took several weeks of patient work for the newcomer to grasp the symbolic meaning of the tapping sounds.

All cultures are learned in much the same way. Children see their elders doing things they do not understand. Through imitation followed by correction from the adults, the child slowly begins to catch on to the system of coded meanings. Once a POW learns the code, he can begin learning other things about life in the POW camp more rapidly. Once a child learns the cultural code of a native language, learning the larger cultural code speeds up.

A central task of every species is to transmit information for survival from one generation to the next. The genetic code is a device that enables all animals to encode specific information and pass it from one generation to the next. Although some animals also teach things to their offspring, biologically coded messages are responsible for the greater part of behavior. With hundreds of species, the offspring hatch from eggs and never interact with the parents and yet, because of genetic inheritance, their adaptive behavior is the same as the parents'.

Human survival, on the other hand, depends as much on cultural inheritance as on biological inheritance. Throughout our lives we receive new information, integrate it with previous learning, and rearrange our total store of knowledge. Unlike social insects whose patterns of interaction are determined by genetically coded messages, human social relations in every society are governed by acquired cultural knowledge. Because culture is learned in a social context, much of what anyone knows is shared with other people.

Take the matter of cleanliness in our own culture. Long before you learned to talk or understand what others said, you knew that some things were "clean" and others "dirty." You acquired these concepts in various ways. Your father or mother rewarded you with warmth and security after a bath or at other times when your odor and appearance were clean. This experience was not forthcoming when you soiled yourself; you were, at these times, washed with a rough cloth, and clean diapers replaced dirty ones. When you played with your food, placed it in your hair, or smeared it on your clothing, you sensed parental disapproval. Objects and places acquired meaning as you sensed the anxiety of a parent when you ate dirt in your yard or reached into a garbage can. By a thousand subtle cues, such as a wrinkled nose, a tone of disgust, or rough physical intervention, you acquired this early knowledge. With increased language facility, the term "clean" or "dirty" was attached to words, stories, clothes, places, smells, and people. You had acquired the cultural code for cleanliness in our society.

Culture Is a Tool
for Accomplishing Human Purposes

It is important to recognize that people are not pawns of their culture. Cultural knowledge is not a rigid mold, but rather like a set of tools used by a craftsman in his work. The tools used depend on goals, available material with which to work, the immediate situation, and many other factors. Old tools can be set aside temporarily or discarded; new ones can be created or modified to meet a specific need. For example, one of the authors was told by the people of a Bhil village in central India that on the second day of one annual festival, two ritual specialists toss a bundle of colored strings over the cooling ashes of the fire. This is done nine times in order to bless the strings, which are then tied to cattle to keep them healthy and productive. When the tossing of the bundle was observed, however, one man dropped the bundle and it was thrown over the ashes 12 times instead of 9. Later, when asked about these deviations, the informant explained that the specialists had been drunk, which caused one to drop the bundle and both to lose count of the times it had crossed the fire. Therefore they threw "a few extra times to make sure it was blessed properly and would work on the cattle."

This incident shows how variation occurs within the limits of culture. Both men knew what they wanted—to bless the strings in order to protect the cattle. Because they were drunk, a condition expected of people at the festival, they failed to perform the ceremony in the prescribed way. Their cultural knowledge was used to evaluate this failure, to plan other courses of action, and finally to behave as they did. They finished their ritual satisfied that the original goal had been met. They *used* their culture; they were not regimented by it.

One way culture handles variation from what is considered appropriate is by means of *rules for breaking rules*. In the United States it is appropriate to drive cars on the right side of the street, but many conditions can make this undesirable. For example, cultural rules for breaking this rule include conditions such as road construction, passing other vehicles, creating humorous situations for motion pictures, and passing animals that block the roadway. Variation also occurs because people are not always motivated to interpret situations or to behave in ways that are appropriate. Cultural knowledge is a dynamic system that changes, in part, because people deviate from their cultural rules.

Culture Exists at Different Levels of Awareness

Once people have acquired a specific cultural heritage it seems like second nature to them. Indeed, most people tend to confuse their cultural heritage with "human nature." In part, this is due to the fact that much of our culture is outside of awareness. We have learned elaborate cultural rules for acting, feeling, and even thinking, but the rules remain hidden from view. When someone points them out it is easy to feel that we act or feel a certain way because it is "natural," not because it is cultural. Anthropologists distinguish between two levels of awareness: explicit and tacit.

The cultural knowledge that people discuss, explain, and talk about is called explicit culture. Parents instruct their children in the proper ways to behave and feel; they give them reasons for doing things in one way and not another. As tramps talk about their behavior and the meaning of experience, newcomers to the world of skid row acquire this cultural knowledge. Earlier we noted that a man entered the Ace Blood Bank, stayed a few minutes, and then left to return again for a longer period several hours later. If you could listen to this man talk about the meaning of his actions he would say something like this.

I went in there to sell a pint of blood. You can give only whole blood every eight weeks, but you can give plasma three times a week. They pay you $5 a pint for both. They test you and if you've got high blood pressure, or if your pulse isn't right, you can't give blood. When you have the shakes you can't give blood because the girls at the blood bank will see you are shaking and nervous. What I usually do is drink some red port wine so my blood pressure and pulse become normal, but I couldn't make a jug this morning 'cause I was broke. When I came to the blood bank this morning they checked me and said I couldn't give blood. Well, I know the girls there pretty well and one of them says to me, "Here's 75¢, go down and get yourself a bottle and drink it and then come back." When I came back, they took my blood and then took the 75¢ out of the $5 I got for the blood.

This account includes cultural knowledge widely shared by tramps that they use in making the blood bank. Like the other ways to make it, some features of this strategy involve explicit culture that tramps talk about in the course of daily life.

But in every society people acquire cultural knowledge that they cannot communicate about with verbal symbols. Tacit culture refers to this shared knowledge that people cannot talk about.[8] Although the members of all societies know how to

---

[8]See Edward T. Hall, *The Silent Language*, Garden City, N.Y.: Doubleday, 1959; and Michael Polanyi, *The Tacit Dimension*, Garden City, N.Y.: Doubleday, 1966.

make the sounds necessary for speaking their native language, hardly anyone can talk about this knowledge. Native speakers also acquire a precise knowledge of the rules for putting sounds together in the proper sequences and using them as symbols that carry information. But most native speakers cannot enumerate the entire set of cultural rules they have acquired. Tramps know how to identify at least 15 kinds of tramps; some men can observe another tramp and tell whether he is a mission stiff, an airedale, a box car tramp, or some other type of tramp. Although they can offer a great deal of verbal information about the cultural concept of "tramp," they cannot fully explain the code rules for identifying the various kinds of tramps.

Tacit culture is acquired partly by paying attention to the nonverbal messages people use to communicate meaning. The newcomer to the tramp world carefully observes the behavior of oldtimers, listens to other men as they identify various kinds of tramps and talk about specific persons who have been identified, and then begins to use the same terms in a tentative way. Oldtimers will correct him and before long he has come to share the tacit rules for this part of tramp culture. In much the same way that children learn the grammar of some unwritten language, tramps acquire tacit culture by making inferences from several sources of information.

When we say that people cannot talk about some of their cultural knowledge, this is only partly true. The boundary between explicit and tacit cultural knowledge is a *permeable* one. That which is tacit in one situation may become explicit in another. This fact is extremely important to anthropologists who set out to describe another culture. When people are confronted with naïve individuals, such as children and anthropologists, they often talk about things that ordinarily remain tacit. Some settings also facilitate this kind of verbal communication. For example, a hunter may be able to explain much more about how he tracks animals through a dense forest while he is doing it than at some later date in a place remote from the hunting territory. A skilled woman can talk about making pottery while she eats an evening meal, but a verbal explanation might be greatly enriched if she talked while engaged in the process of making a ceramic container. Anthropologists encourage people to talk about every dimension of their knowledge. For example, in every society people can talk about <u>ideal culture</u>, knowledge about what people ought to do; they can also talk about <u>real culture</u>, knowledge of what people actually do. If they cannot enunciate specific code rules, they can often relate experiences or tell the stories and myths to communicate cultural knowledge. In Chapter 2 we will discuss some of the discovery procedures that facilitate the process of describing both explicit and tacit cultural knowledge.

CULTURAL ADAPTATION

The primary function of culture is <u>adaptation</u>. Adaptation refers to the process of coping with a specific physical, biological, and social environment to meet the fundamental requirements for survival. Cultural knowledge has become the basis for human survival, distinguishing humans from all other animals. But adaptation has not always been achieved by means of culture, nor is it the only basis for adaptation now.

Cultural and genetic codes both enable humans to adapt, but it was the selection of genetic characteristics that gave culture its start. Our primate ancestors apparently lived in social groups. Several million years ago some of them began to adapt to the savannah grasslands of Africa and to run about on two feet instead of the customary four. By the time we catch a glimpse of these bipedal creatures some 2 million years ago, they are making tools in conjunction with hunting. The archaeological evidence of the development of humans from that time to the present shows a dramatic increase in brain size, social cooperation, and the manufacture of complex tools. Apparently, cooperative hunting acted as a selective force on biological evolution. The ability to survive shifted gradually from biology to culture. Adaptation became a matter of acquiring cultural knowledge for making tools, coordinating the hunt, and defending against predators.

Although the genetic code continues to be an extremely important determinant of behavior, human adaptation depends largely on the cultural code. The acquisition of culture is made possible by our genetic inheritance, but survival in such places as the tropical jungles or the far reaches of outer space is made possible by our cultural knowledge. The Eskimo, for example, are able to adapt to the rugged environment of the far north because of what they know. They share this extremely cold, bleak habitat with other animals, but their means of adaptation are quite different. The polar bear, for example, has adjusted to the cold by a process of genetic change. Only those animals with heavy fur coats and the capacity to sustain a thick layer of fat survive the cold to produce offspring. The Eskimo, fairly recent migrants to the area, show the effects of genetic adaptation. Among other things, they tend to have short arms and legs in relation to their bodies, a physical form that reduces skin surface and thus conserves body heat. But such minor physical changes are insufficient for adaptation to the Arctic climate. Survival there depends on cultural knowledge. The Eskimo do not grow hairy coats but make them out of sealskin. Their culture also prescribes how to hunt the seal successfully, how to skin it properly, and how to render the skin pliable in the coldest weather.

Adaptation and Comparison

If we merely *describe* the cultural knowledge of earth's societies, we would be struck by the differences among human beings. The knowledge that men on skid row have learned about tramps and the intricate strategies for making it, for example, are probably not exactly duplicated anywhere in the world. A description of these codes in their own terms, while a necessary starting point, does not provide a firm basis for cross-cultural comparison. If, however, we ask how these practices function for tramps in the process of adaptation, it becomes possible to make comparisons with other cultures. The various ways of making it are employed by tramps to secure goods and services to meet biological and social wants. As we will see in Chapter 10, for comparative purposes, they constitute part of the *economic system* of tramps. Although we will present specific cultural descrip-

Without culture, people would be limited to life in temperate parts of the world. By use of their cultural knowledge, however, individuals such as the Eskimo hunter shown here are able to adapt to a broad range of environmental conditions.

tions in later chapters, we will organize much of this book around the way culture functions for people in the process of adaptation.

Underlying such comparisons lies a recognition that there are certain universal human needs. Although cultural systems are all different, they can each contribute to the satisfaction of universal human needs. Human beings everywhere have common <u>physical requirements</u> that we all must meet if we are to survive. We must eat and drink, maintain our body temperature at about 98.6°, and protect ourselves against predators. The Eskimo live in igloos; Navajo Indians dwell in partly sunken hogans made of wood and earth; pygmies in the Congo shelter themselves in leaf and sapling huts; tramps find stairwells, parked cars, and all-

People everywhere must meet their physical requirements if they are to survive. Eskimo culture includes knowledge of the construction of shelters that enable these far northern people to stay warm under the coldest conditions.

night theaters where they sleep. Although each structure is different, they all serve the same function: they protect their inhabitants from the weather. Every culture includes knowledge of shelter, clothes, weapons, food-getting techniques, cures for illness, and a host of other things to enable people to meet their physical requirements.

All individuals have a variety of psychological requirements. They must manage fear and anxiety. They need affection from others and rationales with which to account for good and evil in human experience. An African Nyakusan explains his upset stomach as an effect of witchcraft; Americans blame theirs on overeating or excess acidity. These contrasting explanations function to relieve the anxiety aroused by the illness. In addition, every culture provides ways to manage intense emotional states such as grief or hostility. Although there are common psychological needs, the cultural forms in which they are expressed and satisfied change from one society to the next.

Human beings are social animals whose continued existence depends on living in a social group. As a newborn infant, you could not survive without many years of care and training. In every society, food-producing and defensive capabilities are immeasurably increased by cooperative efforts. But this has created a whole set of social requirements that can only be met by culture.[9] Some kind of organization is necessary in order to coordinate activity and assign the tasks that must be done. New members must be recruited by sexual reproduction or some other means if the social group is to continue. Every culture prescribes the manner in which recruitment is to take place. Most new members who enter a society are infants who must be taught to behave in ways that fit in with older members. Thus every culture includes ways to *enculturate* the young or the newcomer. The goods and services for meeting physical and psychological needs must be distributed throughout the society. Markets, taxes, gift giving, pooling, and hourly wages are some of the ways this occurs, each culture defining what is appropriate. One of the most important requirements of social life is communication. Indeed, it is an intimate part of the activities in every society. Every human culture includes a language that is the primary means for linking members of a society together.

Function

When anthropologists examine the consequence of culture for adaptation, they analyze its function. The concept of function refers to what things do. Your heart, for example, circulates the blood throughout your body and thus supplies food and oxygen to the cells. We can say that one function of the heart is to circulate the blood. This does not explain how the human heart develops within a single organism nor how it evolved within the human species. Instead, it is a functional statement about the role of the heart in the survival of the organism.

The study of cultures often leads to understanding specific and limited consequences for cultural practices. In order to understand the lives of tramps, we begin by asking, "What cultural knowledge have they acquired?" Once we discover the meaning of an activity such as "making a run" and the rules for generating it, we can turn to another question, "What are the consequences of this feature of tramp culture?" Making a run functions, in part, to supply a group of men with something to drink. It also creates a special kind of reciprocity among tramps that binds them together in a loosely organized society. The man who makes the run is giving his service to other men; the group that provided the money gives the runner a share of the beverage. A simple kind of exchange has occurred, and one function of this exchange is to strengthen the bonds that link these men together. Sometimes a man who makes the run decides to "beat" the other men out of the jug, and he does not return. He has changed his behavior from one symbolic meaning, "making a run," to another, "beating some tramps out of a jug." This second kind of behavior has a different function; its consequence is to create distrust and alienation among tramps.

The function of any cultural practice refers to the consequences it has for the members of the society, their physical environment, or for people beyond the boundaries of their society. One part of every culture is a knowledge of some such

[9]See David F. Aberle, et al., "The Functional Prerequisites of a Society," *Ethics, 60,* 1950, pp. 100–111, for a discussion of such requirements.

consequences or functions. When the members of a society recognize a particular function, we refer to it as a manifest function. Tramps, for example, recognize that making a run functions to provide them with something to drink. They also recognize that when a man "beats you out of a jug," it creates distrust. These are manifest functions. For example, one kind of tramp, known as a "rubber tramp," travels from place to place in his car. This gives him a decided advantage over other men to leave quickly from one location and to travel to another city. Tramps believe that rubber tramps are more prone to "beating" other tramps for money, clothes, or a jug. This belief has developed from recognizing the manifest function of all those actions referred to as "beating," and men will say, "You gotta be careful with a rubber tramp 'cause you can't trust them."

Many functions of specific cultural practices go unrecognized by the people involved. When the anthropologist, as an outside observer, identifies these consequences, we refer to them as latent functions. For example, a latent function of "making a run" is that the bonds that link tramps together are strengthened, a consequence that tramps do not generally recognize. Sometimes the latent functions of some cultural practice affect people in other segments of society and even beyond. Take, for example, making the blood bank. Blood is a valuable and expensive commodity in the modern world; as the supply of whole blood and plasma is used up, it must be replenished. Most people in our society are not eager to give blood or sell it for a profit; those who market blood have capitalized on the willingness of tramps to sell their blood. As a result, in addition to the Red Cross supply from voluntary donors, much of the blood in our society comes from the skid row men who are "trying to make it." Many tramps are afflicted by illnesses such as hepatitis, a disease carried in the blood and transmitted to transfusion recipients in other parts of the country or even in a foreign country. One of the latent functions, then, of tramps making the blood bank in considerable number is to keep such banks in operation and to spread hepatitis, causing illness and death.[10]

SUMMARY

In order to account for the enormous diversity in human behavior from one society to another, anthropologists employ the concept of culture. Culture is the acquired knowledge people use to interpret experience and generate social behavior. Culture is like a recipe for organizing the necessary ingredients for a viable social life.

Cultural knowledge is learned and shared. The knowledge that people talk about is explicit; knowledge that cannot be articulated is tacit. The boundary between explicit and tacit cultural knowledge is a permeable one, and anthropologists work to assist people in making their tacit knowledge explicit.

Cultural knowledge systems provide the basic means of adaptation for the human animal. Underlying the process of adaptation are important physical, psy-

[10]For a detailed examination of blood donors and the consequences of skid row men making the blood banks, see Richard M. Titmuss, *The Gift Relationship: From Human Blood to Social Policy*, London: George Allen & Unwin, 1971. The dangers of serum hepatitis are discussed in Chapter 8.

chological, and social requirements for survival. The function of culture refers to what a specific cultural practice does in general and its consequences for human adaptation.

MAJOR CONCEPTS

ANTHROPOLOGY	REAL CULTURE
CULTURE	ADAPTATION
CATEGORY	FUNCTION
CULTURAL CODE	MANIFEST FUNCTION
EXPLICIT CULTURE	LATENT FUNCTION
TACIT CULTURE	GENETIC CODE
IDEAL CULTURE	

SELECTED READINGS

Freilich, Morris (editor): *The Meaning of Culture: A Reader in Cultural Anthropology*, Lexington: Xerox, 1972.
A collection of 21 articles by a variety of anthropologists on the culture concept.

Goodenough, Ward H.: *Description and Comparison in Cultural Anthropology*, Chicago: Aldine, 1970.
A discussion of the culture concept in terms of two major tasks of anthropology, cultural description and cross-cultural comparison.

Harris, Marvin: *The Rise of Anthropological Theory*, New York: Crowell, 1968, Chapter 20, "Emics, Etics, and the New Ethnography."
A critique of approaches that define culture as knowledge.

Martindale, Don (editor): *Functionalism in the Social Sciences*, Philadelphia: American Academy of Political and Social Sciences, 1965.
A critical evaluation of the concept of function.

Schneider, Louis, and Charles Bonjean (editors): *The Idea of Culture in the Social Sciences*, London: Cambridge University Press, 1973.
Social scientists from six different fields each contribute a chapter that discusses the culture concept in their field.

White, Leslie A., and Beth Dillingham: *The Concept of Culture*, Minneapolis: Burgess, 1973.
An introduction to cultural evolution.

CHAPTER TWO

Fieldwork
and Ethnography

Fieldwork is the firsthand experience of studying another culture. It encompasses all the activities anthropologists undertake when they go to a new society to discover and describe the culture. Fieldwork has come to have an almost sacred significance to anthropologists; for many it is like a rite of passage into the discipline because it is the single most important factor in acquiring the anthropological perspective. More than anything else, the experience of fieldwork distinguishes anthropology from other social sciences.

When anthropologists leave their own society, travel halfway around the world, and settle down to live in a remote community, they literally exchange their own way of life for a new one. They eat new foods, follow new time schedules, speak new languages, and become intimately acquainted with people who live by different values. The challenge is more than merely studying another culture, although that is the primary goal. In addition, every anthropologist who does fieldwork must overcome numerous barriers intrinsic to living in an alien society. In this chapter we want to examine several hidden barriers to fieldwork and then discuss ethnography, the actual task of studying another culture.

BARRIERS TO EFFECTIVE FIELDWORK

Strange as it may seem, the most important problems in doing fieldwork come from the anthropologist's culture, not the culture of those studied. In a real sense every fieldworker must become sensitized to the tacit culture learned during the process of growing up. In another cultural context one becomes acutely aware of how important that tacit cultural background is for everyday living. Let us consider three barriers to fieldwork that arise, in part, from the conflict between the anthropologist's own culture and the alien one being studied.

Culture Shock

The first major problem in doing fieldwork is culture shock. It is a common experience and one that cannot be avoided if you work closely with members of the new society. <u>Culture shock</u> is a form of anxiety that occurs when one is required to interact with others in a cross-cultural situation. When you leave behind those who share your perspective and your knowledge of appropriate behavior, you will find you have lost your cultural bearings. In such a situation it is impossible to predict what others will do or to know how you should act. Many investigators begin fieldwork among people with an unwritten language and this makes it impossible to ask questions about what is going on. The end result is a feeling of isolation, anxiety, and frustration.

Culture shock is not merely a novel experience that comes from living in a strange community with people who act in unfamiliar ways. More important, culture shock involves a significant loss for ethnographers. The small but important cues that we constantly use to orient ourselves in a complex social world are suddenly gone. The reactions of other people that we constantly monitor for feedback information in order to adjust our behavior to meet prevailing expectations have all disappeared. In their place are strange looks, unfamiliar facial expressions, and body movements whose meaning cannot be understood by the ethnographer. Culture shock renders a person ineffective for studying a culture. Fortunately, there is a way to reduce the effect of culture shock and the distortion it creates for ethnography. That solution is to be found in the passage of time and in learning the new culture.

Kalvero Oberg, one of the first anthropologists to discuss culture shock, suggested that there are four stages to the experience and that if one remains in the field, the effects of culture shock wear off (see Figure 2-1).[1] First, there is a honeymoon stage that lasts a few weeks and is characterized by feelings of elation and optimism. This phase quickly gives way to the second stage, in which individuals feel hostility toward and are critical of their hosts. The ability of ethnographers to hide a superior attitude decreases at this stage, and it becomes difficult not to express criticism about the people they are studying. Some ethnographers find it necessary at this juncture to escape or withdraw for a time from the intensity of contact with informants. The third stage of culture shock is one of initial recovery characterized by humor, especially the ability to laugh at themselves. Finally, there is a period of adjustment and acceptance of the new culture. Although the people they live among accept them, ethnographers realize that the people will always see them as different and that they cannot become full members of the society. They learn to accept their place as outsiders, marginal individuals between two worlds. Most important, they learn the implicit cultural rules for behavior.

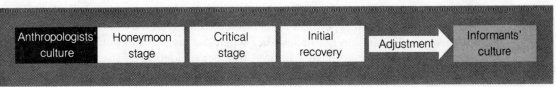

FIGURE 2-1
Stages of culture shock.

[1]"Culture Shock" first appeared in mimeograph form and copyrighted in 1954. Now published as A-329 in the Bobbs-Merrill Reprint Series in the Social Sciences, Indianapolis: Bobbs-Merrill.

Cross-Cultural Misunderstanding

The second major problem in doing fieldwork comes from a failure to grasp new cultural meanings. As we said in Chapter 1, much of your cultural knowledge is tacit, outside of awareness. When you leave the familiar social settings you are used to and take up residence in another society, you must behave in a cross-cultural situation. In this setting there is a temptation to believe that you left your cultural rules at home, but many misunderstandings that occur during fieldwork come from the hidden influence of the ethnographer's own culture. One of the most important ways to prepare for doing fieldwork is to become aware of your culture.

Take the following example. A man who was working with American Indians as a 4-H program organizer on a large reservation announced that he would be holding a meeting for young people to launch a cattle-breeding program. The response was very good; a large number of boys filed into the meeting place, and when they were seated he explained the plan to them and answered their questions. Because he wished to encourage their interest and to appear friendly, he smiled often when members of his audience spoke. It was with some consternation, therefore, that he became more and more aware that the boys were growing sullen and unresponsive. Finally, they began leaving in an unpleasant mood. He was mystified by their change in attitude and concluded that they did not like his program. It was only later that he discovered what had happened. To these boys smiling did not mean support and interest, as he had assumed. In the context of the meeting they had interpreted his friendly smiles as a form of ridicule! Without intending to, he had followed his own cultural rules for conveying interest and friendliness and had made fun of his audience. Then he had misunderstood their response to his behavior. Cross-cultural misunderstanding such as this is an ever-present pitfall in all ethnographic fieldwork. It can occur whenever the anthropologist fails to be aware of his or her own cultural interpretations.

One aspect of your culture is especially important as a source of misunderstanding, your identity in the field situation. For instance, a fieldworker conceives of herself as a scholar, an anthropologist who has a place in the institutions of higher learning. She knows what her role is and others have treated her as an anthropologist. She has other conceptions of herself, she is a friendly person whose interest is to learn about others without changing their way of life and without trying to exploit them. When she sets out to do ethnographic fieldwork, she carries with her these conceptions of her own identity. But the people from whom she wishes to learn do not share these definitions of who she is and yet must give her some identity in order to relate to her. They watch what she does and interpret it according to their own cultural experience. It is often the case that they have never heard of anthropologists and do not believe her when she says she has come to study their way of life. They may have a limited number of identities, such as missionary, government official, policeman, prospector, trader, or soldier, with which to classify strangers. But these identities all have attributes that the ethnographer may wish to avoid; they are labels for people who have frequently caused trouble. As a result, an ethnographer is often unable to establish an identity that permits mutual trust.

One of the authors went to live in a village in India and was first thought to be a missionary. After several weeks, the villagers realized that he was not acting like the missionaries they had known, and they now decided he must be an agent from the Central Intelligence Agency of the U.S. government. He had come to gather information in their village and to use it to compete with the Russians in a kind of college bowl contest. Finally, this identity, with all its problems for gathering cultural information, began to fade, and the villagers decided the ethnographer was really a prospector. He reinforced this diagnosis by walking in the hills and photographing the community from above. In another instance, a group of women who had recently heard a lecture on family planning thought the anthropologist had entered the village to castrate the men and himself sire a new generation of babies!

When you are given such threatening identities, people's reactions to you are guarded, and they will tell outright lies in order to thwart what they perceive to be your intended purpose. The anthropologist in another culture who is identified as a missionary is likely to hear some astounding things about the Christian-like nature of the local religion while a sacrifice and curing ritual are going on behind his or her back.

To cope with these problems, most anthropologists examine the way they conceptualize their own identity and the ways in which their informants might see them. Then they will spend weeks, even months, carefully establishing rapport and trust, constantly explaining the nature of their endeavors. Often they must search for some clue in the native culture or some concern of informants that can be meaningfully linked to explanations about their work. One of the authors who conducted ethnographic research among skid row tramps was suspected of being a "bull" in disguise. Informants had good reasons to be suspicious because some policemen actually dressed as bums in order to circulate more freely among these men and arrest them for begging, urinating in public, and other minor crimes. Such officers were referred to as *ragpickers*. It was possible to gain trust among informants by making it clear that the investigator was from the nearby university and that he hoped to use his findings to change conditions in the local jail. When some of his findings were published in the local newspaper, thus making public the conditions that tramps endured in jail, informants gained even more reassurance that the ethnographer was not a member of the police force. All fieldwork requires that ethnographers be aware of their own cultural background, the identities they have assumed, and the possible identities informants might confer on them without their knowledge.

Ethnocentrism

A third hidden barrier to doing effective fieldwork is ethnocentrism. Ethnocentrism is a mixture of belief and feeling that your own way of life is desirable and actually superior to others. A deeply ingrained attitude found in every human society, it is a central problem faced by anyone who seeks to understand another culture. You can even know that you are behaving in terms of your own culture and that others are acting in terms of theirs and yet still find it extremely difficult to control your feelings about what you see others doing. Because of ethnocentrism you feel surprised, disgusted, horrified, amused, or skeptical when you encounter another life-style. All such reactions arise because you are *evaluating* the behavior that is generated by another culture.

Americans express their ethnocentrism in many ways. Some will come right out and say that everyone else in the world would be better off if they lived like Americans. A politician who later became president of the United States claimed that people all over the world went to bed nights wishing they could become Americans. But many other statements, although less direct, reflect this prevailing attitude. Americans refer to "underdeveloped" areas of the world; they consider tribal groups to be "primitive" and peasants "backward." People who believe in gods and spirits other than one's own are "superstitious." Even the people of industrialized nations in Europe and Asia are characterized by such terms as dirty, lazy, ill-mannered, sneaky, unenlightened, hot-blooded, or unambitious.

Ethnocentrism is rooted in the human tendency to become overcommitted to one set of values to the exclusion of all others. This can sometimes express itself as inverted ethnocentrism when people laud a foreign culture and denigrate their own.

Often, some subgroups within a society openly reject and downgrade the traditional values and customs of their elders and argue for the inherent superiority of some new life-style. In situations where there is contact between the West and smaller, less complex societies, for example, the youth have sometimes adopted this attitude. They are ashamed of the backward ways of their parents and do not feel a sense of pride in their own language and customs. At the same time, they overestimate the value of Western culture and its technological accomplishments. A similar inverted ethnocentrism has been observed among some youth in American society. The "noble savage" is idealized as being more natural and authentic; magical practices are considered more valuable than the religious belief of one's own parents; beads and amulets are worn to symbolize this new life-style; communal living is proclaimed a more desirable arrangement than the nuclear family. But inverted ethnocentrism is no less an ethnocentrism merely because it glorifies new life-styles or some strange and exotic culture. All ethnocentrism is based on the claim that one culture is inherently better than others. It makes no difference whether one downgrades and ridicules the behavior and beliefs of "primitive savages" or "middle-class parents." In both cases it is evidence of an ethnocentric attitude in which one declares the essential superiority of his or her own or another culture.

Ethnocentrism is certainly not limited to Americans. Africans are frequently horrified by the lack of respect American children show to their parents. Many people from India who visit this country are aghast and physically repelled by American pets; dogs actually live in the house with people, and cats, which are despicable animals, are underfoot everywhere. Many other people in the world are convinced that the United States is a backward nation because supermarkets do not offer really fresh produce. And some visitors to this country are appalled because many American youths reject their parents' concern with religion.

But this attitude does not merely pervade the international scene; we find it at home as well. For example, most parents find their children's popular music records offensive. And some young people cannot imagine why their parents advocate loyalty to America first. The civilian who deprecates those who have chosen to be career soldiers is saying that his or her own way of life is best. So is the intellectual who derides the factory worker for watching television instead of reading. The teacher who chides students for their poor grammar and tries to get Mexican-Americans, American Indians, or children from Appalachia to speak "standard" English because it is better is expressing ethnocentrism. Even anthropologists are subject to the influence of this attitude despite their place as major opponents of it. When they criticize a missionary for teaching converts to wear modest Western clothing or to give up the custom of polygamy, they are suggesting that their own relativistic point of view is, in fact, the best one. As long as people hold values, they will continue to be ethnocentric.

There are several things anthropologists can do to reduce the distortion effect of ethnocentrism. First, they can recognize the pervasive existence of this attitude as a human phenomenon that cannot be eradicated. To deny feeling that one's own way of life is superior to any other is to be blind to a major source of distortion. Second, they must make themselves aware of the wide range of human customs and values. Anthropologists study the many ways to be human in order to reduce the intensity of their own ethnocentrism. Finally, they adopt a temporary perspective in which they accept alien customs as desirable. This attitude of suspended judgment is important to reduce the distortion of ethnocentrism during ethnographic research.

ETHNOLOGY AND ETHNOGRAPHY

Ethnography refers to the task of describing a particular culture. But ethnographic research is not the final goal of anthropologists, who also seek to classify, compare, and explain the similarities and differences among many cultures. This broader set of comparative activities is referred to as **ethnology**. We can distinguish these two important and overlapping activities in the following manner:

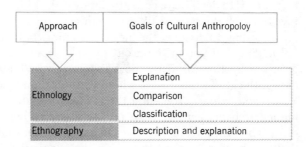

Approach	Goals of Cultural Anthropoloy
Ethnology	Explanation
	Comparison
	Classification
Ethnography	Description and explanation

Ethnology begins with comparison of two or more cultures; ethnography focuses on a single culture. In order to make comparisons and to do ethnology, the anthropologist must create categories that apply to more than a single society. It is through ethnological research that anthropologists seek to isolate and explain general aspects of human culture and behavior as well as human variation.

Yanomamo often engage in formal chest pounding duels as a sign of their fierceness. Such duels require that one man raise his arm, leaving his chest open to a blow from the other. The two alternate roles until they have had enough.

Perhaps the best way to understand the nature of ethnography is by analogy to the work of cryptographers, people who seek to decipher codes. The goal of cryptography is to decipher a code, to discover the hidden meanings that people are using. In much the same way, every ethnographer is trying to "crack the code" people are using, to discover the hidden meanings of their culture.

Imagine that you have set out to make an ethnographic description of a small group of horticulturalists, the Yanomamo of Venezuela.[2] You are flown to the damp, thickly forested area where you meet a missionary who will take you to a Yanomamo village. You enter the village through a gate in a tall stockade and are immediately challenged by six men with drawn bows. They appear to relax, however, when they recognize the missionary who accompanies you, and it is then that you have a moment to size up the people you hope will be your hosts. The men are naked except for a string around their waists. Green mucus flows freely from their nostrils, and later you observe them blowing a green powder up each other's noses through a hollow tube. Each man has a wad of green leaves stuffed behind his lower lip, and you notice that they all spit green juice onto the ground

[2]This description of the Yanomamo is based on Napoleon A. Chagnon's discussion of his initial contact with this group appearing in *Yanomamo: The Fierce People*, New York: Holt, Rinehart and Winston, 1968, pp. 4–5.

from time to time. As you sit down and the village activities resume, you observe men shouting at one another. Later they take turns striking each other on the chest with their fists and finally on the tops of their heads with clubs.

Like the cryptographer's task, yours is not merely to describe the activities you see but to understand the hidden meanings of these activities. Cryptographers seeking to crack some code observe things such as marks on a paper, sounds blipped over the airwaves, taps on a wall, or different colored flags waved from a hill. At first glance these things do not appear to have any meaning for the cryptographers. Merely describing them from their own perspective does not constitute the completion of their job. Instead, everything they see is treated as a coded message, and they attempt to decipher the rules used to produce it and the meaning it contains. To decipher Morse Code, for example, cryptographers have to discover that there are two kinds of sounds, long ones called dashes and short ones called dots. Then they must find out that dots and dashes are arranged in a limited number of patterns that stand for Roman letters and that these are arranged to spell out words from a particular language. Once they have inferred these underlying rules, cryptographers can decipher any coded message and unlock the meaning it contains. If they do their job well, they will be able to understand any transmission in Morse Code and to use the code to transmit messages themselves.

The behavior of the Yanomamo villagers also carries coded information. The threats, green powder, shouts, green leaves, and blows delivered by the villagers at first seem to have no more meaning than a series of dots and dashes heard for the first time. But if you persisted in the community as an ethnographer you would discover that the villagers were fearful of being raided by members of another community at the time you arrived, that green powder caused men to see visions and to communicate with spirits from a lower world, that the green leaves were chewed on most social occasions, and that shouting and the delivery of blows were typical expressions of fierceness, the valued male identity of the Yanomamo. Your success as an ethnographer would be measured by your ability to understand the actions you saw and to anticipate the behavior of Yanomamo villagers. Eventually, as your ethnographic research progressed, you would not be surprised at what people did unless some action was inappropriate and surprising to the Yanomamo also.

ETHNOGRAPHIC FIELD TECHNIQUES

Ethnography is both science and art. The fieldworker discovers the meanings of another culture by total immersion in the daily round of life. By listening, asking questions, watching people, working, participating, and always writing down each day's experiences, the ethnographer slowly gains a working knowledge of the new culture. Techniques that work in one society often yield little new information in another society. New strategies for gathering data are developed while doing fieldwork. In the following discussion of the most important techniques it must be kept in mind that each ethnographer adapts them to the situation at hand.

Participant Observation

The most important field technique involves *participating* in activities and at the same time *observing* what is going on. We can better understand this technique for doing ethnography if we contrast it with detached observation.

In their desire to be objective some social scientists have argued that the study of social behavior requires detached observation. Based on the model developed in the physical sciences, detached observers seek to remain emotionally uninvolved and neutral while making observations. They create their own categories for classifying and describing things observed. As an anthropologist studying a remote tribal village, you could make detached observations to construct a map of the village. Walking around the village you would begin to take notes, measure distances, draw buildings, sketch in trees or other landmarks and slowly develop a complete map of the village. You might discover paths, for instance, by noting where the earth was hard packed and worn smooth as well as by watching people travel from one place to another. The size and shape of open spaces could be charted and drawn to scale. An aerial photograph of the village would probably be an invaluable aid. When your map was completed, you could use it to find your way around the village. Although this kind of map, based on naturalistic observations, would certainly be useful, it would not necessarily tell you very much about the village from a cultural perspective. That kind of information could only come through participant observation.

How would you develop a map of a village by this ethnographic technique? First, you would recognize that the inhabitants of the village each had a complex set of mental images of their community. They know the location of many different places, they can locate themselves at any given time, and they are able to go from place to place without getting lost. An ethnographic map could only be constructed by tapping the knowledge of the residents. Through participant observation you would seek to discover how they perceive their village. In some ways an ethnographic description that resulted would be similar to the map drawn from naturalistic observations. But it would include additional important information. For example, villagers might include objects or beings, such as dwelling places of ancestral ghosts, things invisible to the anthropologist. Instead of merely noting paths and trees, the ethnographer would find out which ones were sacred, which ones taboo, and other meanings these things hold for the people. In short, doing ethnography means searching out the meaning of places, objects, pathways, and arrangements in the village *from the native point of view*. Once the anthropologist has acquired this knowledge, it could be represented graphically. The map would be a composite of all the informal maps, both explicit and tacit, that the villagers have acquired and are using to understand their world.

The goal of ethnography in general, and participant observation in particular, is to construct ethnographic maps, not merely of the geography in which people live, but also of their social relationships, economic activities, religious beliefs, and every other area of culture. Participant observation requires personal involvement with other human beings. This involvement is a fundamental ingredient of anthropological fieldwork. Every ethnographer must learn to take the role of other people, to look at life through their eyes, to share their experiences. This

In this picture Margaret Mead is shown with some of her informants during a field trip to Manus Island in 1928. Her written ethnography reflected Manus culture as it was then, treating 1928 as the ethnographic present.

The fact that cultures change is amply illustrated by this photograph of Margaret Mead on Manus Island in 1964. She is greeted by some of the people she knew well in 1928, but the culture of the islanders has changed in many ways. They no longer wear traditional clothes, for example, or live in pile houses built over the water in the lagoon.

means a partial detachment from one's own perspective on life, but not a detachment from those whose culture is being studied.

Ethnographic Interviewing

The second field technique involves a special kind of interviewing. In most forms of interviewing one person formulates a series of *questions* and presents them to another person. The second person provides *answers* to these questions. This procedure can often yield useful data in social science research. However, when doing cross-cultural research, the questions can often distort the answers to a considerable degree.

Ethnographic interviewing is a procedure by which the anthropologist begins by searching for questions that are meaningful to informants.[3] This often takes weeks of listening even after one has learned the native language. It is important for the ethnographer to discover *folk concepts* and to avoid prematurely introducing *analytic concepts* into interviews. Indeed, an awareness of the difference between these two kinds of concepts is crucial for ethnographic interviewing.

Any concept that is part of the ethnographer's culture and is employed to describe or explain the experiences and social behavior of other people is an analytic concept. It may be a technical term such as "culture," "symbol," or "latent function"; on the other hand, commonly used words such as "smoking," "talking," and "fighting" can be analytic concepts if they are used in reference to another culture. When anthropologists make cross-cultural comparisons, they must employ numerous analytic concepts, and while some are necessary for ethnographic description, it is important to begin with folk concepts.

A folk concept is one that is locally defined by members of a society; it makes up part of their cultural knowledge. Ethnography begins with the search for folk concepts.[4] But after you have identified the more obvious ones in a culture, there is a temptation to create your own categories to describe their experience. At any stage in ethnographic research it is possible to introduce the categories and concepts that you know as an outsider. When it is done prematurely, this practice acts as a barrier to exploring fully the cultural knowledge that informants are using to interpret their experience and generate social behavior. Franz Boas, one of the founders of anthropology in the United States, pointed to this problem long ago.

We know what we mean by family, state, government, etc. As we overstep the limits of one culture we do not know how far these may correspond to equivalent concepts. If we choose to apply our classification to alien cultures we may combine forms which do not belong together. . . . If it is our serious purpose to under-

[3]See James P. Spradley, *The Ethnographic Interview*, New York: Holt, Rinehart and Winston, 1979.

[4]See Harold Conklin, "Lexicographical Treatment of Folk Taxonomies" in *Problems in Lexicography*, F. W. Householder and S. Saporta (editors), *International Journal of American Linguistics*, 28 (2), Part 4, 1962, pp. 119–141, Bloomington: Indiana University Research Center in Anthropology, Folklore, and Linguistics, Publication 21, for a detailed discussion of the nature of folk concepts and how they are organized.

stand the thoughts of a people the whole analysis of experience must be based upon their concepts, not ours.[5]

Ethnographic interviewing begins by discovering folk concepts and formulating questions that are meaningful to informants. Then, in asking questions, the ethnographer must be sensitive to the ability of many informants to translate their answers into a form acceptable to the investigator. In the days when anthropologists went to remote societies where people had little information about outsiders, informants could *not* translate their concepts into terms familiar to the researcher. Communication was almost entirely based on one culture: the anthropologist had to employ the folk concepts and terms of the informants and work to find out their meaning. Informants could not be relied on to assist by explaining things in *the categories and terms of the ethnographer's culture.* Through contact with missionaries, traders, and others, people in remote areas began to acquire the ability to translate their cultural knowledge into the culture of outsiders. In the last 50 years this phenomenon has spread rapidly as people all over the world have attended schools, learned foreign languages, and traveled widely beyond their own communities. Furthermore, when anthropologists work within their own society, almost any informant can translate what they know into the researcher's categories.

Translation competence is the ability to translate the meanings of one culture into a form that is appropriate to another culture. In the process of translation considerable distortion can occur. Take the case of an anthropologist mapping the culture of skid row men. If he asks a rather simple question like, "How much income did you earn last year?" something like the following occurs. First, unknown to the ethnographer, the informant translates this question into, "How much *money* did you get last year from *working* at a *steady job*?" Because he only "worked" for three weeks picking apples during the year, he replies, "A couple hundred dollars." Then the ethnographer may ask, "Where do you live?" Again, because the informant knows the anthropologist's culture, he translates this question into something like, "He wants to know if I have a home or apartment where I stay all the time," and the reply is, "I don't have a place to stay." These same answers could then be elicited from other informants, leading the ethnographer to conclude that these are "homeless men" who live on less than $500 per year. Yet hidden from view is the extensive cultural knowledge that tramps have about ways to make it, about the sums of money they acquire yearly by such actions as junking and panhandling, and about hundreds of places they "flop," and "homes" such as cars and under bridges. This same process can occur with informants anywhere and with similar results. The ethnographer may thus unconsciously guide informants to conceptualize their own culture from the perspective of an outsider!

Collecting Genealogies

In every society the relationships among relatives is of great importance. In the small, non-Western societies studied by anthropologists, such relationships are of-

[5]Franz Boas, "Recent Anthropology," *Science, 98,* 1943, pp. 311–314, 334–337.

ten the most important ones. An early anthropologist, W. H. R. Rivers, originally developed the genealogical method to study kinship identities and relationships. He suggested that informants be questioned about their relatives, naming all those they could remember, living or dead, and stating their relationship. In order to proceed, one must find out the folk concepts for various relatives. Collecting genealogies by this method is actually a form of ethnographic interviewing. This kind of questioning quickly leads to cultural information about marriage patterns, descent rules, inheritance patterns, living arrangements, adoption of children, and many other things of interest to anthropologists.

Collecting Life Histories

Even the longest period of fieldwork only allows the anthropologist to observe a short period in the lifespan of any person. One valuable technique for gaining a broader perspective and for discovering the insider's experience of his or her culture is to collect life histories.

The ethnographer must first develop a close relationship to an individual. Then one can pose the question, "Would you be willing to tell me your life story, everything you can remember from childhood until the present?" As an individual recounts the events of his or her life, a great many folk concepts and their meanings are revealed. Those who recount their life story cannot help but interpret it by reference to the culture that has shaped their life. This reveals many ways that the individual, and by extension, other members who share the culture, perceive their world. Life histories also provide data about how individuals adjust to the restraints placed on them by their culture and to events that happen in their lives.

Life histories can also be used in studying special topics in ethnography. One of the authors became interested in the influence of culture change on individuals and asked a Kwakiutl Indian chief, James Sewid, to recount his life story. This man was born in 1913 and had lived through a period of far-reaching changes in the Kwakiutl way of life. This life history provided insight into the way this individual experienced those changes and adapted to them.

Projective Testing

Projective tests were originally developed by psychologists as a means for getting at hidden dimensions of personality. Borrowed early by anthropologists concerned with culture and personality, projective techniques such as the Rorschach ink blot test and the TAT (Thematic Apperception Test) have been administered to people in many different societies. Although they have been difficult to interpret crossculturally, they nonetheless provide a stimulus on which to get informants talking about various aspects of their lives.

Collecting Case Studies

Case studies represent stories that informants tell about particular kinds of events. Often used by anthropologists interested in particular areas of cultural knowledge (e.g., the anthropology of law), case studies provide a record of behavior and its interpretation particularly valuable to those who wish to study and analyze the decision-making process.

Taking Photographs

Typically, anthropologists take photographs, slides, and movies as an aid in illustrating their ethnographic accounts of a people's culture. But photography can be useful in the ethnographic field process as well. For example, John Collier has suggested that anthropologists can photograph places, things, and events, then show these pictures to informants for comment.

Informants and Questionnaires

Anthropologists often rely heavily on what are called *key informants,* or individuals who talk regularly with field investigators and from whom much of what the anthropologist learns is discovered. However, there comes a time when things people have been saying must be checked out for a wider population. How widespread is a particular individual's viewpoint? To check out such information, anthropologists may use a questionnaire, prepared questions administered to a large population of respondents.

It is difficult to gain an understanding of ethnographic fieldwork by merely reading about it. For this reason, we encourage students to undertake a field project in the study of some cultural scene. We have had students do first-rate ethnographic studies of health clinics, garbage collection companies, dog breeders, courtrooms, police officers, schoolrooms, and dozens of other scenes. In the process they learned how anthropologists do fieldwork and the concept of culture came alive for them. In order to assist those who wish to undertake ethnographic fieldwork, we have included specific instructions at the end of this book. In a special section called "How to Do a Fieldwork Project" you will find a guide to show how to begin, how to collect ethnographic data, how to analyze your data, and how to write it up as an ethnographic description. The work can be done within the time span of a single semester.

SUMMARY

In this chapter we have examined the importance of fieldwork experience to anthropology. This experience is a common theme in the culture of anthropology and refers to all the activities that are necessary when you go to an alien society to describe their culture. We examined three hidden barriers to effective fieldwork: culture shock, cross-cultural misunderstanding, and ethnocentrism.

The primary task of fieldwork is ethnography, the specific task of describing a culture. While ethnology focuses on cross-cultural comparisons and making broad generalizations, ethnography focuses on a single society seeking to describe and explain its culture. The ethnographic approach aims to discover the hidden meanings that lie behind behavior. In this chapter we discussed some of the more important ethnographic field techniques. Participant observation is one means for discovering the native point of view and it contrasts sharply with the detached observation of the natural scientist. Ethnographic interviewing seeks to discover folk concepts and questions meaningful to informants. Collecting genealogies is a special form of ethnographic interviewing that focuses on the area of kinship. Collecting life histories provides a view of the life span of individuals adapting to life events. Other techniques discussed included collecting case studies, taking photographs, projective testing, and using questionnaires.

MAJOR CONCEPTS

ETHNOGRAPHIC FIELDWORK	CASE STUDIES
ETHNOGRAPHY	GENEALOGICAL METHOD
OBSERVATION	PROJECTIVE TESTS
PARTICIPANT OBSERVATION	THE PHOTOGRAPHIC METHOD
CULTURE SHOCK	QUESTIONNAIRE
CROSS-CULTURAL	FOLK CONCEPTS
ETHNOCENTRISM	ANALYTIC CONCEPTS
INVERTED ETHNOCENTRISM	TRANSLATION COMPETENCE
DETACHED OBSERVATION	ETHNOLOGY
LIFE HISTORIES	

SELECTED READINGS

Berreman, Gerald: *Behind Many Masks*, Society for Applied Anthropology Monograph No. 4, 1962.
A warm personal account of fieldwork in a Himalayan village analyzed in terms of Erving Goffman's dramaturgical model of impression management.

Epstein, A. L. (editor): *The Craft of Social Anthropology*, London: Tavistock, 1967.
This book brings together a group of articles on several field techniques, research problems, and solutions associated with particular field research projects.

Golde, Peggy (editor): *Women in the Field: Anthropological Experiences*, Chicago: Aldine, 1970.
This is a collection of papers that treats the woman's experience in anthropological fieldwork. Papers focus on personal, ethnographic, and methodological problems faced by women researchers in various male-controlled field situations.

Kimball, Solon, and James B. Watson (editors): *Crossing Cultural Boundaries*, San Francisco: Chandler, 1972.
A collection of detailed reports on how some anthropologists have met and handled the fieldwork experience.

Pelto, Pertti J.: *Anthropological Research: The Structure of Inquiry*, New York: Harper & Row, 1970.
This book discusses a wide range of research topics including ethnography, the scientific method, and research design.

Spindler, George D. (editor): *Being an Anthropologist: Fieldwork in Eleven Cultures.* Prospect Heights, IL: Waveland Press, Inc., 1970 (reissued 1986).

In this series of reports, anthropologists discuss how they and their families adjusted to fieldwork in a variety of societies. These studies include treatment of particular personal and methodological problems in the field.

Spradley, James P.: *The Ethnographic Interview*, New York: Holt, Rinehart and Winston, 1979.

A step-by-step guide to doing ethnographic interviews. Examines the three basic types of ethnographic questions and shows how to use them in the field.

Spradley, James P.: *Participant Observation.* New York: Holt, Rinehart and Winston, 1980.

A step-by-step guide to doing participant observation. Examines the three basic types of observation and shows how to use them in the field situation.

Spradley, James P., and David W. McCurdy: *The Cultural Experience: Ethnography in Complex Society,* Prospect Heights, IL: Waveland Press, Inc., 1972 (reissued 1988).

An introduction to fieldwork for undergraduate students, which contains 13 ethnographic studies done by students.

CHAPTER THREE

Language

Every society, whether its members are honeybees, chimpanzees, or humans, depends on communication for its existence. Individuals communicate to each other about the location of food and water. They signal one another regarding natural predators and other dangers. Information about individual desires, emotional states, and intentions are transmitted from one organism to another. Social life of every kind requires frequent communication among individual members.

Human societies operate with numerous communication systems. A traffic policeman blows his whistle, signaling an automobile driver to stop; he motions with his arm to inform drivers to proceed. An Ibo village elder in Nigeria beats on a hollow metal object, an *ogene*, and the booming noise tells other villagers to listen for an important announcement. A father in Chicago dials his telephone and speaks to a physician, asking her to come and examine a sick child. Sirens pierce the stillness of the night in a New England town, telling everyone that firemen are rushing to deal with an emergency. On an American college campus a girl waves to a friend to communicate an informal greeting. Human beings have devised a host of ways to communicate, but the most important system in every culture is language.

LANGUAGE

Language is a system of cultural knowledge used to generate and interpret speech. It is a universal feature of every culture and a distinctive characteristic of the human animal. *Speech refers to the behavior that produces vocal sounds.* If you watch someone speaking you will quickly see that speech always occurs with other actions. At a minimum, we inhale and exhale while speaking; the eyes are focused on the listener or shift from place to place; hand gestures emphasize what is said; eyebrows are raised; head movements signal agreement or other nonverbal information. All these actions help to convey meanings from one person to another. The distinction between language and speech is especially important and is based on the more general contrast between competence and performance.

Competence and Performance

Competence refers to the possession of knowledge for interpreting experience and generating social behavior. When individuals learn the cultural knowledge of their society, or some part of that knowledge, they have acquired a degree of competence. Language competence refers to the possession of rules for encoding and decoding speech messages. Like all of our cultural knowledge, this competence is based on the physiology of the brain, yet it is acquired by social learning. It means that an enormous mass of information has been stored within the central nervous system of every native speaker. This information bank contains categories and rules for recognizing the sounds of speech, for identifying the basic elements in sentences, and for interpreting what people say. Language competence carries with it the potential for producing an infinite number of sentences. It enables adults and children alike in every society to produce novel sentences never previously spoken and to comprehend instantly utterances never heard before.

But cultural competence provides us with more than the ability to generate or interpret *appropriate* behavior and *grammatical* sentences. In every society people act inappropriately; they say things that do not make sense, and cultural competence is the basis for interpreting such behavior. We feel embarrassment when a close friend is socially inept; we laugh when someone utters an ungrammatical sentence; such responses are based on our cultural competence.

Performance refers to two kinds of activities: (1) interpreting experience and (2) generating social behavior. It is, in part, a product of a person's cultural competence. Language performance refers to the act of encoding and decoding vocal messages. Performance is endlessly varied as people say new things, recombine words into new sentences, and talk about their daily experiences. In order to speak grammatically or perform in other ways that are meaningful and appropriate, we have to acquire that complex system of knowledge that constitutes competence.

SPEECH MESSAGES

The anthropologist seeks to understand the competence of native speakers who freely generate and interpret speech messages. Our goal is larger than merely knowing how sounds are put together or describing the grammatical rules for sentences. We want to know how meanings travel from one mind to another by means of sound. In order to describe this kind of communicative competence, we must pay attention to things such as who is speaking to whom, the place where speech messages occur, the time of day, and a host of other contextual matters. At the same time, we cannot overlook the intricate structure of vocal symbols and the rules for combining them appropriately.

In order to understand as many factors as possible that influence the sending and receiving of speech messages, we will take a single example from our own society and follow it through this chapter. You are the ethnographer, unfamiliar with American culture; your task is to listen to people talking in natural settings and decode the messages they utter. To assist in this project we will discuss the elements of language and the nature of communicative competence. Together we will carry out an analysis of language and an ethnography of speaking.

A College Bar[1]

Brady's Bar sits obtrusively on East Sixth Avenue, an old and busy street in a large Midwestern city. Unlike the surrounding buildings with their peeling paint and dirty windows, Brady's new brick walls gleam in the midday sun. Across the street on an old frame building rests a sign, "Victoria's Sauna and Massage Parlor." Next door, in the same building, is a used-furniture outlet. A small grocery store and gas station can be seen farther up the street. In the other direction there is a vacant, weed-strewn lot, an empty house, and a dilapidated liquor store. The noise of traffic rises and falls on East Sixth with the daily rush hour, and buses fill the air with noxious fumes. From the outside Brady's looks more like a new, windowless office building than a bar.

As you go through the double set of doors, designed to protect the inner world of Brady's from the bone-chilling blasts that crowd in with each newcomer on a cold winter night, you immediately face the end of a long horseshoe bar. It runs clear to the back of the room with only enough space along the left side of the horseshoe for a row of tall bar stools. To the right of the bar there are six or seven small tables; on the same side toward the back of the room in a smaller, raised section there are four or five more tables. The room itself could hardly be more than 30 feet square. A deep red carpet adds warmth to the darkness, which is broken here and there by candles on each table and low, soft lights behind the bar. Four middle-aged men are sitting at the bar, an older couple occupy one of the tables in the back. They all appear to be working class or perhaps local businesspeople. Within the hour most of them will head for home and family or to dinners alone in some dilapidated apartment.

Within a few miles of Brady's there are several small colleges; much later in your research you will discover that nearly everyone who comes to Brady's after eight or nine o'clock at night attends one of these schools. At half past nine on a cold Friday night you push your way through the swinging doors and quickly survey the scene before you. Loud music blares from the jukebox; laughter, low voices, and the clink of glasses come from the bar and most of the tables. You quickly note that there are nearly 40 people, mostly young, sitting at the tables and the bar. Later you will wonder how nearly 100 more students are able to crowd into the remaining space; they will stand behind the bar, along the end of the horseshoe, kneel between tables, sit on the steps to the upper section, and fill every available inch of space. Tonight this place is strange to you. You do not know what kinds of people are here. You are not sure what activities will take place, perhaps some ritual or ceremony. Two young women clad in short pants and net stockings move from table to table; each one carries a tray, sometimes empty, sometimes filled with glasses and bottles. There is an atmosphere of relaxed congeniality. One table on the far side of the lower section is empty and you take the chair against the wall so you can see what goes on in the rest of the bar. By now your eyes have become well accustomed to the dim lighting, and you see

[1]This case study is based on James P. Spradley and Brenda J. Mann, *The Cocktail Waitress: Woman's Work in a Man's World*, New York: Wiley, 1975.

Drinking in a nearby bar provides college students with a break from school routine, opportunity to meet other students, and a place that seems especially designed for talking.

that there are two young men at the next table. You will observe their behavior and, if possible, record what they say.

One of the women with a tray walks up to their table and stands in silence looking at these two men. One looks up at her, and you clearly hear him say,

Two double sloe screws on the rocks . . . uhhh . . . for Joe and Bill . . . uhhh . . . yaaa.

The woman smiles, quickly goes to the bar, speaks to the man behind it, and soon returns with two tall, dark bottles and two glasses. She places these on the table, they give her a piece of paper, she offers them a few pieces of metal, which are placed on the table. You have quietly written down what was said and made a mental note of the interaction. No one gives any hint that anything unusual has happened. You think that the strange sounds you heard constituted a speech message of some kind. The young woman's actions suggest that she grasped the meaning of the sounds, which were unintelligible to you. What did this coded message mean? At this point you cannot begin to realize how difficult it will be to decode the full meaning of the simple utterance made by the man at the next table.

Within minutes the woman with the tray approaches you and, instead of standing silently, much to your surprise, she says, "Would you care to order?" an utterance you cannot understand. The only clue you have to what might be appropriate to say comes from your observations of the next table, so you look up and mimic part of what the young man had said.

Two double sloe screws on the rocks . . . uhhh . . . yaaa.

You sense immediately that you may have said the wrong thing, although you are not sure why. The woman flushes for an instant, raises her eyebrows in surprise, and says, "What was that?" but, of course, you cannot understand her question and so you again mimic what you heard.

Two double sloe screws on the rocks . . . uhhh . . . yaaa.

She heads for the bar, obviously confused, and you see that she is talking intensely with the man behind the bar. He looks over at you for an instant; you do not know what they are saying, but you feel certain they are talking about you. She returns with two glasses filled with purple liquid and *not* the tall, dark bottles you expected. After she has gone you begin to sip your drink, wondering what it is that the two men are drinking from the tall bottles. So, brushing aside your embarrassment, you turn to the one nearest your table and point toward his bottle with a questioning look. He simply says, "Hamm's." Now you are even more confused. But you do think you may have learned something. The words used do seem to refer to the drinks that the woman brought to each table. But you cannot understand why they received tall, dark bottles of "Hamm's" and you did not. And why did the woman seem confused and embarrassed at what you said, but not when they said the same thing?

These questions bring you back to your central problem: *how are these people constructing and interpreting vocal symbols, combining them into verbal messages?* In order to answer this question we must look more closely at the nature of vocal symbols and the elements of language.

Vocal Symbols

Social life in a bar or in any other setting requires that people know what others mean when they talk, gesture, or communicate by other means. But how does meaning get from one mind to another? All social animals must perform some kind of behavior that signals information; meaning must "hitch a ride," so to speak, on actions that can be perceived. A man in a bar says, "Two double sloe screws on the rocks" to convey his desire for a certain kind of liquid to drink. His spoken words represent a performance of social behavior that acts as *symbols* to carry information.

A symbol is any object or event that refers to something else. Vocal symbols are the sounds produced by our vocal organs that refer to something. The sounds "a double sloe screw on the rocks" refer to something. This sequence of sounds is a sequence of vocal symbols. For a sound to act as a symbol it must be perceivable. In the bar you could hear the man at the next table say "Hamm's." But the noise produced by the high-frequency whistles used to call dogs are outside our auditory range and cannot be used as symbols to communicate to other people. For a sound to act as a symbol it must also have a *referent*. Symbols may refer to objects, events, actions, ideas, or anything else that is conceivable in human experience. Not all the sounds that human beings make have referents, and each of us continually monitors incoming sounds made by other people for their communicative value. Later you will learn that the sound "uhhh . . ." made by the man when he ordered drinks did not have any referent. You suspect that the other sounds did have referents, but how these symbols are linked to their referents and which referents go with which sounds remains a mystery at this point.

It is important to note that the relationship between symbols and their referents is *arbitrary*. Symbols are assigned their meaning by convention and this means there is no necessary relation between sounds like "Hamm's" or "sloe screw" and one or another kind of drink. These symbols could refer to people, places, gods, or anything else conceivable by human beings. But although the symbol–referent relationship is arbitrary, we must emphasize that *in daily use this relationship is not random*. You cannot assign some vocal symbol to a new referent every time you use it. As your research at Brady's Bar continues, you will test your understanding of speech and discover if you say "Coke" or "coffee" when you really want a "Hamm's," no one will comprehend your meaning. There are conventions for constructing vocal symbols, combining them in appropriate sequences, and attaching them to referents. In order to understand these conventions in any culture, we should know the basic elements of language.

ELEMENTS OF LANGUAGE

Every language is composed of three subsystems for dealing with vocal symbols: *phonology, grammar*, and *semantics*. Phonology deals with sounds and the *relationships between symbols and sounds*. Grammar concerns the *relationships among vocal symbols*. Semantics deals with meaning, the *relationships between symbols and referents*. The rules contained in these three subsystems of every language are used to encode information into speech messages and to decode the sounds of speech to get at their meanings. The people you overheard in Brady's Bar could do both of these things because they had mastered the phonology, grammar, and semantics of their language. As an outsider without this knowledge, you could mimic the speech sounds but not encode or decode the message contained in the sounds.

Every cultural code is a set of rules for *forming, combining*, and *interpreting* symbols. Language is one kind of cultural code. Phonology refers to rules for *forming* symbols; grammar is the rules for *combining* symbols; and semantics refers to rules for *interpreting* symbols. In Figure 3-1 we have summarized the major features of language and how it relates to speech.

Phonology

Phonology, as we said, is a particular kind of cultural knowledge; it is knowledge about speech sounds. The <u>phonology</u> of any language consists of the categories and

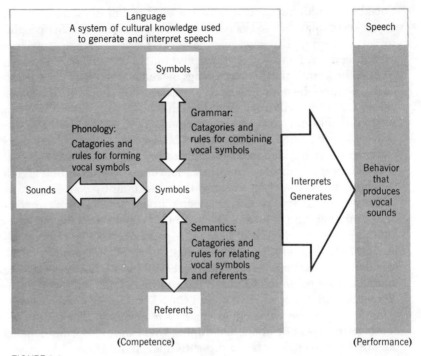

FIGURE 3-1

A Generative Model of Language. Phonology, grammar, and semantics are presented as three distinct subsystems for analytic purposes only. In the actual production and interpretation of speech all three are closely interrelated.

rules for forming vocal symbols. These categories and rules show considerable variety from one culture to another, and so any description of a phonological system will therefore be based on what some local group of people recognizes and uses. We cannot, for instance, describe the sounds of Eskimo speech by using the vowels and consonants of English speech because some sounds in Eskimo have no English equivalents.

Phonemes

It is possible for human beings to distinguish thousands of different speech sounds. Every language categorizes distinct sounds into a small number of units that people learn to produce and recognize. Most languages contain between 30 and 45 such units or phonemes, which are the minimal categories of speech sounds that signal a difference in meaning.

Every phoneme is a category of numerous sounds that people treat as if they were equivalent. As you listen to people talk at Brady's Bar, the phonemes of their language would not be immediately apparent. As an outsider, you would hear many fine distinctions in sound that go unrecognized by the people there. For example, the word "Hamm's" consists of four phonemes: /h/, /a/, /m/, and /z/. (Slash marks indicate that these symbols refer to sounds, not to letters.) But as you listened to people say this word you would notice more than four different sounds. Sometimes the /h/ sound occurs with a strong puff of air; at other times the word sounds like "amm's." When people at the tables utter this word, it has a long, drawn-out /a/ sound; when the young women say it to the man behind the bar, it has a short, clipped /a/. When "Hamm's" occurs alone, there is a noticeable puff of air after the /z/ sound; if it is followed quickly by the word "beer," there is no puff of air.

The way to discover phonemes is to see if they signal a difference in meaning. In all the various ways that "Hamm's" is pronounced, it always seems to refer to tall, dark bottles of liquid. Although you cannot know for sure, at this stage of your research it seems that all the different sounds you can hear do not signal any differences in meaning. They are *nondistinctive*.

You return to Brady's Bar several nights later for another visit only to find it rather crowded. You find a seat at a table, and when the young woman comes to your table, you use the one word you feel confident has a specific meaning, "Hamm's." She smiles, goes to the bar, and returns through the crowded aisles with a tall, dark bottle on her tray. As she turns to go, a young man at the next table reaches out and puts his arm around her waist. To your surprise the young woman quickly removes it and says, "Watch the *hands!*" Although "hands" sounded much like some of the variants you had heard for "Hamm's," the context and behavior involved seemed so different that you felt sure the difference was probably meaningful. Much later, after you had secured the assistance of one of these women to act as an informant, you would test this hunch and find it correct. The two words differ in only one phoneme, a difference referred to as *distinctive*.

$$/h/ \ /a/ \ /m/ \ /z/$$
$$/h/ \ /a/ \ /n/ \ /z/$$

It would be possible to learn all the phonemes of English by going to Brady's Bar each night and listening to people talk, trying to imitate them, allowing them to correct you, and slowly learning to speak appropriately. That, in fact, is similar to the way children learn to distinguish the phonemes in their native language. Because this process is slow and does not make the phonemes explicit, you would probably want to work with informants getting them to *contrast* words that were similar. Whenever you discovered a minimal category of sound that signaled a difference in meaning, you would identify it as a phoneme. The sets of words you used to contrast are called *minimal pairs*. The following are examples of minimal pairs for English and the phonemes isolated by the contrast.

1.	bet	/t/	2.	kill	/k/
	bed	/d/		will	/w/
3.	food	/f/	4.	bet	/e/
	mood	/m/		bit	/i/

Phonological Rules

In addition to categories of sound, the phonology of a language includes rules for arranging these sounds into patterns. English, for instance, has rules that govern which phonemes may occur at the beginning and at the end of a word, and the kinds of sequences that may occur. For example, the /ng/ sound that occurs at the end of *sing* and *tang* is never used to begin an English word, although it occurs in this position in many other languages. Vowels and consonants generally alternate in words, and some sequences of consonants, such as /mktb/, are excluded from English speech.

Phonemes act to signal meaning, but they are not meaningful categories in themselves. Phonological rules are instructions for putting phonemes together into minimal units of meaning, and thus act as a bridge between the phonological and grammatical system of any language.

Grammar

Grammar refers to the categories and rules for combining vocal symbols. If all the symbols of a language could be combined randomly, there would be no need for a grammar. But every language places restrictions on the way words and phrases can be put together. You could go into Brady's Bar and tell one of the young women, "Screw double sloe a rocks the on," and although each word would be recognizable to her, they would not form an appropriate English sentence. Without the competence that comes from learning grammatical categories and rules, you could not tell that this string of sounds was incorrect. The sounds are appropriate; the combination of symbols is not. Linguistic competence enables people to interpret grammatical sentences and also to recognize ungrammatical ones.

Morphemes

No grammar contains rules for combining every word or element of meaning in the language. If this were the case, grammars would be so unwieldy that no one could learn all the rules in one lifetime. The number of possible combinations in any language is infinite. Every grammar deals with *categories* of symbols; they contain rules that tell us how to combine these categories. Take the symbols of chess, for example. You do not have to learn how each of the 32 pieces of carved ivory can be combined with others in order to play chess. Instead, chessmen are grouped into several categories: pawns, knights, bishops, and so on. Once you learn how knights can move, you can apply the rules to any specific knight, no matter how it is shaped or where it is on the chessboard. Grammars involve similar categories of vocal symbols.

Morphemes are the smallest meaningful category in any language. They are minimal units of meaning that cannot be subdivided. There are complex procedures for segmenting the stream of speech into morphemes that all employ the use of *contrast* in both form and meaning. For example, at first you might guess that each of the words in the phrase "on the rocks" constituted a single morpheme. But as you listened you would discover that *rock* contrasted with *rocks*, leading to the discovery that it was a combination of two morphemes: /rak/ and /s/ (plural morpheme). In a similar manner you would find that *screws* in the phrase "two double sloe screws on the rocks" contrasted with *screw*, and you could then isolate /skruw/ and /z/ as two morphemes.

Some words such as *rock*, *two*, *sloe*, and *on* are composed of a single morpheme. Others, such as "undoubtedly," contain several (un-doubt-ed-ly). Some morphemes never occur alone as words, but must be attached to other morphemes or words. The *plural morpheme* in English takes several forms and provides an example. The forms /en/, /s/, /z/, and /es/ are symbols that refer to *number*, but they must be attached to words, changing them from singular to plural (as in ox*en*, rock*s*, screw*s*, and hors*es*). There are numerous kinds of categories of words and morphemes in every language. All such categories, such as noun, pronoun, verb, and adjective, in English are based on the way we use words, not on their meaning. In your research efforts to understand the speech messages in Brady's Bar you would want to map all the classes of words and understand the ways they functioned. But even this would only be a preliminary step to the discovery of meaning. Equally important are the rules for combining all the different kinds of grammatical categories.[2]

Grammatical Rules

The most important developments in the study of language during the last 20 years have concerned the nature and function of grammatical rules. Led by the linguist Noam Chomsky, this movement has proposed that the great significance of grammatical rules is their *generative* capacity. This approach has focused attention on the way a limited number of rules and symbols can be used to generate an infinite set of speech messages. The theory of generative grammar is highly complex, and we shall characterize it only in general terms.

First, generative grammar focuses on a fundamental feature of human speech: the ability of native speakers (1) to create effortlessly new arrangements of words in acceptable combinations and (2) to reject instantaneously unacceptable sentence arrangements that they have never heard before. How can we account for this unique ability? It is clear that people do not learn all the possible combinations of words and then use them in speech. Apparently we use a small number of basic elements (sometimes called kernel sentences) and several kinds of rules. In combination, these are capable of generating the infinite set of grammatical sentences in any language.

The first set of rules, called *phrase structure rules*, is used to identify the underlying base of a spoken sentence. For example, "Two double sloe screws on the rocks, uhhh . . . for Joe and Bill, uhh, yaaaa," was an acceptable utterance to the young woman in Brady's Bar, but it contains no *verb*. The application of phrase structure rules fills in this missing category but not the specific verb. The underlying kernel sentence probably takes a form like, "We want drinks."

At the same time, certain *transformation rules* operate on the kernel sentence to add, delete, rearrange, and do other things to create appropriate combinations. For example, a *context sensitive rule* in the bar would instruct a listener to *add a verb* to utterances in which they are absent when spoken in the context of ordering drinks in the bar. As you listened to people talk in Brady's Bar, you would note that utterances such as "Hamm's," "scotch and soda," and "two double sloe screws on the rocks" only occurred without verbs at tables or at the bar when people were *expected* to want something to drink. No one ever used these noun phrases in isolation from verbs as they walked out the door after an evening of

[2]For a discussion of the major grammatical categories in English, see H. A. Gleason, "Outline of English Morphology," in *An Introduction to Descriptive Linguistics*, New York: Holt, Rinehart and Winston, 1961, pp. 92–110.

drinking. For a speaker this particular transformation rule would be an instruction to *delete a verb* from sentences if spoken in the context of ordering drinks.

The study of phonology and grammar is necessary in order to understand the speech messages used among people. But they are not sufficient. Once you mastered the phonology and grammar of English, you could produce the right sounds and combine categories of words appropriately. You would know, for example, that "Give me a Hamm's," "I want two rocks," and "I want a sloe screw" are all grammatical. You could quickly reject as ungrammatical such utterances as "Hamm's two rocks sloe want."

Although this level of competence is necessary, it would not be sufficient for knowing what these speech messages mean. Furthermore, it would not allow you to judge, as all native speakers in the bar could, that although "I want two rocks" is grammatical and meaningful, it is not appropriate. In order to understand fully the way people talk in any society, we must study the semantic system of language and the sociolinguistic rules for using language in appropriate ways.

SEMANTICS

One subsystem of every language is <u>semantics</u>. It is the categories and rules for relating vocal symbols to their referents. We will examine how these rules function to create referential meaning. Like the rules of grammar, semantic rules are simple instructions to combine things; they instruct us to combine words with what they refer to. A symbol can be said to *refer* because it focuses our attention, it makes us take account of something. For example, the words *Brady's Bar* focus your attention on the building, the setting, and the activities that take place there. At this bar, the word "Hamm's" will make someone pay attention to this particular kind of drink. If you wandered around some night at Brady's, going from table to table, standing at the bar for a while, watching the women talk to the man behind the bar, you would hear words like "Hamm's," "scotch and soda," "brandy alexander," "Smith and Currants," "Harvey Wallbanger," and "Brandy Seven," each causing people to pay attention to a particular kind of drink. After you left Brady's that first night you thought often about how you had used the same symbols as the man at the next table, but for some reason the woman did not bring tall, dark bottles of Hamm's. Now you have formulated a rough hypothesis as to what happened when you said, "Two double sloe screws on the rocks." This phrase and "Hamm's" must refer to things that are so similar that the woman made a mistake and confused them.

Let us go back to Brady's Bar on East Sixth Avenue. Your goal is to investigate the meaning of speech messages in their natural context. Tonight you decide to go to the bar earlier than usual, and at 5:30, just as dusk is settling over the city, you open the heavy outer door at Brady's and go in. Someone is behind the bar and several people sit at the bar, but there is no one at any of the tables. You immediately sense that it might be inappropriate for you to take a table, so you crawl up on one of the tall bar stools with your back against the wall. This provides you with a nice view of the other people and of the entire area. You order a "Hamm's," and wonder whether Bill, the man behind the bar, will bring you a sloe screw. But he gives you a tall, dark bottle of Hamm's beer and a glass.

At about 10:00 you leave your place at the bar and go to the restroom, where you hurriedly jot down a few observations and decide to sit somewhere else. The upper section is quieter, and you notice there is one empty seat along the bar immediately adjacent to where Sandy, one of the women, works. It looks like a good place to see what she does and perhaps even talk to her about different kinds of drinks. Although you know that "Hamm's" and "a double sloe screw on the rocks" are both kinds of drinks, you are not sure how similar or different they might be. As Sandy moves back and forth between tables and the bar, you can listen to many different names being used. For instance, she tells the man behind the bar, "I need four *beers*, two Hamm's and two Millers." Again, she says, "All four of those girls want *fancy drinks*: rusty nail, banana daiquiri, sloe screw, Smith and Currants." And so you begin to sort things out, noting that *beers* and *fancy drinks* are probably two terms that designate larger categories of drinks. Whenever things are slow you find that Sandy is willing to talk about different kinds of drinks.

It turns out that there are four major categories of drinks: *fancy drinks, bar booze, beer,* and *wine*. Much to your surprise, Hamm's and a sloe screw are not even in the same category. One is a *fancy drink*, the other is a *beer* (see Figure 3-2). This probably means that no one would confuse these two drinks, but you cannot tell for sure until you have examined some of their attributes.

Before the evening is over you have managed to discover quite a number of attributes for 10 or 15 drinks. You find the following dimensions of contrast.

1. Use of ice.
2. Kind of glass.
3. Price.
4. Type of liquor.
5. Fruit or nuts added.
6. Additional liquids.
7. Appearance.
8. Odor.

You are certain there must be others, but these seem to be ones that were used repeatedly on different drinks throughout the evening, and they are sufficient to distinguish among all the kinds of drinks you know. When you asked, "How is that drink different from the other one?" the woman would reply, "Oh, it has no ice," or "This one has fruit in it," or "That one looks bubbly, but this one is fizzy."

It is now possible to test your hypothesis that Hamm's and a sloe screw were confused because of their very close referential meaning. Much to your surprise, they only share two of these attributes. The likelihood that the woman confused these drinks seems highly implausible, as you can see from the following comparison.

Drink	Dimensions of Contrast							
	Ice	Glass	Price	Liquor	Fruit/ Nut	Other Liquid	Appearance	Odor
Hamm's	No	Beer	.50	Beer	None	None	Bottle	None
Sloe screw	Yes	Short	.85	Sloe gin	None	Orange juice	Purple	None

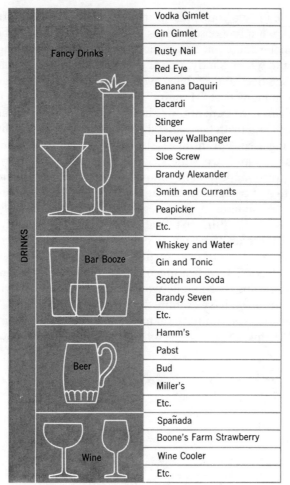

DRINKS	Fancy Drinks	Vodka Gimlet
		Gin Gimlet
		Rusty Nail
		Red Eye
		Banana Daquiri
		Bacardi
		Stinger
		Harvey Wallbanger
		Sloe Screw
		Brandy Alexander
		Smith and Currants
		Peapicker
		Etc.
	Bar Booze	Whiskey and Water
		Gin and Tonic
		Scotch and Soda
		Brandy Seven
		Etc.
	Beer	Hamm's
		Pabst
		Bud
		Miller's
		Etc.
	Wine	Spañada
		Boone's Farm Strawberry
		Wine Cooler
		Etc.

FIGURE 3-2
Kinds of drinks.

LANGUAGE AND SOCIAL CONTEXT

Tonight you have clarified the ethnographic problem but not solved it. Your hypothesis that it was a chance mistake because of similarity in drinks cannot be verified. It now appears that the woman did not confuse drinks but interpreted what the man said in a special way. How did she make this interpretation? How did she know to bring them "Hamm's beer" when they ordered "sloe screws on the rocks"? And why do people who come to Brady's Bar engage in this kind of double-talk? In conducting your ethnography of speaking, in order to make further progress, you will have to take a holistic perspective and go beyond the study of vocal symbols and their referents.

The Holistic Perspective

A basic tenet of anthropological research is that in order to understand any aspect of a culture, you must examine the larger whole. Those who abstract tiny bits and pieces from a culture and try to make sense out of them will fail to crack the cultural code. Ethnographers must take a holistic perspective and seek to relate language to religion, economics, the social structure, and every other area of a culture. Those who study religious rituals will find it necessary to examine their relationship to things such as subsistence, kinship, and language.

In your study of Brady's Bar you would soon realize that your search would have to go beyond the elements of language and beyond referential meaning. Symbols do more than refer; in every society, people use speech messages for a variety of purposes besides naming things and making direct references. Already you have seen that phonology and grammar alone are insufficient for interpreting messages. But even semantics cannot show us the way to interpret everything people say. And it cannot tell us why people talk the way they do, why they speak to some individuals and not others, why things are said at certain times but not at others, and a great many other things about speaking. In order to understand what people mean when they talk, we must find out the sociolinguistic rules that connect language use to the social context of speaking. You will have to discover the sociolinguistic rules for talking at all. This will involve things like when to speak, how to distinguish teasing from ordering, how to talk to different people in the bar, and what people take for granted when they talk because they already know about it.

Let us contrast briefly the various sets of cultural rules that people use to communicate in any society.

Phonological Rules: ⟶ For forming vocal symbols
Grammatical Rules: ⟶ For combining vocal symbols into appropriate sequences.
Semantic Rules: ⟶ For combining vocal symbols with their references into meaningful utterances.
Sociolinguistic Rules: ⟶ For combining meaningful utterances with social situations into appropriate messages.

In order to discover the sociolinguistic rules you will need to study many other aspects of Brady's Bar. After many more weeks of observation and interviews you would find out that the people who come to the bar are organized into a small community. When you first came to the bar the woman classified you as a "loner" but the other two men you overheard were "regulars" (see Figure 3-3). She knew they did not want two sloe screws on the rocks but really did want Hamm's *because* they were regulars. Waitresses soon learn the regular drinks of regular customers. Later you would discover the cues that people use to signal whether they are *ordering a drink* or *teasing*. You would discover that the drink "sloe screw" has sexual connotations and that regular male customers make use of these tacit meanings to tease female waitresses. A *loner* off the street would never attempt such teasing and your actions on that first night elicited the strange responses from the waitress. Slowly, over the months of participant observation, you would develop a holistic perspective on the culture of Brady's Bar. And this holistic view would en-

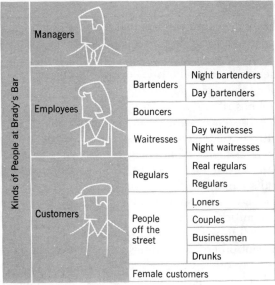

FIGURE 3-3
The speech community at Brady's Bar.

able you to understand the various facets of culture from language to economics and social structure.

Talking and Drinking: A Cross-Cultural Example

It may appear that places like Brady's Bar are primarily for drinking, but such is not the case. As the analysis in this chapter shows, talking is equally important. The importance of drinking and talking has also been observed by anthropologists in other societies. One of the best studies of talking and drinking was done in the Philippine Islands by the anthropologist Charles O. Frake. The scenes pictured here as well as the description of talking are based on his elegant description "How to Ask for a Drink in Subanun" (1964).[3]

Deep in the tropical rain forests of Zamboanga Peninsula on the Island of Mindanao, the Subanun live in small family groups, practicing swidden agriculture. Social ties outside the family are maintained by networks to kin and neighbors rather than through some larger formal organization. Social encounters beyond the family occur on frequent festive occasions that always include the drinking of an alcoholic beverage. The Subanun taxonomy of beverages includes "toddy," "wine," "liquor," "juice-broth," "water," and an alcoholic beverage that we can call "rice wine." We are interested here only in this last drink. In a personal communication Professor Frake has discussed the nature of rice wine: "What the Subanun drink is technically neither wine nor beer, nor is it always made of rice.

[3]We are indebted to Charles O. Frake for the pictures that appear here as well as the material on which the captions are based.

55

Since it is most akin to Japanese sake, which we usually call "rice wine," it is probably best to call this Subanun beverage rice wine."

A drinking group gathers around a large Chinese jar and drinks from this common container by using a long bamboo straw. There are elaborate rules for these drinking sessions that govern such activities as competitive drinking, opposite-sex partners drinking together under the cover of a blanket, and games where drinking is done in chugalug fashion. But the drinking is secondary to the talking on these occasions and what Frake has said about the Subanun could easily apply to Brady's Bar:

> The Subanun expression for drinking talk, . . . "talk from the straw," suggests an image of the drinking straw as a channel not only of the drink but also of drinking talk. The two activities, drinking and talking, are closely interrelated in that how one talks bears on how much one drinks and the converse is, quite obviously, also true. . . . Especially for an adult male, one's role in the society at large, insofar as it is subject to manipulation, depends to a considerable extent on one's verbal performance during the drinking encounters (pp. 128–129).

Frake concludes his discussion of Subanun drinking with the following observation:

> The Subanun drinking encounter thus provides a structured setting within which one's social relationships beyond his everyday associates can be extended, defined, and manipulated through the use of speech. The cultural patterning of drinking talk lays out an ordered scheme of role play through the use of terms of address, through discussion and argument, and through display of verbal art. The most skilled in "talking from the straw" are the de facto leaders of the society. In instructing our stranger to Subanun society how to ask for a drink, we have at the same time instructed him how to get ahead socially (p. 131).

A typical Chinese jar used for making and drinking rice wine. Rice (or some other starchy staple) mash and yeast are sealed in this type of porcelain jar and left to age for several months or more. Jars of fermented mash are often kept hidden in the fields so that visitors to a house will not know how much stock the householders have in reserve.

Cultural rules govern the way people drink rice wine on any festive occasion. First, water is poured into the jar of mash. As it makes its way to the bottom of the jar it picks up both flavor and alcoholic content. The resulting liquid in the bottom of the jar is extracted by the drinker as shown here through a bamboo straw. To begin with the jar is filled to the brim with water, but the drinker lowers the level of the water and when it is replaced, everyone can tell how much any individual drinks. There are three major kinds of drinking recognized by the Subanun: tasting, competitive drinking, and game drinking. When people are drinking they must follow this order of activities. No one would think of beginning a particular drinking bout with game drinking, for example.

While competitive drinking continues, the conversation shifts away from the "jar talk" to discussion. This involves local gossip and often moves on to important disputes. The drinking talk thus becomes a kind of legal institution for settling disputes; the decisions made and their legal force, depend in part on the verbal ability of those involved in the discussion. If drinking continues long enough, those who remain at the jar shift to other topics, engaging in a kind of display of "verbal art" that involves drinking songs, verse competitions, and game drinking. In shifting away from discussions of disputes, there is a new air of festivity. This scene shows the wee hours of a drinking party. Two surviving drinkers gossip and sing drinking songs while exchanging turns at the drinking straw. The can at their side holds water to add to the jar after each turn. A couple plays gong music in the background while others sleep off the party amidst empty jars.

Many different occasions can bring together people from diverse families for drinking and talking. Here a curing ceremony has become the occasion for bringing out one of the large Chinese porcelain jars of rice wine. The rice wine is being offered to the supernaturals as a part of a festive meal along with meat and rice. The supernaturals are being called to the meal by the rhythmic striking of a Chinese porcelain bowl.

There are four kinds of talk that occur during the drinking of rice wine. The first occurs during an initial round of tasting. The person who provided the jar starts the tasting round by inviting someone to drink. That person squats before the jar and asks permission of all the others who are sitting around the jar as part of the drinking group. This invitation and asking permission involve subtle expressions of deference and social rank.

After everyone has tasted, each time with new water being poured into the jar to make up for the amount drunk, "jar talk" begins and competitive drinking. As Frake has noted, "Measurement is an important aspect of competitive rounds, participants keeping a mental record of each other's consumption. Within a round, successive drinkers must equal the consumption of the drinker who initiated the round. In later rounds, as the brew becomes weaker, the measure tends to be raised" (p. 128). Most of the "jar talk" centers around the quality of the drink being consumed.

Here preparations are being made for an offering to a variety of supernaturals during a major ceremony of the agricultural cycle. Each supernatural requires drink and specific kinds of food. Onlookers must wait for the conclusion of the ceremonies before they too can eat and drink what the supernaturals leave over.

During the last stage of a drinking encounter there is a marked shift in the atmosphere. The Subanun see it as a time to engender good feelings among all present. "Participants who have displayed marked hostility toward each other during the course of drinking talk may be singled out for special ritual treatment designed to restore good feelings" (p. 131).

SUMMARY

Language is a system of cultural knowledge used to generate and interpret speech. Speech refers to the behavior that produces vocal sounds. Competence is the possession of cultural knowledge, in this case the categories and rules of a language. Performance is the behavior that this knowledge generates. Competence accounts for the fact that native speakers can produce novel utterances that have never been heard before and can interpret them appropriately.

Language is used to generate and interpret vocal symbols. A symbol is any object or event that refers to something. The relationship between a symbol and its referent is an arbitrary one. Language is composed of three sets of categories and rules: phonology, grammar, and semantics. Phonology consists of the categories and rules for forming vocal symbols. The minimal categories of sounds that signal a difference in meaning are called phonemes. Phonological rules are instructions for forming and combining phonemes. Grammar consists of the categories and rules for combining vocal symbols. The smallest meaningful category in any language is called a morpheme. Semantics refers to the categories and rules for relating symbols to their referents.

In order to understand how people use their language and how they speak appropriately as well as grammatically, anthropologists take a holistic perspective.

This means that they study the relationship between language and the entire social context in which speech messages occur. An ethnography of speaking examines the many relationships between language and the rest of a culture.

MAJOR CONCEPTS

LANGUAGE	SEMANTICS
COMPETENCE	PHONEME
SPEECH	MORPHEME
PERFORMANCE	MINIMAL PAIR
SYMBOL	SOCIOLINGUISTIC RULES
GRAMMAR	HOLISTIC PERSPECTIVE
PHONOLOGY	REFERENT

SELECTED READINGS

Birdwhistell, Ray L.: *Kinesics and Context: Essays on Body Motion Communication*, Philadelphia: University of Pennsylvania Press, 1970.
A collection of essays on the study of body movements in communication by the anthropologist who has done the most to develop a rigorous science of kinesics.

Burling, Robbins: *Man's Many Voices: Language in Its Cultural Context*, New York: Holt, Rinehart and Winston, 1970.
An introduction to the major issues in anthropological linguistics.

Gleason, H. A.: *Introduction to Descriptive Linguistics*, New York: Holt, Rinehart and Winston, 1961.
An introductory text to descriptive linguistics that covers phonology, grammar, language classification, and communication theory.

Greenberg, Joseph H.: *Anthropological Linguistics: An Introduction*, New York: Random House, 1968.
A well-written, nontechnical discussion of the nature of language, the field of anthropological linguistics, and the subsystems of language.

Gumperz, John, and Dell Hymes (editors): *Directions in Sociolinguistics: The Ethnography of Communication*, New York: Holt, Rinehart and Winston, 1972.
This book presents some of the major directions of research on the social meaning of verbal communication. The kinds of studies represented aim to examine the nature of communicative competence. The introductory chapters by the two editors provide an excellent review of concepts and research strategies.

Hall, Edward T.: *The Silent Language*, Garden City, N.Y.: Doubleday, 1959.
The author examines how we communicate with other aspects of culture in addition to language. He discusses how such things as time and space are structured by our cultural knowledge and communicate information.

Hymes, Dell (editor): *Language in Culture and Society: A Reader in Linguistics and Anthropology*, New York: Harper & Row, 1964.
A large collection of previously published articles in the field of anthropological linguistics.

CHAPTER FOUR

Social Structure

We Americans often underestimate the importance of our society, the culture-bearing organized social group in which we anchor our lives. We value, instead, a freedom of personal action and a self-reliance aimed at personal independence. We train our children to stand on their own two feet, to stick up for themselves. We condemn others who rely on government or family support. We accuse people of giving in to social pressure when they appear to yield too easily to the wishes of those around them. Our schools often strive for individualized instruction. We read books that teach us how to "look out for number one." We measure the course of our lives in terms of personal growth.

Yet, despite our value on independence, we continue to live in a highly complex society. Far from becoming hermits, we live out our lives in association with other people. We depend on the cooperative efforts of countless individuals to meet our physical needs, our requirements for food, clothing, shelter, and transportation. And other people are essential for our self-image, for it is their judgment of our actions that contributes to our sense of personal identity and self-worth. Indeed, our very value on independence is a social one, taught to us and reinforced daily by others. If we are to understand the forces that impinge on our lives, it is essential that we learn about the structure and dynamics of society.

Social life is a universal human condition; with few exceptions, human beings everywhere live in social groups. But the way human social groups are put together—the organization of their parts and relationships and the form this puts on social behavior—is not the same from society to society. Although there are some basic elements from which all human societies structure themselves as we will see later, wide variation is still possible, and, in fact, necessary for human adaptation.

Rural Indian society seen from the perspective of a young married woman illustrates a little of this variety. Instead of moving in with her new husband in a separate residence as she might in the United States, the Indian bride goes to live with her husband in his parents' house. There she lives in a world of other women, her mother-in-law, her husband's brothers' wives, her husband's younger sisters. She sleeps with them in the women's quarters, helps them grind wheat for the day's unleavened bread, watches their children, helps them with cleaning, and joins in the task of cooking. Although she sees her husband and his male relatives from time to time, her interaction with these kin is formally restricted.

This Rajput bride's experience reflects a difference in the structure of high-caste Indian society. Whereas an American bride lives with her husband separately and eventually starts a group called a *nuclear family* when she has children, the young Rajput woman enters an *extended family* made up of several married couples and their children. The needs of this large family and its place in the wider community affect the way its members must relate to each other and outsiders. Thus these relationships and the social structure they define are different from those found in the United States.

The significance and variety of human social structure has had an enormous impact on anthropology. Early anthropologists like E. B. Tylor and Lewis Henry Morgan sought to classify and compare different social arrangements from around the world. Emile Durkheim, Radcliffe-Brown, and Bronislaw Malinowski looked at particular social structures in an effort to define their parts more completely and to understand the functional relationships that held them together. Today many professionals call themselves social or sociocultural anthropologists and seek, as a primary goal, the understanding of human society.

In this chapter we will discuss the basic dimensions of human social life. We start with a review of the social behavior of primates, our nearest living relatives. Then we turn to the concepts of social interaction, social structure, status, role, social situation, and social group.

PRIMATE SOCIAL BEHAVIOR

Human beings are primates, a taxonomic order that classifies over 200 different living animals on the basis of homologous traits (features that are similar and that imply common ancestry). No single characteristic defines all primates; the order is too physically divergent. But many display features such as large brains, opposable digits, stereoscopic vision, poor sense of smell, and fingernails—characteristics that apparently reflect adaptation to life in the trees.

The order *primata* contains such varied animals as lemurs, lorises, and tarsiers, called the *prosimii*, and *anthropoidea*, the new- and old-world monkeys, apes, and humans. Chimpanzees and gorillas are most closely related to people, followed by orangutans and gibbons, old-world monkeys, new-world monkeys, and the *prosimii*. Until recently most of our information about primates came from observations of captive animals in zoos. Such observations, however, reflected the behavior of animals adapting to life in captivity, not behavior in the wild. Within the last 20 years this situation has been remedied by firsthand field studies of many monkey and ape species in their natural wild habitats. Primatologists, many of whom are also trained anthropologists, have conducted field studies that often last for years and require patient observation and a building of trust between the ob-

In recent years, there have been many firsthand studies of monkeys and apes in their natural habitats. This primatologist carefully records the behavior of a baboon.

server and his or her subjects. The result has been an enormous increase in our knowledge about these bright and complex animals.

One feature of primates that quickly emerged from these studies was the importance of social organization. Although not every primate species is social, and primates who live most of the time in trees seem less intensely organized than ground dwellers, social adaptation is a hallmark of the primate order. The adaptive advantages of social living are clearly indicated by the defensive strategies of ground-dwelling baboons.

Baboon Defensive Strategies

Baboons live on the grassy African savannah and are, like us, primarily ground dwellers. Because they are so exposed in the open, baboon troops must guard against lions, leopards, and other predators. Even with its huge canine teeth, which are designed for fighting, no single baboon is a match for these large enemies. Baboons that become separated from their troop, a group of about 50 to 100

Social organization is clearly an advantage for baboons. When a troop moves from one place to another, the ordering of its members provides defense for the entire group. This troop was photographed as it moved across the open savanna.

animals, rarely last more than a few days in the open by themselves. But how do baboon social relationships increase the individual animal's ability to defend itself against danger?

When the troop moves, the females, young juveniles, infants, and two or three dominant males stay together in a cluster. Subordinate males station themselves at the front and rear of the group as outriders. In this position one of these males is most likely to spot a predator. When he does, he gives a warning bark along with an appropriate facial expression. The dominant males assess the warning and the danger, and if they repeat the alarm, the group moves into action. The subordinate male who gave the alarm and the other outriders near him are already interposed between the group and the danger. Females, infants, and juveniles move away from the danger toward the safety of the nearest clump of trees. The dominant males, whose job it is to lead the defense, move quickly into the line, followed by the subordinate males who were stationed at the other end of the troop. Together they put on a threatening display to frighten the predator. If this strategy fails, they may actually attack, utilizing their greater numbers to best advantage.

This defensive social arrangement is clearly advantageous to baboon survival. Adult males, experienced in fighting and unencumbered by infants and children, face the predator. Employment of subordinate animals on the periphery of the group ensures that some adult males are always between the troop and danger.

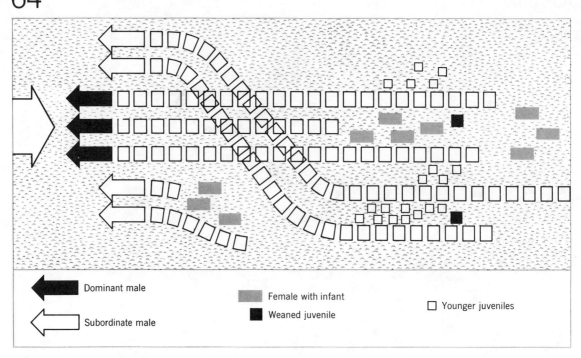

Dominant male

Subordinate male

Female with infant

Weaned juvenile

Younger juveniles

The central location of the dominant males enables them to receive an alarm, assess the intensity of the threat, and reach the site of the trouble quickly, no matter from what direction it appears. By banding together, baboons are able to give themselves a measure of security that would be impossible for any isolated individual.

Primates and Humans

In addition to social adaptation, primates manifest several other important behavioral characteristics. They learn much of their behavior and require an especially long time between birth and social maturity for their education. They have a complex system of communication marked by vocalizations, facial expressions, gestures, and touches. They are unusually protective of their young. With a few exceptions, they lack permanent mating pairs; females and their offspring usually form basic social units. They indicate social support and goodwill through grooming, the act of searching one another's fur for parasites and dirt. Their groups are partially organized by dominance hierarchies among males and of males over females; however, dominance is more noticeable among ground dwellers such as baboons and other species organized for defense. Baboons are not fiercely territorial, although they do have a home range containing core living areas.

In one sense we humans reflect many of these primate characteristics, but with differences in intensity and structure. Learning our cultural heritage is especially important to us and we require an even longer childhood to accomplish it. As we have already seen, human language is extremely complex and permits the communication of much more information than can be managed by other primate groups. We are protective of our young but in the context of relatively permanent mating pairs. We are capable of much more complex social arrangements. Some people actually do groom one another, but verbal grooming, as some call the spoken pleasantries that so often mark human interaction, seems a more common way to signal social support. Finally, humans reflect a tendency toward dominance hierarchy, although the way we define rank varies culturally from one group to the next. In fact, our primate heritage is everywhere modified by culture.

Above all, one thing stands out about humans in comparison to other primates—our complex social organization. Although we often complain about our social shortcomings, the high crime rates, poverty, and public indifference that seems to afflict our society, the very size and complexity of our country and other human groups imply a special emphasis on social living. Human society demonstrates a high degree of cooperative interaction—we share things more willingly; we are even relatively unaggressive. Social interaction is a crucial and highly organized feature of human life.

SOCIAL INTERACTION

Social interaction is systematic behavior that occurs between (or among) two or more people. Whenever we act in some way vis-à-vis another, we are in some kind of social relationship with that person. Thus social interaction is the behavioral side of every social relationship. It is what people do in relation to other people, both in and out of their presence. Social interaction is what the anthropologist observes in the field situation. In the following description the late anthropologist Carlton S. Coon describes behavior that constitutes social interaction.

Mohammed, Hamid, Ali, and a dozen other men like them wash, put on clean clothing, and walk to the mosque. It is a bright, clear day and the congregation meets out of doors. The leader of the mosque, Si Abd el Kadher, a fine old man with a white beard, is there to greet them. He shakes hands with each of the men, one by one, kissing his finger and touching his forehead in each case. While they are waiting for all to arrive, the men chat with each other informally, mostly in pairs, although a group of five listens for a short while to the narrative of one man.

Si Abd el Kadher now takes his place at one end of the little terrace in front of the mosque and the others face him. In a fine, well-modulated voice Si Abd el Kadher begins to pray, and the others pray after him. He kneels, prostrates himself, and comes back on his haunches, then arises. Each part of this sequence of actions is accompanied by elements of his prayer. He does this several times, and so do the men who face him. When they are through he delivers a sermon to which they listen attentively. When he has finished some of them stop to speak to him briefly, and all go home.[1]

[1]Carlton S. Coon (editor), *A Reader in General Anthropology*, New York: Holt, Rinehart and Winston, 1948, p. 577.

Social interaction is *systematic*, although to the outsider interactions among people may not always appear to have form or order. Collective behavior may seem like a flowing stream in which one event shades into the next, without beginning or end, unique to the moment, unprecedented. If you casually witnessed for the first time the events described by Coon, the internal order of existing social relationships would not immediately strike you. You might see men arrive, touch, talk, kneel, listen, and leave in the course of your observation, but you could easily miss the systematic arrangement of parts. Each act would merge with the next. But if you watch carefully, the orderliness of social relationships will become apparent. You might notice, for example, that as men arrived, they grasp the hand of one particular individual. You might see that talking between pairs of men occurred simultaneously. They all kneel together, all listen, all respond to the speaker. Each departs with similar gestures and words. This *repetition* of action provides you with a sense of order, a feeling that the behavior does not occur by chance but is somehow organized.

Another indication that social interaction is systematic is that it is *recurrent*. If you stay at the mosque to observe for several days, weeks, or months, you would discover that the collection of men interacting there was not a chance occurrence. Men would come to the mosque repeatedly, and you could not fail to notice that the same sequence of actions occurred. Each time men arrived, they would shake hands, talk, kneel, pray, and leave in the same way. You would come to expect things to happen in a particular order, and you would be surprised if they did not. Although you would not know the meaning of what was going on, you could see that the interaction was patterned and systematic.

The patterns of social interaction become second nature to the participants so that we can instantly recognize when behavior fits the patterns we know and when it does not. Because social interaction is systematic, it is *predictable;* we can anticipate how other people will act and how we should respond to them. Each man who comes to the mosque recognizes that there is an orderliness to behavior, he anticipates what others will do, and he knows when his own actions are appropriate. If the leader of the mosque were to greet each man with loud laughter and kiss him on the cheek instead of touch his forehead, all would be shocked at such inappropriate behavior. If any man were to sit with his back to Si Abd el Kadher as he spoke to the group, the others would immediately wonder what was wrong with this individual. It is their culture that enables these men to interpret the experience of social interaction and to generate behavior. We call this part of culture the social structure.

SOCIAL STRUCTURE

Social structure refers to the culturally defined parts and their relationships that make up a society. The structural description of a society is a little like the physiologist's description of the human body. The physiologist looks for distinctive parts of the body by carefully dissecting it. The results of this investigation can be found in any anatomy text. For page after page, there are long descriptions of the body's parts, its bones, organs, muscles, and nerves. And along with the descriptions are discussions of how various parts are connected and related: how the organs are situated in relation to each other; how they contribute to bodily processes; how the muscles are attached to the bones; and how they work for the entire body.

In the same sense, anthropologists dissect societies, looking for their basic parts and relationships. Anthropology texts are filled with descriptions of social parts, clubs, presidents, fathers, neighborhoods, friends, families, and their relationships with each other.

As part of this search for structural parts, many anthropologists have sought out basic, universal elements of social structure, the fundamental building blocks out of which other parts are constructed. Just as the physiologist might argue that the body's parts are constructed from a basic element, the cell, anthropologists find certain features of human social life that seem to be fundamental elements of social structure everywhere. Although there is considerable disagreement over what categories should be considered its basic units, we have chosen to divide social structure into four elements—status, role, social situation, and social group—because such units appear to be both universal and useful for the analysis of any particular social structure. We will look at these elements primarily within the context of a single social structure, that of the Kwakiutl living along the northwest coast of Canada.

STATUS

North Americans often use the term "status" to label the degree to which people are given esteem by others. They speak of someone's "high status," or the fact that he possesses "status symbols," like a large mahogany office desk, because he is "status climbing." But most anthropologists use the term status in another way. Instead of using it as a label for esteem (they usually employ the term "rank" for this purpose as we will see in Chapter 8), they define statuses as culturally defined positions associated with particular social structures. Status positions are usually named, and people fill them. From the perspective of the individual, statuses are the categories of people who interact.

The structure of the typical Western nuclear family illustrates how statuses work. If they are not extended in any way, such families contain eight statuses: mother, father, husband, wife, son, daughter, brother, and sister. In order to interact with each other, family members must assume at least one of these statuses.

But it is important to realize that people are not themselves statuses. Statuses are social positions; people fill them. Indeed, a person often assumes several statuses in a usual day depending on the statuses of those with whom he or she must interact. For example, the nuclear family, as we noted, has eight possible statuses. Imagine that it has four actual members, a married couple and one male and one female offspring. The female child of the couple will take the status "daughter" when she interacts with her mother or father, and "sister" when she deals with her brother. Although she is a single person, she moves from one social position to the other, and with each social position go different rules for behavior, as we will see in the next section.

Statuses always occur in pairs, and there are cultural rules for which statuses can go together. For example, within the nuclear family "son" pairs with "mother" and "father," but one cannot be a son when he interacts with husbands, wives, brothers, sisters, sons, and daughters. Such rules are even clearer in other structural contexts. A woman who lectures to students in a college classroom cannot take the status "mother," for the members of her audience are "students."

Ascribed and Achieved Status

Every society limits access to particular statuses. Stated another way, an individual must possess certain criteria before he or she can legitimately assume a designated status. Jobs, which are statuses often found in the social structures of economic organizations, reflect such criteria. Company job descriptions usually contain a list of requirements, such as previous experience, levels of education, and special training, that limit access to particular job statuses. Ralph Linton was one of the first anthropologists to recognize the importance of the criteria giving access to statuses, arguing that there were two basic kinds.

Societies have . . . [developed] two types of statuses, the ascribed *and the* achieved. *Ascribed statuses are those which are assigned to individuals without reference to their innate differences or abilities. They can be predicated and trained for from the moment of birth. The* achieved *statuses are, at a minimum, those requiring special qualities, although they are not necessarily limited to these. They are not assigned to individuals from birth but left open to be filled through competition and individual effort.[2]*

Linton's ascribed statuses are based on biological attributes over which people have no control, such as age, sex, kinship, and caste (rank acquired permanently at birth). "Child," "woman," "brother," and "white person" are examples of statuses that are ascribed. Statuses such as company jobs depend on achieved criteria—education, experience, training—and are not assumed automatically. These are achieved statuses.

When anthropologists investigate and analyze the social structure of a particular society, they look for sets of social statuses, the rules by which these are paired, and the criteria by which individuals gain access to social positions. Let us illustrate such a description by looking more closely at part of Kwakiutl social structure.

Kwakiutl Statuses[3]

Eons ago, in the dim geological past, the high and rugged mountains of British Columbia, Canada, settled slowly into the Pacific Ocean. Today the coastline of this beautiful province drops into the sea with such an abruptness that it has left

[2]Ralph Linton, *The Study of Man*, New York: Appleton-Century-Crofts, 1936, p. 115.

[3]The material on the Kwakiutl included in this chapter is based largely on the following works of Franz Boas: "The Social Organization and the Secret Societies of the Kwakiutl Indians," Washington: Report of the U.S. National Museum for 1895, 1897, pp. 311–738; *Ethnology of the Kwakiutl*, 35th Annual Report 1913–1914, Bureau of American Ethnology, 1921; *Kwakiutl Culture as Reflected in Mythology*, New York: G. E. Stechert, 1935; and *Kwakiutl Ethnography*, Chicago: University of Chicago Press, 1966.

Kwakiutl villages were built facing the water. This one at Fort Rupert is where Franz Boas conducted much of his field work during the 1890's and the early part of this century.

hundreds of narrow fiords and inlets that reach their long fingers inland. All that remains of many of the mountains are their peaks, which rise above the water to form thousands of islands. Some, like Vancouver Island, stretch for more than 100 miles north and south and reach nearly 5000 feet above the sea. Others are so small they look like large boulders jutting from the dark green water. Cormorant Island, which lies between the mainland and the north end of Vancouver Island, is only a few miles long. On this island is a small community of native Americans and others who have come during the last century. Although Alert Bay, as the town is called, creates the impression of being a single town, it is actually two towns, one Indian, one white, divided by an invisible line. Part of the island is an Indian reservation, the Nimpkish reserve, to which the Kwakiutl Indians from more than 15 surrounding villages have come during the last few years. Nestled in protected coves on the mainland and on other islands are other Kwakiutl villages. Some have a few residents, others are merely a row of empty houses with a totem pole house post here and there, relics of an earlier day.

More than 80 years ago Franz Boas began his ethnographic investigation of the Kwakiutl. He visited them nearly every year for 40 years, learned their language, and recorded their culture. When he first visited Fort Rupert, a small village near Alert Bay, one of the major Kwakiutl villages at that time, their culture was still flourishing. In order to understand the complex patterns of behavior he observed,

Boas sought to discover the categories the Kwakiutl employed to organize their experience. He recorded many different statuses. Some were based on their kinship, some on their fishing activity, and others on their rich ceremonial life. This last aspect of Kwakiutl culture provides us with an elaborate set of statuses.

Each winter, the time for certain ceremonies, the Kwakiutl took up their statuses as either *seals* or *sparrows*. The seals were the more important, and there were at least eight different kinds, one of which was the *hamatsa*, or cannibal. In order to become a cannibal, it was necessary to go through a long involved initiation, an experience long remembered by those high-ranking chiefs who alone had the privilege.

The class of sparrow statuses consisted of the following categories: *nuisances* and *killer whales* (see Figure 4-1). The sparrows organized the ceremonies and filled certain official positions during the evening performances. For instance, one sparrow would be the master of ceremonies, one group of sparrows would be *singers*, another would be *composers*, and still another would be *dancers*. The various sparrow statuses have many attributes, some of which are shown in Figure 4-2.

FIGURE 4-1
Some Kwakiutl statuses.
(Source. *Adapted from*
Franz Boas, Kwakiutl Eth-
nography, *Chicago: Chicago*
University Press, 1966,
p. 175.)

FIGURE 4-2
Some defining features of sparrow statuses. (Source. Adapted from Franz Boas, Kwakiutl
Ethnography. *Chicago: Chicago University Press, 1966, p. 175.)*

Sparrows	
	Nuisances
	Killer whales
	Sea lions
	Whales
	Eaters
	Crows
	Hens
	Cows

Sparrows	Sex	Age	Rank
Nuisances	Male	Juvenile	None
Killer whales	Male	Young	None
Sea lions	Male	Older	None
Whales	Male	Older	Chief
Eaters	Male	Middle age	Head chief
Crows	Female	Juvenile	None
Hens	Female	Adult	None
Cows	Female	Old	None

ROLE

Role refers to the culturally generated behavior associated with statuses. Statuses are social positions; roles are the expected behaviors associated with status positions. Role may vary for a person in a particular status when that status is paired with different social positions. A professor's role will include lecturing, discussing, and advising in the professor–student relationship. It usually will not involve gossiping and deciding department policy, which is part of the professor's role in the professor–professor relationship.

The hamatsa *of the Koskimo, a tribe of Kwakiutl, at a feast at Fort Rupert. The "rings around the mens" necks are woven from cedar bark and have special ritual significance that mark the individuals' identities as* hamatsa.

The significance of role can be seen in family interaction as well. It is breakfast time in a typical middle-class home. People are emerging from different parts of the house to gather for the early morning meal. Each knows his or her status and also who the other people are. Together they form a family group and will interact in the familiar setting of a shared meal. The eldest male in this group has two statuses: *father* and *husband*. He will probably take a seat at the table that signifies the authority belonging to these statuses in the family. As he interacts with others around the table, he will behave in ways that are appropriate to these statuses. If his 12-year-old daughter holds her spoon incorrectly or chews the toast with her mouth open, he will correct her. No one will be surprised at his actions because everyone has learned it is part of his role as father. If, however, he corrects his wife or instructs her to "clean up her plate," everyone will be surprised. Furthermore, if his daughter or his 6-year-old son points out serious flaws in the manners of their father and insists that he correct his behavior, the breakfast will quickly become a battlefield. The roles we learn are the rules for play in social interaction.

In our discussion of the Kwakiutl winter ceremonies we have already discussed numerous roles associated with the various statuses. We can now be more specific. A feature of one role, associated with the status of seal, was to keep certain information secret from others. The sacred winter season was known as "the secrets" for this reason. Only persons who had been initiated into one or more of the seal groups were to know about these secrets. Most of the secrets dealt with the simulated nature of the supernatural elements in the ceremonies. It was the role of some seals to go out into the woods and blow the sacred whistles to simulate the voices of spirits. Others carefully planned the disappearance of each new initiate so it would appear that he had evaporated into thin air. And everyone who knew the secrets was expected to keep this information from those who did not know.

Each night as the seals were dancing and singing to attract young men back from the land of spirits, the sparrows would jeer and mock their performances. The role of the seals, in turn, was to become suddenly possessed by their spirits and rush on the sparrows, driving them from the dance house in mass confusion. Again, only the initiated knew that these aggressive acts were done to simulate states of possession.

The most important role was played by the young cannibal initiates. During their stay in the woods, each would fast and bathe in icy pools to prepare himself for his return to the village. In the early days of his confinement, a female relative was assigned to prepare food for each young man as he lived in a small makeshift shelter in the woods. During this time his possession by the cannibal spirit created in him an intense desire for human flesh. Sometimes the decomposed body of a dead relative would be placed on the roof of the lean-to shelter in which the young man lived. When the time came for his return to the village, he had to be coaxed back. In addition to the songs and dances having this effect, the young female relative might aid in the process. She would disrobe and carry the decomposed corpse ahead of the boy; his lust for human flesh would cause him to follow her. When he approached the village and saw people there, he might suddenly lose control and rush at someone to bite a piece of flesh from an arm. Generally, it would take many days to attract the boy eventually into the dance house where he would be "tamed" by the other cannibals. In the final act of the ritual the decomposed corpse would be brought into the house, and the sight of it would excite all the other cannibals, who would rush on it and appear to devour it. Finally, the older dancers would succeed in assisting the young initiate in controlling the spirit that had possessed him. After a purification ceremony, he would be a full member of the cannibals.

Much of this activity was also simulated, but this fact was kept secret from many of the villagers. Instead of a human corpse, a dead bear might be substituted; although the boys would bite people as they returned from the home of the cannibal spirit, the ones they attacked were carefully selected ahead of time and paid well for their part in the drama. During the ceremonies there were other simulated feats that were attributed to spirit possession. For example, a dancer would come in and dance around the fire. Suddenly someone would attack this dancer with a sword and cut off his head. Blood would spurt out for all to see, and then the severed head would somehow move of its own accord around the fire. Later the dead man would be brought to life. To accomplish such a masterful drama, an expert carver created a mask that looked identical to the person who would wear it. Then a seal bladder, filled with blood, was placed on top of the dancer's head, and the mask was fitted over the bladder. In the semidarkness of the community house it was a simple matter to swing the sword above the dancer's head to burst the seal bladder of blood and thereby disengage the mask from the dancer. Then, by prearrangement, someone high in the rafters of the dance house would swing the head slowly around the fire by means of an attached string. Finally, the

Masked dancers performed according to their special roles at the cannibal ceremony. Compare the dancers shown in this picture with the contemporary Kwakiutl dancers depicted on page 305, in chapter 15.

dancer who had been "killed" would be brought to life in an equally elaborate ritual performance.

Sometimes individuals failed to perform their expected roles appropriately. If a dancer made a mistake he would often be initiated again to make up for his mistake. At a minimum, his failure to perform his role properly would create great excitement among cannibals and other seals. Boas observed such a mistake in one of his early trips to Fort Rupert. A dancer was performing with a large double mask that was supposed to open in the course of his dance.

When the wearer of the mask opened it, one side of the cover broke. Although the attendants rushed up to the mask immediately, trying to cover it, the hamatsa had seen what had happened and became excited at once. The hamatsa rushed down into the middle of the house, the fool dancers struck and stabbed the people and pelted them with stones, and the bears scratched them. The greatest excitement prevailed.[4]

[4]Franz Boas, "The Social Organization and Secret Societies of the Kwakiutl Indians," Washington: Report of the U.S. National Museum for 1895, 1897, pp. 565–566.

Soon after this mistake occurred, someone entered carrying a child who appeared to be dead and the following speech was made before attempting to bring him to life.

Friends, if you have a mask for the winter ceremonial which you want to show, do not let a stranger use it. Teach your people to show it, that no mistake may occur. Only because a stranger showed your mask a mistake happened and brought about our great difficulty.[5]

After this speech there was a demonstration of supernatural power and the child was brought to life again.

SOCIAL SITUATIONS

Social situations are the settings in which social interaction occurs. Social situations consist of a combination of culturally appropriate *times*, *places*, *objects*, and *events*. We see the interplay of these factors in the context of the Kwakiutl winter ceremonial of which seals and sparrows were such an integral part. It is impossible to understand fully these statuses and roles without looking at this annual event.

The northwest coast of North America is one of the richest environments in the world. Thus, although they had no agriculture, each summer the Kwakiutl were able to harvest enough salmon to supply them for the entire winter. During the summer each small family group left the larger villages to live at their fishing sites. There, by means of traps and spears, they caught as much as half a ton of salmon. King salmon, silver salmon, spring salmon, and other varieties were cleaned and boned, and then the large slabs of pink meat were dried in the sun or smoked to preserve them. Berries and clams were stored in large wooden boxes and covered with a thick fish oil from the oolachen fish to preserve them. This small fish was so rich in oil that after it was dried it would burn like a candle and was often referred to as a "candle fish." As the mild winter approached, families returned to their villages to live in huge cedar plank houses. The dried fish were hung from the rafters, and the boxes of berries and clams were stored on shelves around the outer perimeter. The winter months brought the Kwakiutl at Fort Rupert and other villages much time for leisure. Men hunted occasionally, repaired canoes, and carved masks or totem poles. Women repaired clothing and helped the men prepare the food. But most of the time was spent in the elaborate rituals of the winter ceremonial.

Everyone knew when the winter ceremonies were drawing near. Then, as the days grew colder, the leading men at Fort Rupert would gather together to decide when to begin: the day had to coincide with the first steps in initiating a young man to become a cannibal. Finally, the elders would visit all the houses in the village at an appointed time and announce that the season of "secrets" was to begin in a few days. Later that same day a young man would disappear into the woods in the midst of great commotion, and everyone would hear the voices of spirits that had returned. Everyone now celebrated for a brief time, continuing to use their summer names, sing their summer songs, and enjoy the freedom from com-

[5]Franz Boas, "The Social Organization and Secret Societies of the Kwakiutl Indians," p. 567.

Kwakiutl houses were constructed of cedar beams and planks. They often housed several families. The Kwakiutl were expert woodworkers, fashioning smooth planks from large cedar trees. House paintings and pole carvings symbolized the mythical creatures encountered by important ancestors. These crests were owned and passed on according to strict rules of inheritance.

ing restrictions. Then, on the morning of the first day of the ceremonies, 12 elders made their rounds, waking up all the people very early, calling, "Don't sleep! Go and bathe in the sea. We are walking around to call you. It is the time of secrets." Everyone arose and went to the nearby shore for a cold swim to cleanse themselves for the assembly that morning and the official commencement of the ceremonial season. At the assembly everyone was reminded that they could no longer use their summer names, which were part of each person's kinship group. Summer songs and dances were now taboo. Everyone must assume his or her ritual status; people must act like seals and sparrows, sea lions and whales, fools and cannibals. They must use the names that they received long ago, names that are part of these ritual groups.

Everyone knew this was a solemn time, a time when the supernaturals who had been traveling around the world return to the village. There was an atmosphere of sober respect for the spirits; life for everyone was sacred. Certain houses were off limits to those who were not ritually clean; everyone was forbidden to engage in sexual intercourse; ritual bathing in icy water for purification continued. From time to time everyone could hear the voices of the spirits, especially at the north end of the village where they returned each year. Their voices were like sharp piercing whistles, reminding everyone that somewhere out in the woods at the home of the cannibal spirit was a young man who was becoming a *hamatsa*.

Then, each night throughout the winter, everyone gathered in a large community house to sing and dance to coax the young man back from the home of the cannibal spirit. Men of power performed mighty feats, killing dancers and bringing them to life again, or performed equally miraculous deeds. But even as they performed, other young men and boys disappeared, abducted by one or another spirit. Some were taken into the woods, others into seclusion at special places in the village. Because a single person could assume a number of different statuses, a boy who last year became a *bear* might become a *cannibal* this year. To understand this social situation and its associated statuses, we must also look at some of the *social groups* connected with the ceremonial.

SOCIAL GROUP

Social group refers to collections of people organized by means of categories and rules. Some groups, such as the Republican party, the Rotary Club, the Mormon Tabernacle Choir, and the American Motorcyclist Association, are named. Others, such as people who band together to try to prevent the building of a nuclear power plant, are not. Anonymous or named, groups are composed of people holding related statuses that use numerous kinds of social relationships to form larger units of the social system.

Common Features of Groups

There are several distinctive features of groups that serve to distinguish them from crowds or other classes of people. First, *the people who belong to a group recognize their common membership.* They have a sense of shared unity and interest. The seals among the Kwakiutl recognized they were seals; this status gave them membership in a large group each winter. Some of the statuses people assumed during the winter ceremonies did not lead to group membership, such as the *master of ceremonies*. But everyone had some status that automatically meant he or she was a member of a social group.

A second feature of groups is that *social interaction occurs between members.* Not everyone in the group interacts with everyone else, but there are recognized interaction patterns. The set of identities referred to as "middle class" is not a group; neither is the crowd of people watching a fire. People who have these identities may form groups, as when several people watching a fire join together to assist the firemen in reviving someone overcome by smoke. But without social in-

The fool dancers at Fort Rupert studied by Franz Boas, formed a group during the winter ceremonies. They went frequently to the woods to prepare for their appearance in the dance performances.

teraction, a category of people is not a group. When the winter ceremonial commences among the Kwakiutl, people change their interaction patterns significantly to conform to the new groups. Instead of living together in kinship groups, everyone now associates with the other members of his or her sparrow or seal group. *Hamatsas* live together for a good part of the winter, as do the members of the other groups.

A third feature of groups is that *they are organized internally in some way:* tasks are divided among members, and lines of communication and authority emerge. Members recognize that this internal organization is present. The winter groups of the Kwakiutl divided up the work of preparing for each night's ritual. Some persons practiced their dances, others their songs. Some carved or repaired giant masks that the dancers for a particular group would show at night. There were groups of men who beat on drums and logs to provide a rhythm for the dancers.

Finally, *groups in every society are linked together because individuals often have overlapping membership in two or more groups.* In our society when two individuals marry, not only do they create a new family group but they also create links between their parents' family groups. In the Kwakiutl culture everyone was a member of some village such as Fort Rupert, New Vancouver, or Cape Mudge.

In addition, everyone was a member of some large group of kinsmen and also of a smaller family group. Members of a single family had ties to numerous other groups during the winter ceremonies: a father and eldest son might be in the cannibal group, a younger son in the nuisances, a wife in the hens, and a daughter in the crows. You can see how these overlapping memberships created a larger networklike structure in Kwakiutl society.

Principles of Organization

The study of cultural groups has led anthropologists to identify a small number of principles that are used again and again for organizing sets of statuses. We will examine many of these in greater detail throughout the remaining chapters of this book, but some of these principles should be identified here. Although we will distinguish each principle from the other, it should be kept in mind that cultural groups can be formed by using several principles at the same time.

Kinship

Every society contains groups formed on the principle of kinship. This was one principle used among the Kwakiutl for their seal and sparrow groups. It was impossible to become a member of the seals unless you had an older relative in this group. And in order to become a *hamatsa* a young Kwakiutl generally had to receive this identity from his mother's father. Kinship was, however, not the only principle for joining the various groups. Some men became a cannibal by killing someone in another village who was a cannibal and claiming the dead man's membership. Because kinship groups are so important in every human society, we will examine them in much greater detail in the next two chapters.

Age

Most societies employ the principle of age to form groups, even if they are only informal play groups among children. In our own society age is often an important criterion for group membership. For example, a new group of older retired people called the Grey Panthers now lobbies for the rights of senior citizens. Most of the Kwakiutl ceremonial societies used this principle, so that members of each sparrow group, for example, were about the same age. Perhaps the most famous case of age-related groups comes from the Nyakyusa of East Africa. Nyakyusa children, after they are five or six, begin to play in an area adjacent to their natal community.[6] Soon they build small huts there, spending more and more of their time away from home. When the boys reach puberty, they marry girls from other communities and bring their wives to the village they have been developing adjacent to their parents' village. Meanwhile, younger brothers have gone off to build their own huts in another area. When one looks at Nyakyusa society as a whole, there are numerous villages, each with a membership of people about the same age. Political power is vested in villages of mature men who live with their wives and very young children. As they grow old, power is transferred to a village of younger men.

[6] See Monica Wilson, *Good Company: A Study of Nyakyusa Age-villages*, Prospect Heights, IL: Waveland Press, Inc., 1951 (reissued 1987).

Sex

Most of the Kwakiutl ceremonial societies used sex as one of their principles for organization. All the seal groups were composed of males except in very rare cases. And even though the sparrows included both sexes, the groups within the sparrows were strictly segregated by sex. This principle is used often within our own society and in most others. Women form informal work groups; men hunt or fish together. In the highlands of New Guinea the organizing principle of sex is carried to the highest degree. Among some groups in this area each village has a men's house that excludes all women. All adult males and children over five or six sleep in the men's house and carry on many of their activities there. Groups of related women live in separate dwellings. Their husbands and sons come daily to eat meals at these houses, but even then the males sit apart from the women.

Common Goals and Interests

Although all groups have a degree of shared interest, some have highly specialized purposes that become an organizing principle for the group. Contemporary Kwakiutl fishing groups are of this type. The Kwakiutl have abandoned their use of fishing traps to catch salmon and instead use various kinds of boats. A *gill-netter* is a small boat that can be operated by one or two men. Large *seine boats* are more efficient, and many Kwakiutl Indians spend their summers on a seine boat fishing the waters along the coast of British Columbia. Each boat is manned by a group with a common goal: to bring in a large catch of salmon. One man is *skipper*, another *engineer*, and several others are simply members of the *crew*. A wife or daughter may work as *cook*. Together these people have identities that form a group called the *crew*. The group may be partially based on kinship ties, but the fundamental principle for a fishing crew is a common goal. In the past the Kwakiutl seals and sparrows formed a larger, unnamed group with a common purpose: to reenact the myths in which ancestors had been abducted by the cannibal spirit. Part of this goal involved the performance of nightly rituals in order to attract the young cannibal initiates back from the home of the spirits. Many of the groups organized on this principle will be considered in detail in later chapters on religion, economics, politics, and so on.

Hierarchy

In every society people recognize differences in relative status and rank. Some people are considered more important than others by virtue of the statuses they assume. Hierarchy organizes the members of groups as well as the relationship between one group and another. The Kwakiutl used the principle of hierarchy in many ways, only a few of which can be considered here.

To begin with, members of a family were not considered equal. The firstborn children were accorded higher rank and status than others according to the principle of *primogeniture*, that is, the eldest son in every family received special treatment and eventually inherited the wealth and status of his father. If his father was a high-ranking chief, he could look forward to being of equally high status. His younger brothers, on the other hand, would be of low status, what Boas called "commoners." It is easy to see that this situation might create tensions within the family, and the Kwakiutl did recognize that a younger brother might be tempted

Today many Kwakiutl work together as members of a fishing boat crew. Here James Sewid, a Kwakiutl chief whom we will discuss in Chapter 15 and members of his sein boat crew haul in a net used to catch salmon.

to perform witchcraft against his older brothers, since if the elder died he could then take over the high-ranking position.

During the winter ceremonials there was a strict hierarchy among the seal groups. Only chiefs and the eldest sons of chiefs could ever belong to these groups, and one usually started at the bottom, working his way up to the highest, the cannibals. The sparrows, on the other hand, were a heterogeneous lot, made up of retired chiefs, young boys who would someday inherit high positions, many high-ranking women, and male and female commoners. Each of the groups in the winter ceremonial had its own supernatural spirit, the highest ranking of which were associated with the highest-ranking groups. Much of the ceremonial was oriented around rituals that reminded everyone that the chiefs and others of high status were of great importance. Gifts were distributed at various points throughout the winter ceremonial, and these were always of different value, the best ones going to the men at the top of the hierarchy. It is impossible to understand Kwakiutl society without taking into account this hierarchical principle of organization.

SUMMARY

In this chapter we have examined the nature of human social structure. We have seen that we are social animals; our survival depends on life in society. Our social nature has its roots in our primate past, where we have seen its utility for defense and for general primate adaptation.

Social life is marked by social interaction, the systematic behavior that occurs between (or among) two or more people. Such interaction involves recurrent and predictable behavior between individuals.

Underlying social interaction is social structure, the culturally defined and interrelated parts that make up a society. The social structure is composed of at least four primary elements: status, role, social situation, and social group. Statuses are the culturally defined positions in a social structure that people fill. Roles are the expected behaviors associated with particular statuses. Social situations are the settings in which social interaction occurs. Social groups are organized collections of people. They are defined by consciousness of membership, social interaction between members, and internal organization. Groups may be organized around kinship, age, sex, common goals, and hierarchy.

MAJOR CONCEPTS

PRIMATE	STATUS
SOCIAL INTERACTION	ROLE
SOCIAL RELATIONSHIP	SOCIAL SITUATIONS
SOCIAL STRUCTURE	SOCIAL GROUP
SOCIETY	PRINCIPLES OF ORGANIZATION

SELECTED READINGS

Firth, Raymond: *Elements of Social Organization*, London: Watts, 1956.
   A series of lectures by a British social anthropologist on the concepts and analysis of social anthropology.

Goffman, Erving: *The Presentation of Self in Everyday Life*, New York: Overlook Press, 1959.
   The author describes the elements necessary for meaningful social interaction.

Goodenough, Ward H.: "Rethinking 'Status' and 'Role': Toward a General Model," in Michael Banton (editor), *The Relevance of Models for Social Anthropology*, New York: Praeger, 1965, pp. 1–22.
   A detailed reformulation of Linton's concepts of "status" and "role."

Murdock, George Peter: *Social Structure*, New York: Macmillan, 1948.
   This book presents a systematic review of concepts used by anthropologists to describe human social structure as well as a theory of change explaining the transition from one kind of structural type to another.

Nadel, S. F.: *The Theory of Social Structure*, New York: Free Press, 1957.
   This book presents an early criticism of Linton's distinction between status and role and presents a more comprehensive definitional system for the basic elements of social structure.

Service, Elman R.: *Primitive Social Organization: An Evolutionary Perspective*, New York: Random House, 1962.
   A comparative study of different kinds of social organization at different levels of human evolution.

CHAPTER FIVE

Marriage and Family Structure

Marriage and family are basic social institutions that occur as elements in every society's kinship structure. Kinship refers to the complex system of culturally defined social relationships based on marriage (the principle of affinity), and birth (the principle of consanguinity). The study of kinship requires the discovery of a society's kinship statuses and roles such as father and sister; kinship relationships like marriage; kinship groups such as the family; and the fundamental processes that flow through the system and serve to hold kinship structures together.

The importance of kin in the lives of human beings cannot be overestimated. Even in our own society, where we often stress personal independence and striking out on our own, kin play an essential role in our lives. We grow up in close intensive nuclear families that are children oriented. The impact our parents have on us lasts throughout life. Although many of us will establish our own households when we reach maturity, family and kin remain important. Family reunions are common experiences for many. Kin often provide entrance to jobs and may also provide a source of support to fall back on during hard times.

Kinship has been especially important in anthropology, partly because it has such immediate impact on people and partly because it serves as a major principle of organization in numerous societies encountered by anthropologists. As we saw in the last chapter, a principle of organization is the point around which groups are organized. In our society kinship is the principle of organization for families and for variously structured groups of cooperating kin. But by and large, most groups in Western society are organized by other criteria such as territory and common interest. Thus most of our important social activity takes place outside the world of kinship. We work in organizations like factories, corporations, businesses, and agencies. We play at clubs, dine at restaurants, relax at concerts, and chat with neighbors, activities none of which are based on the principle of kinship. But the majority of groups in many societies are organized on the basis of kinship and it is interesting to reflect on why this is the case.

KINSHIP ORGANIZED SOCIETIES

The importance of kinship may be related to the way human society and culture have evolved in response to adaptive pressures. This is the view taken by John Pfeiffer in his book *The Emergence of Society*.[1] Pfeiffer argues that humans have been in a technological and social race with their own expanding population. The ways societies are organized reflect human attempts to meet an increasing need to produce more food through more and more complex technology. The extension of kinship organization represents a step in this process.

Humans originally adapted by hunting and gathering the wild foods that grow in the natural environment, a mode of subsistence that favored a particular kind of social organization. Since wild foods are rarely concentrated in one place in large amounts, hunters and gatherers tended to live in small groups of about 25 people called *bands*. Band size reflected the number of people wild foods could support. Bands were subdivided into nuclear families, the group made up of a married couple and their children. Families were loosely affiliated with bands and might move from one to another over the years. Hunter-gatherers had little

The Kung! San of the Kalahari Desert are one of the few remaining hunting and gathering peoples left in the world. The band shown here resides in a temporary camp near trees that provide them with mongongo nuts, a dietary staple.

[1]John Pfeiffer, *The Emergence of Society: A Prehistory of the Establishment*, New ed., New York: Harper & Row, 1977.

property because their life-style required mobility in the quest for food, making goods difficult to carry. The band was so small that formal political and legal systems were not needed. Leadership was informal and rank absent. Studies of the few remaining hunting and gathering groups, like the !Kung of the Kalahari Desert, indicate that such people eat a balanced diet, rarely meet privations, live relatively long lives, and in most ways seem successfully adapted.

About 12,000 years ago, according to Pfeiffer, the way humans could subsist in the world began to change. Over the preceding years there was a slow but steady increase in the number of people living in most parts of the world. Responding to population pressures, groups moved into marginally productive areas where hunting and gathering were more difficult. Perhaps the most serious problem arose when melting glaciers released huge quantities of water to the oceans, raising sea levels and flooding almost 20 percent of the world's productive land. The loss of prime hunting territory in conjunction with rising populations forced people to find new ways to subsist. Archaeological evidence shows more and more intensive collecting and hunting occurring during these transitional centuries. Eventually people began to farm as a way to support their growing numbers, and farming, and in some places, herding, presented a new set of requirements for social structure.

Instead of small bands numbering only 25 people, there were now communities consisting of hundreds. Settlements were more permanent. Farming required food storage, the manufacture of implements, and more concentrated labor. People came to have more property in the form of land, tools, and animals. Later, irrigation came to some parts of the world, requiring construction of canals and the management of water rights. Political and legal systems emerged to control these enlarged groups, and for the first time there was war and the need for defense. To organize so many people into cohesive groups required a powerful principle of relationship that could command loyalty and cooperation. Kinship, a system that was already important among hunter-gatherers, could be expanded to fill this need. Families could be enlarged to hold land and to provide the labor to work it. Descent groups could grow to tie thousands of people together on the basis of common ancestry. Complex marriage relationships could work to tie descent groups together. Larger societies emerged in which kinship was an important, often dominant, principle of group organization.

When anthropologists first started to collect data about other cultures, most societies in the world were agrarian and organized at least partially around kinship. Fieldworkers wrestled with the complexities of a vast variety of kinship systems and, in the end, developed classifications of these systems and a better understanding of how they work.

Although it is still important both formally and informally in industrialized societies like ours, kinship no longer works as the primary organizing principle. Families and extended kin groups, although they initially formed the basis of industrial groups and businesses, are increasingly less able to provide labor, management, and capital for manufacturing and marketing. Common interest, rather than kinship, has taken over as a primary organizing principle. Yet kinship remains an important factor even in our own society and is still a key to understanding many other groups where it is a dominant principle of organization. A knowledge of kinship is essential in order to understand human social organization.

Let us now turn to a discussion of two important elements of kinship systems, marriage and the family. We will look at these elements in the context of a particular society, the Bhils of Rajasthan, India.

THE BHIL MANDA CEREMONY[2]

India is known for its dry, flat, dusty expanses and for its innumerable villages dotting an almost treeless agricultural plain. But India is also a land of mountains, hills, forests, and steep ravines. This is the country of Kipling's *Jungle Books*, the habitat of tigers and leopards and of many different groups of people, which more educated Indians refer to as tribals. Bhils are such a tribal people. They live in the forested hills of west central India, protected from the full influence of life in greater India by the steepness and impenetrability of the terrain. One of their villages, Ratakote, rests in a highland valley of the Aravalli Hills in the southern part of Rajasthan State. It is large, even for a Bhil community, its population numbering over 1150 individuals, and like other Bhil communities, it looks different from most typical Indian villages. Where the houses of the latter cluster together, divided only occasionally by narrow, dusty, winding lanes with open drains, those of Ratakote dot the countryside, overlooking the fields that lie wherever there is room for them in the ravines or against the hillsides.

Imagine that you are an anthropologist and that you have chosen Ratakote as a site for field research. Your goal is to map Bhil social structure so that you can understand their life-style and social interaction. When you arrive in the community after a slow and precariously bumpy trip, you sense a mood of tranquility, almost inertness. It is the Indian month of Vaisakh (April–May), and nothing grows at this time of year save a few broadleafed evergreens. Margashirsh (November–December) was the last time the community saw any rain, and none is expected until the monsoon reappears in the month of Ashad (June–July). The land shimmers a dusty brown under the hot morning sun, and the day shows promise of warming up to over 100°F.

Because it is so warm and because the land will produce nothing at this time of year, the people of Ratakote are hardly in evidence. They sleep at midday to escape the heat; they repair their farm equipment in the shade of their courtyards; they work slowly at constructing walls to retain new hillside fields for later planting; above all, they visit and talk with one another.

You have already made arrangements for the use of a house, and it stands ready now, its new split bamboo, mud and dung-plastered walls, and roughly tiled roof shimmering brown and red in the sun. As you unpack the jeep and settle into your new home, you wonder how you will go about the study of village social structure. You have already seen some people sitting by the road and walking about other parts of the village, but you have no way to understand who they are or how they structure their relationships with each other.

[2]The description of Bhil culture presented in this chapter is based on one of the author's field study of Ratakote (not the village's real name), Rajasthan, India, from 1961 to 1963.

Dispersed Bhil settlements rest among the hills and ridges of west central India. This is a picture of one of Ratakote's wards taken during the summer monsoon season. The anthropologist's house and jeep can be seen on the small hill at the left of the photograph.

Your first clue comes when your efforts at unpacking are interrupted by the sound of a drum beating regularly at a nearby house on the ridge farther up the valley. One of your new neighbors, who has offered to help you unpack, tells you that at this time of year weddings take place. The drumming you hear announces that a *manda* ceremony will begin within an hour, and this rite is part of a wedding. Nanaji Katara, the owner of the house from which the drumming can be heard, is marrying his son Kanji to a girl from the village of Palia, some 12 miles distant. Most of the guests arrived the day before, and they will gather now in Nanaji's walled-in cattle yard. Your neighbor goes on to say that you are liable to be awakened at night by dancing and singing somewhere in the village for the next several weeks, because there will be three more weddings in the valley in addition to this one and it is too hot to dance during the day.

As you continue to unpack, you realize that weddings must be an important part of social activity in Ratakote and that they probably involve family and kin. As in all societies, kinship is an especially important feature of social structure for the Bhils living in this village.

You have learned enough from your neighbor to know that the *manda* ceremony sounds like something you should see, so you drop what you are doing and hurry to view the event. You arrive at the courtyard to find it filled with people. There are girls and women standing and sitting on the covered front porch. Chil-

Guests look on as a Bhil groom, assisted by his father, exchanges an orni *(woman's shawl) with a female relative during the* manda *ceremony. Such exchange, called* peravni, *occurs between the groom and scores of his kin.*

dren perch on top of the stone wall enclosing the yard. Men and women crowd together in the yard itself, their attention focused on what is about to happen. In the middle of this throng, standing before the porch, are Kanji and his proud father, Nanaji. Kanji is dressed in his wedding clothes, a bright crimson coat striped with metallic silver bands, a long, white *dhoti*, the usual men's lower garment, draped about his waist and legs and extending to his ankles, and a red turban decorated with a piece of cardboard on which is pasted red, silver, and gold foil.

Just then the drummer changes his rhythm slightly and three girls, dressed in colorful green and blue skirts and shirts with flowing red *ornis* worn over their heads and tucked in at their waists, dance forward with baskets of clothing on their heads.[3] Nanaji removes each basket as the girls dance before him, placing it in readiness on the ground next to his son. Then a man, dressed in a coat, long *dhoti*, and white turban steps forward carrying a *dhoti*. Kanji clasps his hands together as though in prayer and greets him, saying, "Ram Ram mamaji." The older

[3]An *orni* is a woman's shawllike garment worn over the head and tucked in at the waist. It is similar to the better-known Indian *sari*.

man replies, "Ram, Ram bhanej, I have brought this dhoti in honor of your wedding." He drapes the garment about Kanji's shoulders and Kanji, turning to Nanaji for the necessary item of clothing, does the same thing to him. Both embrace warmly and the older man retires to his place in the crowd. Others, both men and women, now come forward in similar fashion to exchange clothing with Kanji. Over 100 pieces of clothing pass through his hands in this way before the ceremony ends. But not all the people who are there make such an exchange. Many simply watch.

When the *manda* ceremony is over and you are walking back to the chores that await you in your new home, you cannot help being curious about the scene you have just witnessed. What is the significance of the ceremony? Who were the people there? What was the meaning of the exchange? To answer these questions you must first turn to the concept of marriage.

MARRIAGE

As we saw in the last chapter, humans differ from almost all the other primates in respect to the relative permanence of their mating pairs. By themselves, however, even stable mating relationships do not constitute marriage. To be married, a mating couple must receive the legitimate approval of other members of their society according to the cultural standards of the group. A common definition of marriage states that it constitutes a socially recognized union between a man and a woman that accords legitimate birth status rights to their children. Thus marriage not only legitimizes mating, but ensures that children are treated as normal members of a society. (There are some interesting exceptions to this definition that have caused some anthropologists to modify it. It will do for our purposes here, however.)

The definition of marriage helps to clarify the purpose of the *manda* ceremony that you witnessed in Ratakote. This ritual is part of the long, 11-day wedding process that starts with the consultation of the clan goddess, continues through feasts, daily annointments of the bride and groom, and the *manda* ceremony, and ends with the final wedding ceremony. One of the functions of this long process is to certify that a legitimate marriage has taken place. By going through the many parts of the wedding ceremony, Kanji gains the right to become a husband. The *manda* ceremony and other wedding events also publicly announce his change in status.

Plural Marriage

Societies differ in the number of spouses they permit someone to wed. In the United States we follow the rule of monogamy, which stipulates that we can only marry one person at a time. Many societies permit or value polygamy, the simultaneous marriage of one person with two or more individuals. The most common form of polygamy is polygyny, the marriage of a man with two or more women at the same time. Infrequently we also encounter polyandry, the simultaneous marriage of a woman to two or more men. Some anthropologists argue that the high

Toward evening when the manda *ceremony and other activities are over, the groom and his wedding party,* jai., *walk to the bride's village. The wedding party is led by a drummer and includes all the kin and neighbors present at the* manda *ritual. The two grooms shown here are to marry girls from the same community and elected to combine their wedding festivities.*

rate of divorce and remarriage in the United States leads to something called <u>serial polygamy</u>, meaning that we may marry more than one spouse as long as we do so one at a time.

The people of Ratakote permit, but do not particularly value, polygyny. Most men are monogamous but about 10 percent marry two wives and one man is married to three. A few polygynous marriages occur when a first wife asks her husband to take a second to help with household and agricultural work. Most occur when men marry younger women who attract them. This second situation often results in family dissension that Bhils find difficult to manage.

In traditional Ibo society, a group living in Nigeria, jealousies among wives were managed more effectively. The Ibo valued polygyny and structured their families accordingly. Husbands set up each wife in separate huts within family compounds, and visited each in turn. Wives cooked separately and farmed their own plots of land. Their labor, however, contributed to the strength of the whole family and its male head. In this case polygynous marriage results in the formation of a larger economic unit in a society based on horticulture.

The Incest Taboo

The <u>incest taboo</u> is a cultural rule that prohibits sexual intercourse between certain classes of relatives. Every society prohibits sexual relations between primary relatives, an individual's parents, siblings, and children, and the reason for its universal application has created a long-term issue within anthropology.[4] Some anthropologists feel that the taboo results from a human instinct against intercourse with immediate relatives. A variation of this view is that the taboo results from a lack of sexual interest among people who are raised together from the time they are infants. Others have claimed that the taboo prevents sexual competition within the family and that it blocks harmful inbreeding. A final explanation concerns the effect of the taboo on marriage. The taboo, it is argued, came into being because it forced kin to marry outside their own families. Families exchanged partners and became linked by marriage into larger, more powerful, groups.

If you interview the people of Ratakote, you will quickly learn something else about the incest taboo—it is often extended to other relatively large classes of people, many of whom may be quite distantly related. Not only do Bhils prohibit intercourse between people who know they are related by blood, they also include members of the same patriclan, a large group of relatives linked through males who believe they are descended from a common ancestor (see Chapter 6), one's mother's patriclan, and one's father's mother's patriclan. The effect of these far-reaching taboos is to require marriage among more distant groups. In this way larger kinship units can be tied together through marriage.

Exogamy and Endogamy

Whereas the incest taboo reflects people's prohibitions on sexual intercourse, the terms exogamy and endogamy apply directly to marriage. Exogamy means marriage outside any specified group. For example, we could restate the Bhil incest taboo on sexual relations with one's own clan members as "clan exogamy," since marriage involves sexual rights and since marriage must not take place with fellow clan members. Among Bhils, exogamy is also applied to the people living in one's own village. The result is a rule prescribing village exogamy. Again, we see the function of exogamy in terms of group linkage. By requiring villagers to marry outside their community, the rule serves the cause of regional solidarity—it ties communities together through intermarriage.

Endogamy means marriage within a specified group. Bhils usually practice a rule of tribal endogamy, since they marry within their tribe rather than with members of other castes or tribal groups. Instead of linking groups together, endogamy promotes internal solidarity for a particular group. Tribal endogamy permits Bhils to retain their identity by preventing foreigners from entering their society through marriage and by strengthening bonds between members.

Preferential Marriage Rules

Some marriage rules specify particularly desirable marriage partners. These so-called preferential marriage rules are found in a great many societies and also work to tie groups together.

---

[4]Some anthropologists feel the incest taboo is not universal. Some exceptions, such as the royal marriages of brothers and sisters in ancient Egypt and Hawaii, have long been noted. An apparent recent increase in incest relations in the United States has also been used to challenge the idea of universality.

These Bhil girls will marry out of their village because of the Bhil preference for village exogamy.

Levirate and Sororate   The levirate is a preferred marriage rule that gives a man the right, and sometimes the obligation, to marry his dead brother's widow. During your fieldwork in Ratakote a man who lives nearby dies suddenly in his field at the age of 35. Within days after his cremation and funeral one of his three brothers marries his widow and takes on responsibility for the bereaved children. The operation of the levirate, in this case, has at least three effects. It provides economic support for the widow and her children; it perpetuates the original relationship between the wife's family and her husband's group; and it keeps the fatherless children with their close paternal relatives and in a position to inherit the land that normally would have come to them. The sororate works like the levirate except that it suggests marriage between a woman and her dead sister's husband.

Cousin Marriage   Unlike some Western countries including our own where marriage with cousins, particularly first cousins, is considered incestuous, many societies prefer marriage between these close relatives. Explanations of cousin marriage are complex and beyond our scope here, but such an arrangement also serves to tie different kinship groups together or, in one variation, to promote the solidarity of a single group.

Marriage by Arrangement

In many societies, parents arrange their children's marriages. Often this occurs without consultation with their offspring, and it is not unusual for a bride and groom in such societies to be total strangers. Parental arrangement of marriage was, and in many cases still is, the rule in India and Japan, and was also the usual practice in traditional peasant China.

The people of Ratakote prefer to arrange marriages for their children, usually when the latter reach sexual maturity. The reason for urging marriage on their children when they are so young is a practical one. Bhils feel that once they are mature, young people will make liaisons and enter into clandestine sexual relations, a feeling that appears to be borne out in practice. Since these relationships may result in unwanted pregnancies or worse, elopements, parents hurry to get their children married if they can possibly afford the costs of the wedding. Mates are sought by passing the word to relatives in other villages. These kin act as go-betweens, looking for suitable spouses among the families of their own villages and carrying word of prospects back to the original source. Once an attractive possibility is found, the parents of the bride and groom enter into complex negotiations that end in a formal betrothal.

The people of Ratakote insist that it is improper for the bride and groom to enter these negotiations or express an opinion about their forthcoming union. For them marriage is a union of families as much as of young people. In their evaluation of prospects they are more concerned with the reputation of possible in-laws than they are with how the bride or groom looks and acts. Of utmost importance is the strength a marriage brings to the kin groups that are a part of it.

FAMILY

In his classic work *Social Structure*, George Peter Murdock defined the family as a kinship group consisting of at least one married couple sharing the same residence with their children and performing sexual, reproductive, economic, and educational functions.[5] Although there are some familylike groups that are not covered by this definition, it will serve our needs here.

Functions of the Family

One of the essential features of Murdock's definition is the concept of function. People in every society must meet certain needs such as the regulation of sex, the support of reproduction, the organization of economic activities, and the cultural education of the young. Murdock argues that only the nuclear family, out of many possible groups, can function to meet these needs adequately.

As you observe Kanji's marriage in Ratakote, you are witnessing the birth of a family that fulfills these functions. The wedding leads to a state of marriage, thus legitimizing sexual relations and leading to the birth of children. Kanji and his bride, Nani, will raise their children by teaching them Bhil culture. Together, the members of the new family will work in economic cooperation, attending to household chores, fieldwork, and obligations to neighbors and other kin.

[5]George Peter Murdock, *Social Structure*, New York: MacMillan, 1949, p. 1.

Nuclear and Extended Families

As we talk with Kanji about his family and observe other family groups in Rata-kote, we cannot help but notice some puzzling variations. On the other side of the stream that runs near Kanji's place is another house in which live a man, his wife, and their two children. Nearby is a large dwelling inhabited by an older couple, three of their married sons and their wives, and the children of two of these couples. Anthropologists refer to the first, simple arrangement, as a nuclear family. The second is termed an extended family, for it is composed of more than one married couple. But how can such different family arrangements exist side by side in the same community? The answer is simple for Kanji and other villagers. The ideal of every man is to head up a group of his married sons all living under one roof. Together they can acquire and farm more land, so that in abundant agricultural years their surplus is great enough to tide them over hard times. And while his sons and daughters-in-law work in the fields, the household head can spend time dealing with village public affairs. Kanji can point to a man who lives on the western edge of Ratakote who has eight married sons living with him. They can farm over 50 acres of land and maintain a herd of 150 cattle, water buffaloes, and goats. They pool these resources and, as a group, live in greater prosperity than could any one of them by himself.

But this extended family ideal is rarely met, a fact that explains the prevalence of nuclear families in Ratakote. Again, consider Kanji's case. When he marries, his wife joins him, and they live in his father's house. Kanji's mother and father sleep on the verandah so that the newlyweds can have the inner room of the dwelling all to themselves. Even after this sleeping arrangement ceases, Kanji and Nani continue to live as part of Nanaji's family, and the unit remains an extended family. But friction soon arises between Nani and Kanji's mother. They argue over who is to perform the household chores, go to the well for water, sweep the front porch, husk the tiny grains of millet, and milk the cattle. Before long, Nani tells Kanji that she wants a house of her own, and Kanji, who is tired of carrying an extra heavy load of the agricultural work, agrees. They announce that they will build nearby, and when it is finished they move, dividing the family land and establishing themselves as a separate economic unit. Once again, Nanaji heads a nuclear family, although it will become extended once more when his other son marries, and Kanji and Nani establish a new nuclear family. This cycle affects most village families, and it is only the rare man who manages to hold his married children together in a single extended unit for any length of time. Part of the reason for this pertains to the degree of personal economic dependence.

As we saw at the beginning of the chapter, members of hunting and gathering societies tend to live in nuclear families. Such families hold no real property and the children, when they grow up, do not have to depend on their parents for continued support. Nuclear families work well because the division of labor between husband and wife is complementary and serves to support the couple and their children.

Similarly, nuclear families are most important in our own society. As our children mature, they can find their own jobs and become economically free of their parents. With the exception of some farmers, very poor people, and the very weal-

*Bhil family membership
changes over time. The man
in this picture grew up with
his sister who stands on the
left, but now lives together
with his wife and daughter,
standing on the right.*

thy, families do not hold resources to which children must have access when they grow up. Nuclear families are the result.

It is interesting to note that as women gain greater access to the public world of work in the United States, they become economically independent of their husbands. The labor of husband and wife is no longer complementary, but is instead equivalent. The resulting lack of interdependence leads to more frequent divorce and to a new sort of family consisting of a single parent and children.

Agricultural people like those living in India experience a different economic reality. There, economic security depends on farming and herding, and land and animals are often scarce resources, impossible for most people to acquire on their own when they reach adulthood. Instead, land is held by families on whom maturing young people must depend for their future economic security. The result is the formation of extended families that can be maintained as long as there is a single household head who controls access to the land and other resources.

Extended families are short-lived among the Bhils precisely because land and animal resources are still available. Unlike other parts of India, the hilly terrain in which Ratakote lies contains small slopes and valleys that can be reclaimed. Although Bhil sons inherit land from their fathers, they almost always reclaim additional fields for their own use. As a result, they depend less on their families for future economic success and break away to establish nuclear families more easily.

Postmarital Residence

When people marry, they have to live somewhere, and the variety of possible places they can reside has been elaborated into several postmarital residence rules. Since the family is a residential group, residence rules correlate closely with different forms of the family.

Patrilocal (virilocal) Residence Patrilocal residence means that a married couple will reside with or near the groom's parents. If you took a census of Ratakote families, you would discover that about 90 percent of them were patrilocal. Coupled with village exogamy, patrilocal residence means that most of the married women in Ratakote have come from other communities, usually those within a walking distance of about 25 miles. Conversely, most daughters born to Ratakote families move away from the community when they marry. When Bhils travel in their local area, they almost always can count on staying with affinal relations (those related through marriage) or with daughters of their own village. It is this same class of relatives who exchange clothing at the *manda* ceremony. Before the wedding begins the family of the groom (or the bride in her village) invites the women from their family line who have married away from Ratakote and their husbands, children, and sometimes other relatives. They also invite the families of women who have married into their family. These people bring gifts of clothing for the groom and receive similar items from him in return. The male members of the groom's family line and neighbors do not make this exchange.

Matrilocal (uxorlocal) Residence Matrilocal residence means that a married couple will reside with the parents of the bride. Matrilocal residence is much less common than patrilocal residence but still may occur where there are descent lines traced through females (matrilineal descent) or in patrilineal societies under special circumstances.

Residence rules	
	patrilocal
	matrilocal
	neolocal
	bilocal
	avunculocal
	matri-patrilocal
	duolocal

Surprisingly, the concept of matrilocality helps with an understanding of Bhil society. Despite the fact that Bhils trace descent through males and prefer patrilocal residence, about 10 percent of all marriages end in matrilocal residence. The reason for this has to do with the sex of children born to some families, for some of them fail to produce living male heirs. If such a family's daughters all marry normally and go to live with their husbands in other villages, the parents will be without support as they grow old and will have no children to inherit their land. To compensate for a lack of sons, parents attempt to persuade at least one son-in-law to leave his own village and move in with them. The man forms a matrilocal extended family with his wife's parents, farms their land, supports them when they grow old, and inherits their property, which he is then free to bequeath to his own sons. Usually the men who agree to matrilocal residence are those from land poor families. Since they stand to inherit so little from their own parents, they accept lower prestige by moving to their wife's community.

Neolocal Residence   When a couple establishes residence apart from either set of parents or other relatives, we call the arrangement neolocal residence. Neolocal residence is preferred or at least common in societies such as ours where nuclear families are most common. Neolocality indicates that newly married couples are economically independent and can strike out on their own.

Other Residence Forms   Anthropologists have recognized several other residence rules in addition to those we have already discussed. These include bilocal residence, which occurs when a couple may live with either the parents of the groom or the bride. Avunculocal residence names a situation where a married couple resides with the maternal uncle of the groom, an arrangement that correlates with matrilineal descent. Matri-patrilocal residence occurs when the couple first lives with the parents of the bride, then moves permanently to live with the parents of the groom. Finally, duolocal residence is when the bride and groom continue to live with their respective parents.

Familism and Personal Identity

The relative importance of family and kinship has a significant effect on the personal identities of people in different societies. Although our families play a crucial role in raising us and shaping our personalities here in the United States, few of us derive our sense of identity and self-worth from this domestic unit. When asked who we are, we are more likely to identify our occupation than our family position. We are motivated to work hard and succeed by the prestige of success in the world of work, not by a need to acquit ourselves of family and kinship obligations. Even American women, who were always the exception to this rule, now increasingly seek to establish themselves by taking roles outside the domestic group.

But this is not the case for kinship-oriented societies. In such societies, families exist in close communities where their reputations are well known. Family members strive to maintain and increase their reputation by meeting their kinship obligations and extending their network of kin and other associations. Although this emphasis on familism is hard for us to understand, it is crucial to the lives of people in many other parts of the world.

Margery Wolf illustrates this point nicely in a book about a traditional Chinese extended family living in Taiwan. In one chapter she describes how Lim Han-ci, the dour, hardworking founder of the Lim household, purchased a little additional land.

He had made a permanent contribution to the welfare of his family. A peasant farmer does not think in terms of his own welfare and that of his immediate family; he calculates his accomplishments in terms of their benefit to all of his descendants. Lim Han-ci's little land would not produce many catties of rice in his own lifetime, but it would help support his children, his grandchildren, and his descendants for generations to come.[6]

The value of family and kinship and its importance for the personal identity of Bhils and for their motivation is clearly evident in Ratakote. The *manda* ceremony, for example, is not only part of a wedding, it is a family obligation that if handled well, will bring prestige to Kanji and his father and all the members of his family. Such events symbolize family strength and enhance family reputation. Kanji and other Bhil men do not work for success in an occupation; they labor in their fields and in their herds to provide the necessary material resources to meet family obligations. As they say when you ask them about family and kinship, "Now that is a good thing to ask us about. Our relatives make our lives."

SUMMARY

In this chapter we have discussed two important elements of the kinship system. Kinship refers to the complex system of culturally defined social relationships based on marriage and birth. Kinship-organized societies, those based on agriculture and herding that fall between hunter-gatherers and urban and industrialized groups, are most likely to demonstrate social organization based primarily on kinship.

Marriage is a socially recognized union between a man and a woman that accords legitimate birth status rights to their children. Societies may favor monogamy, which limits the number of spouses a person may have to one at a time, or they may permit or favor polygamy, the simultaneous marriage of a person to more than one spouse. Polygyny defines the simultaneous marriage of a man with more than one woman and polyandry means the simultaneous marriage of a woman with more than one man. The incest taboo is a cultural rule that prohibits sexual intercourse between certain classes of relatives. It and exogamy, marriage outside a particular group, serve to tie different groups together through marriage. Endogamy, or marriage within a specified group, enhances that group's solidarity. Many societies practice preferential marriage such as the levirate, the marriage of a man to his dead brother's widow, and the sororate, or marriage of a woman to her dead sister's husband. Both arrangements maintain marriage relations between the same two kin groups. Finally, marriages are often arranged by parents in order to create bonds between families.

The family is a kinship group consisting of at least one married couple sharing the same residence with their children and performing sexual, reproductive, economic, and educational functions. Hunting and gathering and industrialized societies tend to have nuclear families, consisting of a married couple and their children. Agriculturally based groups often manifest extended families, including

[6]Margery Wolf, *The House of Lim*, New York: Appleton-Century-Crofts, 1967, pp. 37–38.

more than one married couple and their children. Residence rules often correlate with these different kinds of families. Patrilocal residence stipulates residence of a married couple with the parents of the groom. Matrilocal marriage requires residence with the bride's parents. Neolocal residence indicates an entirely separate place of residence. Finally, in agrarian societies as opposed to our own, the family may be the major source of a person's identity and motivation.

MAJOR CONCEPTS

KINSHIP	COUSIN MARRIAGE
KINSHIP ORGANIZED SOCIETY	ARRANGED MARRIAGE
HUNTING BAND	FAMILY
MARRIAGE	NUCLEAR FAMILY
POLYGAMY	EXTENDED FAMILY
POLYGYNY	POSTMARITAL RESIDENCE
POLYANDRY	PATRILOCAL RESIDENCE
SERIAL POLYGAMY	MATRILOCAL RESIDENCE
INCEST TABOO	NEOLOCAL RESIDENCE
EXOGAMY	BILOCAL RESIDENCE
ENDOGAMY	AVUNCULOCAL RESIDENCE
LEVIRATE	MATRI-PATRILOCAL RESIDENCE
SORORATE	DUOLOCAL RESIDENCE

SELECTED READINGS

Bohannan, Paul, and John Middleton (editors): *Marriage, Family, and Residence*, Garden City, N.Y.: Natural History Press, 1968.
A collection of articles on such areas as incest, marriage, marriage forms, family, residence, and household.

Evans-Pritchard, E. E.: *Kinship and Marriage Among the Nuer*, London: Oxford University Press, 1951.
This work is an account of Nuer kinship organization with an especially clear description of kinship groups and their importance to the Nuer.

Fox, Robin: *Kinship and Marriage: An Anthropological Perspective*, Baltimore: Penguin, 1967.
An analysis of the way that descent rules and marriage work to form kinship systems.

Murdock, George Peter: *Social Structure*, New York: Macmillan, 1949.
One of the original detailed attempts to categorize elements of the kinship system and to show the systematic relationships among such elements.

Radcliff-Brown, A. R., and Meyer Fortes (editors): *African System of Kinship and Marriage*, New York: Oxford University Press, 1950.
A collection of articles describing several African kinship systems.

Schusky, Ernest L.: *Manual for Kinship Analysis*, 2d ed., New York: Holt, Rinehart and Winston, 1972.
This book treats most basic aspects of kinship analysis in terms written for the student. A useful compilation of terms and explanation of various aspects of the kinship system.

CHAPTER SIX

Kinship
and
Descent

In the last chapter we saw how family and marriage arrangements can be extended to enlarge the scope of kinship systems. Here we look at the principle of descent to see how it, too, has been used to create more extensive kinship associations. Specifically, we will discuss three different rules of descent and see how these relate to kinship terminology, roles, and larger kinship groups.

DESCENT

Descent is based on the notion of common heritage. It is a cultural rule of relationship that ties together people who may or may not actually be relatives on the basis of reputed common ancestry. In keeping with our general deemphasis of kinship, we North Americans have a weak sense of descent. We usually know the identity of our grandparents and occasionally our great-grandparents, but we quickly lose track of our ancestry. Only recently has interest rekindled in the discovery of family genealogies. But in most so-called intermediate kinship-oriented societies, descent is of crucial importance. It governs rules of incest prohibition and exogamy, as discussed in Chapter 5. It also assigns ultimate responsibility for children and channels the inheritance of land, goods, and formal authority. Descent may be reckoned in two basic ways: unilineally through one sex or the other, or bilaterally through both sexes at the same time. Patrilineality and matrilineality are the two basic forms of unilineal descent (see Figure 6-1).

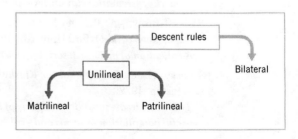

FIGURE 6-1
Kinds of descent rules.

Patrilineal Descent

Patrilineal descent occurs when people believe that they are descended from a common ancestor through males only. The essential line of inheritance, as is clear from Figure 6-2, is from father to son down through the generations. Females belong to their father's patriline, but cannot bequeath line membership to their children. Our surname (last name) is assigned on a patrilineal basis, although North Americans are usually considered to be bilateral, as we will see presently.

Patrilineality is the most common descent rule and is found in almost every part of the world. Middle Eastern societies are almost all patrilineal; so are the peoples of north and central India, China, and Japan. Although the popularity of patrilineal descent is not entirely understood, its preference seems to be related to a couple of factors. First, it specifies exactly every person's descent group because it is a unilineal descent rule. Children belong to their father's descent group and may not usually choose another. Second, it seems to be related to situations where males control resources, particularly resources that can be publicly shared. Such control seems evident in peasant societies such as those of the Middle East, India, and traditional China.

Returning to your ethnographic study of Ratakote, you will find the concept of patrilineal descent would help you understand Bhil kinship arrangements. You have already noticed that clan and village exogamy and patrilocal residence combine to add women to families. As you interviewed more extensively, you would also learn that the women who have married into Ratakote families continue to keep their father's surname. They remain members of their father's descent line and do not join their husband's.

There are other indications of the importance of patrilineal descent in Ratakote. Bhils like Kanji want sons, not because they value special masculinity among children but because sons continue to live in the village, help them work their land, inherit from them, care for them when they are old, and eventually see to

FIGURE 6-2
Patrilineal descent. Shaded figures indicate ego's patrilineal descent group.

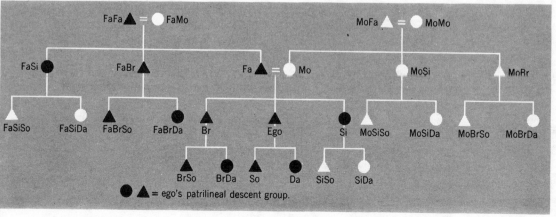

their souls when they are dead. Each year on a special ritual day, ancestors of each descent line found in Ratakote possess *shamans* (religious specialists who in this case act as mediums) and speak to their living descendants.

Patrilineal descent is evident in other ways. A family's land and goods are inherited equally by sons, not daughters. The latter must depend on the inheritance of their husbands. Children, too, stay with fathers in case of a divorce. Infants remain with their mothers as long as they are nursing, but find a permanent place in their father's family. And, as we have seen in the last chapter, patrilineal descent limits the range of potential marriage partners.

Matrilineal Descent

But patrilineal descent is not the only way kinsmen can be linked together from generation to generation. In some societies people trace descent through females only. This rule is called matrilineal descent and is represented in Figure 6-3. In matrilineal descent the line of ancestry is traced from mother to daughter. Males belong to their mother's line but cannot pass membership in it along to their own children.

The distribution of matrilineal descent systems has concerned anthropologists for decades. Much rarer than patrilineal systems, matrilineality appears to be associated with horticultural societies (those that employ shifting agriculture and gardening). Some anthropologists argue that this association is related to the important place women hold in these societies, in which they often perform more of the essential field labor than men. The correlation, however, is far from perfect for there are many patrilineal and bilateral horticultural societies as well.

Some of the first Westerners to encounter matrilineal descent concluded that it led to matriarchy, or female authority and political dominance. Subsequent studies show that even in matrilineal societies, men continue to hold formal authority.

FIGURE 6-3

Matrilineal descent. Shaded figures indicate ego's matrilineal descent group.

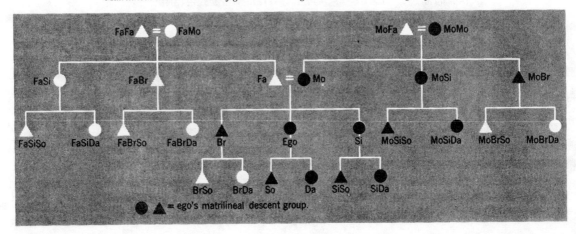

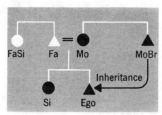

FIGURE 6-4
Inheritance in matrilineal societies.

Males also continue to dominate the system of inheritance. Land and goods do not usually move from mother to daughter and cannot pass from father to son, because a man's sons belong to his wife's line. Instead, property usually flows from a man to his sister's sons, an arrangement that leads to some interesting kinship relations in matrilineal society (see Figure 6-4). This form of inheritance only makes sense when one remembers that both males belong to the same matriline.

The exercise of authority within the matrilineal extended family and matrilineages (lineages will be discussed later in this chapter) follows the same pattern. Males usually hold formal authority. Patrilineal families and lineages complement this rule of authority, for normally it is the eldest member of the group who serves as its head. But in matrilineal extended families the women all belong to the same descent group, but the men, their spouses, do not. Since a woman does not head the family, who is to do so? The only males who can exert such authority are those belonging to the female line, the brothers of the women living in the household. Although they usually live in other households, often the brothers assume formal responsibility for kin-group decisions. It is common for a woman's son to move in with her brother to facilitate the exercise of such authority over her children. The boy will inherit from his maternal uncle and, in turn, pass along his property to his own sister's sons.

Bilateral (Cognatic) Descent

In North America, we follow neither unilineal rule of descent. Instead, we recognize descent from ancestors through both males and females, the resultant rule being termed bilateral descent. Like matrilineality, bilateral descent is also less common than patrilineal descent. Bilateral descent leads to greater flexibility. In place of assignment to a particular unilineal descent group, people in bilateral societies often have a choice of groups, all of which have members to whom they are somehow related. Such flexibility seems to correlate with lighter control of scarce resources, like land, by families and other kinship groups. In agricultural societies where land is scarce, families or lineages exercise control and unilineal descent is most common. But where individuals are less dependent on families for access to land and other resources, bilateral descent is more likely.

As in our own society, bilateral descent may lead to equal inheritance by both sons and daughters. (Legally, of course, an individual may designate heirs, but the general expectation is as we have stated it.) Bilateral societies, however, often demonstrate a patrilineal or matrilineal bias, as they do to some extent in North America.

KINSHIP TERMINOLOGY

The study of kinship terms, the words such as our English "mother," "father," "brother," and so forth that label different kin, has occupied anthropologists for many years. The reason for this interest is that kin terms designate statuses that define the social positions in a kinship system. They also divide up a range of possible kinsmen differently from one society to the next. The discovery of kin term systems is an important part of any ethnographic field study.

The Bhil Kin Term System

Kin terms would be an immediate object of investigation for you in your study of Ratakote. When you witnessed the *manda* ceremony, for example, you heard people refer to each other by such words as *mamaji*, *bap*, *beta*, and *bhanej*. You suspect that these are terms for kin and by using a genealogical method in which you ask Bhil informants to identify all the kin they know and to tell you what they call them, you begin to learn additional kin terms. By this process you can discover the terms and the particular kin they denote.

You start by approaching Kanji after his wedding, and using the genealogical method, you quickly discover that he has one living brother, two sisters, cousins who are his father's brother's children, his mother's brother's children, and his father's sister's children. His mother has a sister, but as yet she has had no children (see Figure 6-5). When you ask Kanji what he calls each of these relatives, he responds with two terms, *bhai* and *bai*. The first designates his brother and his male cousins; the second indicates his two sisters and his female cousins. You have found out part of the meaning of the terms *bhai* and *bai* by simply discovering the range of kin to which they refer. Completing the interview, you are surprised to discover that Kanji knows of 79 different terms that he and his neighbors use to identify their kinsmen. Clearly this system is more complicated than your own.

Once you have the entire set of kinship terms used by villagers, you can return to your original problem, the identification of the people who were present at the *manda* ceremony. You learn, for example, that *bap* is a term that refers to father. *Beta* is the term for son, *bhanej* refers to one's sister's son, and *mamo* (the "ji" affix

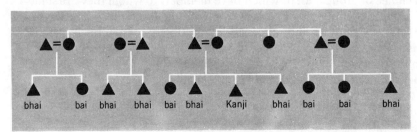

FIGURE 6-5
Terms that Kanji uses to refer to his cousins and siblings.

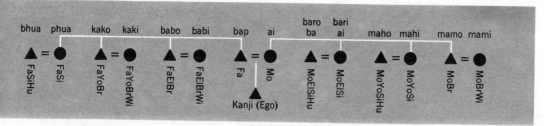

FIGURE 6-6
Kin belonging to Kanji's father's generation.
Note: *El = older than; Yo = younger than. Relative age can be shown by placing the oldest kinsman to the right. This convention is not followed here for reasons of space.*

you earlier heard attached to the word is an honorific) indicates one's mother's brother. You ask Kanji what other relatives were present at the ceremony, and he gives you a long list of kinship identities, part of which appears in Figure 6-6. If there is any doubt in your mind before going to Ratakote that the same relatives can be culturally categorized in more than one way, it is dispelled by this arrangement of Bhil kin terms. In our own kinship system we class all of our parents' siblings (brothers and sisters) and their spouses by two terms: *uncle* and *aunt*. For Bhils, these same kin are terminologically divided into 12 different identity categories!

Kin Term Systems

As anthropologists have collected kin terms, diagramed them for particular societies, and compared them from one group to the next, they have discovered that terms usually form patterns that may be classified on the basis of the way kin terms label cousins. Although it is not always easy to explain the reasons that terms fall into this limited number of patterns, some systems clearly relate to particular descent rules. Let us look at these systems briefly.

1. **Hawaiian terminology.** Hawaiian terminology assigns two kin terms to ego's cousins and siblings, one for males and one for females. The system repeats this principle throughout, labeling kin in each generation by only two terms. Bhils, like other people living in north and central India, use an Hawaiian system to label cousins, but employ a much more complex approach to uncles and aunts.

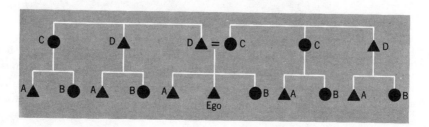

2. **Eskimo terminology.** Eskimo terminology is similar to Hawaiian, except that ego terminologically separates his lineal relatives from all others. The Eskimo system appears to correlate with bilateral descent and, not surprisingly, characterizes our own kin term system.

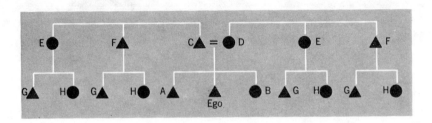

3. **Sudanese terminology.** Sudanese terminology assigns a different term to each cousin.

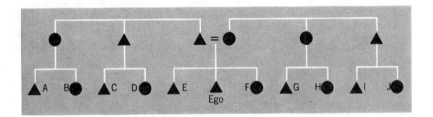

4. **Iroquois terminology.** Iroquois terminology classes cross-cousins together and distinguishes them from parallel cousins and siblings. While parallel cousins are usually classed with siblings, they are not always found associated in this way. Parallel cousins are children of ego's father's brother and mother's sister. Cross-cousins are children of ego's father's sister and mother's brother. (We will let the letter *X* stand for cross-cousins and // represent parallel cousins in the following diagram.) Iroquois terminology is generally associated with a unilineal rule of descent.

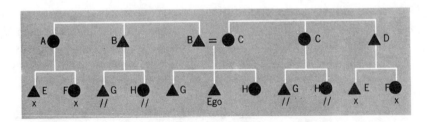

5. **Crow terminology.** Crow terminology is complex because it classes relatives of different generations together by the same terms. The system is most easily understood as an outgrowth of matrilineal descent (see the previous discussion of descent), for it classes all the kin of ego's father's matriline together by two terms, one for male and one for female, and all the children of males of ego's line by two terms according

to sex. It also follows an Iroquois pattern for designating parallel cousins and siblings.

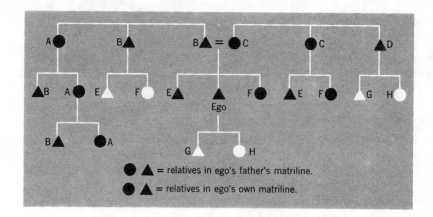

= relatives in ego's father's matriline.

= relatives in ego's own matriline.

6. **Omaha terminology.** The Omaha system is the reverse of Crow terminology because it is based on a patrilineal rule of descent.

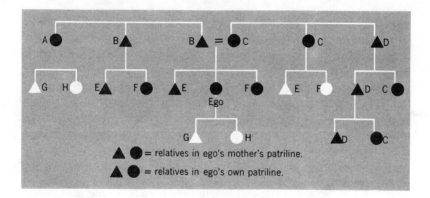

= relatives in ego's mother's patriline.

= relatives in ego's own patriline.

KINSHIP ROLES

Kin terms are labels for <u>kinship roles</u>, which indicate special roles. When Kanji and his mother's brother (*mamo*) exchanged *dhotis* at the *manda* ceremony, they based their behavior on a set of rules that made up part of their role on that occasion. Kanji's *mamo* must initially approach Kanji. Kanji should greet him first, then receive the gift of the *dhoti* before he reciprocates. The parting embrace is clearly defined by their culture as mandatory in the situation.

Role behavior is clearly defined and valued. For example, at the *manda* ceremony everyone would have been surprised, even shocked, if Kanji had criticized the way his father passed him the pieces of clothing for the exchange or had asked his father to give the clothing directly to the relatives. For a son (*beta*) must show

The relationship between a father and son among the Bhils emphasizes paternal responsibility and authority, and fillial loyalty. Here a father symbolizes his rights and obligations by placing a hand on his son's head.

his father (*bap*) respect, listening to his advice and accepting his decisions. This respect is expected at all times—when they are at home working together on the wooden frame of a new plow; when they discuss who is to walk the 20 miles to the district capital to buy ritual items for an upcoming festival; or when they are in public, caught up in a discussion of how to handle the government forest guards who are trying to prevent villagers from cutting bamboo. In addition, Kanji knows that he has an obligation to support his father when the man becomes old and unable to guide a plow. Similarly, Kanji has the right to expect financial cooperation from his father as long as he is able. Kanji should support his father in disputes, help his father to become prominent in village politics, and loan his father money if he has need of it.

Perhaps a better way of viewing and understanding the nature of kinship roles is to look at what a new bride must learn on entering her husband's village. Consider Kanji's bride, Nani. On the day of her wedding, Kanji arrived in her village before sunup with his large wedding party. Their families exchanged water, food,

A wedding establishes a new set of kinship ties for a bride and groom, while simultaneously altering some original relationships with relatives. The bride, shown completely veiled sitting by the groom, must leave her parents and siblings, and weeps throughout the ceremony to dramatize her love and respect for them.

and clothing, and Nani donned the wedding clothes Kanji had brought to her, entirely covering her face to avoid being harmed by the forces of the evil eye. She cried at this time to show her sadness at leaving the parents who had so lovingly raised her, even though secretly she was glad to marry Kanji. She had arranged to see him at a fair after their parents had betrothed them, and he was truly a handsome boy, tall, light, with a clear skin and strong body. When the sun was about to rise, Kanji and his party approached her courtyard where her mother met him. It was her mother's role to honor him with fire and a plate filled with wheat balls, engaging in a little ritual that served to bless the groom. Then Kanji, wearing silk slippers, rushed into the courtyard of her house with drawn sword, and Nani was brought out, still weeping, and tied securely by her left hand to his right hand and wrist. Her mother's brother and her father's oldest brother both spoke about her obligations to her new husband, and her relatives and Kanji's relatives, who had followed him into the yard, made off-color comments about the probable quality of their sexual life together. Then she and Kanji were led seven times around the wedding fire, and after his party had been feasted and Kanji had exchanged *peravani* with her kin, she was stolen by her new husband in a mock battle and followed him at some distance, weeping all the way to Ratakote.

Formal Kinship Roles

Thus began the second phase of her life, one in which she had to learn a whole new series of roles. For example, she discovered, although there were no formal restrictions on how she could interact with Kanji's kin before she was married, now that she was a bride she had to be careful, particularly of her father-in-law. Her new identity of daughter-in-law required that she cover her face with the border of her *orni* before her husband's father. She should not address him directly or joke or laugh while he was there. The second day after she arrived to live in Kanji's house, she forgot about this new restriction in her nervousness and joked about the flirtations of Kanji's youngest sister. Her father-in-law immediately left the room, and Kanji's mother gave her a stern lecture on the virtues of being respectful and a proper member of the household. Nani quickly learned that the same respectful behavior was required in the presence of any of her husband's older male relatives. She discovered that, more and more, she must cover her face and hold her tongue when they were around.

But on one occasion she followed this rule of behavior when Kanji's younger brother came into the room, and he laughed, explaining to her that she need not be reserved when he was around. In fact, it was quite proper for them to joke with each other and, if they were quiet about it, to sleep together.

Even her relationship with Kanji was not what she thought it would be. Once she attempted to display her affection for him in public, and promptly received a second lecture from his mother on how to show proper respect. For either her or Kanji to pay too much attention to one another in public was to claim that their relationship was more than that between Kanji and his parents. Thus his mother was rightfully offended.

Avoidance

These kinds of roles, involving formal rules for behavior that Nani had to learn, have their counterparts in many societies, and anthropologists have classified them into several types. When Nani covers her face and refrains from speaking with a relative, this behavior expresses an avoidance relationship. In the United States we may avoid other people when we have been fighting with them, but such a state of affairs develops in the course of the relationship and may disappear as quickly as it started. For Nani, however, the avoidance of her father-in-law is culturally expected behavior; it is defined as part of her role. A similar kind of avoidance relationship is described in the words of a young man by anthropologist Morris Opler in writing about Chiricahua Apache kinship roles.

If you come where your sister is alone, you put disgrace on the whole family. If the mother and father aren't at home and the sister is alone, you must leave the camp. You must stay somewhere else. You must go to the sunny side of the hill or in the shade and sleep until your parents come home. Also, when the whole family is together, you must show respect for your sister. This feeling begins when you are about six or seven years old, when you are first big enough to understand what is being said to you.[1]

[1]Morris E. Opler, "An Outline of Chiricahua Apache Social Organization," in *Social Anthropology of North American Tribes*, Fred Eggan (editor), Chicago: University of Chicago Press 1955, pp. 193–194.

It is common for North Americans to interpret avoidance in a negative light, as though it represented the outcome of a fight. But in most societies where it is found, avoidance means respect for another person. The Apache boy would offend his sister if he failed to avoid her when she was alone.

Joking Relationship

The easy interaction Nani displays with her husband's younger brother is usually termed a joking relationship. It, too, is found in a great many societies and tends to appear between people who are possible mates. In Ratakote, Kanji's younger brother is expected to marry Nani if Kanji should die (see the levirate, p. 000). Sexual relations are possible between the two even while Kanji is still alive.

Roles and Descent

Many kinship roles fit particular descent arrangements. We have already seen that one's mother's brother holds a special position in matrilineal society. Because it is his sister's children, and not his own, who belong to his descent line, the mother's brother becomes responsible for their proper upbringing. Years ago, anthropologist Bronislaw Malinowski reported on this relationship for the matrilineal Trobri-

Kinship roles regulate behavior in many social settings. At the manda *ceremony the groom is carried by his mother's brother* (mamo) *to a special stool where he is washed and perfumed before donning his wedding clothes.*

and Islanders. There he noted that mothers' brothers were authority figures, responsible for the proper upbringing of their sister's children. Fathers, on the other hand, could be friendly and warm to their own children, for whom they bore no direct responsibility.

This order is reversed in patrilineal society. Fathers are often the disciplinarians and mothers' brothers are warm and supportive. You would learn quickly after your arrival in Ratakote that the patrilineal Bhils followed this pattern. Despite all the precautions of their parents, many young Bhils elope, either with neighbors or someone encountered at a fair or in the hills grazing cattle. Inevitably, the young couple incurs the wrath of both the bride's and the groom's parents and takes refuge with a mother's brother, usually of the groom. This maternal uncle attempts to talk them out of their marriage. If he fails, he will have them married in a small ceremony and will act as a mediator to reconcile the parents to the new union. This friendly support is repeated under several other circumstances as well.

DESCENT GROUPS

One of the most striking features of many kin-organized societies is the large kinship groups made possible by the organizing principle of descent. In societies such as traditional China, for example, a single patrilineal clan might include millions of people, all of whom felt they were descended from a common ancestor. Large descent groups formed the basis of several precolonial African kingdoms as well as those found in Polynesia. Anthropologists classify descent groups on the basis of their size and the rule of descent on which they are based.

Unilineal Descent Groups

Groups based on a unilineal descent rule are called <u>unilineal descent groups</u>. Membership in such groups is assigned at birth; however, in some patrilineal societies women tend to be cut loose from their own patrilines and, although not full members, are attached to their husband's descent group.

Lineage

Anthropologists typically define three basic unilineal descent groups: the *lineage*, *clan*, and *phratry*. In societies where such groups are highly developed, all three may be found. The normal relationship among them is one of inclusion. Lineages are smallest in size, a number of them constituting the next largest unit, the clan. Two or more clans make up a phratry. At each level members of these groups recognize a rule of unilineal descent from a common ancestor.

The Bhils of Ratakote exhibit all three groups, although phratries are rare among them. Again, marriage and wedding arrangements are instructive. Kanji's father began to worry about getting his son married when Kanji reached his eighteenth birthday.

His first step in the marriage process was to approach other members of his lineage. A <u>lineage</u> is a group of kin related to each other by a unilineal descent rule who can trace the actual relationships between one another. Normally the group

Lineage mates cooperate in several ways. Here two brothers, members of the same lineage, plow land together.

is small, as it is in Ratakote, so that its members can trace their connection with one another exactly. Kanji's father's lineage is composed of his living brothers and their children, the same people who would have made up his extended family if they had been able to keep it together. There are a few lineages, however, composed of two or three sets of brothers, their married children, and the children of these. The tendency is for such large groups to break apart into smaller lineages, much as extended families do because of conflict among their members.

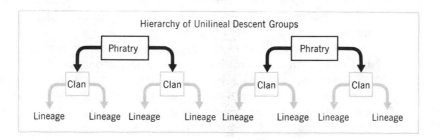

Hierarchy of Unilineal Descent Groups

When Kanji's father called the members of his lineage together to discuss plans for the wedding, the eldest brother acted as convener and exerted the most authority in the group. All had heard about the proposed wedding, but they discussed the matter thoroughly before agreeing to the plan, for they are all expected to contribute money, food, and time to the venture. It will cost them all dearly; it is nearly impossible to hold a wedding without the resources and support of lineage mates. In this sense the lineage represents a corporate body with control over certain aspects of its members' lives. In fact, the group has other responsibilities. It must decide about the inheritance and transfer of its members' land and forms a cooperative economic unit when harvesttime is at hand. Thus these functions characterize lineages in many societies.

Clan (sib)

Clans are larger unilineal descent groups composed of lineages. Clan members recognize descent from a common ancestor, but because of the clan's size, cannot usually trace their actual relationship with other than local clan members. As we noted earlier in this section, clans can be enormous in some societies. For Ratakote Bhils, they are very large. Bhils refer to clans by the term aṛak. Members of the Kaṭaṛa clan founded Ratakote and today over 60 percent of the household heads living there belong to this clan. The Kataras, however, are also found in many other Bhil villages, some as far as 200 miles from Ratakote. At the local level, they form Katara lineages; viewed as a whole, they make up the Katara clan.

Like members of every Bhil clan, the Kataras believe they are descended from a common ancestor. No Katara will marry another; to do so, as we have already seen, would be incestuous. In addition, there is a single goddess who represents clan members everywhere. Beyond these few functions, however, Bhils have little to do with members of their own clan outside their immediate area. When traveling they stay with affinal relatives or daughters of the community who have married elsewhere.

Phratry

Phratries are even larger unilineal kin groups composed of clans. Although members of phratries often recognize descent from a common ancestor, such ancestry is often thought to be distant. It ties people together but is not so close as clan membership, and marriage between members of different clans belonging to a single phratry is often permitted.

There are phratries among the Bhils, but they are rare, the result of clans splitting rather than a preferred pattern. For example, about 100 years ago, a famine drove some Kataras living in a place called Hiravat to the Aravalli Hills and they settled in many villages including Ratakote. At first they were treated as Kataras but called Hiravat Kataras because their customs were slightly different. Over time they came to be known as Hiravats, and now Kataras may marry them. But both clans recall their common heritage and still consider themselves to be descended from a common ancestor. For the time being, at least, they form a phratry.

Bilateral (Cognatic) Descent Groups

Because it is more flexible and not usually the basis for the organization of really large societies, bilateral descent does not yield such clearly defined or extensive kin groups. Anthropologists generally recognize two bilateral descent groups, the personal kindred and the rammage, or cognatic descent groups. Personal kindreds are not defined like the groups we have discussed so far. Instead, they are figured from the point of view of a particular individual. Kindreds tend to be made up of relatives someone knows about and interacts with. They may never all come together at once, but they will be people with whom one exchanges Christmas cards, wedding and holiday dinner invitations, and occasional aid. Unless they are brought together for family reunions or are in some other way forced to interact and cooperate, kindreds hardly represent organized groups at all. Because they are identified in relation to a particular individual, their membership changes from one person to the next. They also change over time. Small kindreds characterize kinship relations in North America.

Cognatic kin groups are more formally constructed, although they also seem loosely structured by comparison to lineages and clans. Cognatic kin groups resemble lineages in some ways, however, for they are localized and have corporate responsibilities.

SUMMARY

In this chapter we have looked at a major organizing kinship principle, descent, reviewing its subtypes and relationship with kin terms, kinship roles, and descent groups. Descent, a rule of relationship that ties people together on the basis of reputed common ancestry, may be unilineal or bilateral. Unilineal descent is patrilineal when people trace descent through males and matrilineal when they trace descent through females. When descent is traced through both males and females we call the arrangement bilateral descent.

Kin terms identify classes of relatives who hold specific roles. Kin terms fall into several patterns based on their classification of cousins. Kinship roles may be formalized into roles of respect, avoidance, and joking.

Descent leads to the formation of several descent groups. The smallest unilineal descent group is the lineage, followed by the clan and phratry. Bilateral descent results in personal kindreds and cognatic descent groups, or rammages.

MAJOR CONCEPTS

DESCENT	PARALLEL COUSIN
HAWAIIAN TERMINOLOGY	KINSHIP ROLES
ESKIMO TERMINOLOGY	AVOIDANCE RELATIONSHIP
SUDANESE TERMINOLOGY	JOKING RELATIONSHIP
IROQUOIS TERMINOLOGY	PATRILINEAL DESCENT
CROW TERMINOLOGY	MATRILINEAL DESCENT
OMAHA TERMINOLOGY	LINEAGE
CROSS-COUSIN	CLAN

PHRATRY	UNILATERAL DESCENT
PERSONAL KINDRED	BILATERAL DESCENT
RAMMAGE	COGNATIC DESCENT

SELECTED READINGS[2]

Bohannan, Paul, and John Middleton (editors): *Kinship and Social Organization*, Garden City, N.Y.: Natural History Press, 1968.
This book contains a number of useful articles on various aspects of the kinship system.

Fox, Robin: *Kinship and Marriage: An Anthropological Perspective*, Baltimore: Penguin, 1967.
An analysis of the way that descent rules and marriage work to form kinship systems.

Pasternak, Burton: *Introduction to Kinship and Social Organization*, Englewood Cliffs, N.J.: Prentice-Hall, 1976.
This book presents an approach for determining and analyzing kinship.

Schneider, David M., and Kathleen Gough: *Matrilineal Kinship*, Berkeley: University of California Press, 1961.
In this book, six anthropologists treat various theoretical aspects of matrilineal kinship systems.

Schusky, Ernest L.: *Manual for Kinship Analysis*, 2nd ed., New York: Holt, Rinehart and Winston, 1972.
This book treats most basic aspects of kinship analysis in terms written for the student. A useful compilation of terms and explanation of various aspects of the kinship system.

[2]See also the list of "selected" readings for the previous chapter.

CHAPTER SEVEN

Groups, Associations, And Age Sets

In every society the bonds of marriage and descent link people together. We all acquire numerous kinship statuses, learn to play various kinship roles, and belong to several kinship groups. As we saw in Chapter 6, some kinship systems have such a wide range that they seem to engulf the entire society; almost everyone is a kinsman. In other societies the multiplicity of groups outside the kinship system seems to make kinship insignificant in comparison. In fact, both kinship and nonkinship principles are important in most societies. In this chapter we focus on territory, sex, and age as principles of the social structure that go beyond kinship.

KINDS OF SOCIAL UNITS

In Chapter 4 we identified the following principles of organization: (1) kinship, (2) age, (3) sex, (4) common goals and interest, and (5) hierarchy. Other principles will be examined here and in Chapter 8. Every social group and every set of identities employ multiple principles of organization. Kinship groups nearly always have common goals and interests, often occupy a common territory, and may be structured on the basis of age and sex. A college football team is organized around a common goal, but it also is made up only of males. The Kwakiutl kinship group is internally ranked and also arranged in a hierarchy of other such groups. A kindergarten class meets daily in a common place (territory) and is made up of children of about the same age. Several combined criteria form the basis of any group or set of related identities.

Anthropologists classify social units on the basis of a *primary organizing principle*. Thus, although we recognize that the basic group in Eskimo society has a common shared interest and occupies a common territory, the principle of *kinship* is primary, and we call it a *family*. We recognize that members of an Indian caste are all kinsmen, but the principle of hierarchy, or rank, seems to be primary. Although the men's club in a New Guinea society has the common goal of performing certain religious rituals, the fact that it only includes males underscores the primary importance of sex as an organizing principle for this group. On the basis of the primary principles we can construct a partial taxonomy of social units for cross-cultural comparison (Figure 7-1). This taxonomy represents part of the shared knowledge that anthropologists have developed in their attempt to understand human social structures; it is part of anthropological culture.

The set of terms in Figure 7-1 labeled *associations* is distinct from the other three sets because it employs several different primary principles. Kinship groups are quite clearly based on marriage and descent; territorial groups share a common locality; ranked groups are hierarchically arranged. Associations constitute a catchall category that includes social units based on sex, age, networks, and common purpose.

TERRITORIAL GROUPS

A territorial group is one in which the members inhabit a common locality over time and recognize that they share this locality. Your family probably shares a house and yard, and thus territory is one feature of this group. In some societies, such as that of the Eskimo and of the Shoshonean Indians of the western United States, the local group and the nuclear family are coterminous. These families are *nomadic*. Instead of sharing a house on a 100×75 foot lot, they hunt and gather food over an exceedingly large territory. Nomadism refers to regular seasonal or cyclical movements of groups from one locale to another.

Kinds of Social Units		
	Kinship groups	Family
		Lineage
		Clan
		Phratry
		Etc.
	Territorial groups	Band
		Homestead
		Village
		City
		Etc.
	Associations	Men's and women's associations
		Age set
		Network
		Association (common purpose)
		Etc.
	Ranked groups	Caste
		Class
		Etc.

FIGURE 7-1
A partial taxonomy of social units.

There is no agreed-on taxonomy of territorial groups, but we may briefly contrast four kinds that are widespread throughout the world's cultures. Bands are nomadic groups in which kinship ties predominate. The Bushmen of Africa live in patrilineal bands in which a father, his sons, and their sons make up the core of the band. When the father dies, such a band may continue, or it may split into several smaller bands. Composite bands are made up of several unrelated families, and members may therefore marry someone within the band. Patrilineal bands, in contrast, are exogamous. Most bands subsist by hunting or hunting and gathering. Labor is usually divided between the sexes, but there is little specialization of roles such as full-time craftsmen or religious practitioners.

Probably the smallest settled community is the homestead. The Karimojong, a cattle-herding society in northern Uganda, live in homesteads, which may be the residence of a single extended family (a man and his wives, with his sons and their wives, and the unmarried children). In Karimojong culture this is ideal because a man is thus surrounded by his own human group and the animals that sustain them. But success is neither quick nor easy to achieve in any society, and a homestead may, in fact, be occupied by brothers or friends and their families, sometimes even sisters and their families if the husbands get along. In any case, every homestead will be divided into separate living compounds marking the separate households of each woman and her children. Karimojong homesteads are permanent settlements that contain not only livestock pens but also granaries and storage houses for the sorghum and other crops grown in the nearby fields. The stored grain is the main food of the women and small children.

Villages are larger units of settlement. The Karimojong do not have villages in this sense, only clusters of homesteads that see themselves as "neighborhoods" because their inhabitants interact and help each other to some degree. Villages also are usually associated with agricultural land and the storage of agricultural products, except in rare cases. The Kwakiutl, for example, could harvest enough salmon to support settled village life without agriculture. With the advent of agriculture in rich alluvial plains, villages increased in size to produce *cities* with many thousands of members. Here we find a high degree of role specialization, and nonkinship ties tend to predominate. There are a vast number of attributes that could be used to distinguish these and other kinds of territorial groups. Some of the more important ones are shown in Figure 7-2. But it is one thing to list terms for territorial groups and to identify the attributes; it is quite another to understand how such groups channel social behavior. For that we must turn to a case study of some territorial groups among the Karimojong of Uganda.

Karimojong Territorial Groups: A Case Study[1]

The Karimojong live in an area of about 4000 square miles in northern Uganda, Africa. This tribe of about 55,000 members has been studied extensively by the an-

---

[1]The case study developed in this chapter is based on the many published writings of Neville and Rada Dyson-Hudson. See especially Neville Dyson-Hudson, "The Karimojong Age System," *Ethnology*, 2, 1963, pp. 553–401; "Subsistence Herding in Uganda," *Scientific American*, 220 (2), 1969, pp. 76–89; and Neville Dyson-Hudson, *Karimojong Politics*, Oxford: Clarendon Press, 1966.

	Dimensions of Contrast			
	Nomadic Settled	Primary social ties	Subsistence	Role specialization
Bands	Nomadic	Kinship	Hunting/ gathering	Unspecialized
Homesteads	Settled	Kinship	Agriculture/ pastoralism	Unspecialized
Villages	Settled	Kinship or nonkinship	Agriculture/ pastoralism	Partly specialized
Cities	Settled	Nonkinship	Agricultural base	Highly specialized

thropologists Neville and Rada Dyson-Hudson. In order to see how cultural practices related to territory influence behavior, we want to focus on a single young man in Karimojong society.

If Loput had grown up in American society, he would probably be studying at some university, working at his first job, or perhaps would have joined the army. Instead, as a Karimojong, he has left his father's homestead and traveled to a cattle camp with part of his father's herd. With the onset of the dry season in September, grazing is getting scarce near his father's homestead, so Loput, with the help of two younger brothers, is moving the cattle that do not provide milk to the eastern grazing grounds. With his father's permission, he is joining two of his friends who have built a thorn corral in which to keep the cattle safe from hyenas, lions, and other predators. This camp will gradually grow to include several separate corrals. As grazing becomes scarce near the homesteads, more and more herdsmen will move their herds from various parts of the tribal land, to mingle in the dry season grazing grounds. Eventually the herds of half a dozen families could gather here and be corralled together for as long as it suits their individual owners to cooperate. When the girls finish with the agricultural work, they will join their brothers or boy friends and build small, temporary shelters.

It is growing dark now and the milking is finished. Loput selects a large ox. While two of the other boys hold the horns and lower jaw, a third holds the tail and Loput tightens a noose around the neck of the ox. As soon as the neck vein begins to bulge, he aims a blocked arrow. Much to his annoyance, and his friends' amusement, his first shot misses the jugular vein. He aims again, and a stream of warm blood gushes into a wooden bowl, filling it within minutes. The cord is released and the animal, shaking its head, ambles off in the direction of the herd. Loput stirs the warm blood with a stick to remove the fibrin that clots the blood. He gives this to the tan dog, which helps to guard the livestock at night and herd them during the day.

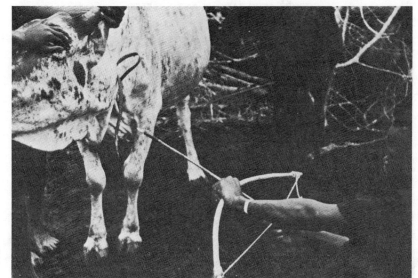

The Karimojong use their cattle as a source of blood for drinking and mixing with other foods. Here a blocked arrow is prepared to pierce the vein of an ox being held by other boys.

A cord tied tightly around the neck of the animal increases the pressure on the neck vein so that when the arrow is removed, a steady stream of blood flows. Here a Karimojong youth catches the blood in a basin. As soon as it is full, the neck cord will be loosened and the animal released.

The rich dark liquid contains fibrin, *an insoluable fibrous protein that is involved in the clotting process. This material is removed before the blood is ready for drinking.*

Loput passes the basin. It moves slowly from one person to another until all have drunk long and deep from this rich liquid. The boys build a fire, talk of the day's journey, and discuss the cattle. Before going to sleep, Loput, stroking a back here, rubbing a tail there, wanders among his father's herd. In his mind, he names the animals one by one, checking that they are all, indeed, there. He stops to sing softly to his ox from which he has taken his honorific name—Apalomeripus (the father of the blue roan with small spots like a leopard). Loput is 18, and although he has been tending the livestock since he was 4 years old, this is the first time he has had full charge of a part of the family's herd. That responsibility, and the nearness of the Upe enemies to the east, who sometimes push their camps to within 20 miles of this place, make him anxious.

As he lies down to sleep, it is the sweet smell of the cattle and their soft night noises, as much as the warmth of the fire, that reassure him and enable him to sleep. All his life, it has been nearness of cattle and closeness of people that made home. He wonders who he will encounter this particular dry season, since every year seems to bring a different mixture of people together. He drifts off into a light sleep from which he will frequently wake to listen for noises of wild animals, look to see that the fire remains bright, and check the well-being of the cattle and his brothers. Although he must still wait for the ritual that will make him an adult man in the eyes of his own people, Loput feels good tonight to be doing a grown man's job, to be away from his kinsmen and on his own.

Loput has lived much of his life surrounded by kinsmen. In the homestead on any day Loput could play or work, not only with his own brothers and sisters, but also with the children of his father's other wives and his father's brothers' wives.

Other relatives lived nearby and visited frequently. As he began to understand the discussions of the adults, he found that not all of these were equally important. Some—"our water kin"—you had to be courteous to and show hospitality to. But others—"our cattle kin"—could be depended on for support in times of misfortune and for contributions of cattle for marriage gifts. These could just as surely ask for a share when Loput's family had good fortune and request contributions toward their marriages.

But the ties of kinship are supplemented for Loput with ties to people who share the same territory. If each of us belonged to a single territorial unit, life would be much simpler. But such is not the case. Even a student in college will share certain areas with roommates, still larger territories with those in the same house or dormitory, and other areas with members of the same college. Beyond that, such a student is a participant in the life of a city or town, a state, and even a nation. All such territorial groups influence some of our behavior.

Loput's maximal territorial group, the largest and most inclusive territory and its inhabitants, is the Karimojong tribe. It includes the 55,000 people living in homesteads scattered over 4000 square miles. But this maximal territorial group is flexibly defined and rarely operates as a mobilized group. True, Loput knows that there is such a thing as *Karimojong*, "the place of the Karimojong people," but he knows this refers to wherever the Karimojong people happen to operate, and that the borders of this territory expand and contract as conditions make moves to new grazing necessary. Loput knows the Karimojong are different from other surrounding people, whether they are friends like the Nyakwai to the northwest, or simply people the Karimojong treat with indifferent contempt, such as the little tribes living on the volcanic mountains that rise steeply out of the plains. He certainly knows the Karimojong are different from their numerous enemies to the north (Jie), east (Upe), and west (Teso), enemies who also occupy flexible territories.

But even when "the Karimojong" go to fight the Jie, Loput knows it will be mainly people from the northern divisions of the tribe who will be there. People from the southern division have their own enemies on whom to concentrate, although anyone who happens to be in the area is welcome to join in a raiding group. Phrases such as "all the Karimojong" are used only when people talk of "the sacred camp" (*nawiamuros*) and the ritual of "dividing the haunch" (*akidung amuro*). Like the Fourth of July celebrations for Americans, this ritual periodically reminds the Karimojong that they are indeed one people, with one place, one way of life, and one future.

Loput has never seen the ceremony himself, because it only takes place once in a generation. Last time, indeed, there was almost 50 years between two performances of the ceremony, and it caused many difficulties. But around the fire at night Loput has heard his father speak of how people from all the tribal divisions went toward the northeast—"the Karimojong direction"—to Apule. They drove their herds before them and everyone who could wore finery. Freshly mudded headdresses of bright blue, orange, and gray were topped by tossing plumes of ostrich feathers, made fresh and shining by cleaning them in river sand. Shoulder capes of white cowhide mingled with cloaks of leopard skin. Carefully matched pairs of sharp and shining spears were carried with negligent skill in one hand. And the clink and jingle of iron dancing bells, strapped below the knee, could be heard from far away. The tribal elders were there in their old-fashioned baboon-skin capes and heart-shaped nose ornaments, come to retire themselves and to promote the men of Loput's father's generation.

Loput's father had the honor of spearing the first ox, a brindled brown and white one, and for the first time was allowed to eat that part of the meat reserved for the elders. Everyone ate the roasted meat and drank milk and blood, but one part, the "haunches" had to be saved. The oldest of the elders took a specially long shafted spear and, joined by younger men holding it behind him, they divided the haunches. When the meat was roasted, all ate together and the elders blessed their young replacements, who could then return to their home areas to initiate young men into adulthood. Weeks later, Loput's father and his contemporaries went back again to the tribal ceremonial center to complete the lengthy rituals, whereby the title of "the elders" and the power to bless the tribe—or curse it, if need be—finally passed to them. Loput has heard the story many times from his father, and each time tries to absorb the details because he knows that some day another ritual of "dividing the haunch" will take place, his father will retire, and he, Loput, must go to Nawiamuros to become a man of influence and power in Karimojong society.

Loput and his friends awake the next morning at the *stock camp* near the eastern border of Karimojong territory. These camps are only temporary settlements, and only parts of families live in them. Women and their young children and older men usually remain in the homesteads or visit the camps for brief periods only. At the camp Loput will meet young men from other neighborhoods, even other sec-

The temporary stock camps, located in the eastern part of the Karimojong territory, are usually used for only a small part of each year. Boys from different neighborhoods will meet here during the dry season, expanding their contacts beyond the local homestead area in which they have grown up.

tions, and he will participate in guarding cattle from the dangers of Upe raiders and hungry lions, leopards, or hyenas. From wherever they come, all these herders will, in principle, have equal rights to graze their animals because this is Karimojong territory, and each member of the tribe is free to move in it according to his view of what will benefit his own family and its livestock.

In addition to the tribal territory and the small temporary stock camps, Loput is a member of three progressively smaller territorial groups: *section*, *subsection*, and *neighborhood*. To understand how they operate, we must go back to Loput's homestead—or as the Karimojong would see it, his father's homestead. Oval in shape and bounded by a 6-foot stockade of thorn trees dragged together as a wall, the homestead sits on a low ridge. There are gates into the cattle corrals and into the part of the homestead where the people live, allowing for the daily movement of cattle and people to pastures and gardens. Inside, the homestead is divided into smaller areas, each with a sleeping house for one of his father's wives and their children, granaries, and storage houses. Within the stockade there are a large corral for each herd of cattle and smaller pens for the goats.

The airview of a Karimojong homestead makes the spatial arrangements clearly visible. The gardens are usually in the immediate vicinity of a homestead while cattle may be grazed many miles away.

Ten years ago the Upe raided a friend of Loput's father, making off with all his cattle and killing most of his family. The friend came to live with Loput's father, and set out to build up his herd by begging from friends and relatives. Livestock were given, sometimes grudgingly, sometimes willingly, by cattle kin and close friends. Now a bulge in the oval stockade around the homestead marks the area where this friend has his cattle corral, calf pens, granaries, storage houses, and sleeping huts for his two wives. There is a sense of inner security in the homestead, the high stockade clearly marking the boundaries between the outside and the 50 relatives and friends inside.

At the homestead Loput would care for his father's cattle, taking them out of the corral to nearby pastures every day after the morning milking, and returning with them in the evening. During the rainy season, his mother and his sisters, along with other women, left almost every day to tend the gardens of sorghum, millet, and corn. As his father used to say, "Sorghum is the cattle of women." While each sex can, and when it is unavoidable will, do the other's work, people are happiest doing the tasks they are trained for and feel themselves to be good at. They see this as part of the balance of life. Men with few animals will spend considerable time in the fields. However, Loput's time is fully occupied with caring

Boys begin to assume responsibilities in herding their fathers' cattle as early as 5 years of age. From that time until they die, cattle are a central feature of their lives and a focus of their interest.

for his father's livestock, and he only helps with the agricultural work when the sorghum harvest is particularly abundant and his mother and sisters cannot handle the work alone. It is far more rare for girls to help with herding the livestock, and they are ashamed and embarrassed to be seen doing a boy's work.

To Loput, the homestead was part of him, the hard earth, the gates of the cattle corral, the beaten paths between the internal sections, the sorghum fields surrounding the compound, the smell of smoke arising each night from the 10 huts inside the stockade. He could see it now in his mind's eye, as he and friends got up, shivering in the distant stock camp, ready to drive the herds out to graze.

If you climbed up on the outcropping of rocks to the south of Loput's father's homestead, you could see a dozen other homesteads come into view to the north and west. These all belong to a single *neighborhood*, "homesteads that go together," as the Karimojong say. The Karimojong like to have company, and an isolated settlement would for them be an abnormality and a misfortune. The other young men who are with Loput at the stock camp this morning are from other homesteads in this neighborhood. These were boys he used to see when, as a young child, he went with his mother to draw water from a well in the riverbed; everyone in the neighborhood shared this common water source. Herd boys from all the homesteads of the neighborhood would line up with their cattle to wait their turn for water.

Long before he became a herd boy more than 13 years ago, Loput knew that one way or another he was related to people in nine of these other homesteads. He

A Karimojong woman offers beer to a visitor in her compound.

visited them often, playing with children, carrying messages. Often enough he heard his mother and father clapping and singing at whatever homestead was holding a beer party. Sometimes he heard the wailing lament of distress signaling a death or tragic misfortune and had joined his family at a run so that they could console the grief-stricken, as neighbors should.

Sometimes there were raids from the Upe, and the men in the neighborhood banded together to defend their cattle or later raided in retaliation to increase the size of their own herds. And when cattle are slain for sacrifice, it is most often the people of the neighborhood who gather together for the ritual meal and prayers and dancing.

Although the neighborhood is important to Loput, he will not always belong to it. He might remain a member until he has married a wife or two, but also he might not. He will always belong to *some* neighborhood, but homesteads are moved every few years. If social relations are strained, a move out of one neighborhood

Each Karimojong homestead is surrounded by a thick wall of sticks, seen here from the interior in the men's place of the homestead.

and into another is easy to arrange. A man must first ask all the elders of the neighborhood he wishes to join because his women will need garden land in the vicinity. Some neighborhood will certainly agree. Loput knows that when he and his brothers finally inherit their father's herd, differences of opinion may, in time, lead them to split off from each other. By the time he is old, the people in Loput's present neighborhood could well be scattered to the four winds.

Beyond his homestead and his neighborhood, Loput lives in a *subsection* and a *section*, larger, more inclusive territorial units. For each there is a permanent ceremonial center where rituals occur, and sometimes the men of a subsection or the entire section might join together in a raid. When the ceremony for "dividing the haunch" must take place, it is as section and subsection groups that men will travel to Apule for the important tribal ritual. The subsection is not a clearly bounded area and generally concerns Loput only for some ritual matters—how many people and their cattle should gather to be blessed or to pray for rain, and at which dancing ground. His section membership is much more important, and he will carry it until he dies. As a member of this group, he will prefer some grazing areas and waterholes to others; he will have unquestioned right to settle and appropriate free land for gardens anywhere in the territory associated with his section. He can move into the land of other sections with no trouble, but he must always ask there for what he needs, and however long he lives there, he will be distinguished by the name of the section into which he was born. At big gatherings his section membership involves him in identifying dances—miming the giraffe or the elephant, perhaps. And there will be comments, cheerful or malicious, on the supposedly well-known character of his section as thieves, dancers, singers, or whatever. Formally and informally, socially or politically, Loput can no more leave his section membership behind than he can change his skin.

Despite his continual movement, Loput, like all young Karimojong men, is to some degree anchored in space by his membership in a series of territorial groups that will continue to influence his social behavior throughout his lifetime (see Figure 7-3).

ASSOCIATIONS

Membership in a territorial group is based on location in space; marriage and descent, on the other hand, provide the basis for membership in a kinship group. But in nearly every society there are other kinds of groupings based on common interest, shared purpose, or some attribute such as age or sexual gender. We call such groups associations. This category is not well defined and includes a diverse collection of groups. There are a vast number of types of associations, and any classification depends on selecting a single organizing principle.

Voluntary associations refer to groups where membership depends on choice. Secret societies include groups that restrict their membership and maintain secrecy about their rituals, group practices, and special esoteric knowledge. Military societies, such as those that existed among the Cheyenne, refer to groups whose members have a common interest in warfare or a common experience in combat. Men's and women's associations include groups and clubs that restrict

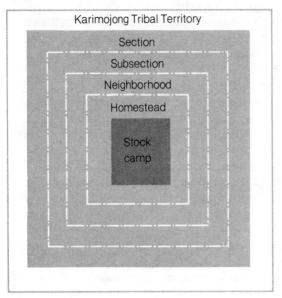

Karimojong Tribal Territory
Section
Subsection
Neighborhood
Homestead

Stock camp

FIGURE 7-3
Karimojong territorial groups.

their membership to one sex. Age sets are groups whose membership is determined by age. It is often difficult to find pure types of associations and, as we will see, the associations to which Loput belongs involve age, sex, and even secrecy. In the remainder of this chapter we will examine associations based primarily on sexual gender and age.

Men's and Women's Associations

No human society fails to make clear distinctions between men and women. Members of each sex almost always wear different clothing, engage in different activities, speak in perceptibly different ways, and are even thought to have different natures. And, on some occasions, in every society, men associate with other men while women meet with other women to work, play, or talk. Loput has always been aware that boys and girls could not do the same kinds of things. Whereas both sexes carried names based on the circumstances of their birth without regard to gender, Loput and his father took formal names from their favorite oxen. If circumstances allowed, they might also get names from killing any member of an enemy tribe. Women took their formal names from bearing a child: "Mother of so-and-so." Only males could fight enemies, guard herds, own livestock, compose cattle praise songs, kill animals in sacrifice, offer public prayers, and give ritual blessings.

But sexual gender can also be used as an explicit, primary principle for creating formal social groups. When this occurs, a men's or women's association is formed. Such groups may have many different purposes. In our society there is an endless list of such groups: boy scouts, campfire girls, Daughters of the American Revolution, the Vikings football team, the Faculty Wives' Bridge Club, the Masonic Lodge, Lions Club, Association of University Women Professors, Hell's Angels, Girls' Glee Club.

Among the Karimojong, men's associations are numerous and of great importance. Women's associations are shadowy and minor; generally women are aggregated on the basis of their husband's associations, and when they do make up associations of their own, they seem to be fragmentary imitations of male behavior—play (perhaps satiric) activities.

Principles of Recruitment

Ideally, it may seem, a men's or women's association should be open to all members of one sex in any particular society. But this is not often the case, even when a society has only a single men's or women's group. Sexual gender is the limiting criterion for membership, but other principles, such as wealth, age, birth order, and voluntary choice, also operate. Let us examine the men's associations among the Karimojong, and see which principles of recruitment operate. Their men's associations are made up of numerous smaller groups nested within them. This complex internal structure means that you can be in the association generally without belonging to more than a few of the smaller groups within it.

No single Karimojong term identifies the totality of men's associations. In theory there are four possible units, each known as *anyamet* (roughly translated "eating group," because members feast together at sacrifices) and distinguished from each other by name: Zebras, Mountains, Gazelles, Lions. For reasons that are perfectly clear to Loput and everyone who knows him, he will one day be a Gazelle.

Kinship ties are important among the Karimojong for joining men's associations. To start with, the four *nganyameta* are arranged in a fixed order and, generally speaking, you must join the *anyamet* that follows that of your father. The reason Loput will join The Gazelles is that the fixed order is Zebras-Mountains-Gazelles-Lions, and Loput's father's *anyamet* is Mountains.

But your mother is important, too, because most men have several wives, each with several sons, and to have them all initiated at the same time would be impossibly expensive. In deciding who goes first and who follows, the usual rule is "order of birth in order of mother's marriage." That is, the first son of the first wife is followed by the first son of the second (third, fourth, etc.) wife; then the second son of the first wife, followed by the second son of each other wife, in order; then the third sons similarly; and the fourth sons, and so on.

These domestic rules are just guidelines, of course, because the Karimojong are pragmatic people and, in any case, a father's decision on family affairs is final. So, if one son is physically more mature, and involved in more responsible jobs than another supposedly more senior but (because preceded by many sisters) actually much younger son, the father will take this into account. If he wants to show favor—or annoyance—to one wife by changing the order so that her son benefits or suffers, he can also do that (as long as he is willing to live with the resultant nagging and quarrels).

Kinship can count in other ways and has to be acknowledged even if it brings strange results. His friend Tyeko is 2 years younger than Loput but, when barely a teenager, was initiated as a Mountain just before the big ceremony at Apule cut off recruitment into that group. Tyeko's father is a Mountain, like Loput's father. Why, then, would Tyeko become a Mountain also? Because Tyeko's mother was not really married by her present husband (not "married with cattle"). She was first married to an older man, a Zebra, and when he died, she was inherited by her present husband, who was a relative of the old man's. All her sons, whoever fathers them, will be counted as children of a Zebra. Since Mountains follow Zebras, Tyeko was entitled to become a Mountain.

Membership fees of one sort or another constitute a widely used principle of recruitment. In order to join you have to pay. Among the Karimojong, new members must sacrifice an ox. Loput knew that he could have been initiated at least a year ago, but two of his half brothers had the right to precede him, and his father was reluctant to sacrifice three oxen in a single month. The Karimojong never kill and eat their cattle except for ceremonial feasts of this nature, and it is no small expense to a family. Once an animal is dead it cannot supply milk or blood.

Because of the importance of membership in these associations, the Karimojong clearly delineate a dividing line between members and nonmembers by means of an *initiation* ritual. This ritual not only announces publicly to everyone that Loput is a member of his men's association, but it also gives him an inner sense of identity. When his initiation is over, Loput will identify himself as a Gazelle. His initiation will be an important *rite of passage* that will ensure a permanent identity change in him. Because these rites of passage are extremely important and because they relate more specifically to certain age groups within the larger men's associations, we will discuss them at length after identifying the age sets in this culture.

Not all men among the Karimojong are initiated. A young man must choose to join his men's association. Loput has known all his life that someday he will become a man, one recognized by others as an adult with rights and responsibilities. In part, his manhood will depend on his age but, more important, it will depend on his initiation. For only those males who are initiated into one of the *nganya-meta* are considered men. At any time a few physically adult men remain uninitiated because they lack an animal to sacrifice at the initiation ceremonies. This is usually because their families have been impoverished through enemy raids or natural disaster. At certain chronological periods, as we will see, some physically adult men are just not allowed to be initiated because their grandfathers have not yet retired. In both cases, being physically mature but not being socially adult is a cause for anger for the men concerned and of embarrassment for the others with whom they deal. Such a man cannot be called *esorokit* (adult) and anyone can indeed call him *ediya* (boy). So while choice is involved, for Loput it is a matter of when his father chooses to judge him ready for initiation. The only people he has ever heard of who "choose" *not* to be initiated have been some of the boys at the European school. For reasons Loput does not understand, some missionaries insist that traditional ceremonies are bad and must be avoided. Even some of these schoolboys will be initiated later when they are away from missionary contact to avoid being perpetually stigmatized as "boys."

*Headdresses and hair or-
naments of various kinds
symbolize the age grades in
Karimojong society. Here
two agemates are working on
their headdresses.*

AGE SETS

People, in the normal course of life, progress through *biological maturation.*
Every society deals with this process culturally, identifying various stages in the
life cycle, assigning different roles to each stage, and placing different values on
each stage. Age grades refer to the cultural categories that identify the stages of
biological maturation. Infant, preschooler, child, teenager, adolescent, young
adult, adult, middle aged, retired, past his or her prime, elderly—the list of age
grades in our own society could be greatly extended. All cultures contain similar
categories, but they divide the cycle of life from birth to death in various ways. Although age grades sometimes approximate biological age, they often classify people into social ages that can be quite different from their biological age. Initiation
into manhood in some New Guinea societies occurs at intervals of several years, at
which time boys from 10 to 18 years of age can be initiated. Thus it is possible to
have a "boy" of 17 or older and an "adult" who is little more than 10 years old in
the same community. Age grades always refer to local cultural definitions, not to
exact biological age.

Age sets are organized groups of persons who are in the same or adjacent age
grades. A seventh-grade class is an age set with members who elect a class presi-

dent, secretary, and other officers. In many communities the students in a junior high school make up a large age set. Many churches are divided into age sets from the kindergarten class to a group of old members. Age sets usually have an internal structure of identities and roles, and they also have well-defined relationships to other age sets. The several classes in an elementary school constitute age sets where, as in most systems, the older ones have higher rank and greater privilege than the younger ones. Karimojong culture contains age sets. When Loput becomes a member of his men's association, he will also be joining an age set. Let us look more closely at these groups.

Loput returned from the stock camp late in April with the other herd boys. Their fathers' cattle were sleek and strong after grazing on the nutritious grass in the eastern highlands. Loput's father had visited him at the camp several weeks earlier, and Loput had again asked him, "Is it not time for my initiation?" His father assured him that if the grain harvest was good, in late September he would visit the elders in their section to see if they would be willing to come to the neighborhood ceremonial ground for the sacred ritual.

At last the time was near, the day Loput had dreamed of and talked about for many seasons. Soon he could exchange the beads he wore for yellow ornaments made of brass. Several other boys at the stock camp would also be initiated and together they shared the excitement of anticipation.

The rains during April and May were regular and abundant, and large fields of grain were planted. In June there was a 3-week drought, and Loput watched anxiously as the leaves of the sorghum plants curled up from lack of water. But July brought more rain. By mid-August the children were standing on platforms chasing the birds away from the ripening grain. In September everyone helped to bring in the huge harvest, even the herdboys, who usually do not help in the fields.

Loput began to prepare himself for the long-awaited initiation ceremony. He cut off the tall red headdress that had symbolized his status as a grown but uninitiated boy. He was to be initiated into an age set (*asapanet*) that included all the young Karimojong men who had been initiated during the last 4 years and those who would become men in this, their final year of recruitment. Their distinguishing name—across the entire tribe—would be "The Bat-Eared Foxes." Loput would also become a member of the much larger group, an *anyamet*, or *generation set*, composed of five age sets spanning a period of 25 years.

Together, the five age sets make up *The Gazelles*, the junior generation set in the Karimojong tribe who wear yellow (brass) ornaments. Loput's father is an *elder* (*ekasikout*—roughly "a man made wise"), a member of *The Mountains*, the senior generation set that alone can wear the red ornaments fashioned from copper. The other two *nganyameta* are inactive now: Loput's grandfather is still alive, an old man who belongs to *The Zebras*, and Loput's own sons will someday join *The Lions*. Boys who will later be recruited into *The Lions* generation set are now satirically called "little mice," because, say the elders laughing, "Lions is a name for men, while these are small creatures that swarm all over the place squeaking."

The four men's generation sets, each with five age sets, revolve slowly and perpetually as if they made up a huge waterwheel moved by the river of time (see Figure 7-4). Although the members change, the age system goes on forever. Someday, when Loput is much older, there will be another tribal ceremony of "dividing the haunch." *The Gazelles* will become elders; the men who are still alive in his father's generation set (*The Mountains*) will retire from public life; and the "little mice" will be initiated as *Lions*. But until then Loput must live in obedience and submission privately to his father and publicly to all the members of his father's generation set.

Rites of Passage

The Karimojong age cycle is like all social structures: the groups and status positions are occupied for a time by individuals, they die, and others come to take their place. Each of us enters a social system at birth to assume one or more identities. Our life trajectory can be seen as a series of movements from one status to another, from one position to another. We keep some identities throughout the life cycle; others will be taken up for a few years and then discarded. We move from child to adult, from single to married, from independent to fraternity brother, from student to alumnus, from nonparent to parent, from parent to grandparent, from worker to retired, and someday all of us will make the transition from living to dead.

A status passage occurs when any individual moves from one position in society to another. Some status passages are more significant than others, both for the person who goes from one identity to another and for those who make up his or her social world. Marriage, death, and the birth of a child are all important status

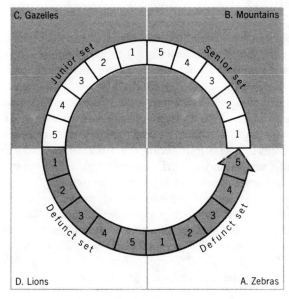

FIGURE 7-4

Karimojong age organization. The four generation sets succeed each other in a cycle (A, B, C, D); there are always two functioning generation sets. When the junior generation sets succeeds the senior set, a new set is formed for younger men (from N. Dyson-Hudson, "The Karimojong Age System," 1963, pp. 359-360).

passages. A birthday or graduation from junior high school is a less significant status passage to most of us.

In every society some status passages are accompanied by rituals called <u>rites of passage</u>. These ceremonies serve a variety of functions. They symbolically mark the transition from one position to another, acting as a public announcement that someone is not what they were before the ritual. Their identity has changed, and they must be treated in accord with this new identity. There are many theories to account for the cross-cultural variations in rites of passage, especially those that occur when the youth of any society become adults. These ceremonies, called <u>puberty rites</u>, are often the most elaborate, but they should not lead us to overlook the rites of passage for numerous other status changes. The *manda* ceremony, for example, which we examined in Chapter 5 in connection with a Bhil wedding, is one part of the elaborate rite of passage that occurs when a young man and woman move from the status of unmarried to married. Among the theories to account for rites of passage, the one that has stood the test of time stresses the *function* of these ceremonies. It was first proposed by Arnold van Gennep in his classic study, *The Rites of Passage* (1908). Van Gennep asserted that there were three major phases in rites of passage: *separation*, *transition*, and *incorporation*. The individual undergoing a status passage is first *separated* from his previous position, then there is a *limnal period* during which one is neither in the old nor new status, and finally one is ritually *incorporated* into the new position.

In his functional analysis of these ceremonies van Gennep suggested that transitions affected both the individual and the society. Each person who makes the transition must assume a new identity and the role that accompanies it. He must know the content of this new role and be able to perform it appropriately. He must gain acceptance from others and come to feel within himself that he has become an adult, a husband, or some other new identity. This change and the tasks it presents create anxiety and insecurity. The rites of passage serve to facilitate the accomplishment of these tasks and to reduce the anxiety brought on by the status passage.

But other members of the society also feel the affects of such a status passage. When a child is born, it adds new identities to others; someone becomes a sister, a mother, a father, a grandfather, an uncle. Loput's father is the head of a large homestead, and his death will affect more than 50 other people and could lead to a reorganization of the compound. Sometimes a status passage on the part of one or more persons can disturb the underlying values of a society. When youths become adults they assume new authority, and the value of submission to elders may be questioned. Patterns of social interaction are always based on our positions in society, and a status passage may disturb these patterns. The young woman who marries generally changes her relationship to all the previous suitors with whom she interacted. Every society is a functioning unit, and the equilibrium is upset when individual members change their positions within the social system. Rites of <u>passage</u> serve to reinforce the values on which a society is founded and restore the equilibrium of the social order. They enable us all to deal appropriately with the changes that occur in our own social worlds. Thus there are individual and social tasks or requirements that must be carried out whenever a status passage occurs.

As we examine in more detail the rites of passage that Loput goes through, we will look for the functions these ceremonies serve for Loput and the others in his social world.

Asapan: A Karimojong Rite of Passage

An air of excitement has swept through Loput's homestead; everyone knows that today *asapan* will begin. The same sense of anticipation runs through several compounds in the neighborhood where other boys hover on the brink of adulthood, eager to be men. At 18 Loput feels he has had to wait long enough for this ceremony, but there will be other "boys" much older. Apuun, from the nearest homestead, is many years older than Loput. His initiation was delayed because his father is very poor and he is the youngest son of his father's last wife.

Elders gather from all parts of the section. Some got up early to walk 15 or 20 miles to participate in the ceremony, but most of the men are from nearby. Loput's father greets his friends in formally chanted antiphonal greetings:

> *Blessings. Blessings be well.*
> *Blessings on the cattle.*
> *Blessings on the people.*
> *Blessings on the homestead.*
> *Blessings on the camp.*
> *Blessings on the grain.*
> *Blessings on the sheep and goats.*
> *Blessings on tomorrow, also.*
> *And again blessings. Blessings forever.*

Loput and the other boys who will be initiated gather leafy branches to mark off a large horseshoe-shaped enclosure and collect wood for cooking fires. Loput does not have time to be nervous about spearing his ox, which walks freely with the herd on the ceremonial ground. The spear must enter the right side between the ribs and pierce the heart so that the animal dies quickly. To spear it far back in the belly would be bad because it might penetrate the stomach sac and pollute the sacred chyme. If the ox and boy panic, so that the animal is speared in the left side, that would be truly disastrous. "Hold your spear high" was his father's only advice.

Spearing the Ox

Asapan, as the initiations are called, is actually a series of three named ceremonies. The first is called "spearing the ox," and it is followed the next day by the second, "eating the tongue." The last stage occurs up to 2 or 3 weeks later and is called, "cooking the stomach." Toward midday on the first day of *asapan*, the senior men, all members of The Mountains generation set, arrive at the ceremonial grounds and take their places around the enclosure of leafy branches. The eldest, members of the first age set, sit on the ground facing the open end of the enclosure; on each side of them all the others take their places in rank order according to their age sets: The Rocks, The Warthogs, The Colobus Monkeys, and The Red

The asapan *ceremony begins when the elders gather at the ceremonial site and sit in a large circle around the area where the initiates will each spear his ox. The elders shown here are seated according to rank, an arrangement largely based on age.*

Feather Headdresses. The representation of these groups is far from equal, for men do not die neatly, in batches. As at a college reunion, the groups may be of different sizes, and some might be missing altogether. But everyone knows the precise ordering of the seating arrangement. Younger initiated men who belong to the junior generation set, The Gazelles, remain in back of the elders. Loput walks into the ceremonial grove, accompanied by his father, who is acting as his sponsor. Six friends, who will be initiated at the same time, join him. Each has a 7-foot spear, which he is holding high.

The herd with the ox that has been selected for Loput's initiation is moved slowly near the elders' circle, for to try to drive the ox alone would make it panic. Loput moves quietly among the herd, raises his spear, and thrusts it into the ox. He pierces the heart of the huge animal, which slumps to the ground heaving a great sigh. Apuun is less skillful and has to spear his ox several times before it dies. The oxen killed by the five other initiates lie in different areas of the sacred grove. Each dead animal represents a childhood that is finished and a manhood begun.

Loput and the others begin to butcher the animal with the assistance of elders. They start by cutting the head and neck from the body; these are carried off by

Each animal that is killed is carved up by the initiates and their fathers. The division of meat is very important with some sections being saved for later parts of the initiation ceremony. Here a mother waits in the background for her part of the sacrificial animal.

Loput's mother and sisters to be eaten in the village. The stomach sac is carefully removed by one of the elders and placed on a bed of leaves, the half-digested chyme to be used as a symbolic marker of the change in status. Loput can see the flies on his father's back as he works beside him, carving up the animal. No hide can be removed from a sacrificed animal, and the carving follows a ritual pattern. First, the tender meat beneath the tail, the *elamacar*, is cut out and placed on the leafy branches in front of the elders; then the right foreleg is cut free from the body. The hind legs are separated from the rest of the body, but kept as a single undivided haunch. The haunches from all seven sacrificed oxen are stacked together on a pile of branches within the elders' enclosure. When the carving is nearly completed, initiated men are publicly called to the carcass to drink the blood that has accumulated in the stomach cavity.

The senior elder takes his spear and slits the stomach sac, which lies nearby. The thick chyme, scooped up in handfuls, is smeared on Loput's head, shoulders, and belly. The elder calls out loud enough for all to hear, but speaks to Loput: "Be well, grow old, become wealthy with stock, become an elder, be made wise." He then takes the right foreleg, which has been cut free from the carcass, and holds

The initiates pile up the portions of meat from the sacrificial animal. This meat will be cooked, distributed to the elders and initiates, and then eaten at the conclusion of the first stage of asapan.

the hoof so Loput can bite some of the hoof material. A few grains give away and Loput spits them upon his own body, in self-annointment. The senior elder then moves on to Apuun and the others, repeating the procedure. All the time Loput stands with his arms folded, holding the chyme against his chest. It is caking on his body; the sweet odor fills his nostrils; unnoticed flies crawl on his head and back.

When the last boy has been blessed and all are standing in line, the senior elder leads a litany of prayers, all the seated members of the senior generation set responding in unison.

The Gazelles—are there not gazelles?
There are!
Are they not many?
They are!
The Bat-Eared Foxes are many!
They are many!
The people in this place—will they not be well?
They are well.

The leader then blesses the section in which the ceremony takes place, the neighborhood in which Loput lives, and the cattle of all the people. Then Loput and the others arise and cook the chunks of meat, which the elders eat, sharing pieces as it suits them with the younger men as well as with the new initiates. The meat is passed out with careful attention to the order of rank. After they have eaten, the assembly disperses; everyone goes to a cool place to spend the rest of the day; they talk about the slain oxen, and some argue about the relative skill each initiate showed in spearing his ox.

The first stage, "spearing the ox," has come to an end.

Eating the Tongue

The next day, the second stage of *asapan*, "eating the tongue," is held at each boy's homestead. The elders visit each one in turn. At the time of the spearing of the ox Loput's mother waited on the outskirts of the ceremonial ground to drag away the severed head of the ox. Then, in her own compound at the homestead, she carefully boiled the windpipe, the tongue, and the lungs of the sacrificed ox. When the elders arrive now they are invited in. The whole family is wearing their best ornaments for this ritual occasion. The elders talk with Loput's father as they eat the cooked meat. When they have finished, they offer a special blessing for Loput and leave to visit the homesteads where the other newly initiated boys live.

Dividing the haunch is a central focus of the ceremony and has great symbolic importance.

Cooking the Stomach

The last stage of the initiation is "the cooking of the stomach." This occurs some days, and maybe even several weeks, after the killing of the ox, because the women of the homestead must gather and prepare the food for the feast. Loput's mother grinds sorghum from her granary and accumulates it in a skin sack. But she needs special kinds of food and does not have them all in her storage house. The day before the feast she starts shortly after sunrise to visit her kinsmen and friends in other homesteads of the neighborhood and tell them of her needs. At the door of each compound she requests and is granted permission to enter. It is late September, a bumper crop of sorghum has been harvested, and people are relaxing and drinking beer. Loput's mother takes her turn taking a long drink from the huge clay beer pot and, after a period of drinking and casual conversation, announces the purpose of her visit.

"I have come to beg," she announces. "Oh, you have come to beg," comes back a chorus from the others in the compound. "Yes, I have come to beg," repeats Loput's mother, taking her turn again at the pot of warm, muddy water with its fer-

The mothers of Karimojong initiates participate in the initiation ceremony, gathering a supply of food and preparing it in a ritual fashion. Here, a mother grinds grain in preparation for the last part of the initiation ceremony.

Karimojong women cooking a thick porridge that will be eaten during that part of the initiation ceremony known as "cooking the stomach."

mented gritty grain. "What have you come to beg?" someone ventures. "I have come to beg food for Loput's initiation." "Oh, you have come to beg food for Loput's initiation," comes back the chorus. She tells her friends and kinsmen that she needs sorghum flour, pumpkins, beans, cucumber seeds, fat—all the traditional Karimojong foods—for the feast the following day.

The next day all the women gather in the compound of Loput's mother. They pound cucumber seeds, cut up pumpkins, collect wood, and wash out huge wooden tubs. The children are busy grinding grain and fetching water. At midmorning women come from all the homesteads of the neighborhood; some bring large clay pots; some bring fat in shining gourds; others carry pumpkins and green gourds, one under each arm, one balanced on the head; still others come to find out what was still needed so that they can go home and get it.

By midmorning the cooking begins. The dried stomach of Loput's ox is cut into long strips. For three hours, it simmers in huge clay pots placed on small, efficient fires that have to be fed every half hour and blown up into a tiny, hot flame. In midafternoon the cooked meat is removed and the beans and pumpkins are added to the bubbling meaty soup. As the day grows cooler the sorghum flour is shoveled in. It makes such a thick porridge that two women must hold the pot, and five stir it, each taking a five-minute turn. Sweat pours from their bodies as they struggle to make the solid mass smooth. Finally, in the late afternoon, as the elders of the neighborhood begin to gather outside the settlement, the steaming mixture is piled high onto wooden trays, the meat and fat mixed in with the porridge, and the pounded roast cucumber seeds sprinkled on top as garnish.

Six of the women struggle into the cattle corral with a high platter of food and serve it to the elders. The presence of the elders in this enclosure symbolizes the unity of initiated men as a group and their close identification with cattle. Not far away in the calf pen, as if still children, sit Loput and the other boys. Had he for any reason speared his ox alone, he would still be accompanied by several young Bat-Eared Foxes who had become men in recent years. Loput's mother comes with a calabash filled with animal fat, dips a large handful, and pushes it toward Loput's mouth. He swallows the sticky substance, and then his mother smears it on his neck, repeating the process for each of the others seated in the tiny calf pen. "May you grow old," the old men pray for Loput after the feast is finished. "May you grow rich in cattle." "May you have many children." "May your family prosper."

And now Loput is a man, a full member of both his age set, the Bat-Eared Foxes, and a member of The Gazelles, his generation set. Tonight there will be a dance and all the young men initiated this year or in recent years will join with the girls of the neighborhood. They will sing and dance long past dark, and some young men will take their lovers into the bush until the early hours of the morning. For Loput this day will always remain a vivid memory. His status passage is complete; today he has become *ekasapanan*, an initiated man (see Figure 7-5). Now he can start shaping his hair into a close-fitting headdress covered with purple mud. From the back of the headdress will dangle a metal chain that marks his new status as an adult.

FIGURE 7-5
Karimojong rite of passage.

Boy (ediya)	"Spearing the ox" (akicum emong)	"Eating the tongue" (akinyam angajep)	"Cooking the stomach" (akipo aboi)	Man (ekasapanan)
	Neighborhood ceremonial ground	Father's homestead (in mother's compound)	Father's cattle corral (preparation in mother's compound)	
	First day	Second day	Eighteenth— twenty-fifth day	
	Asapan period			

A Karimojong elder smears himself with chyme from the sacrificial animal during the asapan *ceremony. The symbols used during initiation not only announce the initiates identity change, but also link initiates to the elders in a common identity.*

Rites of Passage:
A Functional Analysis

It would be easy to underestimate the importance of rituals such as *asapan*. They do far more for the participants and the social groups involved than it might first appear. *Asapan* is *not* merely a strange set of activities announcing that boys have become men. Like the rites of passage that take place in every society, it serves important personal and social functions. No doubt you have already noted some of the functions served by these rituals. We will now summarize eight general functions rites of passage serve for any society, although the extent to which they are all served by a particular rite varies.

1. **Rites of passage serve to facilitate the transition from one position to another.** Loput and his friends moved from uninitiated boys to *ekasapanan*, initiated men. These transitions were facilitated by the rituals in which they participated. Their status passages received public attention. Significant others in the lives of each initiate were reminded by these ceremonies to treat them in accord with their new status. Parents, friends, age mates, and brothers would now accept the change that had occurred.

2. **Rites of passage serve to provide emotional support.** As indicated earlier, status passage can often create insecurity and anxiety. When a husband dies, a funeral ceremony provides emotional support for his widow during the period of transition. Loput and the others are not required suddenly to begin acting like initiated men; instead they go through a transitional period when others give them emotional support. It is difficult to know the extent to which these transitions create anxiety, and it would probably vary from one initiate to another. But there is considerable evidence that any status change, whether desirable or undesirable, causes stress to the individual. Rituals bring people together and provide social support for those undergoing this stress.

3. **Rites of passage serve to establish an inner sense of identity.** If people are to perform new roles effectively, they must do more than intellectually accept a new identity. Boys must set aside the feeling that they are children and acquire an inner sense of manhood. Manhood among the Karimojong has many rewards, but it also carries responsibilities to work and fight and participate in tribal rituals. *Asapan* forestalls backsliding by giving young males a deep sense that they are now men. One way in which rites of passage create this inner sense of a new identity is through difficult and even painful experiences. Circumcision, hazing, beatings, long periods of isolation all function to inscribe a new identity indelibly on the consciousness of the individual.

4. **Rites of passage enhance social cooperation.** The rituals that Loput went through bring part of his age set together in cooperative action. They create the enclosure on the sacred ceremonial grounds, gather the wood, prepare the meat, and work together in other ways. This foreshadows the cooperation that will continue during the rest of their lives—cooperation in guarding cattle, making raids, staging rituals, and settling disputes. A cooperative unit beyond the family, beyond the homestead, is thus begun through the rite of passage in each case.

5. **Rites of passage serve to increase social solidarity.** These rituals bring people together from distant places, reinforcing social ties and creating a sense of unity. The age set among the Karimojong, the generation set, and all local members of the men's association gather for initiation. Old stories are retold, old friends renew acquaintance, and the bonds of kinship, territory, and age are reinforced.

6. **Rites of passage serve to reinforce common social values.** Through symbol and ritual, the values of society are brought to each initiate's attention. Older members of the age sets and men's associations are reminded by the ceremonies that cattle are the center of a man's life, that submission to authority is important, that fathers are to be respected. No society can exist for long without a shared commitment to basic values that act like the foundation stones of social life. These can be restated publicly and thereby reinforced and given sacred authority through status passage ceremonies.

7. **Rites of passage serve to enculturate the initiate.** Loput not only learned about the fundamental values of his society, but he was also taught many specific cultural rules.

8. **Rites of passage serve to integrate the social order.** The bonds that link human beings together, that bind one segment of society to another, are tenuous, easily broken strands. We have discussed how rites of passage enhance cooperation and increase

Initiation ceremonies serve important functions for the elders who participate as well as those being initiated. People from other parts of the section come to participate in the ceremonies, renewing old ties. Here an elder is being smeared with fat during one part of the Karimojong initiation ceremony.

social solidarity; they also link individuals to the society at large. They help create patterns of wider integration. Loput's age set is integrated with all the other age groups in his society as they sit, encircled by ranked groups of elders. However formally separated the generations may be, they cannot be isolated or alienated; *they need each other to do what must be done.* Furthermore, Loput's age set is linked to men of similar age who are being initiated in all parts of Karimojong territory. Apart from reminding them of age set and generation set affiliations, men are reminded that they are, above all else, the Karimojong people. Crosscutting kinship ties and territorial exclusiveness, age and generation sets serve important integration functions. This is especially important in this society, where the environment continually scatters people into small groups that must often compete for survival. In the rituals Loput and his age mates are linked to the past history and future of Karimojong society: they wear in their ears the sort of ornaments worn by their grandfathers before them, and to be worn by their grandsons after them. For the Karimojong as for the French: *in changing, things remain the same.*

SUMMARY

Every social structure contains statuses, roles, and groups outside of the kinship system. Anthropologists have classified these on the basis of some primary organizing principle. The most important groups identified by this means are kinship groups, territorial groups, associations, and ranked groups.

A territorial group is one in which members inhabit a common locality over time and recognize that they share this locality. Territorial groups may be nomadic, such as bands, or settled, as in the case of homesteads, villages, and cities. Generally, the smaller the territorial group, the more frequent and intense the social interaction.

Associations are groups based on common interest, shared purpose, or some other attribute such as sexual gender or age. There are many types of associations including voluntary associations, military societies, secret societies, age sets, and men's and women's associations.

One type of association is formed when sexual gender is used as the primary organizing principle. Such groups are called men's and women's associations. They often serve to integrate kinship and territorial groups.

Biological maturation sets the stage in each society for categories and groups of people based on age. Age grades refer to the cultural categories that identify the stages of biological maturation. Age sets are organized groups of persons who are in the same or adjacent age grades.

Status passages occur when any individual moves from one position in society to another. The passage from one age grade to another is a status passage. These movements accompanied by ceremonies are called rites of passage. Rites of passage involve three major stages: separation, transition, and incorporation. Rites of passage serve many functions for the individual as well as the group. They facilitate the transition from one position to another, provide emotional support, establish an inner sense of identity, enhance social cooperation, increase social solidarity, reinforce common social values, enculturate the initiate, and integrate the social order.

MAJOR CONCEPTS

PRIMARY ORGANIZING PRINCIPLE	MILITARY SOCIETIES
TERRITORIAL GROUPS	MEN'S AND WOMEN'S ASSOCIATIONS
MAXIMAL TERRITORIAL GROUPS	AGE SET
NOMADISM	AGE GRADE
PATRILINEAL BAND	GENERATION SET
BAND	RITES OF PASSAGE
COMPOSITE BAND	STATUS PASSAGE
HOMESTEAD	SEPARATION
ASSOCIATIONS	TRANSITION
VOLUNTARY ASSOCIATION	INCORPORATION
SECRET SOCIETIES	

SELECTED READINGS

Alland, Jr., Alexander: "Is Territoriality Imperative?" Chapter 3 in *The Human Imperative*, New York: Columbia University Press, 1972.
A critique of Robert Ardrey's theory on aggression and territoriality.

Dyson-Hudson, Neville: "Territory and Society," Chapter 4 in *Karimojong Politics*, Oxford: Clarendon Press, 1966.
A detailed examination of the way space and territory influence the political life of the Karimojong.

Gluckman, Max: "*Les Rites de Passage*," in *Essays on the Ritual of Social Relations*, Manchester, England: Manchester University Press, 1962.
A theoretical discussion of rites of passage.

Goodenough, Ward Hunt: "Identity Change," Chapter 9 in *Cooperation in Change*, New York: Russell Sage, 1963.
An examination of the requirements for identity change. Because this is a major function of rites of passage, this chapter sheds light on the nature of such rituals.

Hall, Edward T.: *The Hidden Dimension*, Garden City, N.Y.: Doubleday, 1966.
An eminent anthropologist examines the way people use space.

Van Gennep, Arnold: *The Rites of Passage*, Chicago: University of Chicago Press, 1960.
A recent edition of the classic work on rites of passage. This book examines the wide range of forms taken by such rituals and their function for the individual and society.

CHAPTER EIGHT

Rank
and
Stratification

Inequality is a regular feature of complex societies. In the complicated social arrangements that organize such large groups, some people inevitably rank above others, controlling scarce resources, wielding power, and receiving special treatment. Even Marxist societies, which are supposedly founded on an ideal of equality, display formal systems of privilege and prestige.

Some find the roots of human inequality in our primate past. They observe that most species of apes and monkeys display hierarchical order, led perhaps by baboons whose troops are controlled by a group of two or three dominant males. In baboon troops, dominant individuals control other members of the group, stopping quarrels, initiating movement, and directing defense. They wield power over other males, females, and juveniles; they have first pick of the best feeding sites by virtue of their high status; they are groomed by other baboons more than they do the grooming; they monopolize estrous females when the latter are most receptive.

The function of hierarchy is clear for baboons and other primates. It facilitates the exercise of authority and control leading to better organization and cooperative effort. Such close social organization is especially important to ground dwellers, like baboons, because group defense must often replace the relative safety of trees when the troop is threatened by a leopard or lion. We are ground dwellers as well, and it seems logical that we retain an inherited tendency for hierarchy to ensure cooperation and defense.

Although it may be true that people do inherit a potential for dominance hierarchies, a number of groups, often termed egalitarian societies by anthropologists, show little difference in social status. Most egalitarian societies are small hunting and gathering groups. Usually no man in a hunting band has the authority to tell another what to do. Although some people may gain high prestige through their actions, there are no formal hierarchical arrangements. There are, however, differences in status between men and women and adults and children. Such inequality may not be obvious to the casual observer, but men often have the right to command the actions of women and both men and women, the activities of children. Even then, group members tend to lead by example, not command, and cooperation and personal freedom are both valued.

Anthropologists also encounter groups that they label rank societies. In rank societies there may be a formal system that assigns prestige unequally, but people with high prestige still do not control scarce resources, economic power, or authority over others in a way that gives them unequal access to these things. The Bhils described in Chapters 5 and 6 seem to fit this category. A Bhil headman holds a hereditary position that is clearly prestigious. He calls meetings, serves several ceremonial functions, and represents the village in dealings with outsiders. But his position confers little economic advantage and, if Ratakote's headman is to be believed, actually costs its occupant money because of his need to entertain visitors, underwrite village festivals, and be generous to other members of the community.

SOCIAL STRATIFICATION

Social stratification exists when people regularly experience unequal access to valued economic resources as well as prestige. In stratified societies the chance in life to obtain economic resources and/or prestige is much higher for some individuals than others. Stratified societies tend to be large and complexly structured. They are characterized by the existence of property and other economic resources. Unlike egalitarian hunting and gathering bands, stratified societies manifest formal political structures; authority tends to be vested in the hands of a political elite. Resulting economic and political differences result in inequality, in differences in rank that produce groups on different social levels. Anthropologists usually recognize two basic forms of social stratification—*class* and *caste*.

In rank societies chiefs possess a high degree of prestige without a similar degree of access to economic resources and wealth.

Class

Class stratification is defined by unequal access to both economic resources and prestige, but permits individuals to alter their rank within the system. Class systems usually do not involve organized ranked groups. Class boundaries are extremely difficult for social scientists to determine, and classes themselves may not even be represented in the folk concepts of a particular culture. This does not mean, however, that people who live in class-stratified societies are unaware of rank or that such ranking does not systematically affect an individual's life chances.

For example, there is a town in New York State where conversations in the grocery store often focus on the community's residents. Such talk eventually yields two general terms for local people, those from the "hill" and those from the "village." Additional statements make the implications of these terms clear. People from the hill are rich, educated, and snobbish. They think they are superior to villagers in the context of their local scene. This kind of division in the United States does signal a difference in access that people born in the village or on the hill will have to economic resources and prestige. All the children from the hill go to college. Most have found jobs that pay substantially more than the employment taken by people from the village. The family background and expectations of people from the village make it unlikely that they will attend college or strive for better paying jobs. Since employment in our country is one of the main sources of prestige, the chances of villagers to gain prestige are much slimmer than those for hill dwellers.

This does not mean, however, that it is impossible for people from the village to increase their social rank. Some village children have attended college and gone on to succeed in the American economic system. Because ours is a class system, their upward mobility is approved. In fact, such movement lies behind the increasing number of people who have improved their status in this country. Despite such movement, class continues to confer greater chances for success on individuals born at higher levels in the system, making it difficult for people of low rank to move ahead.

Caste

Some social scientists consider caste a form of class. However, the characteristics of caste systems justify treating them as a separate type of social stratification. A caste system is characterized by (1) a ranked hierarchy of groups, (2) recruitment to such groups by birth, and (3) a permanence of membership. Both class and caste systems define a hierarchy of groups. However, while birth in a particular class may limit an individual's chances in life, mobility from one class to another is possible, while birth in a caste is the sole means of recruitment to such a group, locking an individual to his caste for life.

Defined in this way, caste systems are found in several countries. For example, in Japan there is a group of people called *Buraku* who form an untouchable group. Other Japanese think of them as genetically inferior, as people unable to hold a normal place in regular society because of their rude manners, defiling background, and meager intellectual ability. *Buraku* must live in their own communities and stay away from other Japanese. No matter what a *Buraku* does, he or she must carry the stigma of his or her birth around forever. In the United States racial groups appear to be ranked in a caste system as are, to some extent, certain ethnic groups. While members of such groups may succeed in a manner that would normally gain them status in the American class system, their accomplishments can do nothing to rid them of their original racial or ethnic classification and of the limits it places on the acquisition of economic resources and prestige.

Let us now look at social stratification in the context of one of its most formal expressions, the Indian caste system. Imagine that you are an anthropologist whose task it is to study a small market town. You will quickly learn that you can only understand this Indian society if you recognize the importance of social stratification in the form of a complex caste system.

CASTE IN INDIA[1]

It is hot and humid as the bus on which you are riding comes to a halt next to a swollen stream 10 miles from Udaipur in southern Rajasthan, India. You had wanted to reach the village of Nagar directly, but the monsoon rains have filled the usually dry stream bed, making passage across it by bus impossible. You take off your shoes and begin to wade, assured by a fellow passenger that the stream is still shallow enough to traverse on foot. You have embarked on your first field experience, the study of the social structure of Nagar village, a large community of 1500 people.

As you enter the village for the first time you find yourself walking down a narrow lane lined by small, mud-plastered stone dwellings with tile roofs. A dirty stream trickles down the middle of the rocky path, and several children play in it, damming the water with mud and sailing sticks in the resulting puddle. As you reach a place where several lanes converge, you ask your companion from the bus if he can direct you to the headman's house. Smiling, he leads you down one of the narrow roads through a part of the village where houses are larger, two-storied structures, some even constructed of brick. Your journey ends as you walk into a small plaza and spy a group of men sitting, smoking, and talking in the shade to your right. The headman, you are told, is sitting on a string cot talking with the others in what you later learn is a village council meeting.

You walk toward the group to enlist the headman's aid in establishing your residence in Nagar, and you cannot help but notice how its members are arranged. Three sit on the string cot, several more squat on the ground near the cot, sharing a small clay pipe by passing it around the circle, and four more sit and smoke about 9 yards from the others, apart but still included in the conversation. These latter, however, speak little, for conversation seems dominated by one man sitting at the foot of the cot and by one or two others in the immediate group around him.

[1]The information for the description of an Indian caste community presented here is drawn largely from the field experience of one of the authors who conducted research there from 1961 to 1963.

Bhangis *(sweepers) inherit the task of cleaning houses, streets, and latrines for other people. Municipalities also hire them to clean city streets.*

As you will quickly learn after you have lived in Nagar for a short time, the arrangement of the men in this group is no accident. The individuals sitting there are guided by a set of rules for interaction based on their unequal status in the community. All belong to named castes that are ranked in a hierarchy. Ranking, in turn, confers privilege, wealth, and power on those who hold it, and guides, among other things, the way people must sit, talk, and smoke in public. In Nagar, as in most of India, social status is a key to social organization.

Village Caste Structure

The great number of caste groups found in India makes the system there unique. Even the smallest hamlets will have two or three castes living within their boundaries, and large villages, particularly those that serve as trading centers like Nagar, may contain as many as 30 or 40 different caste groups.

As you settle into the room rented to you by a landowning family in Nagar, you will immediately learn the castes that are represented in the village. Your host family belongs to a group called *Rajputs,* the members of which typically own land and politically dominate their villages and regions. In the past all the kings and nobles ruling the Rajasthan were *Rajputs,* and *Rajputs* continue to think of themselves as rulers and warriors today.[2] But *Rajputs* are not the only caste pres-

[2]In many parts of India, members of different service castes no longer follow their traditional occupation. Instead, they work as cash laborers for landowners, farm as sharecroppers, or work in government jobs. Despite this fact, most Indians still associate them with their traditional occupations. In Nagar most caste members continue to work at their hereditary occupations because the villagers serve clients in a number of surrounding communities.

ent in Nagar. There are *Chamars*, the men who sat apart at the meeting and who live in a separate hamlet at the edge of the village. *Chamars* cart off and skin dead animals and, from the leather, make shoes and other useful items for others in the village. They are, as you surmised from watching their isolation at the meeting, of lower rank than *Rajputs* or anyone else present at that gathering. Other castes present in Nagar include low-ranking *Dholis*, who drum at festivals and weddings, high-ranking *Brahmins*, who are the priests of the community, *Kumars*, who make pottery and roof tiles, *Dhobis*, who wash the village laundry, *Lovars*, who work iron, and *Nai's*, or barbers, who cut hair, shave people, and clip nails. All these groups are ranked in Nagar. All confer social worth on their members and a place in a hierarchical system (see Figure 8-1).

When the people of Nagar rank one another's castes, they use more than a simple knowledge of hierarchical position: they employ a complicated system of information that explains and justifies unequal status and defines how individuals of different social position should behave toward one another. Such information makes up the criteria of rank and may be divided into two related aspects, *attributional rank* and *interactional rank*.

Attributional Rank

Attributional rank refers to the social position of individuals or groups based on their association with other ranked items and behavior. In Nagar, as well as the rest of India, such items and behavior fall along a continuum of people's ritual (religious) purity. Ritual pollution and its opposite, ritual purity, refer to someone's eligibility to approach the gods. *Bhangis*, not surprisingly, are ritually polluted people who may not enter any of the village temples except their own. *Brahmins*, on the other hand, are ritually pure (although they may be polluted by other substances or people) and conduct many rituals for people in the community.

Jatis (castes)	
	Brahmin (priest)
	Rajput (warrior, landowner)
	Mahajan (trader, moneylender)
	Kisan (farmer)
	Nai (barber)
	Lovar (smith)
	Kumhar (potter)
	Dhobi (washerman)
	Dholi (drummer)
	Chamar (tanner)
	Bhangi (sweeper)

FIGURE 8-1
Some castes of Nagar village.

Indian castes hold a particular rank assigned partly on the basis of their association with polluting substances. Dhobis *(washerman), for example, often rank quite low in the caste hierarchy because they must clean other people's soiled clothes.*

One's state of ritual purity, however, depends largely on his or her association with polluting things, for villagers divide up their world into substances that defile and substances that purify. Bodily transitions and processes such as death, excretion, perspiration, menstruation, and childbirth, are most polluting. Thus things associated with these states—corpses, meat, leather, feces, urine, sweat, hair, and nail clippings among others—cause defilement. The people of Nagar assign others rank at least partly on the basis of their association with these substances.

One crucial setting for such association is occupation. *Bhangis* are untouchable because they work with human feces and other leavings. *Brahmins* are high because they are priests who work with the gods, not polluting substances. Barbers are impure because they cut hair and nails, but these things are not terribly defiling, so barbers hold an intermediate rank. The rank of washermen is lower because these people must wash clothing that has been contaminated by sweat, urine, and perhaps menstrual blood.

A second setting that defines attributes of ritual purity is dining. Because the ritual purity of foods varies, people can be rated according to what they will eat. Vegetarians usually are rated purer because they avoid meat, which is defiling because of its association with death. Cows, because they are so especially pure and sacred during life, are particularly defiling in death; thus beef is an extremely contaminating food and eaten only by untouchables. Pork is also unclean because pigs eat human feces. Chickens fare a bit better, but are still dirty because they peck at almost anything they come across on the ground. Only goats have clean eating habits, making their meat the purest kind of flesh. This ranking of meat reflects itself in the way meat-eating castes are ranked.

Other factors also indicate levels of ritual pollution. Drinking liquor is not a particularly pure thing to do. People who customarily encourage widow remarriage instead of requiring a bereaved woman to spend the rest of her life praying for her dead husband, are more impure than those groups whose widows remain unmarried. Premarital sexual intercourse and the free, unveiled movement of

The Brahmin *shown with a cow in this picture will take cooked food only from other* Brahmins, *demonstrating his high rank. Members of all non-*Brahmin *castes, however, will accept food from him.*

women in public are also signs of low status, to be avoided by higher ranking groups. Figure 8-2 represents some of the attributes used to establish levels of ritual pollution and caste rank in Nagar.

It is clear from Figure 8-2 that the rank of some castes, notably *Rajputs* and to a lesser extent potters and drummers, do not always fit the ritual pollution model. For example, *Rajputs*, who enjoy high rank, eat meat, while *Mahajans* and *Kisans*, who are lower, do not. *Kumhars* work in clay to make pottery, something that is not especially polluting, and *Dholis*, while the heads of their instruments are made from skin, are not ranked by their association with the drum. In the case of *Rajputs*, rank can be attributed to *economic position* and *power*. *Rajputs* politically dominate in Nagar and control most of the land. Although they eat meat and drink liquor, *Rajputs* are especially careful about protecting women from public view and take pains to remember the gods regularly and pray for themselves and their ancestors. The low status of potters is not made clear by typical attributes in Nagar, and drummers are considered to be low because they have a reputation as shiftless and good-for-nothing beggars, undeserving of high status.

Thus part of the explanation for why you have been categorized as a *Rajput* by villagers stems from the things attributed to you. You eat meat and drink; thus you cannot be a *Brahmin* or *Mahajan*. You are rich by local standards and powerful and, although you have told inquirers that your society does permit widows to remarry and that females are not secluded, people feel that you are most like a *Rajput* and accord you this general rank in their community.

Caste	Occupational association with polluting substance	Food	Widow remarriage		Seclusion of females	Twice born
Brahmin (priest)	None	Vegetarian	Prohibited	No	Secluded	Yes
Rajput (landowner)	None specific	Goat	Prohibited	Yes	Strictly secluded	Yes
Mahajan (trader)	None specific	Vegetarian	Prohibited	No	Veiled in public	Yes
Kisan (farmer)	Dirt	Vegetarian	Prohibited	Yes	Veiled in public	No
Nai (barber)	Hair and nail clippings	Goat and chicken	Permitted	Yes	Sometimes veiled	No
Lovar (smith)	Iron	Goat and chicken	Permitted	Yes	Sometimes veiled	No
Kumhar (potter)	Clay	Goat and chicken	Permitted	Yes	Sometimes veiled	No
Dhobi (washerman)	Dirty clothes	Goat and chicken	Permitted	Yes	Rarely veiled	No
Dholi (drummer)	Drum	Goat and chicken	Permitted	Yes	Usually unveiled	No
Chamar (tanner)	Dead cattle, leather	Any meat carrion	Permitted	Yes	Unveiled	Untouchable
Bhangi (sweeper)	Human feces	Any meat carrion	Permitted	Yes	Unveiled	Untouchable

FIGURE 8-2

Aspects of ritual pollution and caste rank in Nagar.

Interactional Rank

Interactional rank refers to the social position of individuals or groups signaled by unequal privilege and by priority in social interaction. You have already discovered that a group's attributes do not always indicate the level at which it will be ranked in the caste hierarchy. You soon learn that caste groups may also be stratified according to their interactional rank. In India several forms of interaction serve to indicate relative rank, the most important being *commensality* and *proximity.*

Commensality

Commensality refers to the rules that govern who may dine with whom. The people of Nagar believe that pollution is contagious, moving from one person to the next like a communicable disease. Water and food, particularly food that is prepared by baking or boiling, transmit pollution most readily. Consequently, villagers exercise care to avoid contamination in accepting such food from others. They will only accept a meal from castes of equal or higher status, and this form of interaction provides a readily observable symbol of their place in the village hierarchy. *Brahmins*, for example, will take food from no other castes, indicating their superior position to all other groups. *Bhangis* accept food, including table scraps and other forms of garbage, from every other caste, vividly demonstrating their depressed status. Because of these restrictions, it is not unusual for you to see members of different castes cooking their food separately at a village feast. And if you ask someone the rank of a caste that is on about the same level as his in the village hierarchy, he may have to stop and think whether or not people from that group took food from him the last time they visited his house.

Proximity

Proximity, which refers to physical distance between persons, is another interactional measure of rank. *Chamar* leather tanners are classified as untouchables because physical contact with them will pollute members of higher castes. That is why the *Chamar* tanners sat apart from the others at the meeting you witnessed when you first entered Nagar, and it also is why this depressed caste must live in a separate hamlet at the edge of the community. Proximity is a feature of ranked interaction in other situations as well. At a wedding feast to which members of a number of castes are invited, the guests sit in separate lines, each eating apart from the others. Such separation signals differences in rank that must be observed during a meal for, just as it is unwise to accept food from lower castes, so is it improper to sit next to them while you and they eat. Only caste groups of relatively equal rank will sit together in lines at a feast.

Smoking groups also observe such rules. When you first entered Nagar and observed the meeting taking place in the plaza, you noticed that three men sat on the cot while others, besides the *Chamars*, who we have already discussed, sat nearby on the ground smoking. It is customary for members of the highest castes present to sit at the head of a cot while other members of clean castes may occupy its foot or sit nearby on the ground. In Nagar, so long as the pipe is not touched to the lips, all members of clean castes may smoke it. However, the pipe will not be shared with the untouchables, who sit in their own groups and must provide for their own smoking needs.

In addition to commensality and proximity, there are several other ways that villagers interact to signal superior or inferior status. *Bhangis* act in a humble and self-effacing manner in the presence of higher caste members. *Chamars* will not try to dominate a political discussion, as we have seen, speaking only when others clearly ask for their opinion. Interactional ranking says little to villagers about your own status in Nagar. You try to talk to everybody, you appear to accept food and water from a variety of groups, and you seem undaunted by untouchables. If anything, your actions are confusing and contradict the notion that you are a *Rajput*. Some villagers will even cease to speak with you because of your unclean habits.

In India, untouchables are often required to live in separate hamlets or on the edge of villages. Because being poor often accompanies low status, they usually live in small, cheaply constructed houses. This photograph shows the thatched houses of a South Indian untouchable group.

SOCIAL MOBILITY

Social mobility refers to the process of gaining rank in a system of social stratification. One of the most difficult things to understand about systems of rank and stratification is why people put up with them. The interest expressed by people of high status in such systems is understandable. People of superior rank appreciate their greater access to economic resources, prestige, and power. But why do people of lower rank accept their status, if indeed they actually are resigned to it? Part of the answer lies in the attributes people use to justify systems of rank. In a broad sense Indian villagers such as those of Nagar learn that ranking is a natural, almost divinely inspired arrangement legitimized by mention in religious texts. It is one's lot in life to hold low rank and, if one lives properly, he or she will be born at a higher level in his or her next worldly existence. A second reason is security. While people of depressed status may have fewer chances to attain scarce resources or prestige, they often are recipients of protection from people of higher station. This was particularly true of India in the past, when members of lower castes inherited obligations to serve landowners. Although their remunerations in such an arrangement were rarely great, they did enjoy the protection of their landlord, who was obligated to help them when they were in need.

Despite these functions of rank, most social scientists accept the notion that people of low rank anywhere in the world resent their status and wish to move up in rank. Such desires are most apt to be acted on when the aspiring individual or group can achieve some economic independence from other people or groups in the system.

In a class system social mobility is a personal matter. To gain status, individuals must acquire jobs that confer higher rank and, if possible, wealth with which to purchase material goods and education, which also signal prestige. Social mobility within the Indian caste system is different. Because people are locked into a caste from birth, no amount of personal effort on the part of an individual will increase his or her status. One of the *Chamars* in Nagar has become quite wealthy because two of his sons now work in a shoe factory in the city of Agra and send a substantial portion of their wages home to him. Despite his new source of income and the visible prosperity it has brought him, other villagers still consider him to be untouchable like other *Chamars* in the community. To improve one's station in the Indian caste system, it is necessary to elevate the rank of the entire caste group, which requires a major social effort.

No movement of this sort seems to have occurred in Nagar, but numerous attempts at caste mobility have been recorded in India. To conclude this chapter, let us discuss a movement that occurred in South India among the Nadars.

The Nadars of Tamilnadu[3]

If we were to have traveled 200 years ago through what is now Tirunelveli District in the south Indian state of Tamilnadu, we would very likely have seen the remarkable spectacle of toddy tapping. Throughout this hot, sandy, and relatively infertile region of India grow stands of the palmyra palm. But these trees are not like other palms. They give off a sap that people make a liquor out of or concentrate into an animal food. It is a caste of toddy tappers, called *Nadars*, who collected this sap. Each morning at daybreak they left their houses and headed for the stands of palms. Once there, they climbed each tree with the aid of short safety ropes and trimmed the flower stalk that grows among the leaves at the top so that it will continue to bleed the precious sap. If the stalks were not trimmed daily, they healed over and the tree became dry. After he trimmed the flower stalk, the tapper collected the night's accumulation of sap from the vessel he had left there to catch it and rapidly descended the tree. Three times each day he climbed all the trees in his care, and three times each day he trimmed the flower stalks, collected the sap, and descended.

The *Nadars* followed their occupation faithfully, enduring the deformation of their feet caused by climbing and other difficulties of an existence dependent on the collection of sap. For the life of the toddy tapper in those days was difficult. Climbing palms, no matter how skilled the tapper, was always a dangerous matter. Men often fell to their death or to life as a cripple. And the occupation was itself an uncertain way of making a living. Toddy flowed only during the summer season when the palmyra palm flowered, a period lasting from March to September. For the rest of the year *Nadars* were unemployed or worked only occasionally in the fields of some landowner. To make ends meet, tappers borrowed money, goods, and food in their off season, but found it hard to pay back the lenders even when the tapping season was in full swing.

---

[3]Information about the Nadars on which this section of the chapter is based is from Robert L. Hardgrave, Jr., *The Nadars of Tamilnad: The Political Culture of a Community in Change*. Berkeley: University of California Press, 1969.

The occupation of toddy tapping is both dangerous and physically taxing. Nadars must scale their palm trees three times each day to trim the flower stalk at the top and collect the sap that has collected there.

The toddy tappers belonged to the *Nadar* caste. They were locked into their group with its low rank and occupation. Although the names given caste groups are different in the south from those of the north and central India, the caste system there was basically the same. The major difference between the two regions is that warrior (*Rajput*) and merchant (*Mahajan*) castes are absent in the *Nadar* area. *Nadars* were treated as untouchables by higher groups and, as a result, lived in their own enclaves slightly apart from the communities to which they were attached. But, unlike the north, they were also required to remain at a prescribed distance from clean castes and could not move within 12 paces of *Brahmins*. However, they also ranked above several other untouchable groups, including barbers, washermen, and sweepers, all of whom endure particularly low status in the south.

Despite their low rank and difficult occupation, most *Nadars* accepted their depressed status stoically. Because their outlook was local and insulated by poor communications, they had little notion of their overall strength in numbers in this region of India. In addition, they had neither the economic base nor a knowledge that mobility was possible, to mount a successful upward movement in the caste system. This situation changed with the arrival of missionaries, starting with the Jesuits who entered the region in 1680 and growing to significant proportions with the Anglican efforts begun in 1771 and reaching full force in 1810. The arrival of Westerners stimulated a group consciousness and awareness of rank that had not existed before among *Nadars* and started the group on a series of steps designed to improve the status of the entire group.

Group Consciousness

Nadars were hardly aware of the context of their ranking system until after the British arrived and began to exercise some measure of political control in their land. Prior to this period, communications in Tamilnadu were rudimentary. Few roads traversed the area, travel occurred on paths and cart tracks that linked one small village with another. In addition, there was always the danger of attack from bandits and marauding bands of a group called *Nairs*, who waylaid travelers and attacked villages. The British put a stop to this raiding by the late 1700s and quickly set about improving the transportation system. The land opened up in a way unknown in the past. *Nadars* could travel more freely, and with travel came a greater sophistication about the nature of their region and of south India in general.

It was during this period that *Nadars* became more and more conscious of their low status. As *Nadars* traveled more often, they discovered that everywhere their caste mates were degraded, living as untouchables. In cities this was not so much the case, however. Urban enclaves of *Nadars* were independent and ran their affairs in a dignified way, although they were still treated with disdain outside of their city wards.

Dissatisfaction increased as many Anglican missionaries arrived. Zealously carrying the teachings of Christ to the rural byways of the district, these Englishmen set up schools and treated *Nadars* with greater respect. Although few *Nadars* were converted at first, many saw how new Christians were treated by the missionaries. The *Nadar* converts received schooling, became wealthier and, most important, received special privileges from the British, who now held power in the area. Thus as *Nadar* dissatisfaction with their depressed rank increased, so did the attractiveness of Christianity with its higher prestige and attendant benefits.

Escape From the Context of Rank

As we have already seen, ranking always occurs within a defined context. One way for an individual or group to be rid of low status is to leave the context of their traditional ranking system for that of a second, where they hope to gain an improvement in status. This was precisely what the *Nadars* tried to do when many, particularly those in the cities who were more independent economically, converted to Christianity in several mass movements. While churches in north India struggled to gain a foothold, those of the south were overwhelmed by new members, most of whom knew and cared little about Christianity. Driven by a desire to escape from their depressed status, they flocked to the new church by the thousands.

Their hope of gaining higher rank was premature, however. Although the missionaries treated them respectfully enough when they were inside the walls of the mission compounds, they continued to live in their original villages and to carry on their traditional work. Members of other castes refused to treat them any differently and, in fact, angered by the defection of *Nadars* to the missions, retaliated by beating them up in the bazaars and burning Christian schools and books.

Claiming Higher Status

Although conversion to Christianity did not permit the *Nadars* to escape the caste system altogether as they had originally hoped, it did provide them with some skills and new access to money and authority. Many *Nadars* received an education and, in their newly literate state, found jobs in the British-controlled government. Others who received schooling entered a mercantile life and began to prosper as merchants. It was these wealthy, powerful, and educated *Nadars* who led the movement toward higher rank, for they were better able to cope with the problems of organizing such a movement and standing up to economic sanctions that higher-caste peoples, eager to protect their status, might apply against them.

The first step in the movement involved a claim to higher status. *Nadars* changed the name of their group, which had originally been *Shanar*, to *Nadar*. But more important, they laid claim to *Kshatriya* status, a general classification of warrior caste such as *Rajputs*. This move was particularly attractive because there were no major *Kshatriya* castes in the area to oppose their claim.

Changing Attributes of Rank

But merely claiming higher status was not sufficient to effect a rise in status for *Nadars*. Members of other castes would dismiss such a claim as empty because, as they could point out, *Nadars* had not changed their dirty habits. To remedy this situation the Nadars took steps to change the attributes by which their social position was judged. First, they adopted the sacred thread ceremony, a ritual in which members of the caste are born again and don a cord that is worn over the right shoulder and under the left arm. They refused to tap the toddy palm any longer, although this occupation by itself is not particularly polluting. They became vegetarians, cremated their dead (to purify the body by fire), forbade widows to remarry, and even asked the women to cease carrying water pots on their heads, a sure sign of low rank.

Nadars also altered their participation in traditional interaction with other castes. They tried to enter village temples from which they had been excluded, and they failed to observe the customary distance of 12 paces when they approached *Brahmins*. They attempted to draw water from wells that were exclusive to the higher castes. The men even wore *dhotis* made of fine cloth tied in the fashion of *Brahmins*, a privilege normally forbidden to them.

One of the most important outward signs of high rank in south India at this time was the wearing of a cloth across the upper torso. Lower castes, particularly untouchables, were required to go naked above the waist. Both men and women had to wear only a simple piece of cloth around their waists, a cloth that was not supposed to come below their knees. When they sought higher rank, the *Nadar* women adopted the upper piece of cloth worn by high-caste women.

People of high rank, as we have previously noted, are often offended by the attempts of individuals of lower status to move up in a ranking system. But often the adoption of higher-ranking attributes by lower-status groups does not bother those at the top. When *Nadars* became vegetarians, members of high castes merely observed and noted that all the pretensions in the world would not raise the *Nadars'* status. But attributes and forms of interaction that publicly symbolize rank are another matter. If people at the top allow those of lower status to get away with changing the obvious signs of rank, it is a tacit admission that higher rank has been gained by these groups. Such changes publicly challenge the place of those who dominate the system. The use by *Nadars* of the traditional breast cloth represented such a public claim and invoked a strong response from high-caste people. *Nadar* women were attacked on the streets, beaten, and stripped of their new badge of high status. Enraged high-caste people carried their actions even further, attacking and burning *Nadar* settlements and even killing some of the tappers who tried to flee.

It was at this point that the *Nadars* used their relationship with missionaries to support their public claim to higher rank. Most missionaries were unaware of the actual issue that motivated the conflict that raged around them in south India. To be sure, they recognized that high-caste members in the region objected to the breast cloth worn by *Nadar* women, but they did not fully appreciate the fact that the *Nadars* actually wore the cloth in order to raise their caste rank. By this time many *Nadars* were Christians. The missionaries were long distressed by the immodest nakedness of the new female converts and were therefore extremely pleased when *Nadar* women began to cover their breasts, assuming that finally their teachings about modesty had been heeded. The negative response of high-caste Indians to the wearing of the cloth outraged the missionaries. They petitioned the English governors to support the *Nadars* by law. After all, they argued, good Christian ladies should be allowed to dress for their new part.

The *Nadars* were aware of the useful potential of these new allies in their quest for rank, and also realized that the English wanted the women to cover their breasts. To gain support in their conflict with high-caste groups, they complained bitterly to the missionaries about the suppression of their desire to dress as Christians, knowing full well that the Westerners did not understand their true passion for the garment. With the missionaries as allies, the *Nadar* women continued to wear the breast cloth, although their action caused riots in 1828 and 1829 and generated continual animosity during the following years. In 1859 the altercation was brought to the attention of Queen Victoria, who stated that her governors in India were not to interfere with local custom, a decree interpreted by the high-caste opponents of the breast cloth as support for them. But she also said that Christians ought to be able to dress in accordance with their new moral enlightenment, a viewpoint that *Nadars* felt favored them. New riots erupted, both against the *Nadars* and against the missionaries. The last series of public disorders occurred in 1899, after which the *Nadar* movement to become *Kshatriyas* ceased.

Since that time the *Nadar* caste organization has focused on the provision of better education and opportunity for its members instead of actions aimed solely at improving their rank. *Nadars* continue to tap palms and hold low-caste rank in rural areas today, but those of the city are more prosperous and of acceptably higher rank.

SUMMARY

Social stratification exists when people regularly experience unequal access to valued economic resources and/or prestige. Prestige normally refers to the degree of deference typically received by an individual. Some groups, labeled egalitarian societies, lack social stratification with the exception of rank based on sex and age. Although social rank exists in egalitarian societies, members of such groups are born with equal chances to attain economic resources and prestige. Rank societies are stratified on the basis of unequal access to prestige alone. Both class and caste systems involve stratification based on economic and prestige factors. Classes produce systems of ranked groups that permit, although they limit, individual mobility from one class to another. Caste systems assign caste membership at birth, making individual mobility impossible.

Every system of rank includes a set of criteria of rank that explains and justifies unequal status and defines how individuals of different social position should behave toward one another. Ranking criteria may be divided into two areas, attributional and interactional rank. Attributional rank refers to the social position of individuals or groups based on their association with other ranked items and behavior. Interactional rank refers to the social position of individuals or groups signaled by unequal privilege and priority in social interaction.

Social mobility is a universal feature of ranking systems. Although hierarchical social systems possess positive functions even for those at the bottom, and despite the fact that high-ranking individuals attempt to maintain the system as it is, people of low status strain toward higher position. Social mobility requires the manipulation of ranking criteria. Such manipulation includes a claim to higher status, the adoption of higher-ranked behavior, and the display of symbols of elevated status.

MAJOR CONCEPTS

SOCIAL STRATIFICATION	RITUAL POLLUTION
EGALITARIAN SOCIETIES	INTERACTIONAL RANK
RANK SOCIETIES	COMMENSALITY
CLASS	PROXIMITY
CASTE	SOCIAL MOBILITY
ATTRIBUTIONAL RANK	

SELECTED READINGS

DeVos, George, and Hiroshi Wagatsuma: *Japan's Invisible Race: Caste in Culture and Personality*, Berkeley: University of California Press, 1966.
A book on caste in Japan containing original contributions by 10 authors with stress on the psychological aspects of caste membership. Of particular interest are Berreman's discussions of caste in Chapters 14 and 15.

Jackson, J. A. (editor): *Social Stratification*, London and New York: Cambridge University Press, 1968.
A collection of nine articles by sociologists on the definition and measurement of social stratification and the nature of class, prestige, and deference.

Kolenda, Pauline: *Caste in Contemporary India: Beyond Organic Solidarity,* Prospect Heights, IL: Waveland Press, Inc., 1978 (reissued 1985).
An excellent discussion of the changing Indian caste system.

Leach, E. R. (editor): *Aspects of Caste in South India, Ceylon and Northwest Pakistan,* Cambridge: Cambridge University Press, 1960.
Five essays dealing with the definition of caste and variations of the caste system.

Lenski, Gerhard: *Power and Privilege: A Theory of Social Stratification*, New York: McGraw-Hill, 1966.
A review of the theory of social stratification that traces the development of rank and stratification through evolutionary sequence of societies beginning with hunting and gathering groups and ending with industrial societies.

Tuden, Arthur, and L. Plotnicov (editors): *Social Stratification in Africa*, New York: Free Press, 1970.
This book contains 11 essays on both contemporary and historic systems of slavery, class, and caste in Africa.

CHAPTER NINE

The Ecological System

It was the winter of 1934 when French Canadian Joseph-Armand Bombardier found himself in a race against death.[1] His young son had fallen ill, and despite the care given him by his mother in their rural Quebec home, the boy's condition became grave. When it became apparent how serious the situation was, Bombardier hurried through the snow to his barn, hitched a team of horses to the family sleigh, and drove up to his house. He placed the boy, bundled up against the cold, beside him on the front seat and set off into the frozen landscape toward a hospital and medical help. At best, however, his team was a slow means of travel, and its progress that day was complicated by the force of the wind and depth of the drifted snow. His son died before Bombardier could complete the journey.

This tragic event illustrates a crucial requirement of human existence: in order to survive people must adapt successfully to their physical environment, adjusting to its features and using its resources to meet their needs. All animal species face this task, of course, but none meets it in quite the same way people do, since people adapt culturally. They use the knowledge that they have learned to define the important features of their environment, to build countless artifacts to help them adapt, and to prescribe the procedures necessary to use these things and to evaluate their place in the world.

To meet his son's needs, Bombardier used his knowledge of the winter environment, of his team and sleigh, and of the routes of travel to move the boy toward help. Given the tools and techniques provided him by his cultural knowledge, he did the right thing. Unfortunately, in this instance, his knowledge was insuffi-

---

[1] See R. Schiller, "Snowmobiles: The Cats That Conquered Winter," *Reader's Digest, 90,* 1968, pp. 49–54.

cient. Stunned by his son's death, Bombardier set out to develop a better means of transportation, one suited to rapid travel in a winter environment. He experimented with designs for motorized vehicles, and in the 1950s managed to produce and market a successful seven-passenger snow bus. Although the bus was an effective mode of rapid winter transport, Bombardier was not satisfied. He wanted to build a vehicle cheap enough for a person of average income to own, one that would meet the needs of a rural Canadian like himself. He found the answer in 1958. Up to that point he could find no engine suitable to drive a smaller, cheaper winter machine, but in that year an Austrian-made, inexpensive, lightweight two-stroke engine became available. He quickly adapted the engine to a small vehicle propelled by a rubber track and steered by two metal skis. Christened the Ski-Doo, the machine went into production in 1960 as the first popular snowmobile.

Bombardier's invention was to have a dramatic effect on the lives of people living in another part of the world.[2] In the winter of 1961–1962 a merchant, drawn by the possibilities of its use in his cold, northern environment, put a Ski-Doo on display in Rovaniemi, the capital of Finnish Lapland. The snowmobile captured the interest of many who saw it and, one of these, a schoolteacher from the northern village of Partakko, bought it to use on the fishing trips he enjoyed taking at that time of year. The next year many Lapps and Finns who had seen the teacher's Ski-Doo or heard about its attributes followed suit, and within 5 years almost all Lapp householders owned snowmobiles, now made and marketed by several companies.

Although it might seem to be a minor change from our point of view, the adoption of the snowmobile dramatically affected the lives of the Skolt Lapps living in Finland. It altered reindeer-herding technology and the availability of these animals for subsistence; it affected the delicate balance of the Lapp environment; it even changed the shape of Lapp social organization. To understand these changes, we should look at a branch of anthropology called *cultural ecology*.

CULTURAL ECOLOGY

Ecology is the study of the way organisms interact with each other within an environment. Ecologists usually study ecosystems, the interrelated plants, animals, and features of a particular environment. Human beings are obviously an important factor in ecological studies. They affect other organisms in countless ways; they adapt to and often alter features of the natural environment; they have a growing impact on ecosystems in every part of the world.

Anthropologists are concerned with the impact of people on their natural surroundings but have probably looked harder at the reverse relationship—the effect of the environment on people. Because they wish to understand human culture better, *anthropologists look at the way people use their culture to adapt to particular environments*. We call this sort of inquiry cultural ecology.

---

[2] A majority of the information on the snowmobile revolution among the Lapps comes from Pertti J. Pelto, *The Snowmobile Revolution: Technology and Social Change in the Arctic,* Prospect Heights, IL: Waveland Press, Inc., 1973 (reissued 1987 with changes).

The natural environment may be culturally categorized in different ways. A tourist might appreciate the view of this Rocky Mountain pass for its beauty; the geologist would also see the work of glaciers in its steep-sided valleys and ridges.

Environmental Determinism

An early view of the environment, one that started at least with the Greek philosophers and continued into nineteenth-century Western thought, claims that the environment actually determines culture. Environmental determinists argued that the humid tropics made people lethargic, infertile soil led to popular government (in Greece), and hot climate caused customs favoring the release of emotions.

Environmental Possibilism

By the turn of the century, anthropologists began to reject the deterministic position. Led by people such as Boas and Kroeber, both major figures in early American anthropology, they argued that cultures showed wide variation, even within the same natural environment. Environment, they asserted, did not cause culture, it merely limited the range of possible forms culture could take. Subsistence based on fishing, for example, would not be found in a waterless desert. Irrigation would not occur on a well-watered coastal plain. The environmental possibilists were probably too cautious about the effect of environment on human life, but their work, particularly the firsthand ethnographic data collected in the field, led to the more balanced view, which we call cultural ecology.

Adaptation

Today the anthropological study of cultural ecology is less concerned with the origin of custom. Instead, research emphasizes how culture adapts people to their surroundings. Studies of this sort involve the analysis of ecosystems, including the food chain, energy exchange, and techniques for resource utilization. They also focus on the adaptive functions of particular customs. Eskimo skin clothing, for example, can be understood as an adaptation to extreme cold. So can the winter division of some Eskimo groups into dispersed family units. Game is too sparse and hard to kill during this intensely cold time to provide support for large concentrations of people.

Recently, some anthropologists have argued that most human customs, no matter how useless they seem to be, have adaptive utility. Marvin Harris, an anthropologist from Columbia University, makes this claim for the "sacred" cows of India.[3] Cows are protected in India by religious custom. Feelings of protection run so deep that drivers of cars and trucks unlucky enough to hit cattle have been beaten and sometimes killed by enraged witnesses. The result seems to be an enormous overpopulation of cattle. Everywhere in India, from the wealthy districts of New Delhi to the muddy lanes of villages, wander emaciated, sickly looking, cattle. They constantly menace food displayed in bazaars and eat unlikely things such as mail (grazed from a postman's bicycle carrier) and a doormat one anthropologist optimistically placed outside his front door.

To many Westerners the sacredness of cattle seems irrational. Why not eat them instead of feeding them in a land where food is already scarce? Harris argues that if anything, cattle are in short supply in India. Bullocks provide the traction for Indian farming and there never seems to be enough to go around when the fields must be plowed. Cattle also produce milk, hides, and manure for fertilizer and fuel; they do not compete directly with people for scarce food. When we view it this way, the custom of cattle protection is an attempt to conserve a valuable resource that might otherwise disappear in crowded India. It is, therefore, adaptive. Let us now look at the environment and the way people use culture to adapt to it.

THE PHYSICAL ENVIRONMENT

All human beings live in a physical environment—the world they can experience through their senses. People can see the features of the landscape and the living things that grow on it. They can touch trees and rocks, feel the wind's force on their bodies, and smell the odors emanating from flowers and grass. Everyone

[3]See Marvin Harris, "The Cultural Ecology of India's Sacred Cattle," *Current Anthropology*, 7, 1966, pp. 51–56; Marvin Harris, *Cows, Pigs, Wars and Witches*, New York: Vintage, 1975, pp. 11–32.

must take these things into account in the course of his or her daily life; every group must adapt to its natural surroundings in order to survive.

The Lapp Environment

Perhaps the most rigorous physical environment, the one that is least forgiving to the people who attempt to survive in its midst, is the far north, the region where the Skolt Lapps make their home. The snow-covered, icy terrain, which makes up this world, rejects most living things. Few, if any, trees grow on the frozen wastes because they cannot survive the many months of bitterly cold temperatures and deep snow. Only a few animals that have adapted genetically to the cold and to the limited food supply manage to stay alive on the barren land.

The Lapps live in northwestern Finland, a land typical of the European northern environment: winters are long, dark, and cold, although the temperatures rarely dip below $-40°F$, modified a bit by the warming action of the Gulf Stream, which runs along the shores of the Arctic Ocean farther north. Part of the land is tundra, devoid of growth except for lichens and moss. The groves of pine trees that manage to exist in the hills and sheltered valleys of the southern portion of the territory become more and more scarce as one moves north. Small clumps of birch trees dot the land, and lichens, the ancient, hardy plants of the north, grow among the pines and in other protected areas. Reindeer are at home in this part of the world, where they occupy the middle of the food chain. They survive by eating the lichens and mosses. Fish are also present, thriving in the hundreds of glacially formed lakes and streams that characterize the countryside. In this relatively simple ecosystem, the Lapps occupy the top of the food chain, subsisting largely on reindeer and fish.

THE CULTURAL ENVIRONMENT

Surely the physical environment is an area of human experience that should give rise to a single set of categories shared by people everywhere. Features of land and climate are obvious. Rocks cannot be anything else but rocks; snow should be snow for all; a mountain is a mountain no matter who views it. Yet just as people from different societies class the same relatives into different status categories, so can they look at the same physical environment and divide it up into distinctive sets of cultural categories.

Consider the mountain terrain that is visible from a lookout at the summit of Loveland Pass in the Colorado Rocky Mountains. This area of the mountains that, because of its high elevation, is very similar in climate to land lying much further north, may appear very different to those who view it, depending on the cultural knowledge that they bring to interpret the scene. A tourist who stops to admire the view sees a spectacular sight of sharply etched, snow-covered mountain peaks, steep-sided valleys, and small lakes and streams. His general perspective is one of aesthetics. He has driven the long, winding road to this pass on his way to Arizona instead of keeping to the more level freeway that skirts most of the mountains because he wishes to see and appreciate the beauty of this view. Thus he notices the lines made by the peaks, the sheer grandeur and size of the landforms, and the clarity of the pure lakes and streams that lie in the valleys below.

A geologist comes to this same scene with a different perspective. She may appreciate the aesthetic impact of what she surveys, but she sees what is before her in terms of her geological training. The peaks that lie before her are glacial peaks, their steep sides eaten away by the alternate melting and freezing of ice. There are not simply valleys below her, but cirque basins and U-shaped valleys, again formed by the action of glaciers that no longer exist at this warm period of geological time. She can see a *paternoster* stream, so named because it flows from one cirque basin to another down the valley like a string of rosary beads. Other features tell her that these mountains, made by the earth's tectonic action, have been eroded and carved by glaciers.

Both the tourist and the geologist look at the same physical environment, but its reality for each is different. Each applies a different set of cultural definitions to classify and understand what he or she sees. Each looks at a different <u>cultural environment</u>.

The Meaning of Ice

The cultural environment reflects what is important to people about their surroundings. They use it to adapt to the special environmental conditions in which they live. The way the Slave Indians of Fort Norman, Canada, classify ice provides a good example.[4] Fort Norman lies about 125 miles south of the Arctic Circle on the east bank of the MacKenzie River. The land around Fort Norman contains many lakes and streams, attesting to its glacial heritage. Winters are long and very cold, lasting from November until April and producing temperatures as low as −60°F. As winter approaches, lakes and streams begin to freeze and are soon covered with a layer of ice.

The Slave Indians have a classification of ice that is much more complex than ours. They acknowledge a general term for the substance, *te*, but they subdivide this category into no less than 13 different types (see Figure 9-1). This involved classification does not exist because the Slave enjoy complexity. Instead, it lists categories that are adaptive, given the conditions under which the Slave Indians must hunt, fish, and travel.

Travel is most important, and the categories of ice culturally defined by the Slave define its suitability for this activity. To begin with, they must recognize the kind of ice with which they deal. Brittle, slippery, blue, and black ice, for example, are different as to physical state, thickness, clarity, and color (see Figure 9-2). The need to determine the safety of ice is greatest when families travel in April to fish and in winter when they move out to hunt moose and caribou and to serve traplines set for fur-bearing animals such as mink, otter, and beaver. Imagine that a Slave sets out to service his trapline during late winter. He harnesses his dogs to the sled, packs the items he needs for the day's work, and sets out into the snow-

[4]This discussion is based on an article by Keith Basso entitled, "Ice and Travel Among the Fort Norman Slave: Folk Taxonomies and Cultural Rules," *Language and Society*, 1 (1), 1972, pp. 31–49.

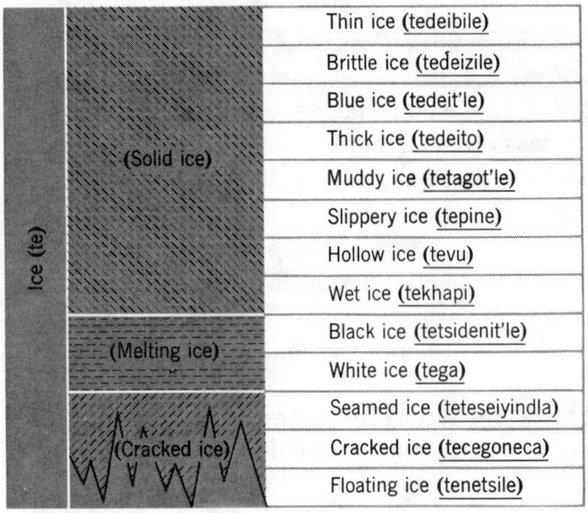

FIGURE 9-1
Slave Indian categories of ice (adapted from Basso, 1972, p. 35).

Type of ice	Physical state	Thickness (inches)	Clarity	Color
Brittle ice	Solid	Between 1 and 4	Transparent	Light or dark
Slippery ice	Solid	More than 4	Transparent	Light or dark
Blue ice	Solid	More than 4	Varies	Light or dark
Black ice	Melting	More than 4	Varies	Dark

FIGURE 9-2
Some observable characteristics of four kinds of ice. (Source: Adapted from Basso, 1972, p. 36.)

covered terrain. One of his traplines lies on the opposite bank of a broad stream that he must cross in order to carry out his day's activities. As he approaches the stream, he pauses to survey its condition, and at that moment must use his knowledge of ice and of different strategies for successfully dealing with it. He is concerned about his own and his dogs' safety, and when he sees that this part of the stream is covered with black ice, he will decide to detour around it. Black ice is ordinarily thick enough to carry the weight of his team and sled but, because it is melting, that thickness is not a reliable measure of strength. He can, if he wishes, cross black ice on snowshoes or on foot and might cross with his sled using extreme caution, but on this particular day he does not like the look of the surface and decides to look for another place to cross.

If he observes brittle ice at the crossing (see Figure 9-3), he will also make a detour with his sled. Again, although it may hold his weight, this kind of ice is too

Kind of ice	Mode of travel		
	On foot	With snowshoes	By dogsled
Brittle ice	Dangerous; use caution	Dangerous; use caution	Not safe; detour
Slippery ice	Safe; travel across	Not safe; detour	Not safe; detour
Black ice	Safe; travel across	Safe; travel across	Dangerous; use caution
Blue ice	Safe; travel across	Safe; travel across	Safe; travel across

FIGURE 9-3

Matrix indicating the evaluation of four kinds of ice in relation to modes of travel. (Source: *Adapted from Basso, 1972, p. 40.*)

thin to carry the combined weight of his team and sled. An encounter with slippery ice does not pose the problem of strength because it is over 4 inches thick; the trouble is its surface, which is too smooth for the dogs to cross. They tend to thrash about, tangling their lines and putting a premature end to a full day's work. Of these four kinds of ice, only blue ice will make a good crossing for a man with his dog sled. It is strong and thick, and its surface is generally covered with snow, which the dogs can easily cross.

Thus the Slave trapper depends on his cultural knowledge of ice to aid him in travel. He avoids ice that might break under his weight. He makes a detour around ice that might injure him and his dogs (wet ice is particularly hazardous in this regard), and he judges whether or not the ice will slow him up, for he is anxious to make the best possible speed during the short daylight hours. His categories of ice are indispensable in helping him to survive in his harsh climate.

TECHNOLOGY

Technology includes tools and the cultural strategies for making and using them. Technology enables a group to exploit its environment. Slave Indian technology, for example, includes rifles, sleighs, traps, fishhooks, and the techniques for hunting, traveling, trapping, and fishing that are associated with them. Using this technology, the Slave are able to subsist in their difficult environment at the top of the food chain.

One aspect of the technological complex, food-getting, has been particularly important to anthropologists. The techniques that groups develop to get their food seem to fit particular environments and shape, in very general ways, social organization and ideology. The significance of food-getting has led anthropologists to classify societies according to basic food-getting strategies. We discussed these types in the context of social organization in Chapter 4 but should note them again here.

Slash and burn agriculture, a form of horticulture, is often found in sparsely inhabited forests. Such shifting agriculture requires that large trees be cut and brush burned to create fields suitable for planting. Here Indians clear a field in the Amazon.

Hunting and Gathering

Hunting and gathering is a process of food-getting in which people employ techniques and tools to hunt and collect wild, naturally occurring foods. The !Kung Bushman, Mbuti Pygmies, some Australian Aborigines, and Eskimos are four of the very few groups that still subsist in this manner. Typically, those hunting and gathering groups that do remain inhabit areas of the world where other forms of food-getting are difficult or impossible to carry out. They are usually small and nomadic, their size circumscribed by the limits of available wild game and vegetable foods in their environments and their movement caused by the need to follow game and to exploit new areas when old ones have been harvested.

Horticulture

Horticulture refers to farming carried out with simple hand tools such as the digging stick. Typically, horticultural societies lack draft animals and plows and exhibit only limited use of irrigation and fertilizer. Many horticultural peoples practice *shifting agriculture*, burning off a patch of land, planting it with the aid of a digging stick, and moving on to clear another patch of ground when brush and weeds make the original piece of land difficult to farm. Horticulture is practiced in heavily forested areas like the Amazon basin where more intensive farming is impossible. It is also commonly employed in Melanesia and several other parts of the world.

Pastoralism

Pastoralism is a form of food getting that depends on the maintenance and control of large herds of animals. The Karamojong described in Chapter 7 are pastoralists, as are several other groups such as the Basseri of southern Iran and the Massai of East Africa. Pastoralists tend to live in relatively arid areas where there is enough vegetation for their herds, but too little rainfall for farming. It is common for pastoralists to establish a regular exchange relationship with neighboring farming peoples, giving meat and milk in return for a variety of vegetable food stuffs.

Agriculture

Agriculture defines a method of farming in which draft animals, plows, fertilizer, and irrigation (if necessary) are commonly used. Intensive agriculture, including irrigation, arose first in the Middle East but is now commonly found in many parts of the world. It is associated with large populations and provides enough surplus to permit significant specialization in nonagricultural occupations.

Lapp Food-Getting Strategies

Like the Slave Indians, the Skolt Lapps developed a technology to subsist off the scarce resources of a northern environment. In their case, however, the reindeer, although a wild animal, could be partially domesticated and herded. Herding and fishing required traveling over large distances, as did hunting and fishing for the Slave.

Reindeer

The Skolts live in two-room cabins built for them by the Finnish government. Almost every family owns some reindeer, which provide the family with a source of meat and cash. Care of the reindeer imposes a yearly rhythm on Skolt life marked by winter roundups, spring calving, and summer freedom for the herds. Typically, the herds are permitted to run free in search of the best feeding spots and shelter from mosquitoes. When the animals are in the wilds, those belonging to different owners mingle with each other. This intermingling poses a problem of identification, and to keep track of their animals, Lapp householders cut special marks into the ears of their deer. In this way the animals can be identified and separated out by their owners when the herds are rounded up in the winter.

Such roundups occur after the animals have grown fat from summer feeding. The Lapp herders have been organized into reindeer associations by the Finnish government, and these groups provide personnel for the roundup. When roundup time is to begin, the men set off into the countryside to find their scattered animals, concentrate them into a large herd, and drive them into a corral that has been prepared in advance. When the reindeer are safely inside the enclosure, individual owners begin the work of spotting and cutting out their own animals. Some of these are sold to meat buyers, others are slaughtered for personal needs, and the

The traditional relationship between a Lapp and his reindeer was close, and the animals were an important source of food, shelter, and transportation. Here a Lapp herdsman watches over his animals.

rest held for return to the wilds. Owners also look for the unmarked calves of their own female deer and earmark them for future identification.

In the past each owner drove his reindeer home following a roundup and watched over the animals near his house for several months. Of particular concern was the spring calving, for the more young animals that could be brought successfully into the world, the greater the herd size for the owner. Once born, the calves were earmarked and the herd freed once again to forage in the open.

Fish

In addition to animal husbandry, fishing is also an extremely important source of food for the Skolt Lapps. There are not enough reindeer to meet fully the subsistence needs of the Skolts, and the abundant supply of fish found in nearby lakes makes up the nutritional difference. Fishing, however, does not follow the same kind of seasonal variation as reindeer herding and remains a popular activity all year.

Space and Travel

To herd and fish, Skolts must travel. Reindeer become scattered over many square miles, and to find them, Skolt herders search the terrain, looking for signs of the deer and driving back those they manage to locate. On skis or by reindeer sled the winter roundups can take 2 or 3 weeks, requiring the herders to camp out in the cold temperatures and deep snow. Fishing also means travel and, although the lakes are relatively close at hand, getting to them takes time and effort.

The Skolt Lapps recognize their need to travel in the ways they categorize their environment. The attributes that define categories for land features, for example, in part reflect the suitability of such features for different forms of human movement. Weather and snow also have meaning for travel, and the Lapps tell many stories of the times they have been caught in particular kinds of storms or found themselves trying to ski in snow that was insufficiently deep or covered with a hard layer of ice after a brief thaw. The hardships of winter trips, frostbite, danger from wolves (although this danger has almost ceased to exist), fatigue, and accident are clearly part of the meaning Lapps give their environment.

INNOVATION AND CULTURAL ADAPTATION

A group's physical and cultural environment, technology, social organization, and ideology do not each exist separately. They form a more or less integrated system designed to adapt a society as securely as possible to its surroundings—it is no accident that the Lapp's cold environment, complex herding and fishing technology, family-oriented social organization, and many other customs and values fitted together. They provided the Lapps with an adaptive stance that enabled them to subsist over a long period of time in a relatively unproductive part of the world.

It is also no surprise to discover that a change in one aspect of this adaptive structure often causes alterations in other parts of the system. Gasoline shortages, for example, affect not only the distances North Americans can drive, but the kinds of cars they can buy, the places where they can live, and even the jobs available that they can hold. The automobile and truck have become such central features of our lives that any limitation on their use affects many parts of the cultural and social system.

Change of this sort often stems from technological innovation. A familiar example is industrialization in the West, which displaced countless cottage industries and replaced them with an even more complex corporate system. This, in turn, has dramatically changed how people live. The adoption of the snowmobile by the Lapps has also had far-reaching implications.

The Snowmobile Revolution

The popularity of the snowmobile stemmed from its ideal design for winter travel in rough terrain and because it relieved so many of the problems the Skolts encountered in herding and winter travel. The Lapps quickly discovered that the machine would cut travel time dramatically during herding operations, fishing trips, and journeys to stores. A 2-day journey into Norway to trade now takes a matter of hours. Instead of a day long trip to the place where winter roundup activities were to start, a herder can reach his destination by midmorning. The

In the past, Lapps depended heavily on their reindeer for transportation. Selecting especially strong and controllable animals, they trained them to pull several kinds of sleds.

snowmobile reduces the amount of time that Lapps have to endure the hardship of cold weather and, because the machines move so quickly, one can always put off a trip for a day or two on account of bad weather and still manage to arrive at his destination more or less on time. Snowmobiles can move over deep as well as over thin snow cover. They make fishing trips an easy day long excursion and hauling wood and other loads fast and sure. Given their perception of the environment and the things that are important to them about it, the Lapps find that the snowmobile is ideally suited to help them cope with their needs. It is a dramatic improvement over travel by reindeer sled, skis, or foot.

Use is reflected in the way Skolt Lapps distinguish among snowmobiles. Take two varieties, the Motoski and the Evinrude, for example. Three major attributional dimensions that serve to define the difference between these two machines are weight, power, and maneuverability, as indicated below.

Brand	Weight	Power	Maneuverability
Motoski	Light	Medium	Great
Evinrude	Heavy	High	Low

Why Skolt Lapps employ these features to define snowmobiles is made clear only when we consider what they use the machines for. The Motoski serves in herding operations. Since reindeer frighten easily and tend to bolt and stray when they are driven anywhere, maneuverability is of utmost importance. The Motoski's lower speed is fast enough to do the job, its power sufficient to climb hills with one herder aboard, and its weight light enough to permit it to be righted by one man if it falls over on its side. All of these features are desirable when one is herding reindeer far from home. The Evinrude, on the other hand, is used to haul wood and other loads and to make long trips. For these purposes, its added weight and power make it more valuable and its lack of maneuverability goes unnoticed.

Snowmobiles, like cars in North America, are especially associated with males, particularly young men. At roundups and other times when men come together, talk inevitably turns to snowmobiles, the techniques for driving them, their maintenance, accidents people have had with them, and stories relating things such as how drivers have become stranded in the woods, been outrun by a particularly fast reindeer, or fallen through the ice into a stream.

Snowmobiles and Reindeer

The use of snowmobiles for herding has not only changed Lapp herding practices, it has also affected the health and vitality of the reindeer themselves. Traditionally, the Skolts went out each winter to collect and separate their herds. The proc-

Today most Lapps use snowmobiles to herd reindeer. The vehicles have been used to locate and collect the animals during this roundup in Swedish Lapland.

ess took 2 or 3 weeks and required the men to move by reindeer sleds and skis and to search out the animals wherever they could find them. The Skolts recognized some important attributes of reindeer in this process. The animals become easier to handle in large groups. The more animals in a herd, the more small groups are attracted to the main body of reindeer. Once collected, reindeer could be led to the corral, following a bell reindeer trained and led by a ski man. The animals were separated and driven home to winter quarters by the owners. New calves were protected and marked, and some animals were gelded and trained to pull sleighs and carry loads. In all, the relationship between Lapp herders and their animals was an intimate one, although not so close as it was when they stayed with their reindeer throughout the year.

The snowmobile has changed this relationship, and with it the general health and vitality of the reindeer. Reindeer are shy animals, easily frightened by noise and disturbances. Snowmobiles are clearly noisy, and their use in herding frightens the deer. A typical roundup these days involves a number of snowmobiles in a rapid search of one portion of the reindeer association's territory. Once collected, the animals are driven at a trot to a temporary corral where they are separated as in the old days. However, the process is hectic and incomplete. Roundups rarely take more than a few days. Snowmobiles are expensive to operate, and there is a point at which further search would not be repaid by the collection of significant numbers of additional reindeer. The animals also shy away from the noise of the machines and hide among the trees and rocks or wherever they can find shelter, so that many are missed during the roundup sweep. Finally, the animals that are caught become frightened. They are extremely difficult to separate once they are in the corral, and it is almost impossible to identify calves who become separated from their mothers in the confusion. Unmarked animals are sold by the reindeer association to cover the added expense of operating the snowmobiles, and herds grow smaller and calves fewer each year. Fright may also be the cause of recent weight loss among the deer, a trend that has started since herding with machines began.

In general, the snowmobile has been responsible for the dedomestication of the reindeer. The animals are now left in the wilds throughout the year because no one takes them home anymore. Geldings and, in fact, tame reindeer, have disappeared from the scene. Instead, the winter is marked by a large number of small roundups during which smaller numbers of wild animals are caught and separated.

Social Change

The Lapp shift to snowmobiles has also deeply affected social relations—most important, their growing dependence on each other and on people living in other parts of Finland. Lapps now rarely travel alone, although they did so happily in the past. Their traditional private world has given way to the necessity of human companionship while driving over open country, for the machines break down from time to time, and it is handy to have a partner who can carry one back to warmth and safety.

The snowmobile has penetrated almost every part of the arctic. In North America Eskimos have often foresaken the traditional sled and dog-team for the faster mechanized conveyance.

The snowmobile means dependence on people in other ways as well. The Lapp owners must have a regular association with someone who can supply them with spare parts and gasoline for their machines. Such support is crucial if the snowmobiles are to be kept running throughout the winter season. Dependence also stems from a need for money to purchase and maintain the machines. To earn money, many owners hire out to haul goods or run errands for their neighbors. They may also act as guides for tourists or take jobs as herders with the local reindeer-herding association. Altogether the snowmobile means increased contact with people. Lapps can now travel great distances quickly; they can get to distant reindeer roundups where they drink and talk with many people; they go to stores and towns too far away for comfortable travel by the traditional reindeer sled. In short, their world has changed from a relatively private, personal one to one of greater social contact, interreliance, and communication.

A second social effect has been the emergence of rank among Lapps. Originally everyone owned reindeer herds of approximately equal size. Now, mainly because of the need for capital to maintain a snowmobile fleet and use it to herd reindeer, some families without money have lost almost all their animals, while others have substantially enlarged their herds. Typically, the people with the most resources are able to claim more unmarked calves.

Part of the movement toward rank stems from mechanical ability. Some Lapps are more clever than others at keeping their machines running. Although many Lapps own snowmobiles, a substantial number of them must forego travel because their machines are broken. In such circumstances, only those who are able to ride get to the roundup where they can claim the ownership of unmarked reindeer and need not depend on their neighbors for other transportation needs.

More and more there are unemployed Lapps, people with few animals and no means of support except government allotments. Some leave the land for work in nearby towns and cities; some try to stay on the land, working for other people in the absence of the traditional reindeer economy. Women, particularly, leave the area for work elsewhere.

Today many forces are at work to disrupt traditional Lapp ecological adaptation, but the process of change was started largely by the arrival of snowmobiles. Lapps recognize some of the problems caused by the advent of the machines and try to do something about them. There are many arguments concerning the way reindeer should be herded by snowmobiles, and some people now claim that, with proper techniques, the animals can be collected successfully without harm. It is doubtful, however, that reindeer will ever again represent the basis of Lapp subsistence. Technological change has propelled these people into a larger social world with a more varied and complex ecological niche.

SUMMARY

Ecology is the study of the way organisms interact with each other within an environment. Ecologists usually study ecosystems, the interrelated organisms and features of a particular environment. The study of the way people use their culture to adapt to particular environments is called ecology. In the past, environmental determinists argued that the environment caused culture. Environmental possibilists held the view that the environment merely limited the range of possible cultural variation for a group. Cultural ecologists see the relationship between the environment and human groups as a complex adaptive system mediated by culture. Harris, for example, argues that most human customs, such as the religious proscription on killing cows in India, have ecological adaptive functions. The physical environment is the world people can experience with their senses. The cultural environment is the particular cultural classification of the physical environment. Slave categories for ice reflect their physical environment and their strategies for exploiting it.

Technology includes tools and the cultural strategies for making and using them. There are at least four categories of societies, based on food-getting technology: hunting and gathering, horticulture, pastoralism, and agriculture. A group's physical and cultural environment, technology, social organization, and ideology form an integrated system, all of which may change when one part of the structure is altered. The introduction of the snowmobile among the Skolt Lapps of Finland illustrates this point.

MAJOR CONCEPTS

ECOLOGY	CULTURAL ENVIRONMENT
ECOSYSTEM	TECHNOLOGY
CULTURAL ECOLOGY	HUNTING AND GATHERING
ENVIRONMENTAL DETERMINISM	HORTICULTURE
ENVIRONMENTAL POSSIBILISM	PASTORALISM
ADAPTATION	AGRICULTURE
PHYSICAL ENVIRONMENT	

SELECTED READINGS

Barth, Fredrik: *Nomads of South Persia: The Basseri Tribe of the Khamseh Confederacy,* Prospect Heights, IL: Waveland Press, Inc., 1961 (reissued 1986).
A detailed discussion of Basseri pastoral nomadism, including analysis of the interaction between the Basseri and nearby sedentary groups.

Cohen, Yehudi A. (editor): *Man in Adaptation: Cultural Present,* 2d ed., Chicago: Aldine, 1974.
A collection of articles by anthropologists organized around the major strategies for food getting, hunting and gathering, horticulture, pastoralism, and agriculture.

Lee, Richard B., and Irven DeVore (editors): *Man the Hunter,* Chicago: Aldine, 1968.
A collection of articles dealing with the social organization, ecology, and demography of hunting and gathering peoples.

Leeds, A., and A. P. Vayda (editors): *Man, Culture and Animals: The Role of Animals in Human Ecological Adjustments,* Publication No. 78 of the American Association for the Advancement of Science, Washington, D.C., 1965.
A group of articles discussing the relationship between culture and environment.

Sahlins, Marshal: "Culture and Environment: The Study of Cultural Ecology" in Sol Tax (editor), *Horizons in Anthropology,* Chicago: Aldine, 1964, pp. 132–147.
A general review of the study of cultural ecology.

Steward, Julian: *Theory of Culture Change: The Methodology of Multilinear Evolution,* Urbana: University of Illinois Press, 1955.
An early important formulation of the relationship among technology, environment, and social structure.

Vayda, A. P. (editor): *Environment and Culture Behavior: Ecological Studies in Cultural Anthropology,* Garden City, N.Y.: Natural History Press, 1970.
A collection of articles by anthropologists on cultural ecology.

CHAPTER TEN

The Economic System

Individuals everywhere in the world experience wants (a word we will use to indicate both what people have to have as well as what they desire) that can only be satisfied by the use of material goods and the services of others. To meet such wants, humans rely on an aspect of their cultural inventory, the economic system, which consists of the provision of goods and services to meet biological and social wants.

Any need related to human physical well-being is a biological want. People must eat, drink, maintain a constant body temperature, defend themselves, and deal with injury and illness. Meeting these physical wants requires the use of material goods—food, water, clothing, shelter, weapons, medicine—and the cooperative services of others.

In addition, social wants are essential to the maintenance of human social relationships and also require the provision of material goods and services. People identify particular social roles with special clothing and bodily adornments and the particular goods that mark associated social settings. In her clinic, for example, a doctor must wear special white clothing, use a stethoscope and other specialized instruments, and work in an antiseptic clinic furnished with examination tables, X-ray machines, and other large pieces of medical equipment. Without these material items and the services of nurses and technicians, the doctor could not play her medical role successfully.

People also use material goods and services to enhance social solidarity by exchanging them with others. Gifts reaffirm kinship ties at Christmas. The offer of a beer on a hot day or the loan of a garden rake in the fall serve to tie neighbors together.

But goods and services do not automatically fulfill human biological and social wants. There must be some organized system of behavior that permits individuals to create and obtain these things. The economic system provides this organization by defining two fundamental areas of activity: a system of *production* and a sys-

Once an Australian Aborigine has quarried a large axe head or procured it from a trading partner, he must polish and sharpen it, and haft the finished stone on a wooden handle. The long manufacturing process contributes to the meaning of the completed implement.

tem of *distribution*. In the remainder of this chapter we will discuss these broad areas, illustrating them with examples drawn from a Tarascan village in Mexico.

PRODUCTION

Production is the activity of rendering material items useful and making them available for human use. There are probably some useful things that require little modification beyond the act of collecting them. Salt, for example, has been available to some people in dry inland lake beds and coastal estuaries; in such cases, production amounts to collecting the substance.

However, many materials people use must be manufactured. A simple tool, such as the polished stone ax used by the aborigines of Australia, required a chain of productive activities. First, stone had to be laboriously quarried in sizes appropriate to the finished item. Next, the raw stone had to be shaped by chipping, then polished by rubbing. Wood for the handle was cut and shaped; sinew for hafting was taken from a kangaroo. Finally, the finished ax was constructed by hafting the ax head onto the handle.

Human productive activities include several factors that require cultural definition and regulation: identification and allocation of the natural resources from which useful goods are derived; technology for extracting resources and manufacturing them into useful items; and organization of labor, because human productive activity is so often cooperative.

Allocation of Resources

People everywhere depend for their survival on a number of material resources, such as foodstuffs and raw materials, for the manufacture of tools, shelter, and transportation. Such raw materials are often in short supply, and humans regularly delimit access to them. The allocation of resources refers to the cultural rules people employ to assign rights to the ownership and use of resources.

The extent of people's rights to own and control natural resources has often been misunderstood by people from industrial societies like ours. In North America we are used to an enormously complex productive system that creates an almost limitless variety of goods. Associated with this system is a strong notion of private ownership, in which the rights to goods and natural resources are exclusive and relatively complete for individual owners. We talk about private property and our rights to its exclusive use. We teach our children to respect the property rights of others, coming down hard on those who take toys from playmates without asking.

However, not every society displays this view of ownership. Among the !Kung of the Kalahari desert, for example, there are few things that one can really call property in our sense. The territory of the hunting band is open to all who wish to hunt there. A family may gain access to other hunting places by simply changing bands. Water holes are nominally the property of band headmen but when asked, they will always grant permission to those who wish to use them. Even tools such as hunting arrows are freely borrowed or exchanged.

Confusion over the degree to which humans hold rights over a resource and the exclusivity of ownership may account for some of the misunderstandings that occurred between the U.S. government and American Indians, particularly those living in the Great Plains. Treaties, which formed the backbone of government policy toward most Indian groups, almost invariably included statements about the ownership and use of land. In the American view, when a treaty was signed giving the land previously used by Indians to the U.S. government, the Indians no longer had any rights to it at all. In essence, the government took over private ownership of the Indian territories, which included complete rights to its use. But the Indians could not understand this kind of agreement. They customarily held the right to use land jointly within the tribal group and sometimes extended that use to members of other tribes as well. The notion that a tribe could voluntarily give up all its rights to land was not part of their experience.

Chiefs often signed treaties thinking that there was plenty of territory to go around and that they would be pleased to share it with others. The Indians were surprised and dismayed when they and their people were confined to "Indian territories" and prohibited from using lands given up in the treaties. In addition, land rights were generally shared by all the members of a group; no one person or group of leaders had authority to prohibit use of this resource, at least not without

When Indians signed treaties with the U.S. Government, they often were shocked to learn that they had given up all rights to their territory. Their own relationship to land and natural resources was not usually so exclusive or complete.

the assent of all the adult men. Thus a treaty signed by his leaders meant little to the Indian who was confronted by hostile settlers as he attempted to hunt on tribal land according to his traditional rights. Eventually, most Indians came to see the loss of their lands as the result of an invasion, not a legal transfer, and often attempted to expel settlers and others from their territory despite the existence of treaties.

Even in North America, property rights are not so exclusive and ironclad as many think. In the name of public good, national, state, and local governments regularly condemn private property. People by the thousands have lost their homes to freeways and various forms of urban development. Minnesota farmers still sabotage electrical power towers that have been built on their farmland without their permission.

The many ways that people hold natural resources and the processes they use to allocate rights are complex and varied. Anthropologists have long been interested in this area of culture, particularly in land tenure and inheritance.

Technology

Technology consists of the cultural knowledge for making and using tools and extracting and refining raw materials (see Chapter 9). Although many people equate technology with tools alone, such implements are only part of this aspect of production. Technology is also the information that people possess about the manufacture and use of tools and the production of goods. For example, when a restaurant cook arrives at work, he or she walks into a world full of equipment. In the kitchen are stoves, broilers, ovens, grills, fryers, coolers, freezers, mixers, slicers, knives, pots, trays, utensils, cleavers, peelers, and literally hundreds of cooking tools. However, the cook does not simply sit down and let these tools do the work. Cooks must learn a wealth of technological strategies before they can use the tools of the cooking trade effectively to prepare a wide range of food for their customers. Everywhere, tasks require technological guidance composed of a knowledge of tools and their function.

There is another aspect relating to technology that should be clarified. Because we are from an industrial society we usually think about our technology as extremely complex. In one sense, this is quite true. Industrial manufacturing processes require the use of ever more complex tools—automatic welders, cutters, stampers, and so forth—and hundreds of specialized activities may go into the manufacture of a particular item. By contrast, the manufacture of a pot by a *Kumar* (potter) in India may appear to be a simple process. Complex machines are absent. In their place are simple tools, a potter's wheel, a pot full of water to be mixed with clay, a simple kiln or no special firing device at all.

However, when viewed from the perspective of individuals in the manufacturing process, technology is complex in all societies. To be sure, some tasks are simple everywhere. A hydraulic press operator in a stamping factory may produce battery plates all day using three simple motions. The Indian potter may collect his clay with a simple digging action. The factory engineer must understand much of a plant's mechanical complexity, and the Indian potter is really a craftsman who must know the properties of different clays, have the skills for mixing and shaping this plastic material, and use the correct techniques for firing the ware that he manufactures.

The Organization of Labor

The need to organize people's labor is felt in every society. No single person can perform all the tasks necessary to his or her biological and social life. And, in fact, many techniques are too complex to be performed by a single person working alone. We have all had the experience of trying to do something that requires a second pair of hands. To meet these needs, people everywhere organize their work by making a division of labor and forming units of production.

Division of Labor

The division of labor refers to the rules that govern the assignment of jobs to people. Most tasks performed in any society are assigned to people on the basis of traditional cultural rules. But occasionally a group of people faces a new situation

*The manufacture of pottery,
although it may seem simple,
involves a complex
technology. Here a Mexican
woman uses her knowledge of
ceramics as she smoothes a
pot before drying it in the sun.*

that demands a freshly devised division of labor. For example, one American family recently traveled across the United States to visit relatives. Because they were short of money, they decided to camp out along their route instead of staying at motels. They bought a tent and some other camping equipment from a discount house and set off on their trip, planning to make camp that night for the first time in their lives.

Their first attempt to make camp was a sobering experience. Not only did they not understand the technology surrounding their camping equipment, but no one knew what job he or she was supposed to do. The problem of using the equipment was solved by reading sets of directions that came with the items. But evolving a smooth-functioning division of labor took several days. The children all wanted to perform the same tasks at the same time or did not want to help at all. The mother was not sure whether she or her husband should draw water at the camp pump. Who would light the stove, blow up the air mattresses, raise the enormous 10 × 12 foot frame wall tent, and wash the dishes? After a long, hot day on the road, arguments over who should perform what tasks became so bad that the family nearly decided to forget the trip and spend their summer in the comfort of their well-regulated home. However, within 4 or 5 days a system was worked out dividing the labor among family members, and making and breaking camp, once a matter of several hours of continuous work, now took only 1½ hours.

Like any set of roles, those associated with work reflect a number of attributes—skill, age, physique, wealth, and more qualities determine how labor is to be allocated. One of the most important attributes governing the division of labor is sex. In virtually every society, from the !Kung Bushmen of the Kalahari desert to the suburbanites of Bayonne, New Jersey, men and women perform at least some tasks exclusively.

Unit of Production

The unit of production refers to the person or organized group responsible for producing something. An individual may represent such a unit in any society. Among the Siriono, a small hunting and gathering band living in the Bolivian rain forest, men usually hunt by themselves. Avoiding cooperation with others, they depend on their own skills to bag game. In most North American cities there are a few craftsmen who work singly to produce such items as guitars, pottery, and paintings.

However, most often, units of production are organized groups. For example, although they may hunt alone, the Mbuti Pygmies of Africa work in small cooperative groups to find and kill game. They may even involve whole bands in communal hunts. Men set up nets and wait to kill wild animals driven into them by a line of noise-making women and children.

Families are usually the most important units of production in kinship organized societies. The Bhils discussed in Chapter 5 illustrate this nicely. From plowing, when Bhil men break the ground and women sow, to weeding and harvesting, agriculture is a family activity. Members of the same lineage, however, will help each other with heavier tasks such as threshing, and large jobs such as the construction of terrace walls may entail the formation of a neighborhood cooperative work group.

Factories serve as units of production in industrial societies like our own. Even preindustrial cities show evidence of factorylike groups. The Indus Valley cities that flourished in South Asia about 4500 years ago show evidence of large buildings where many workers appear to have manufactured goods or processed grain.

PRODUCTION IN MEXICO[1]

Let us illustrate some of these concepts by reference to Mexico. Imagine that you wish to understand the economic system of a small community, Santo Domingo,

[1] The Mexican village described in this chapter is fictitious. The information on which this description is based comes largely from George M. Foster, *Tzintzuntzan: Mexican Peasants in a Changing World*, Prospect Heights, IL: Waveland Press, Inc., 1967 (reissued 1988 with changes); George M. Foster, *Empire's Children: The People of Tzintzuntzan*, Westport, Conn: Greenwood, 1948.

All societies assign at least some productive tasks on the basis of sex. In Mali it is the job of women to pound millet into flour for the day's meals.

that lies at an elevation of 7000 feet nestled in a valley surrounded by volcanic peaks in western Mexico. The village's mixed population of *mestizos* and Tarascan Indians live in one-story adobe houses whose walls and walled courtyards abut the

In order to survive, people everywhere must meet their needs through production. In rural Mexico many people depend on the crops they grow in highland fields for at least part of their subsistence.

several cobblestone lanes that neatly divide the community into a chessboardlike grid. You have as your key informants Miguel Estrada, his wife Maria, and their three children. You try to understand village economics by seeing how this family meets its economic wants.

You quickly learn that the family engages in several productive activities. Mr. Estrada, with the occasional help of a son, farms some scattered fields located in the hills around the village. Yields from agricultural activities are insufficient to meet the family's need for food, however. To supplement, the entire family makes pottery for sale in the village's weekly market. Family members also cultivate vegetables grown in a garden next to their house, and Mrs. Estrada tends lime trees behind the dwelling. The family consumes all the vegetables and limes it produces.

Resources are allocated in a few basic ways in Santo Domingo. Private property exists in the community to which people have exclusive and relatively complete rights. Miguel Estrada owns the few fields he farms, which he inherited from his father. Maria Estrada owns the house and the lime trees. She inherited the land and house from her parents and planted the trees herself. She has exclusive rights to the trees and fruit although, as a dutiful wife, her husband could command that she sell them. Other items of private property include the family cow, chickens, two burros, and farming and pottery-making equipment.

Other resources on which the Estradas depend are owned by their community. The water that Mrs. Estrada so laboriously carries up from the well each morning is a community resource. Villagers all have rights to use the water, but none actually owns it privately. The clay the Estradas use in the making of pottery is also a community property. All have a right to dig clay from the clay beds and village officials may even extend permission to use Santo Domingo clay to others outside the village. Nevertheless, the deposits are community property and the rules governing their use ensure that they will stay that way.

The division of labor within the Estrada family occurs along lines of sex and age. Miguel Estrada farms the land with the couple's oldest son. Both also make pottery when they have time. Maria Estrada works from dawn to dusk at a variety of tasks necessary to the maintenance of the family. She rises early to take corn to the village mill for grinding; she cooks the family's meals, does the laundry, cleans the house, carries the water home from the well, waters her lime trees, tends the vegetable garden, and spends many hours making pottery; she also milks the cow and transports and sells pottery on market day. The two younger children, both girls, help their mother with a number of these tasks.

Within Santo Domingo as a whole there is some division of labor based on economic specialization, but it is not nearly so varied as similar communities in the United States and Canada. Most men in the village farm at least some land. Most families also manufacture pottery because of the fine source of high-quality clay found in the community. Santo Domingo pots and dishes are sold in the market and exported to other parts of Mexico. Thus, although a few people, such as shopkeepers, engage in specialized economic activities, most know how to do the same set of tasks—a feature common to peasant agricultural communities in other parts of the world as well.

The nature of village technology correlates with this relatively undifferentiated division of labor. The manufacturing process is performed from start to finish by the same person. Using pottery molds, pumice for polishing finished ware, and an adobe kiln with a fire pit, Maria Estrada manufactures pottery from start to finish. Although her husband does the heavy work of digging clay, loading it onto the burros, and transporting it to their house, generally Mrs. Estrada herself mixes the clay with just the right amount of water, kneads it into a workable consistency, presses it into the molds, dries the newly formed pieces, polishes away seam marks, and fires the pots in the kiln. The process does not require complex tools and specialized procedures; however, it is not simple. Each step requires a sensitive knowledge of the properties of clay, the techniques for molding, and the conditions for firing. Mistakes lead to broken pots or uneven, inferior wares that bring less on the market.

The most important unit of production in Santo Domingo, like so many other agrarian societies, is the family. Although individuals can work alone in the community, they usually labor as part of a family group. Pottery making usually occupies most of the time that Estrada family members are together. They help each

In many societies, kinship groups form the most important units of production.
Every member of this family in Oaxaca, Mexico, helps to manufacture pottery.

other with the molds, carrying and mixing clay, and polishing and firing. Proceeds from production are shared within the group.

Production is an essential part of any economic system, but by itself it does not meet the material needs of groups. To understand the full process, we must also look at distribution.

DISTRIBUTION

If people kept the things they produced for themselves, the social benefits of cooperation would be lost. A !Kung hunter, for example, would eventually starve without the vegetable foods provided by his wife. She, in turn, might suffer from a deficiency of protein if he failed to give her a share of the meat he obtained from hunting. In every society the fruits of production are unevenly dispersed among people and in relation to time. To cope with this problem, every society manifests a system of distribution, or a set of strategies for apportioning goods and services among the members of a group.

Economic Exchange

By far the most common way people distribute goods and services is through economic exchange. Economic exchange consists of the cultural rules for the transfer of goods and services among people. Exchange occurs when a man gives a waitress money for the hamburger she has brought him to eat in a diner. It takes place when Bhil girls accept one or two coconuts from a householder about whom they have just been singing lewd songs during the Holi festival. It comes about when the family heads of a *barrio* in a Mexican village contribute money for fireworks to a festival committee.

We acquire most of the material support and services that we need to survive and live adequate social lives through exchange. It explains how automobiles made in Detroit find their way to market in other parts of the United States. It accounts for why Londoners can sit down to a cup of tea made from leaves grown on plantations in mountainous Sri Lanka. And it provides the system by which the Estradas exchange pottery for other needed items.

The most notable fact about exchange is that it requires a transaction between people. Exchange systems provide the rules and the motivation for individuals to give one another material goods and to provide each other with services. If we were to view examples of economic exchange from around the world, we would be impressed by their variety. If we look at such instances systematically, however, we will discover that three basic *transaction modes* emerge: *market exchange*, *reciprocity*, and *redistribution*. Each mode embodies a particular system of rules that makes it different from the others, and each gives the transfer of goods and services special meaning. One mode, reciprocity, is found in every society, and the others may or may not be present. All three exist together in many economic systems, including the Mexican economy of which Santo Domingo is a part.

Market Exchange

Market exchange refers to a transfer of goods and services based on price, supply, and demand. It depends on how much people desire particular goods or services, how much they must give to obtain them, and how much they have to give in the first place. Market exchange is familiar to people in the United States. Every time we speak of selling something or of making a trip to the store to buy food or other things we need, we are using terms associated with market exchange. The words buy, sell, discount, price, money, cost, profit, loss, and hundreds of others express various aspects of the many different transactions that characterize our complex market economy. But what is market exchange? What makes such exchange, which seems normal and usual to us, different from the other transactional modes? To answer this question, let us look at the strategies used by the Estradas to sell their pottery.

Selling Pottery

The Estradas sell pottery in three ways. They often take their wares to the local weekly market in Santo Domingo, which is attended by people from nearby villages and by buyers who will purchase pottery in relatively large amounts for re-sale in other towns and cities. There is also a market at a nearby town, San An-dreas; however, transporting pottery the several miles to San Andreas makes those trips less attractive. Finally, a buyer may make a special arrangement with the Es-tradas for pottery of a certain kind. A contract of this sort is appreciated by the family because it ensures them of sales at a guaranteed price. For our discussion here, let us look at the exchange that occurs in the Santo Domingo market.

When the Estradas take their wares to market, several things happen that are features of market exchange. First, buyers approach the Estradas for pottery be-cause of *direct need* or desire for such goods. Similarly, the Estradas wish to ex-change their pottery because they need the money it will bring. When people en-gage in market exchange anywhere, they do so because they have *an immediate need* for goods or resources.

Second, when individuals conduct market exchange, they try to *maximize* by getting the most goods and services for the least expenditure of their own re-sources. If the Estradas have only one water pot left and two customers want it, they will sell it to the one who offers the most money. In this way they get the most

While it is possible for other kinds of exchange to govern the transfer of goods in a market place, most markets, such as this one in Oaxaca Mexico, are characterized by mar-ket exchange.

money for their labor. This also means that the price of a particular item may change from day to day in relation to supply and the demand.

Maximization leads to a third attribute of market exchange, the fact that it determines who will be *parties* to the exchange. Because a seller and buyer attempt to get the most for their limited resources, they will choose to deal with the individual who gives them the most value. There is no need to know the person with whom the transaction occurs. Thus market exchange facilitates the transfer of goods among strangers and is ideally suited for large, complex societies like our own and Mexico's, where most people do not know each other. When we visit a supermarket, we need not know the checkout girl or packer to buy the food we require that week, nor must we be personally acquainted with the president of the regional power company to pay our monthly utility bill. In fact, exchange may actually be easier when it is unencumbered by the obligations that tie together people who know each other well.

Fourth, market exchange leads to a *setting of the value* of goods and services in terms of each other. Imagine that exchange occurs without money, a situation that is possible so long as the maximization principle is applied to the transaction. For example, in Santo Domingo buyers may come forward who wish to exchange grain, in the form of dried corn, for pottery. Hypothetically, let us assume that a set of ten plates normally brings 10 pounds of corn. From day to day this rate may change because the market principle permeates the exchange system. Over time, however, the value of plates and corn and the other things exchanged in the market become related. The worth of plates, corn, baskets, and other exchangeable goods eventually can be stated in terms of each other.

Money facilitates such intervaluation immensely. Normally, money is a market device designed to facilitate exchange by acting as a medium for it. The Estradas, for example, convert their pottery into cash. In turn, they can use that cash to buy other things, such as grain, that they need to meet their economic wants. Because of money, there is no need for the Estradas to find someone with corn who especially wants pottery in order to make an exchange. Cash can be stored and used when something is especially needed. It also is a handy way of stating the value of goods and services.

Although market exchange is essential to the way the Estradas and people in many other parts of the world acquire necessary goods and services, it is not the only way such things can be distributed. There is also nonmarket exchange composed of two closely related types—reciprocity and redistribution.

Reciprocal Exchange

Reciprocal exchange refers to the transfer of goods or services between two people or groups based on their role obligations. Surprisingly enough, reciprocal exchange is important to North Americans as well as to Mexicans. Every time we have the neighbors in for cocktails, visit our grandparents for Christmas dinner, offer a friend a ride to school, or act in thousands of other familiar social situations, we behave according to rules defined by reciprocal exchange. However, just what are the attributes that make reciprocal exchange different from market transactions?

The answer to this question revolves around the notion of *role obligation*. Let us look at this point in the context of an example from our own society. The American family is usually composed of a man and woman and their children. These individuals identify each other by kinship terms and relate on the basis of associated role obligations. One of these is the exchange of gifts at Christmas, an activity that requires days of shopping in the marketplace and hours of concern about whether or not gifts will be appreciated. Imagine that the mother of these children gives her son a slot-car racing set. He presents her with four colorful hot pads to handle dishes that come from the oven. The two engage in an exchange that is fundamentally different from the one they used to buy the presents in the first place. What does this difference amount to?

First, the reason for their reciprocal exchange is not necessarily dictated by the desire for the material goods themselves as it is in the market. Certainly, the mother and son attempt to give each other items they know will be appreciated, but the reason for the exchange is their obligation to one another, an obligation they assume when they take on the status of mother or son. If the boy fails to give anything to his mother, she will be hurt and disappointed. Her husband will probably take the child aside to explain the nature of the transgression and to point out the future occasions on which he, as a son, must give his mother presents. A mother who did not give gifts at Christmas would also have to face some very disappointed children. For this reason, reciprocal exchange does not usually occur between strangers, although it may when strangers can identify themselves in a way that signals the necessity of fulfilling mutual obligations. Such is the case among Australian Aborigines, for example, when two strangers meet and determine how they are related. Once their kinship ties are established, they assume the exchange obligations of the associated statuses.

Second, reciprocal exchange is not dictated by maximization, as we saw this principle operating in market exchange. When the mother gives her son his slot-car racing set, she does not haggle with him first about what he is going to give her in return, nor would she give the set to the boy's sister because the girl has a more valuable present for her. She makes the exchange because it is a culturally defined obligation associated with her role as mother.

There are a few other activities of reciprocal exchange that bear mentioning. For example, as discussed above, the value of goods given need not be the same, but there is a tendency for an equality of value to characterize exchange between individuals of equal rank. Thus the American mother will give her husband something relatively equal in value to what he gives her, but will present her son with a gift that is much more expensive than the one the child will present her. In fact, she may be distressed if the boy gives her a very expensive gift. As long as the value of items exchanged reciprocally is within the range of what is culturally defined as proper, the obligation of the parties to the exchange is met.

Some forms of reciprocal exchange are difficult to recognize because they seem one sided. It is easy to see that Christmas gift giving is reciprocal because the two parties to the exchange give presents to each other simultaneously. However, in

Weddings often require reciprocal exchange. Outside the village of Rumsiki in North Cameroon, a husband and wife pose with the equivalent of the dowry, he was obligated to give at the time of their marriage.

many circumstances we may only witness a one-way exchange, for example, when a neighbor gives a Bhil groom (see Chapter 5) some money at the time of his wedding. The groom does not immediately return something of value to the donor, but will repay the favor when the donor is married or experiences a wedding in his immediate family. *Delayed reciprocity* of this sort functions to tie people together by placing them in a network of outstanding debts.

Finally, and perhaps surprisingly, as we noted earlier, money may be used in reciprocal exchange. This is sometimes a difficult matter because money is usually associated with market exchange and consequently takes on the meaning of market maximization, as though the giver is buying something instead of reciprocating. To circumvent this problem, one grandmother in the Midwest sends her grandchildren money for their birthdays in the form of crisp, new dollar bills, one for each year they have been alive. Somehow the condition and number of dollar certificates give them a nonmarket quality.

Reciprocal exchange serves as the major mode of transfer for members of hunting and gathering societies, such as the Mbutu Pygmies. When the pygmies hunt, they often do so together, setting out nets and driving game into the resulting trap to be clubbed by waiting hunters. Animals caught in this manner, or killed by a solitary hunter, are usually distributed among other members of the camp on the basis of obligations associated with kinship. For the pygmies the basic biological needs are met by a system of reciprocal exchange that in our society accounts for only a small proportion of economic transactions.

Reciprocity is a major avenue of exchange in Mexico and of real use to the Estradas in their attempt to meet economic needs. The family members regularly exchange hospitality with neighbors, which is a form of reciprocal exchange. They can also meet emergency needs for money through this avenue. The Estradas exist in a network of kin with whom reciprocal favors are possible. They also establish fictitious kinship relations with other people. When they are short of money, the Estradas frequently ask relatives for small loans. These kin, if they have money, will lend it with the expectation that, when in need, they can come to Miguel and Maria Estrada and receive the same treatment.

To extend this system of social security to its fullest, the people of Santo Domingo create a number of added fictive relatives through the *compadrazgo* system. For example, when their son was born, the Estradas asked another couple to be godparents for the baby at his baptism. This couple agreed and took on some of the responsibility for supporting the cost of the ceremony and for looking after the child in later life. By far the most important consequence of the arrangement, however, is the relationship between the Estradas and their son's godparents. These people are like kinsmen and take on some of the obligations associated with kinship. Often *compadres*, as godparents are called, are chosen for their financial strength and can be approached on the basis of reciprocal obligation for money in times of need.

Redistribution

The second kind of nonmarket exchange is called redistribution. Redistributive exchange refers to the transfer of goods and services between a group of people and a central collecting source based on role obligation. Like reciprocity, redistributive exchange occurs because people are obligated to each other. The most obvious example of a redistributive system is government taxation. In our role as citizens we are obligated to pay taxes to various governments, both local and national. These governments are obligated to return taxes to us in the form of various services and at times cash. The amount we pay in may not equal the amount we get back and, indeed, it is often difficult to determine the entire value of services that governments return to the people.

Redistributive systems do not always involve a state tax system. For example, in the Indian tribal village of Ratakote, every Bhil householder contributes food and drink to the family of a person who has died. This family redistributes these things at a memorial feast to those who contribute as well as to some guests from outside the community. Such pooling of resources occurs in many forms around the world and presents a major means by which people can gather the necessary goods and services to hold feasts and other communal events.

203

In Mexico redistribution works through a system of taxation. The Estradas pay land taxes to the national government. Their payments, such as giving a gift, are part of their obligations as Mexican citizens. They have no choice about this transfer of money and are in no sense buying anything with cash. The Mexican government is also obligated to redistribute at least some of this tax money in the form of health programs, public works, or direct aid. The most costly service provided by the government to the people of Santo Domingo is the school, which has a payroll of over 150,000 pesos each year, much more than the total sum of the taxes collected from the individual landowners. In such cases there is no requirement in redistributive systems that people get back precisely the same amount as they contribute to the system.

SUMMARY

The economic system consists of the cultural knowledge people use to provide goods and services to meet biological and social wants. It defines human productive activity and the distribution and exchange of goods and services. Production involves an allocation of resources, a technology, and an organization of labor. The allocation of resources refers to the knowledge people use to assign rights to the ownership and use of resources. Technology consists of the knowledge people use to make and use tools and to extract and refine raw materials. Labor is organized according to the division of labor, the rules that govern the assignment of jobs to people, and the units of production—the groups of people responsible for producing things.

Goods and services are dispersed by a system of distribution—a set of strategies that apportion goods and services among the members of a group. Distribution is normally effected through economic exchange, the cultural rules for the transfer of goods and services among people. Exchange takes three basic forms: market exchange, reciprocity, and redistribution. Market exchange refers to a transfer of goods or services based on price, supply, and demand. Reciprocal exchange indicates the transfer of goods or services between two people or groups based on role obligations. Finally, redistribution refers to the transfer of goods or services between a group of people and a central collecting source based on role obligation.

MAJOR CONCEPTS

ECONOMIC SYSTEM	DIVISION OF LABOR
BIOLOGICAL WANTS	UNIT OF PRODUCTION
SOCIAL WANTS	DISTRIBUTION
ALLOCATION OF RESOURCES	ECONOMIC EXCHANGE
OWNERSHIP	MARKET EXCHANGE
TECHNOLOGY	RECIPROCITY
TOOLS	REDISTRIBUTION

SELECTED READINGS

Belshaw, C. S.: *Traditional Exchange and Modern Markets*, Englewood Cliffs, N.J.: Prentice-Hall, 1965.
A discussion of the relationship of the economic system to social and political structure.

Bohannan, Paul, and George Dalton (editors): *Markets in Africa*, Garden City, N.Y.: Doubleday Anchor, 1965.
A collection that includes articles on the nature and development of markets in several African societies.

Dalton, George (editor): *Tribal and Peasant Economies: Readings in Economic Anthropology*, Garden City, N.Y.: Natural History Press, 1967.
A collection of articles drawn from the literature on the economies of Africa, Oceania, Asia, Europe, and America. Articles stress the difference between the formalist and substantivist view in economic anthropology.

Dalton, George (editor): *Economic Development and Social Change: The Modernization of Village Communities*, Garden City, N.Y.: Natural History Press, 1971.
A collection of articles discussing the nature of primitive and peasant economies, the economic impact and consequences of colonialism, and economic modernization and development.

Firth, Raymond (editor): *Themes in Economic Anthropology*, New York: Travistock, 1967.
A collection of papers on the relationship between economic theory and economic anthropology, and four field studies of economies.

LeClair, Edward E., Jr., and Harold K. Schneider (editors): *Economic Anthropology: Readings in Theory and Analysis*, New York: Holt, Rinehart and Winston, 1968.
A collection of articles focusing on the points of difference between the formalist and substantivist positions in economic anthropology.

Nash, Manning: *Primitive and Peasant Economic Systems*, San Francisco: Chandler, 1966.
A review of the theory of economic anthropology.

Schneider, Harold K.: *Economic Man: The Anthropology of Economics*, Salem, WI: Sheffield Publishing Co., 1974 (reissued 1989).
An attempt to integrate various theoretical positions in economic anthropology.

CHAPTER ELEVEN

Politics
and
Government

All people use their cultural knowledge to cope with the situations of daily life. A !Kung Bushman living in the Kalahari Desert of South Africa employs his extensive cultural knowledge about hunting when he tracks a gazelle that has been wounded by one of his poisoned arrows. He uses information he has learned about a gazelle's spoor, typical behavior, and reaction to poison in order to follow the wounded animal until it dies. When the gazelle moves out of sight, the hunter must use his culture to predict its condition and intentions so that he can decide how fast and in what direction he must go to track it. Only in this way can the hunter assure himself of catching his dying quarry ahead of other scavengers.

Groups also use culture to meet their needs. The !Kung survive in small nomadic bands of about 20 individuals. For most of the year the band moves freely about its territory in search of game and vegetable foods, and hunters range over the land confident of finding enough water to meet their needs. However, as winter approaches, the land dries up and only a few reliable water holes remain. Because of this lack of water, the band must make camp near one of the water holes and live there until fresh rains bring new life to the desert in the spring. But which water hole should they choose? The water at some may become brackish or dry up, although it rarely has done so before. Other locations may provide abundant water but lack proximity to sufficient game and plant foods to see the group through the dry period. To make their decision, the !Kung use their cultural knowledge of the environment, reading its signs and predicting its condition. Only in this way can they choose an adequate winter campsite.

However, the lone hunter, on the one hand, and the members of a !Kung band, on the other, make their decisions in different ways. The hunter's choice is personal; he alone assesses the signs and decides in which direction to follow the wounded gazelle. But when a decision affects the entire band, it requires a collective choice. They must set a process in motion that allows for an assessment of environmental conditions, a common interpretation of the situation, and a final decision to act in a particular way. The choice requires the support of all if the band is to function as an effective unit. In short, they must make a political decision.

THE POLITICAL SYSTEM

The political system is the process of making and carrying out public policy according to cultural categories and rules. Every society has a political system. When the Nuer of the Sudan discuss whether or not to hold a religious ceremony to combat smallpox, they must make a political decision. When a Polynesian chief chooses to allow labor recruiters onto his island, his action is political. When the members of a Japanese fishing village find their fishing grounds polluted and devoid of aquatic life and ask their government to move them to an inland farming area, they initiate a political process.

The heart of our definition of the political system is the notion of public policy. Policy refers to any guideline that can lead directly to action. When the !Kung decide to move to a particular campsite, they make a policy that will be acted on. Because of this attribute, policy should not be confused with goals or values. Goals and values label what should be, and although they may bear on the way a public decision is made, they are too general to stimulate action by themselves. The term public refers to the people that a policy will affect. Some publics, such as the !Kung band, are organized social groups. Others, like the people who will receive the fallout from a nuclear test, are simply aggregates of people affected by the same decision. Public policy thus refers to guidelines that lead to action that affects a group.

Political Process

The *structures* for making political decisions, the issues that fall within the public domain, and the rules employed for making and enforcing decisions vary enormously from one society to another. Anthropologists often use general ethnological categories for cross-cultural comparison and the formulation of general theory of political structures. Concepts such as "band," "tribe," "state," "acephalous state," and many others have all been used to this end. Although we will occasionally point out some anthropological categories of political structures, our main task in this chapter will be to discuss the political process. The political process refers to the events and actions that lead to the formulation and enforcement of public policy. In every society, decision-making processes are initiated and pursued, and everywhere public policy, once formed, is applied and enforced. To get at these elements more clearly, we will define them within the boundaries of a single case that occurred in the state of Minnesota in 1969. During that year a public issue arose in the Twin Cities (Minneapolis and Saint Paul) metropolitan area concerning the planned release of nuclear waste materials from a new power plant. Let us look at this case through the eyes of someone who participated in it.

Political structures take many forms. The African king photographed here with his royal family largely inherits his authority to rule.

208

The Discharge
of Nuclear Wastes[1]

On a cold evening in February 1969 Alice Warrick, married and the mother of two, picked up her copy of the *Minneapolis Star*. As she thumbed through the first section, she came across this story, entitled "Plan to Discharge Radioactive Wastes into River Opposed," by Jim Shoop.

There are no "safe" levels of human exposure to radiation and the planned discharge of radioactive wastes in the Mississippi River from Monticello, Minn., nuclear electric plant should be prohibited, a University of Minnesota zoologist said Wednesday.

Prof. Charles W. Huver made the recommendation in a meeting with John Badalich, director of the Minneapolis Pollution Control Agency and several state legislators.

The Monticello plant, now under construction by Northern States Power Co., is scheduled to go into operation early in 1970. The company has maintained that the plant will be operated in a completely safe manner and that there will be no danger to public health from radioactive wastes.

Huver said later he told the group that neither the radiation control standards of the U.S. Atomic Energy Commission nor those recommended by the Pollution Control Agency's consultant, Dr. Ernest C. Tsivoglou, "are any guarantee of public safety."[2]

The article went on to describe Huver's contention that "there was 'mounting evidence' in biological studies over the past 10 years that tritium, the most predominant radioactive isotope found in wastes from nuclear power plant reactors causes cancer in animals." The report also included Huver's assertion that a noted study showed an increase in cancer deaths near the large government reactor and waste storage site on the Columbia River at Hanford, Washington. Pointing out that no amount of radioactivity is inconsequential, Huver urged that the Pollution Control Agency require offsite disposal of all nuclear wastes.

The story disturbed Alice. Wasn't the Monticello reactor upriver from Saint Paul, and didn't the city draw part of its drinking water from the Mississippi River? Was Northern States Power Company's contention true that its nuclear wastes released into the river would be harmless? As Alice thought it over, she wondered if the power company's assessment of the situation was correct. If it was not, as Huver charged, what could be done about it? How might she and other concerned citizens affect the process by which pollution standards were formulated? But above all, she wondered if this were really a public matter in the first place. Perhaps it was an internal problem for the people at Northern States Power to decide.

[1]The information on which this chapter is based is drawn from a study of the Monticello nuclear plant dispute by one of the authors. With the exception of the people and groups named in the newspaper article by Jim Shoop, the names of people and groups discussed in the remainder of the chapter are fictitious.

[2]*Minneapolis Star*, February 20, 1969.

Public Policy
and Nuclear Waste

Company officials certainly implied that the matter of waste discharge was a company, not a public, problem. They argued that any radioactive isotopes they "released" from the plant would be harmless, thus of no concern to the general public. They would carefully "monitor" waste materials from the plant and release them in "controlled batches" into the river. The whole process would be supervised by "scientists" who were "experts" in these matters.

But Professor Charles Huver also seemed to be an expert, and he felt that no radioactive materials should be put in the river. To make his point, he spoke of the company dumping these poisonous wastes into the *public's* water supply. Clearly he felt that the matter was public and thus of political consequence. In the end, Alice came to agree with him and joined a group that organized to oppose the power company's plans. To understand her decision and the framework within which she would later carry on political activity, we should look at the notion of political organization.

POLITICAL ORGANIZATION

People do not make public policy by accident, they produce it in the context of well-defined situations. Typical political situations involve the operation of government, political authority, political conflict groups, and political leaders. Let us look at these concepts more closely.

Government

A government is a political group composed of political specialists and associated with a state. When we consider politics we automatically think of government. We live in a world of government officials, government agencies, government policies, government actions, and government deliberations. One sixth of the American labor force works for the government, doing everything from carrying mail to inspecting meat. As we grow up in this country, we quickly learn that our government is a formal organization specifically constructed to make and carry out policy. It, like governments in other parts of the world, includes a number of special, usually full-time officials or functionaries who carry on its business. Typically, governments are associated with states, or culturally organized populations that control a specific territory.

Our view of what a government is, however, may be colored by a knowledge of our own particular governmental system. We are used to a large bureaucracy, with an elected legislature and administration. But monarchies, many chiefdoms, and some other systems also represent forms of government, for each possesses some full-time political officials, a state, and the authority to make and enforce political decisions.

Stateless Societies

Stateless societies are groups that lack a formal government and clear-cut territory. Such groups possess no full-time political officials or public administrative apparatus. Instead, the members of stateless societies depend on informal leaders with limited authority and an unspecialized system of social organization as a foundation for public decision making.

Many of the smaller societies around the world were stateless at the time of European expansion and colonial activity. To European explorers and the stream of traders, missionaries, and officials who followed them, the notion that people could live without formal government was inconceivable. Thus they tended to overestimate the power of informal leaders, mistakenly expecting that the agreements and treaties they made with such individuals would be binding.[3] When agreements failed to work, Europeans impugned the character of native populations instead of looking for the causes of these difficulties in the structure of local informal political systems.

Harriet Kupferer described a situation something like this in her study of the subarctic Cree living at Rupert's House, Quebec.[4] She discovered that a man, entitled "band chief" by the Canadian authorities, found it almost impossible to lead in the ways Canadians or his own people expected of him. The case represented a classic instance of a Western government's imposing its view of formal political structure on people who had never had one, for the Cree were traditionally a stateless society.

The Cree hunted in small nomadic bands in northern Quebec. They had no tradition of strong leadership and, in fact, had no word for such units as "villages" and "bands." Authority rested in the hands of family heads, although, as Kupferer points out, "A kind of informal leadership was recognized, however, in that a 'good man', wise in the ways of the people or skilled in the hunt, might be sought for counsel, but he did not have the power to coerce. There was no mechanism to enforce a headman's decisions or wishes."[5]

Ignoring this form of political organization and assuming that the Cree had a tradition of formal leadership, the Canadian government established the band chief system. Those who held the new position of chief quickly discovered that their fellow Cree did not know what to expect of them and that the Canadian Indian Agent thought of them as a conduit for his own authority and leadership. As in so many cases, the nature of stateless political systems was misunderstood by a government trying to integrate a group into its larger political structure.

Because they lack government does not mean that the Cree avoid political activity. Many peoples are able to make decisions within a looser system of political organization. We have already seen, for instance, that the !Kung make political de-

---

[3]The word *chief* became the common English term for native leaders and, as its use in such phrases as "commander in chief" and "chief of staff" implies, it is associated with relatively centralized power and authority.

[4]See Harriet J. Kupferer, "Impotency and Power: A Crosscultural Comparison of the Effect of Alien Rule," in *Political Anthropology*, Marc J. Swartz, Victor W. Turner, and Arthur Tuden (editors), Chicago: Aldine, 1966, pp. 61–72.

[5]Kupferer, 1966, p. 62.

Many new nations face the problem of integrating culturally diverse peoples into a nationally structured political system. Here we see a Massai who is Tanzania's minister for defense addressing a group of his own people about national affairs.

cisions, and their political system, with the exception of a more clearly defined headman, is very like that of the Cree.

The Pollution Control Agency

Prior to 1966 there had been no regulatory arm of state government to control pollution in Minnesota. That year the legislature voted to establish the Pollution Control Agency, or PCA as most people had come to know it, giving the group the power to determine waste emission standards and to set up a process for enforcing them. The agency had seven voting members and a permanent staff with a director. Northern States Power Company was now coming before that agency to seek a license permitting the release of some nuclear wastes into the river and air.

For members of the public such as Alice Warrick, the importance of the agency, like the importance of political organizations anywhere, lay in its ability to act. As a legally established arm of state government, it had the legitimate authority to regulate activities that caused pollution. Getting at the problem of nuclear contamination required a knowledge of the locus of such authority.

Authority

All of us have probably said at one time or another that someone else does not have the right to do something. A daughter may argue that her father has no right to choose a husband for her; a student may claim that school administrators lack the right to regulate the length of his hair; a motorist may feel that state legislators do not have the right to require him to wear a seat belt. In each case, these people challenge the authority of those who seek to regulate them. Authority is the right to make and enforce public policy.

Authority is a right that people assign to particular political roles. The degree to which authority may be exercised varies from one society to the next, with one political identity or group to the next, and with one public issue to the next. Americans recognize different limits on authority when they use the terms dictatorship and democracy. In the former we envision a system where a leader or group can "dictate" decisions to a larger public without consultation and where decisions are enforced with strong coercive measures. Our ideal of a democracy is a system where all the people participate in the political process and where authority is regularly conferred by election. We do not like to think of our democratic government as coercive, although it does hold such power.

To those concerned about the discharge of nuclear wastes, access to authority is a crucial matter. Without authority to back it up, public policy will not work. In the case of the Pollution Control Agency, access seemed easy. Professor Huver, for example, found he could talk to the agency's director without trouble, and the PCA held several open hearings to consider limits on radioactive releases from the Monticello plant. In addition, the agency's regular meetings were open so that the vote of board members on this issue could be witnessed and recorded by the public.

The Pollution Control Agency's openness contrasted markedly with that of another governmental body, the Atomic Energy Commission. One of the reasons that Alice Warrick originally had not been too concerned about the Monticello plant was her confidence that something as potentially dangerous as that would be carefully regulated by the national government. However, the Congress of the United States had given the Atomic Energy Commission authority for two things: (1) to develop nuclear power and (2) to regulate the use of nuclear power. Many felt this had created an inherent conflict of interest within this agency. Furthermore, since atomic matters also concerned national defense, most of the commis-

Authority is often vested in hereditary leaders such as King Savang Vatthana of Laos seen here standing among seated dignitaries at his court.

sion's activities were secret. Although the Atomic Energy Commission did hold public hearings, these did not concern the setting of safety standards and limits on the release of radioactive materials. The nuclear scientists employed by the commission, in conjunction with several commission boards, had set those standards in private, and hearings merely functioned to air any questions about enforcement. People who felt that the Atomic Energy Commission's standards were too lax could not approach the commission because they had no ready access to its authority. This is why the people from the Twin Cities who were concerned about the Monticello plant approached the more open State Pollution Control Agency.

Conflict Groups

Conflict is often part of political activity, for people frequently disagree over suggested public policy and struggle to have their ideas adopted by everyone. !Kung hunters, for example, occasionally differ over which water hole will make the most secure winter campsite and argue their positions at length with one another. Minnesota power company officials and environmentalists disagreed over the strictness of standards for the release of radioactive wastes. Their confrontation led to a prolonged conflict.

Conflict often involves more than a clash between a few individuals. It becomes the cause of larger social units called conflict groups, which are any groups that contend with each other over the formulation and application of public policy. Conflict groups typically take a particular viewpoint in regard to a policy decision and attempt to influence those in authority to decide the matter in the groups' favor. They do so in at least two ways. First, they approach decision-making bodies directly, arguing the merits of particular viewpoints and applying pressure to gain support for their positions. Second, they struggle with the conflict groups opposed to them, attempting to cause opponents to modify their positions and come to a compromise.

Conflict groups take several forms. First, any existing group can *become* a conflict group if its members decide to disagree with others about public policy. Kin groups, secret societies, factory organizations, or any other regularly established group may become a conflict group in this way. In his ethnographic account of the Nuer, Evans-Pritchard discusses the part played by kin groups in political conflict and notes that the organization of conflict follows the hierarchical pattern of Nuer patrilineal kin structure.[6] He argues that the patrilineal village is most likely to become involved in political conflict. When a public issue involving two closely related villages arises, these local kinship units are the competing groups. However, if the issue is more widespread, involving people who live at a greater distance, nearby villages will band together in opposition to a similarly constructed unit on the other side of the matter. He named this pattern of conflict group formation, segmentary opposition.

We can see the same kind of process at work in the United States. It is common for members of a family to conflict with each other over family level policy but stand together in the face of conflict with other families in neighborhood contro-

[6]E. F. Evans-Pritchard, *The Nuer*, Oxford: Clarendon Press, 1940.

versy. It is important to note that neither the Nuer patrilineal village nor the American family is designed solely to act in conflicts. Conflict becomes part of the activity of such groups only when their members decide to participate in it.

The power company represents such a conflict group in the dispute over the Monticello plant. It was not formed out of a need to participate in political conflict and acts in the political arena only when it is necessary to reach its goals.

A second kind of conflict group is a faction. Factions are conflict groups that exist solely for the purpose of contesting public policy and that represent divisions of existing social groups. Indian villages are well known for the operation of their factions. In these rural communities, men who wish to be important gather a host of followers around them, using ties associated with kinship, caste, economics, and friendship to recruit their followers. But most important, factions arise over public disputes, such as rights to irrigation water or the inclusion of guests on a wedding invitation. Once formed, the faction may outlive the original issue around which it formed and go on to contend over other public decisions. If, however, additional political conflict fails to materialize, factions usually dissolve.

A third kind of conflict group is the interest group. Interest groups form specifically around political issues. They are not factions because they do not represent a division of a community or society over public issues. Interest groups are most commonly found in complex societies where the political process tends to be impersonal so that people often feel they are cut out of the steps leading to a decision and where interests are liable to vary widely. The U.S. Supreme Court's decision to legalize abortion in the United States gave rise to a large number of locally organized interest groups. People for and opposed to an Equal Rights Amendment to the U.S. Constitution have also formed many interest groups to express their viewpoints.

The Citizens Environmental League

Such an interest group formed over the issue of the Monticello nuclear plant. Interested people organized a meeting of concerned people in a church basement. The gathering featured a professor from the university who had training both in applied physics and radiation biology. Alice Warrick joined about 150 other people to listen. The professor described the events leading up to the construction of the plant at Monticello, the plant operation, and his concerns about plans to release low levels of radiation into the air and the Mississippi River.

The power company, he began, had owned its site near Monticello for many years in anticipation of the time when the growing suburbs west and north of Minneapolis would need additional power. That time had arrived, and the company set about the process of contracting for the construction of a large power plant to be built on the Monticello site. Their decision to build a boiling water nuclear reactor came at a time when nuclear power was a bargain. The price of fossil fuels, used to drive the turbines of conventional electrical generating plants was increasing and had always been high in the upper Midwest because of the region's distance from the sources of such fuels. After authorizing the construction of a number of small, uneconomical, and marginally operational reactors in the late 1950s and early 1960s, the Atomic Energy Commission had approved two new basic designs for larger, more efficient nuclear generating plants to be supplied by Westinghouse and General Electric. Attracted by the economic profile and by the clean appearance of nuclear plants, the board of directors at the power company decided to buy General Electric's boiling water reactor for the job at Monticello, and construction began as soon as preliminary licenses were issued by the AEC.

The professor continued by talking about how the plant operated, what kind of fuel it used, and how wastes were treated. He pointed out that most of the highly radioactive by-products of the fission process in the reactor remained inside the fuel rods. He noted, however, some of the rods leak, releasing a variety of radioactive isotopes into the primary coolant, the water that flows through the pile and is heated by it into steam. The steam drives the turbines and is condensed once again in a heat exchanger cooled by river water. As nuclear wastes build up in the primary coolant, they eventually reach intolerable levels unless this water is replaced from time to time. It was a portion of the primary coolant, once it had been run through a chemical purification system, that was to be released into the river. The speaker went on to note that the amounts of radioactive matter released could get quite large if there was a substantial leakage from the fuel rods and that the AEC standards for human exposure to radiation levels were too lenient, particularly because they ignored the fact that isotopes could be concentrated millions of times over in the natural food chain.

When the professor was done and people finished asking him questions, the moderator requested those who were interested to stay and organize a group to fight for stricter regulations on the plant. Alice Warrick remained, as did about half the people at the meeting, and helped to organize a new interest group, the Citizens Environmental League (CEL). The new group joined several others in the area in a battle for "zero release," the demand that the power company dispose of its nuclear wastes by bottling them and shipping them to an out-of-state permanent storage area.

Leadership

Some people stand out in the political process. They may hold formal political positions such as president or mayor, or they may operate informally. Anyone who is able to influence the members of a group to act together is a leader. When Alice attended her first meeting on the nuclear pollution issue, she quickly noticed that several people in the room stood out. Most obvious was the evening speaker, a board member of another local environmental conservation group. He seemed to know a great deal about nuclear generators and the issues surrounding their operation and was a persuasive speaker when he talked about the problems of nuclear generating plants. There were also other people in the room who seemed to be important. For example, an older lady sat by the door and collected signatures on a petition that asked the PCA to deny the power company a license to release radioactive wastes. Another person, a young man reported to be a lawyer, had opened the evening meeting and seemed to be in charge of it. Less conspicuous, but clearly of some importance, were three or four more people who frequently conferred

An African king with subject. Leaders may be identified formally or they may act informally to affect the behavior of others.

with one another and the other leaders present. These people had organized the meeting, and as Alice was to find out later, they would be instrumental in organizing many of the activities designed to affect the Pollution Control Agency's decision about Monticello.

Leaders have the ability to use their cultural knowledge of social interaction to influence people and enable them to reach satisfactory public decisions. A Bhil headman, for example, must be a leader in this sense. Although his position is a formally recognized political identity, it does not give him authority to act unilaterally. Earlier we noted that in 1962 Bhil villagers living in Ratakote, India, were faced with the problem of a national election and that villagers expected to vote as a block for a particular slate of candidates. However, a great many people were running for a limited set of offices that year, making a decision on a slate difficult. The headman facilitated the process of choice by inviting political candidates to the village and by suggesting various issues that should concern villagers in their evaluation of candidates. When members of the community became confused about the many candidates who sought their vote, the headman discreetly suggested first one, then another slate and observed community reaction to them. When he sensed support forming around a particular candidate, he placed him together with others whom people liked. When consensus appeared to be at hand, he called a general meeting of village householders and, in the context of an open discussion, led those present to adopt the slate and informed them how to recognize party symbols so that they could place their "X" opposite the appropriate candidates. Although the headman was clearly able to introduce some of his own ideas into the decision-making process, he was nonetheless as much an organizer of the public decision-making process as he was a decision maker himself.

THE POLITICAL PROCESS

People who advance different proposals for public policy attempt to generate *support* for them. Support is anything that contributes to adoption of public policy and its enforcement. The two most important kinds of support are legitimacy and coercion, although it is easier to treat these two concepts as poles of a continuum instead of as distinct categories. Legitimacy refers to support that is derived from a people's positive evaluation of public officials and public policy. Some may think that a particular policy is wrong, but accept it because in the long run they feel that the government, which laid down the policy, is a valuable instrument in their lives and worth support. A policy may also be seen as legitimate because supernatural beings have decreed it. Coercion, on the other hand, is a kind of support based on the threat or use of force or other adverse action, or the promise of short-term benefit. Someone may decide to support a public decision because it will cost his or her life if he or she does not. The policy may be repugnant to the individual, but the decision will bring immediate benefit.

The members of the Citizens Environmental League attempted to generate both kinds of support in their quest for strict discharge standards for the Monticello plant. They "put pressure" on the power company and the Pollution Control Agency. For example, the Citizens Environmental League organized what came to be known as the "NSP Picnic." On a chilly day in the spring of 1969 about 200 members of several environmental groups gathered at a shopping center in a northwestern suburb of Minneapolis. The Warricks arrived to find people attaching signs to the 75 cars that had gathered for the drive out to Monticello. Signs carried messages such as "Leukemia Is Penny Cheap at NSP," a slogan based on the company's own advertising about their inexpensive electricity. Another read, "Stop Northern States Pollution Company!," and still another carried a longer message about the harmful effects of radiation.

Public opposition to nuclear power plants has grown steadily over the years. Here a crowd of demonstrators contests the decision to build such a plant at Diablo Canyon.

When the group was ready, the cars pulled out in a line toward their destination, followed by the camera crews of two local television stations. When the caravan reached the inoperative Elk River plant, an earlier reactor that had failed, the group stopped to hold a funeral service, intoning with mock sadness the passing of another fine nuclear facility. On the road once again the caravan pulled up on a hill overlooking the construction site of the new power plant. They were met there by a team of public relations men from Northern States Power Company, who, armed with a small power-assisted lectern, began a lecture on the generation of electricity and the safety of nuclear power plants. The NSP representatives, who seemed to think of their audience as frightened, uninformed people on the order of "fluoride nuts" (as one later put it), were finally shouted down. The Warricks joined the other environmentalists in filling about 100 balloons with helium and launching them into the air. Each balloon carried a message about the danger of airborne radioactive wastes, and the group hoped to show people by this technique that prevailing winds would carry plant effluents right across the Twin Cities area. Unfortunately, the winds were not prevailing that day, and the message carried by the balloons was read by only a few surprised farmers living northeast of the plant. Once the balloons had been launched, the assembly drove to the Monticello village park where people ate lunch to the occasional jeers of the town inhabitants, who looked on the nuclear plant as an asset to their community.

The NSP picnic was only one of a complex set of strategies used by members of the CEL to put pressure on the power company and the PCA. Figure 11-1 represents a taxonomy of many of these strategies. The aims of the Citizens Environmental League, at this point, were to press for zero emissions from the plant.

This list, although partial, is the kind of cultural knowledge that the CEL used to influence the Pollution Control Agency's decision. In specific settings, additional strategies were also employed to pressure the board and the company. For

Political Action Strategies			
Write letters			
Make public appearances	Testify at hearings		
	Talk in public meetings		
	Debate		
	Give TV interviews		
Demonstrate	Hold NSP picnic		
	Picket		
	Perform satirical play		
	Organize marches		
Display signs on cars			
Attack company	Damage IBM card	Knock out bridges between holes	
		Repunch card	
		Wrinkle card	
		Chew on card (baby)	
		Bite card (dog)	
	Pay improperly		
Telephone people			
Telegraph people			
Make press releases			
Attend hearings			
Organize meetings			
Meet with strategic people			

FIGURE 11-1

A partial taxonomy of CEL political action strategies.

example, the CEL attempted to recruit as many people as it could to attend PCA hearings in an effort to get an audience sympathetic to its point of view. Once in place, the audience followed rules of general decorum, although it might groan at opposition points it thought especially egregious or cheer in a refined way for its own spokespeople. One trick used by some people involved cassette tape recorders. When company members testified, or members of the agency publically stated their views, a few members of the audience would angrily hold up the microphones of their tape recorders as if to capture permanently damaging quotes. It also gave agency and company representatives the impression that the audience was hostile, knowledgeable, and well prepared. The object of these many strategies is partly made clear by their definition in Figure 11-2. Above all, mem-

FIGURE 11-2
Some attributes of political action strategies.

Strategies	Get publicity	Persuade people	Show strength	Inconvenience company	Face-to-face contact	Special knowledge
Write letters	No	Yes	Yes	No	No	Some
Make public appearances	Sometimes	Yes	No	No	Yes	Yes
Demonstrate	Yes	No	Yes	No	Yes	No
Display signs on car	No	No	Yes	No	No	No
Attack company	No	No	Yes	Yes	No	No
Telephone people	No	Yes	Yes	No	Verbal	Some
Telegraph people	No	No	Yes	No	No	No
Make press releases	Yes	Yes	No	No	No	Yes
Attend hearings	No	No	Yes	No	Yes	No
Circulate petitions	No	Yes	Yes	No	Yes	Some
Organize meetings	Sometimes	Yes	Yes	No	Yes	Some
Meet with strategic people	No	Yes	No	No	Yes	Yes

bers of the Citizens Environmental League wished to make the nuclear waste issue public. If people heard about it, they reasoned, they would not like the idea of using the river as a "sewer" for nuclear wastes. Thus obtaining publicity was an important function of many CEL strategies. Just as important, however, was making the case for stricter standards, and many activities of the Citizens Environmental League, from writing letters to testifying at hearings, accomplished this end. The company also presented a strong argument, and the CEL found it necessary to counter its position with their own views. The group needed to demonstrate its strength; they reasoned that the PCA would pay little attention to a small fringe group.

In addition to indicating some of the important strategies used by the Citizens Environmental League, Figure 11-2 also points out some organizational problems faced by the group. Some activities required face-to-face contact with people, something that many individuals found difficult to do. Other events required that members have special knowledge about the issue, particularly about the generation of electrical power, nuclear plant design, and evidence about safety hazards. In planning their strategies, the leaders of the movement had to take these factors into consideration to successfully achieve their goals.

An important part of the league's case was its policy proposal and supporting arguments. Although many league strategies were basically coercive, many of its arguments were an attempt to gain legitimacy by persuading others that the plant should, indeed, be required to truck its wastes to offsite burial facilities in other states for reasons of public safety. To underscore this position, league members argued that no amount of radiation was "safe," that radiation caused cancer and genetic damage, that not much was known about low-level radiation, so that the company was really running an experiment on the Twin Cities population, that evidence shows an increase in cancer rates and infant mortality in the vicinity of nuclear plants, that power companies are run by people who want to make money, not safeguard public health, and that existing nuclear plants have far exceeded their projected discharge levels. Again, the main object of these arguments was to indicate that the waste materials were unsafe and to be avoided and that the company was no judge of safety standards and thus an illegitimate agent for its own regulation.

Finally, members of the Citizens Environmental League had to understand the company's strategies. Figure 11-3 presents a list of strategies used by the power company as they were categorized by environmentalists.

The company also developed a line of argument stressing that

1. People receive a lot of radiation through X rays, airplane flights, television sets, and natural background sources—a little more won't hurt.
2. The company is the only party to the conflict with experts on nuclear technology—only the company's word can be trusted on the matter.
3. Existing plants have never harmed anyone.
4. Offsite disposal of wastes would cost more money than it was worth.
5. The Monticello plant has a series of safeguards that make it perfectly reliable.
6. The company carefully monitors conditions in the plant and atomic wastes.

Company Tactics	Spy	
	Speak in public	
	Disseminate propaganda	
	Advertise	
	Pack official hearings	
	Retain Washington lawyers	
	Hire biased consultants	
	Debate	
	Publish propaganda	
	Influence appointments to PCA	
	Oversimplify the facts	
	Invest to create chain reaction	
	Stereotype opponents	
	Lobby	Entertain government officials
		Visit government officials
		Call government officials
		Persuade government officials

FIGURE 11-3
Company tactics as they were categorized by opponents of the nuclear power plant.

7. There is a 10-year doubling period of electrical power needs creating a demand for new plants.
8. The company has an enormous investment in the plant already and asks that this not be wasted by a set of limits that would prevent its use.

PUBLIC POLICY AND ENFORCEMENT

Once public policy is made, people comply with it on the basis of legitimacy or co-ercion. In the case of Northern States Power Company, the Pollution Control Agency finally decided to adopt the recommendations of its own consultant. The consultant suggested that the PCA adopt, as a standard, the emission levels pro-jected for the nuclear plant by its manufacturers. This standard amounted to about 3 percent of the original limit set on the plant by the AEC and, as often oc-curs when there is a controversy, it represented a compromise between the posi-tions of the conflicting parties. The Citizens Environmental League was not satis-fied with the release of any wastes into the environment, while the company claimed that despite the manufacturer's prognostications, the plant could not meet the new standards without adding equipment, a step that the company later agreed to take.

However, the Pollution Control Agency lost its authority to regulate the plant altogether when the power company sued, claiming that only the Atomic Energy Commission was empowered by Congress to regulate nuclear plants and that this power overrode state authority. The matter went all the way to the Supreme Court, and much to the discouragement of CEL members who had worked so hard to bring about strict standards, the high court upheld the company's position. However, the uproar had damaged the local image of the company, and to recover, it tried to comply with the PCA's standards, regardless of the agency's lack of authority.

Despite this outcome, the political process concerning nuclear power continues in the Twin Cities as well as in the rest of the country. To improve its credibility, the Atomic Energy Commission later decided to separate its regulatory from its promotional arms. The resulting Nuclear Regulatory Commission oversees nuclear plant safety today. Since 1969, public opposition to nuclear plants has grown. Orders for new nuclear plants rose in the early 1970s, but many were canceled as plants became more expensive and public resistance grew. Nuclear power plant opponents have gained influence as engineers and physicists have defected from power companies, the Nuclear Regulatory Commission staff, and other parts of the industry. Subsequent studies of radiation effects have also raised questions about plant safety as has the persistent problem of waste disposal. Perhaps the most important event of all was the recent serious nuclear accident at the Three Mile Island plant near Harrisburg, Pennsylvania, which occurred on March 28, 1979.

SUMMARY

The political system is the process of making and carrying out public policy according to cultural categories and rules. Policy refers to any guideline that can lead directly to action; public refers to the people affected by a policy decision. The political system is composed of a political organization and operates by means of the political process. Forms of political organization include several types, two of which are governments and stateless societies. A government is a political group composed of political specialists and associated with a state. Stateless societies are groups that lack a formal government and clear-cut territory. Authority is an important aspect of political organization because it defines the right to make and enforce public policy. It is typically assigned by people to political identities. Conflict groups are those that contend with each other over the formulation and application of public policy. A conflict group may be any group whose members decide to disagree with others about public policy, or it may be specially formed to pursue political conflict such as factions and interest groups. Finally, the political process often includes leaders or people who are able to influence the members of a group to act together.

Underlying the political process is the notion of support, anything that contributes to the adoption of public policy and its enforcement. One common kind of support is legitimacy, which is derived from people's positive evaluations of public officials and public policy. Another is coercion, which is based on the threat or use of force or other adverse action, or the promise of short-term benefit. In this chapter we saw how these forms of support were used by the Citizens Environmental League to effect the formation of public policy concerning a Minnesota power plant.

MAJOR CONCEPTS

POLITICAL SYSTEM	FACTION
PUBLIC	SEGMENTARY OPPOSITION
POLICY	INTEREST GROUP
GOVERNMENT	LEADERSHIP
STATE	SUPPORT
STATELESS SOCIETY	LEGITIMACY
AUTHORITY	COERCION
CONFLICT GROUP	

SELECTED READINGS

Cohen, Ronald, and John Middleton (editors): *Comparative Political Systems: Studies in the Politics of Pre-industrial Societies*, Garden City, N.Y.: Natural History Press, 1967.
A collection of articles on political organization and process. Includes political structure of societies from many parts of the world.

Mair, Lucy: *Primitive Government*, Harmondsworth, England: Penguin Books, 1962.
A discussion of the political system including stateless societies, African states, and politics in the modern world.

Schapera, I.: *Government and Politics in Tribal Societies*, New York: Schocken, 1967. First published in 1956 by Watts: London.
A series of public lectures by Schapera on aspects of the political system with illustrations from Africa.

Swartz, Marc J. (editor): *Local-level Politics*, Chicago: Aldine, 1968.
A broad collection of articles representing a wide range of thinking in political anthropology. Includes sections on basic concepts, the relationship between politics and ritual, the political middleperson, and political contests.

Swartz, Marc J., Victor W. Turner, and Arthur Tuden (editors): *Political Anthropology*, Chicago: Aldine, 1966.
One of the first collections of articles to attempt a broad definition and illustration of the work extant in political anthropology. The book is organized around such concepts as political conflict, authority, and rituals. It includes a final set of selections on political fields and their boundaries.

CHAPTER TWELVE

Law
and
Order

An orderly social life is an astonishing achievement. It requires mechanisms of social control that induce members of a society to keep their actions within well-defined limits. In contrast to other social animals, humans have the potential for a
wide range of behavior; people must limit their behavioral range if a society is to
continue. The primary means of gaining conformity and order from individual
members is through enculturation. As we acquire our culture we learn the appropriate ways to look at experience, to define our existence, and to feel about life.
Each system of cultural knowledge contains implicit values, concepts of what is
desirable, and we come to share these values with other people. Slowly, with the
acquisition of culture, most people find they *want* to do what they *must* do; the requirements of an orderly social life become personal goals. Then, throughout life,
we encounter many reminders that reinforce conformity. Informal social pressures encourage us to abide by cultural rules. Rewards of recognition and praise
motivate us to live in the accepted way. Negative sanctions, such as ridicule, rejection, and criticism, act as powerful forces of social control. Religious rituals and
secular ceremonies of all kinds reinforce our common values and standards as well
as individual commitments to following them.

However, the potential for disruptive behavior always lies just beneath the surface of every society. No culture satisfies the needs of all persons equally; cultural
values are often contradictory, creating frustration and hostility; misunderstandings occur even when everyone believes he or she is living up to cultural expectations. People disagree on the allocation of scarce resources and the goals that
should be jointly pursued. Sometimes individuals violate accepted traditions and
rules; disruptive behavior occurs in all societies, and conflict is a recurrent feature
of social life.

The maintenance of social order and control does not mean the absence of disputes, but instead involves their ongoing resolution. It is when a dispute requires
resolving that law enters the picture. *Every culture contains agreed-on ways to*

settle disputes. The settlement of disputes, however, is not the only function of law in a particular society, and the ethnographer will seek to trace the many relationships between law and other customs and institutions. For example, one consequence of law is that it prevents disputes from occurring by reminding people of appropriate behavior. In addition, law may function to create a group of specialized professionals; it may also result in a stigmatized group of people such as "public drunks" or "ex-cons." Anthropologists study all the functions of law in society, but they use one universal function to define law itself. This universal function of law is to settle some of the disputes that regularly occur in social life.

THE NATURE OF LAW

Law is the cultural knowledge that people use to settle disputes by means of agents who have recognized authority. A young man shovels snow from a neighbor's sidewalks all winter. Before the first snow they agree to a price of $2 per hour. The neighbor then refuses to pay, resulting in a dispute. The young snow shoveler files a petition in small claims court and both parties appear before the judge, who settles the dispute. A recognized authority has intervened and the process of law has been carried out.

The anthropologist who studies law begins by locating trouble cases, the disputes that occur within a society. Instead of looking for courts or legal *forms,* the ethnographer seeks to describe the process of dispute settlement. When did the young man shoveling snow first become aware that his neighbor would not pay him his wages? What did he do to try and settle the dispute? How did the difference escalate into a conflict that led to the small claims court? What processes occurred in this court to settle the dispute? Some of the strategies for resolving conflict in any society will bring in agents such as the judge in this example. The involvement of such persons signals the possible presence of a legal case. Other trouble cases will be more difficult to classify, because the disputes are ongoing and no settlement has been achieved or because certain cases are settled outside the formal legal system. In order to understand the different levels of law in action, we want to examine dispute settlement among the Zapotec of Mexico. The law ways of this group have been studied extensively by Laura Nader.

A Zapotec Case Study

The land rover disappeared in a cloud of dust on its way back to Oaxaca City. The anthropologist adjusted the shoulder straps on the backpack, turned away from the end of the road, and began to follow the two Zapotec Indian guides. The trail led north, climbing along the edge of steep valleys, crossing over mountain ridges, and winding back and forth to make a steady gain in altitude. Accustomed to living at 5000 feet above sea level, the two guides walked rapidly, oblivious to the hard breathing of their American companion. In every direction, scattered over much of the 36,000 square miles of Oaxaca State in southern Mexico, the anthropologist knew there were small Zapotec villages. The three of them headed toward the Rincon district, which means "the corner," calling attention to the fact

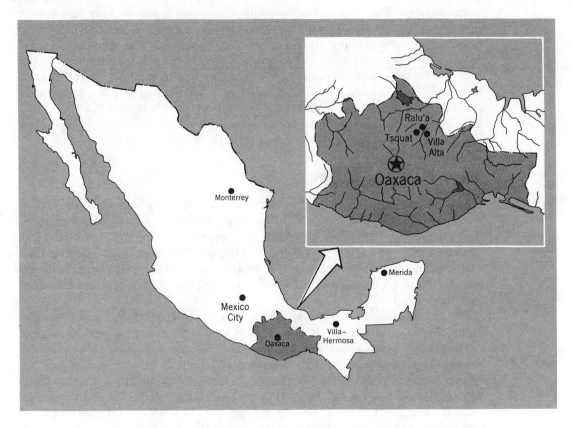

Location of Ralu'a, the Zapotec village discussed in this chapter, is shown here.

that the area is partially encircled by three high mountain peaks. As they walked, the anthropologist could see the distant and formidable Zempoateptl Mountain reaching to more than 10,000 feet; Maceta and El Machin, the two other peaks, would come into view before they reached their destination, the pueblo of Ralu'a. One of the Zapotec men spoke Spanish and had told the anthropologist as they started, "We are called the people of the corner, *Rinconeros*, because we live between the peaks." The sun was high on this day in early May 1957 and the sky clear; it was several weeks before the rainy season would begin. Wild orchids were in bloom everywhere. The mountains had a kind of awesome beauty for the anthropologist, particularly since she had anticipated the sight for many months. As she walked behind the guides, she wondered why no other social scientist had ever come before to this place, to live and study among these people.

The Zapotec guides pushed on, stopping only for water now and then at the edge of fast-flowing mountain streams. During the first hour they had passed scattered fields of coffee plants in bloom and sugarcane, evidence that a pueblo or homestead was nearby, enfolded in some mountain niche. The anthropologist

The Oaxacan village of Ralu'a lies deep in the Sierra Madre. It has the largest population of any of the pueblos in this area. This is a market town where people come every Monday from the surrounding area.

would like to have stopped to inquire about these settlements and to rest, but the two guides never hesitated, pressing on toward their destination. The sun had already disappeared behind the highest peak when, after a 3½-hour walk, they came to Ralu'a, a pueblo of 2000 people. Unexpectedly, as they came over a rise, houses appeared everywhere; children played on the paths, and women could be seen carrying firewood. The anthropologist felt a sense of excitement as she looked down on the town that would be her home for many months to come. Here she would live and work and make friends; from here she would travel to other villages and nearby settlements in her efforts to discover the cultural ways of the Zapotec; and here she would try to understand Zapotec law, to describe the cultural rules these people used when settling disputes.

As they entered the edge of the pueblo, she wondered how these people would receive her. Would they understand why she had come? In Oaxaca City she had met an engineer, a government employee who had friends in Ralu'a. He had made tentative arrangements for her to stay with a family while she conducted her field study. All was excitement at the home of her hosts, for a fiesta was in progress to celebrate the return of religious pilgrims from the Sanctuario in Veracruz. Her hosts seemed polite but not enthusiastic as they invited her to join them in the fiesta meal of special foods. After they had eaten, the head of the household came to her and asked, "Are you a Catholic? If you are not a Catholic, you cannot stay here. We do not want Protestants in our town." Surprised by this question, she explained her role and assured him that she belonged to the original Catholic church (Eastern Orthodox).

It would be many weeks before she would fully appreciate what lay behind this simple question about her religion. She was to discover that it concerned authority, conflict, and the process of law and dispute settlement, the very areas she had come to investigate. Before two weeks had elapsed a message came from the priest: she was to come to his house immediately. She entered and, after a brief exchange in Spanish, he said, "You are a Protestant missionary! Why have you come to our pueblo?" Nothing would convince him that it was not so; even the letter of recommendation that she brought from a priest in Oaxaca was dismissed as a fake, and a wire of confirmation from that priest that she was an anthropologist and a good Christian did not convince him. Although others would eventually accept her, the priest in Ralu'a would remain unconvinced, spreading the word from the pulpit and in the streets that she was really a Protestant missionary. Several years earlier some missionaries had come to Ralu'a and, as a result of winning converts, conflicts erupted that led to burning of Protestant homes. The dispute reached enormous proportions for this small pueblo and was only settled through the process of law when the state government forced the town to pay heavy fines for damage inflicted.

When the anthropologist was called to the home of the priest in the Zapotec pueblo of Ralu'a, she became a party to a dispute. He accused her of being a Protestant missionary; she denied it. Although she appealed to another priest to confirm her identity, he did not have the authority to settle the dispute. Like many troubles that beset human interaction, this dispute was never settled, and the anthropologist had to work around the difficulties it created with other individuals in the village. The dispute remained below the level of the law, but it is conceivable that the priest or the anthropologist could have appealed to some agent whose authority was recognized and who could settle the case. It would then have become a legal matter.

The Case of the Washing Stone

One of the earliest disputes that came to the anthropologist's attention occurred at a Ralu'a well several months after she arrived among the Zapotec. She awoke as usual one morning to the sound of the women in the household getting ready to go to the mill. It was 5:00 A.M., and each morning at this time the women in Ralu'a arose to take their corn to nearby mills. The men were still asleep as the anthropologist dressed and prepared to go with the women. It was not yet light at this hour of the morning, but the daily walk to the mill was exhilarating. Other women greeted them and, at the mill, while they waited to have their corn ground, they visited with each other. Soon each would return home to prepare tortillas, fix breakfast for the family, and make lunches for the men who must walk many miles to their fields for a day of work. But now they caught up on the local news and enjoyed visiting.

This morning two women were earnestly discussing an argument that had occurred on the previous day at Los Remedios, one of the town wells. Carmen had gone to the well to wash the family clothes, and instead of using the flat slab of stone that belonged to her, she selected one near a friend so they could visit as they worked. Like other women she looked forward to this task because it enabled her to visit and gossip with others in the neighborhood, a pleasant change from working alone inside her house. But hardly 20 minutes had passed when the owner of the washing stone appeared, and instead of taking another place she angrily asked Carmen to move. As Carmen began to gather her wet clothes together, she loudly commented on the other woman's generosity. Insults began to fly, and the situation became especially tense when Carmen "accidentally" splashed water on the newcomer's dress as she went off to finish washing on her own slab. Some said Carmen should have moved to her own stone without comment; others declared that the second woman was wrong and should have gone quietly to another place to wash. Someone recalled a similar conflict several years earlier when a woman had taken the matter to the *municipio*, or town hall, where the *presidente* had settled the dispute. Some of the women wondered whether the trouble of yesterday would go that far.

It was the end of the summer before the dispute over washing stones reached the boiling point and became a case of law, but it did not happen in the way the anthropologist had expected, for no one took the dispute to the *municipio*. The incident at the well did not die down; the two women continued to make insulting remarks in public, and others began to take sides. Then a similar conflict arose between several other women who were not using the stones that belonged to them. At night in the *cantina* as the men drank *mescal*, an alcoholic drink made from the fermented juice of agave plants, they talked of the disputes they had learned about from their wives. Some men reported that at the wells where their wives washed clothes no such fights had occurred; everyone agreed that the problem was primarily at Los Remedios.

The bickering and fighting continued until one day people noticed that the water at Los Remedios had begun to dry up. Some said this was caused by the fighting. The men who belonged to the Well Association, a group that worked to maintain the wells, called a special meeting and decided that they must take ac tion to save the water. They formed a work party and improved the well to ensure more water, but they also removed all the slabs of stone used for washing. In place of these privately owned washing places they constructed 24 shallow tubs from cement and announced that no one could own or reserve one of these spaces. They belonged to the well and were to be used on a first-come, first-serve basis. The priest blessed the new well, and the disputes were settled. Although some women complained that they liked the old way better, everyone recognized the authority of the men's Well Association, and the change was accepted.

Three Kinds of Disputes

The conflict over washing stones did not become a matter for the legal process until many weeks after it began. This case illustrates the fact that in all societies some disputes occur outside the law. We can distinguish three kinds of disputes.

Infralegal Disputes

Any dispute that is below the level of the legal process is an infralegal dispute. These conflicts may not be serious enough to require the attention of someone in authority. And even serious disputes may be overlooked, concealed, or patiently endured. The argument between Carmen and the other woman regarding the washing stone, for example, was an infralegal dispute. No one took the necessary steps to bring this single conflict to the attention of one or another authority. It might have died after the first encounter but, because the women continued to insult each other, it stayed alive. Infralegal disputes such as this can last for years, never boiling over, perhaps slowly fading away. The men belonging to the Well Association could have overlooked the matter, hoping it would dissipate in time. Most cultures have numerous ways to deal with infralegal disputes, including avoidance, fighting, verbal insults, prayer, and mutual agreement to end the dispute.

Extralegal Disputes

When disputes remain outside the process of law but develop into repeated acts of violence between groups, they become extralegal disputes. *War* refers to violent extralegal disputes that take place between separate political groups. Feuds, on the other hand, refer to violent conflicts between subgroups of the same society. Several gangs on the streets of Chicago engage in periodic "rumbles," in which they attack each other violently. The police may attempt to stop these feuds, but they often continue for years despite all efforts of law enforcers.

On occasion incipient feuds develop among the Zapotec, but they almost always die or become legal disputes. When the missionaries came to Ralu'a, the town became polarized between Protestants and Catholics. The conflict developed into a feud between these two groups and was only brought to an end by the intervention of the state government. Not long after the Well Association had set-

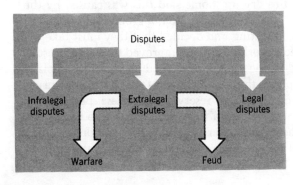

A taxonomy of major dispute types.

tled the dispute over the washing stones, the anthropologist learned about another dispute, an *incipient feud* that was extralegal. One of the pueblos near Ralu'a has a scattered residence pattern in which villagers build their homes at the site of their land. These *ranchos*, as they are called, tend to isolate families from one another. The anthropologist visited these *ranchos* from time to time in the course of her research. On arriving at the Mendozas' *rancho* one afternoon, she found things in an uproar. It was late in the summer, and the fields of corn were ready to harvest. Señor Mendoza had checked his fields the previous week and decided to let them ripen for a few more days; then, with his two oldest sons, he had gone to Ralu'a to work and earn some cash. The day before he returned Señora Mendoza discovered that someone had come during the night and harvested their corn, stealing almost all their crop. She had gone to several of the neighboring *ranchos* to tell them of this misfortune and to see if anyone might know the thief. At the *rancho* of one neighbor, Señor Francisco, she had become angry and accused him of stealing their corn. An argument ensued amidst denials and further insults.

The family discussed the loss and what they might do for many hours, finally going to bed well after midnight. Suddenly, everyone was awakened by someone making noise outside their house. "Ay, ay! Mendozas! Mendozas!" someone was calling. "Firecrackers, firecrackers," the voice called again, using the nickname of the Mendoza family. "If you want to accuse me of stealing your corn come on out here! I have my machete, and unless you can find your corn on my *rancho* I will use it on you!" Everyone was awake and tense; they knew it was Señor Francisco, but no one went outside, and soon he disappeared into the night. The next morning they discovered that he had smashed the washing stones near the house. The Mendozas were very upset with their double loss, but because they could not prove that Señor Francisco had stolen their corn, they decided not to take further action. Had they retaliated, the feud would have become full blown; had they taken the matter to court, it would have become a legal dispute.

Legal Disputes

The ethnographer who investigates the process of law in a non-Western society must collect data on all kinds of disputes. Since any conflict can be transformed overnight into a legal dispute involving some agent with recognized authority, it is important to examine the range of ways that people handle such troubles. By means of various ethnographic discovery procedures, one begins to focus more and more on legal cases, those that are settled by people or groups with authority.

THE STRUCTURE OF LEGAL CULTURE

By examining dispute cases, observing their outcome, and questioning the parties involved, one can describe a goodly portion of the law ways of a community. Such legal knowledge can be analyzed into three different aspects. First, the most explicit aspect of legal knowledge includes *substantive law* and *procedural law*, which are interrelated. At a more implicit level, underlying these rules, are the

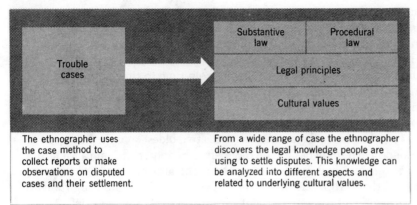

The ethnographer uses the case method to collect reports or make observations on disputed cases and their settlement.

From a wide range of case the ethnographer discovers the legal knowledge people are using to settle disputes. This knowledge can be analyzed into different aspects and related to underlying cultural values.

FIGURE 12-1
The Structure of Legal Knowledge.

fundamental *legal principles* that determine the shape of the law in a particular society. Finally, there is a common core of *cultural values* that influence the legal principles and link the law of any culture to other domains of that culture. These aspects of legal culture are shown in Figure 12-1. We will consider each of them briefly in the context of Zapotec law.

Substantive Law

The term "law" is most often used in our own society to refer to substantive law, the legal statutes that define right and wrong. Phrases such as, "He broke the law" or "It is illegal to bring liquor across the state line," refer to substantive law. It is easy for us to assume that substantive rules can be equated with written statutes, but this is not always the case in our own society, and most of the world's cultures do not have written laws at all. But all people have agreed-on substantive rules. Let us look at an example of an unwritten law from our own society.

Until recently every city in the United States had passed legislation that made it a crime to appear drunk in public. For many years in the city of Seattle this substantive rule was used to make more than 10,000 arrests each year. Although the law against public drunkenness seems clear and simple, ethnographic investigation of individual cases in Seattle shows that many other substantive rules of a complex nature were actually being used. In practice, the police used their own discretion to arrest some drunks but not others. The unwritten rule was, "If you see a poor man on skid row who is drunk, arrest him; those of the middle and upper classes who are drunk in other parts of town need not be arrested." A tramp from skid row who had been arrested many times reported the following experience. Standing outside the University Club located several blocks from skid row, he observed men coming out of the club in states of obvious intoxication. A policeman not only saw the same men, but assisted them into cabs for transportation home.

The substantive law of Ralu'a contains many specific rules. Some are part of a written legal code, others must be inferred from what people say and do in dispute

The municipio *or town hall of Ralu'a. This large, rectangular building has two rooms and two small jails. The various government officials have their offices here and town meetings are held. It is here that disputes are settled of a legal nature.*

cases. Many cases end up in the town hall, the *municipio*, a two-room, adobe building in the center of town. Here certain officials hold a kind of court to settle disputes. Thirteen respected men make up an advisory group for the pueblo, the *principales*. Each year this group nominates three men for the position of village chairman, or *presidente*, one of whom is elected by the village to serve for 1 year. The *presidente*, in turn, appoints these same *principales* for another 1-year term. Working closely with the *presidente* is a man elected to the office of *sindico*, who runs the communal work program of the pueblo and is also head of the town police. There are 12 *policia* who serve under two lieutenants and a chief of police. Each year the outgoing men of this police force nominate other men, generally those who have been the biggest troublemakers during the year, to take over as replacements. They are then elected by the village as a whole, and the roughest man of all becomes the chief of police for the year. The *presidente* and the *sindico*, working together, handle minor disputes such as drunkenness, fighting, flirting, slander, boundary trespass, and theft. There is a third elected official, the *alcalde*, a kind of justice of the peace, who presides over more serious disputes. The *presi-*

dente will often pass more serious cases as well as any cases that he cannot resolve directly to the *alcalde*. More serious cases or those that the *alcalde* cannot resolve are passed on to the district court. While the *presidente* and the *sindico* have various duties, the *alcalde* deals only with legal matters. We can see substantive law in action among the Zapotec if we examine two specific cases.

The Case of the Flirting Husband

The first dispute involves a violation of rules that prohibit flirting. An unmarried woman, Señorita Zoalage, came to the *presidente* early on a Tuesday morning. She complained that a married man, Señor Huachic, had flirted with her. He appeared outside her house and made the equivalent of American wolf-calls shortly after dark on Monday night on his way home from the market. The *presidente* talked over the matter with the *sindico*, and someone was sent to notify Señor Huachic to appear in court that afternoon. It was now 2:00 P.M. and the *presidente* sat behind a long table at the front of the *presidencia*, one of the rooms in the town hall. Both Señor Huachic and Señorita Zoalage sat before him. After presenting the complaint to Señor Huachic, the *presidente* waited for his response. "Yes," he admitted, "I did what she said, but only because this woman here, Señorita Zoalage, flirted with me last week! She even invited me to come with her to collect firewood!" After some discussion about the particulars of the case the *presidente* said, "Señorita Zoalage, I am going to fine you 30 pesos for flirting with Señor Huachic. And Señor Huachic, you are fined 60 pesos for flirting with Señorita Zoalage. You are a married man and should have been at home with your wife." After warning them to refrain from further exhibitions of such behavior he dismissed them, they paid their fines, and returned to their homes. Each had violated a substantive rule that holds flirting to be illegal. In some cases individuals refuse to pay fines and, as a result, may be detained in jail or compelled to work on a community project.

The Case of the Disobedient Son

The second case sheds light on substantive rules involving the relationships between parents and children. It was relatively easy to elicit cultural rules for this relationship. For example, one evening after the anthropologist had been in Ralu'a for 8 months, she was having dinner with a Zapotec family. The father had just told the others about a son who had been sent to jail in the district capital because when his father had beat him he had struck back, hitting his father. The anthropologist asked quizzically, "And for this they sent him to jail?"

"Of course," he said, looking rather surprised that she would ask such a stupid question.

"But," she said, seeking to enlarge on the discussion, "many men beat their wives, and they never go to jail for that!"

"Yes," the father responded, "but wives are one thing, fathers another."

It seemed a good place to introduce a hypothetical question and so she asked, "But what if the father beats his son harshly, and the father is in the wrong? Is it still wrong for the son to strike his father?"

The son in the family spoke up, entering the discussion with a serious tone. "Fathers are never in the wrong for beating their sons. They always do it for their own good."

Still not satisfied, the anthropologist asked one last question. "All right, but sons grow up and become men. Under your law could a father ever be proved guilty for doing wrong to a son, even if he is a grown man?"

The father's answer brought looks of agreement from the others, "A father cannot do wrong with his children." There the discussion ended, but several days later she observed a case in the *presidencia* that underscored this substantive rule of Zapotec law.[1]

Señor Benjamin Mendoza Cruz had complained to the court about his son, Clemente Mendoza, who was 25 years of age. Because the complaint had been made several days earlier, both men were sitting before the *presidente*. Señor Cruz repeated his charge. "I have coffee planted on my land near one of the neighboring *ranchos*. Someone harvested some of my ripe coffee beans, and I thought the thief was from the neighboring pueblo, but a woman who has the land next to mine said she saw my son harvesting the coffee. I demand that he repay me for the coffee he has stolen."

The *presidente* turned to the son, Clemente Mendoza, waiting for him to speak. His eyes were on the floor; he did not look at the *presidente* or his father as he spoke. "Yes," he said, "I admit that I went to his field and cut some coffee. A year ago he allowed me to cut some coffee on his property, and I was confident he would give the coffee to me, but I am at fault, and now he can decide how to punish me. I have committed a crime against him and now I wish he would forgive me." There was a long pause when the son finished speaking. The *presidente* sat silently as the secretary continued writing. Then the father spoke slowly. "I am, as his father, very sad that my son Clemente should have done this wickedness to me. I did not believe that it was he until the woman told me. Now I will leave it to his *Municipio Presidente* to decide what is suitable. As his father I have to help him and look after him, but he should not act this way, disposing of the fruit of my harvest without my consent."

Another period of silence followed; flies buzzed noisily around the room. It was warm and the *presidente* thought about the man and his son, how he would settle the case. He recalled that fathers should provide for their sons when they came asking for a bride price, but Señor Cruz had already given more than once to his son for this purpose; Clemente had spent it on other things. Yes, it was the son who was at fault. He turned to him now. "Now you heard what your father said, and I will tell you that your father does not have an obligation to give you, his son, *anything*." He raised his voice on the last word as if to emphasize the great distance between fathers and sons. He continued, "Nor is a father obliged to give you what is his. If a father loves his son very much, he may give him something, but nobody can force him to do so. Now, you have abused him and, as you have ad-

---

[1]This case is presented in the excellent ethnographic film *To Make the Balance*, Berkeley: University of California Extension Media Center, and also in "Styles of Court Procedure: To Make the Balance," in *Law in Culture and Society*, Laura Nader (editor), Chicago: Aldine, 1969.

Inside the municipio *the* presidente *hears the case of a father accusing his son of stealing his coffee, an unusual instance of filial disobedience. The* presidente *listens first to the father, then to the son as the secretary makes a record of the case. Although it appears that an informal discussion is taking place, a formal court case is in progress.*

mitted, there is no reason why your father should help you because you committed this wrong." Clemente Mendoza had been afraid of his father all of his life. After his mother died, his father remarried, and he found it even more difficult to get along with the old man. Now he sat in silence, his eyes shifting nervously, focused on the floor most of the time as he listened to the *presidente* ask, "Are you now both ready to come to an agreement?" They would accept his settlement.

"Clemente Mendoza," the *presidente* addressed the guilty son, "you shall repay your father for the coffee that you took without permission. Without delay you have to deliver the 25 pounds of dried coffee to your father, and the deadline is Friday, the 21st of this month, and for the wrong you have committed I impose on you a 200-peso fine, which you have to pay today." The secretary prepared an agreement that finalized the ending of the dispute, and it was soon ready for signing. More than an hour had passed since they first appeared before the *presidente*. The agreement showed the amount Clemente would repay his father as well as the fine payable to the *municipio*. The agreement was shown to both parties, and the *presidente* addressed them one more time.

"Clemente Mendoza, you should realize that both you and your father are bound by this agreement; you should not inflict reprisals on your father or step-mother, and you must realize that your father has the right, as a father, to correct any of your faults. You, as his son, must ask him for full permission to harvest some coffee or give you anything else, to avoid being offensive to your father. You should now go and behave as a good son should behave."

Turning to the father he said, "Señor Cruz, whenever you desire you can dispose of your property and give it to your son, you can help him in mutual agreement, but the father does not have any obligation to give his son anything; on the other hand, the son cannot demand his father to give him any of his property. It is entirely in the hands of the father whether he wants to give or not."

The two men, father and son, signed the agreement and turned to walk out of the *municipio*. It had been a rare occurrence for a father to bring his son to court. Most disputes of this sort are easily settled by the authority of the father. Although all sons feel the constraints of the father's authority, they know they will one day marry and have sons of their own and, like their father, require total obedience.

Procedural Law

When a dispute moves into the settlement stage, numerous procedural rules come into play. Procedural law refers to the agreed-on ways to settle a dispute. They guide not only the *presidente*, the *sindico*, the *alcalde*, or other authority agent, but also the parties to a dispute. Take, for example, the unwritten procedural rule about *who* should bring family disputes to the court. Although a large number of family cases are brought to the *presidente's* court, only certain classes of persons would think of settling such disputes in the court. The *principales*, for example, are some of the most respected men in Ralu'a, and they take pride in their respectable families. Undoubtedly their authority in the pueblo enhances their authority within their families, giving them the power to arbitrate and settle any disputes that may arise. If any member complained about family problems in court, it would bring shame and dishonor to the entire family. There is, therefore, considerable social pressure to keep members abiding by the unwritten procedural rule that says that *principales and their families should not use the court to settle family disputes*. If the wife of a *principale* were to appear in court making a complaint against her husband, the *presidente* would be greatly surprised, and news of this event would quickly spread throughout the pueblo. Everyone would know that she had violated an implicit procedural rule of Zapotec law.

Procedural Rules in U.S. Society

Procedural rules in our own legal system are not always clearly specified. The ethnographer seeks to make these rules explicit, thereby shedding light on substantive rules and the entire process of law. The ethnographic research among the tramps in Seattle, Washington, mentioned earlier, revealed an implicit procedural rule that held enormous significance for this population.[2] It involves a procedural rule for sentencing that can be stated as follows.

If a man is poor and has been arrested many times for being drunk in public, he shall be sentenced with greater severity than those with money or with no record of previous arrests for drunkenness.

On the basis of this rule, two men could be arrested at 10:00 P.M. on Monday on the same block in Seattle and plead guilty in court to public drunkenness. One would be given a 2-day suspended sentence and would walk out of the courtroom a free man. The other would be given 90 days in jail. Why this difference? The first man had not been arrested for this crime during the preceding 6 months, whereas the other had been arrested seven times.

The most significant part of this procedural rule, however, involves differences in wealth. Take two men, for example, who were arrested 10 to 15 times each year for public drunkenness. Each time they were picked up by the Seattle police they had to spend several hours in the jail "drying out." Then both men were allowed to post a $20 bail, *if they had the money.* Only one of the men had this amount, and he alone was immediately released from jail. He might be arrested again within a few days or weeks and repeat the process. Over the course of 15 or 20 years such a man might spend several thousand dollars for bail, each time walking away from jail after a few hours of sleep. Although a man who posted bail was expected to appear in court for his arraignment, no one did, choosing instead to forfeit this money than face a judge and possible jail sentence. The man who could not post bail, on the other hand, waited several days in the drunk tank, appeared in court, pleaded guilty, received his sentence, and then returned to the jail to serve his time. Thus violation of the same *substantive rule* can lead to enormously different consequences, depending on the nature of related *procedural rules*.

Cultural Procedures for Settling Disputes

For comparative purposes anthropologists have identified several mechanisms for settling legal disputes. Their presence or absence in a society appears to be related to other aspects of culture such as subsistence, political structure, and stratification, although few systematic cross-cultural studies have examined these relationships. The following are among the most important legal mechanisms for settling disputes.

1. **Self-redress** *Disputes are settled by the individual who has been wronged; community sentiment supports this individual action.* Among the Comanche, for example, "willful killing of a man's favorite horse was an act akin to murder, especially if the horse had been bequeathed to him by a best friend. Retaliation was taken not in killing the favorite horse of the transgressor but in slaying the transgressor

[2]See James P. Spradley, "Beating the Drunk Charge," in *Conformity and Conflict: Readings in Cultural Anthropology*, James P. Spradley and David W. McCurdy (editors), Boston: Little, Brown, 1971, pp. 351–358.

himself. A favorite horse had a legal personality and was equated with a human be-ing. Consequently, no further blood revenge followed, for things were already equal: a man for a horse."[3]

2. **The go-between**   *Disputes are settled by a mediator who negotiates with each side of a conflict until a settlement is achieved.* Among the Ifugao of the Philippines, dis-putes within the bilateral kinship group are settled within the group. Disputes be-tween members of different kin groups are necessarily disputes between the groups. In the case of any interfamilial conflict except homicide cases that require direct blood revenge, a go-between works out the details. He moves back and forth be-tween kinship groups, arguing the case for each, and finally settling on the details of an agreement. It may involve a property settlement at divorce, a fine for failure to live up to a land-rental contract, or other kind of trouble.

3. **The contest**   *Disputes are settled by a game of skill in which the two parties engage in physical or mental combat according to rules.* Several kinds of contests occur among the Eskimo for purposes of dispute settlement. *Buffeting*, in which oppo-nents alternately hit each other on the side of the head, may be used for any dispute except homicide. *Head butting* refers to a contest in which opponents lower their heads and ram them into each other. This often occurs in conjunction with a *song duel* in which each partner alternately scoffs and derides the other in song.

An Eskimo man had married the divorced wife of an old man who wanted her back. The younger man would not give her back and a song duel occurred. The following two songs are only each man's first stanza in a long series in which the audience cheers and laughs, acting as informal judges on the outcome.

OLD MAN:

Now shall I split off words—little,
    sharp words
Like the wooden splinters which I
    hack off with my ax.
A song from ancient times—a breath
    of the ancestors
A song of longing—for my wife.
An impudent, black skinned oaf has
    stolen her,
Has tried to belittle her.
A miserable wretch who loves
    human flesh—
A cannibal from famine days.

YOUNG MAN:

Insolence that takes the breath away
Such laughable arrogance and effrontery.
What a satirical song! Supposed to
    place blame on me.

[3]E. Adamson Hoebel, *The Law of Primitive Man*, Cambridge: Harvard University Press, 1954, p. 140.

You would drive fear into my heart!
I who care not about death.
Hi! You sing about my woman who
was your wench.
You weren't so loving then—she was
much alone.
You forgot to prize her in song, in
stout, contest songs.
Now she is mine.
And never shall she visit singing,
false lovers.
Betrayer of women in strange house-
holds.[4]

4. **The ordeal** *Disputes are settled by submitting the accused to a supernaturally controlled, painful or physically dangerous test, the outcome of which determines guilt or innocence.* Among the types of ordeals are burning, scalding, bleeding, and poison. Ralph Linton reports on a scalding ordeal among the Tanala.

Water was boiled in a large pot and a stone fastened to a cord, like a plumb-line. The stone was dropped vertically into the pot, but was not submerged. The cord was attached to a stick which rested across the mouth of the pot so that the stone hung about 5 mm. above the water. The suspect's hand was washed and examined to see whether he had any scars on it, also whether it had been rubbed with medicine. After the Anakandriana had made the usual invocation, the accused approached the pot and seized the stone from below, plunging his hand into the boiling water. He then plunged his hand into cold water. The hand was bandaged and the accused shut up in a guarded house. The next morning all assembled to see his condition. If there were blisters on the hand he was guilty. If accused of sorcery he was killed on the spot, or, if the king was merciful, he was expelled and all his goods seized.[5]

5. **The moot** *Disputes are settled through a community meeting that provides for an informal airing of the conflict.* Although the Kapelle of Africa have a well-developed court system, they also settle disputes by means of the moot. It is referred to as a "house palaver," and includes the kinsmen and neighbors of the litigants. There are no permanent officials who organize the moot; it is an ad hoc group that usually meets to settle domestic conflicts. The following "case of the ousted wife" illustrates the Kapelle moot.

Wama Nya, the complainant, had one wife, Yua. His older brother died and he inherited the widow, Yokpo, who moved into his house. The two women were classificatory sisters. After Yokpo moved in, there was strife in the household. The husband accused her of staying out late at night, of harvesting rice without his knowledge,

[4]Ibid., p. 94.

[5]Ralph Linton, *The Tanala: A Hill Tribe of Madagascar,* Field Museum of Natural History, Anthropology Series, Vol. 22, 1933, pp. 156–157. See also John Roberts, "Oaths, Autonomic Ordeals, and Power," *American Anthropologist,* 67 (6), Part 2, December 1965, pp. 186–212, for a cross-cultural study of ordeals.

and of denying him food. He also accused Yokpo of having lovers and admitted having had a physical struggle with her, after which he took a basin of water and "washed his hands of her."

Yokpo countered by denying the allegations about having lovers, saying that she was accused falsely, although she had in the past confessed the name of one lover. She further complained that Wama Nya had assaulted her and, in the act, had committed the indignity of removing her headtie, and had expelled her from the house after the ritual hand-washing. Finally, she alleged that she had been thus cast out of the house at the instigation of the other wife, who she asserted, had great influence over their husband.

. . . The Town Chief and quarter elder, and the brother of Yokpo, was the mediator of the moot, which decided that the husband was mainly at fault, although Yua and Yokpo's children were also in the wrong. Those at fault had to apologize to Yokpo and bring gifts of apology as well as local rum for the disputants and participants in the moot.[6]

6. **The court**   *Disputes are settled through formal procedures that involve designated officials with authority to enforce decisions.* The Zapotec court and our own court system provide examples of this type of mechanism for settling disputes.

Legal Levels

In every culture the existence of different kinds of authority agents means that disputes can be settled at different levels. In our own society a dispute between a teacher and a student can be settled by the school principal. If the dispute continues, it could go to the town board of education. If still unsettled, it might go to the local court and even be appealed to a series of higher courts.

Among the Zapotec, several levels for settling disputes exist. Figure 12-2 shows these levels. Disputes can be settled by family elders, witches, local officials, the priest, supernatural beings, or officials in the *municipio*. If all else fails, the dispute can be taken to the district court in Villa Alta. Consider the following case.

Mariano's son Pedro married the only daughter of a family in the pueblo and went to live with her family. Mariano was pleased with the arrangement because he had helped decide the marriage. But soon trouble began to develop between his son and the new wife. It came to his attention directly when his daughter-in-law came to him and complained, "Your son Pedro is always drunk, he does not work now, and he argues with me all the time in the home of my parents." Mariano talked with her for some time and, on the following day, he warned Pedro that he should drink less and live at peace with his new wife. Like any son in Ralu'a, Pedro promised his father that he would change his behavior. However, within a month Mariano's daughter-in-law was back again with the same complaint. This time Mariano was angry. "She is back again so soon," he thought. "This son of mine does not learn from words." Mariano found his son and this time, amidst stern warnings, he whipped Pedro harshly.

[6]James Gibbs, "The Kpelle Moot: A Therapeutic Model for the Informal Settlement of Disputes," *Africa*, 33 (1), 1963, p. 3.

Municipio	District court in Villa Alta	
	Alcalde	
	Presidente	Sindico (property disputes and theft cases)

| Supernatural beings |
| The priest |
| Local officials (such as the Well Association) |
| Witches |
| Family elders |

FIGURE 12-2
Zapotec authority agents.
This hierarchy of levels should not be taken to mean that disputes are first taken to the family elders, then to witches, and so forth. Except for some cases handled in the municipio, the levels of authority can be utilized in almost any order.

The weeks passed and still Pedro did not change. His wife now turned to the *padrinos de pano*, the godparents of the marriage. But their warnings to Pedro were to no avail, and so she went to the priest. He talked to Pedro several times, and it seemed the penitent husband might change with his intervention. Then one night Pedro came home very drunk and began cursing at his wife and threatening her. Then he beat her, and she lay awake most of the night wondering what to do next. The fact that he had beat her was less important than that it was another stage in their deteriorating relationship and evidence that Pedro had not changed. Early in the morning while Pedro was still asleep she went to the *municipio* and made a complaint to the *presidente*. Pedro was cited and appeared in court later that same afternoon. He told the *presidente* that he had been drunk and did not know what he was doing, that he would change his ways, and that he would begin to work regularly in his fields. Pedro paid a fine of 50 pesos and signed an agreement that he would live at peace with his wife.

Disputes such as this can be resolved at various levels and through various remedy agents, such as male family heads, church officials, village officials, and even by appeals directly to supernatural beings and individuals who are witches. For example, a man who is having trouble with his wife may go to a witch and say, "Somebody is gossiping about me and every time I come home my wife is after me because she is so upset. Can you do something about this person who is spreading bad tales about me?" The witch will reply, "Pay me 5 pesos and I'll find out who it is and do something about it." But whether a man goes to a witch or to the *presidente*, or whether a woman goes to her father-in-law is not left to happenstance. The procedural rules of a culture's law help define which authorities should be employed for various kinds of disputes.

Legal Principles and Cultural Values

Underlying the settlement of disputes in every society we find legal principles based on the fundamental values of a culture. A legal principle is a broad conception of some desirable state of affairs that gives rise to many substantive and procedural rules. The witness is asked, "Do you promise to tell the truth, the whole truth, and nothing but the truth, so help you God?" We accept the value of telling the objective truth, getting at the facts, and we believe that humans are capable of telling the truth. In some societies, however, people hold different assumptions, asserting that it is not possible to tell objective truth. In other cultures the value placed on the facts is small when compared to the importance of restoring amicable relationships. In order to understand the decisions authorities make to settle disputes, we need to grasp the legal principles of a culture.

When the Zapotec talk about the characteristics of those wise men who have settled disputes in the proper way, they say, "He knows how to *make the balance*." This principle means that fault-finding in a particular trouble case is not as important as balancing the demands of all parties and restoring conditions of peaceful coexistence. The men's Well Association did not concern itself with seeking culprits who had violated rules about the use of private property. Instead, they sought to restore peace and prevent future conflicts at Los Remedios. Their goal—*hacer el balance*—to make the balance, was achieved.

The principle of balance does not mean people are never at fault, never violate substantive rules. Instead, it means that disputes are not settled merely by establishing the facts of the case, finding the guilty party, and administering punishment. When Clemente Mendoza harvested his father's coffee without permission, he was clearly in the wrong. But the *presidente*, acting as a kind of father to the citizens of Ralu'a, sought to restore the balance, to mend the relationship between father and son, eliciting a signed agreement from them that they would not hold grudges and continue the dispute.

The Case of Fright

To the Zapotec, making the balance means settling disputes with an eye to the future of the relationships involved, not merely an examination of past events. Disputes create difficulties for people, financial losses, bitter feelings, and disrupted relationships. It would be possible to settle disputes without rectifying any of these conditions, but for the Zapotec this would not be sufficient, although the guilty person were given a life sentence for his or her crime. Take the case of Señora Juan. She complained to the *presidente* that she had been working, cutting coffee in the field of Señora Quiroz, when a young boy, Teodora Garcia, had picked on her 6-year-old boy, hitting him. The experience had been so disconcerting to the smaller boy that he had come down with *susto*, or magical fright, an illness involving the loss of one's soul. "My little boy got frightened," she told the *presidente*, "and now he yells during the night and has diarrhea because of the fright. I am asking the *presidente* to help me make my little son well again." The *presidente* asked Teodoro Garcia about the dispute, and he answered that the son of Señora Juan was always calling him names and taunting him while he worked. Back and forth the discussion went, but the *presidente* did not seek to discover what really happened; *his goal was not to find out the facts.* He allowed people to express their feelings in the matter. It was difficult to tell who was at fault, but he could easily see that this upset had disturbed the equilibrium in social relationships of all those involved. A boy had *susto* as a result, and the *presidente* knew he could do something about that, restoring the balance required. The poor mother said she needed 30 pesos for the curer. After negotiation, Teodoro Garcia offered to settle for 20 pesos. The case was resolved, the boy taken to a curer, and the balance restored.

Cultural Values

Underlying the legal principles of a society are the values that form the basis of social life. Making the balance in settling disputes is based on a widely held Zapotec cultural value of maintaining equilibrium. Direct confrontation between individuals in which one loses and another wins is unsettling to Zapotecans. As expressed by Laura Nader:

> *This concern for equilibrium is evident through Ralu'a. Upon my making inquiries as to the motives for witchcraft in Ralu'a an informant reported the following as causes: "because one works too much or not enough; because one is too pretty or too ugly or too rich; for being an only child; for being rich and refusing to lend money; for being antisocial—for example, for refusing to greet people." These are all situations that somehow upset the balance as Ralu'ans see it. It is no wonder that the zero-sum game (win or lose) as we know it in some American courts would be a frightening prospect to a plaintiff, even though all "right" might be on his side. The plaintiff need not worry, however, for the* presidente *is equally reluctant to make such a clear-cut zero-sum game decision for a variety of reasons—among them that witchcraft is an all too possible tool of retaliation for such behavior. If a plaintiff wanted to play the zero-sum game he would go to a witch and not to the courts, where behavior is far too public.*[7]

No doubt on that first day when the anthropologist entered the pueblo she had somehow upset some unseen sense of equilibrium in this Zapotec pueblo. A strange woman, dressed in strange clothes, with a strange reason for being there, asking strange questions; she must be a Protestant missionary, a person with supernatural power, at least someone to arouse suspicion. However, after weeks of persistently defining her role and participating in the daily round of life, she had overcome most of the suspicion and fear. Then one warm day when the excitement of a fiesta filled the air of Ralu'a, she had purchased a large barrel of *mescal* and donated it to the pueblo celebrations. It was a simple token, but the citizens of Ralu'a responded with enthusiasm. Public officials lauded her generosity and declared that she was now a true member of the pueblo. Others apologized for their suspicions and unfriendliness as they drank and laughed together. Without calculation she had *hacer el balance.*

SUMMARY

Human societies have many ways to maintain social control. Law functions in the settlement of disputes that occur in every society despite other mechanisms of social control.

---

[7]"Styles of Court Procedure: To Make the Balance," in *Law in Culture and Society*, Laura Nader (editor), Chicago: Aldine, 1969, pp. 73–74.

Law is defined as the cultural knowledge that people use to settle disputes by means of agents who have recognized authority. Legal disputes must be distinguished from extralegal ones, such as war or feud, and infralegal disputes that never reach the point of needing the legal system for their settlement.

Legal knowledge in any culture consists of (1) substantive law, the statutes that define right and wrong; (2) procedural law, the agreed-on ways to settle disputes; and (3) legal principles, broad conceptions of some desirable state of affairs. Cross-cultural studies have revealed the following cultural procedures for settling disputes: self-redress, the go-between, contests, ordeals, moots, and courts. Underlying every legal system are those shared values that give meaning to a particular way of life.

MAJOR CONCEPTS

LAW	LEGAL LEVELS
INFRALEGAL DISPUTES	LEGAL PRINCIPLES
EXTRALEGAL DISPUTES	COURT
LEGAL DISPUTES	MOOT
FEUD	ORDEAL
WAR	CONTEST
SUBSTANTIVE LAW	GO-BETWEEN
PROCEDURAL LAW	SELF-REDRESS

SELECTED READINGS

Hoebel, E. Adamson: *The Law of Primitive Man*, Cambridge: Harvard University Press, 1954.
This book examines the nature of law in nonliterate societies. It includes detailed case studies of law in five cultures at different levels of complexity.

Nader, Laura (editor): *The Ethnography of Law, American Anthropologist, Special Issue*, 67 (6), Part 2, 1965.
The selections of this special journal issue emerged from a special conference on law sponsored by the Wenner-Gren Foundation for Anthropological Research. It includes case studies, theoretical articles, cross-cultural studies, and an excellent overview of the field by the editor.

Nader, Laura (editor): *Law in Culture and Society*, Chicago: Aldine, 1969.
The most comprehensive book on anthropology and law published to this date. Part I presents a variety of case studies of law in non-Western societies. Part II deals with law and innovation in non-Western societies. Part III shifts to case studies in Western societies. The last section, Part IV, deals with comparative studies.

Nader, Laura, and Barbara Yngvesson: "On Studying the Ethnography of Law and Its Consequences," in *Handbook of Social and Cultural Anthropology*, John J. Honigmann (editor), Chicago: Rand-McNally, 1973.
A review of the anthropology of law with emphasis on needed directions for research.

Pospisil, Leopold: *Anthropology of Law: A Comparative Theory*, New York: Harper & Row, 1971.
This book examines the form of law, proposes a definition of law in terms of four universal attributes, examines change in legal systems, and discusses an approach to the formal analysis of law.

CHAPTER THIRTEEN

Religion
and
Magic

As we examine each aspect of culture it is important to keep in mind a major premise stated in Chapter 1: *human survival is uniquely dependent on culture.* The categories, rules, and codes possessed by each society are like a set of sophisticated tools. They are symbolic tools that people put to work in helping to meet the biological, psychological, and social requirements of existence. As anthropologists we seek to understand this cultural mode of survival. In this chapter and the next we will examine the role that religion, world view, and values play in human adaptation.

THE NATURE OF RELIGION

We can highlight the nature of religion by briefly reviewing the major functions of those aspects of culture discussed in earlier chapters. As we have said, culture is a necessary requirement of human societies. Each cultural code develops out of the collective experience of many generations of people and, in the process, it undergoes constant revision and change. Human social life is possible because of our capacity to employ these symbolic codes. Social life requires predictability and organized patterns of interaction. In Chapters 4, 5, 6, 7, and 8 we saw how culture provides us with the ground plan for social interaction in the categories and rules of the social structure. Human survival also depends on the effective utilization of a physical environment. In Chapters 9 and 10 we saw how culture is used to identify resources, define the physical world, and provide goods and services for social and biological wants. In the distribution of resources and the allocation of responsibilities, choices must be made and disputes inevitably occur. In Chapters 11 and 12 we examined the nature of political systems to see how culture is used to allocate resources, make public policy decisions, and settle disputes.

Each of these aspects of culture provides people with means for coping with the demands of life. Each helps to reduce the world of experience to known quantities, defining the situation and providing plans for action. Each helps to bring vast areas of experience under human control, but always there are problems left over, difficulties unresolved, wants unsatisfied, tragedies unexplained. Social life itself is often a precarious venture that requires people to pay allegiance to values that transcend individual interests. The part of each culture that helps to fill these gaps in a uniquely human way is religion.

Religion: A Definition

Religion is the cultural knowledge of the supernatural that people use to cope with the ultimate problems of human existence.[1] Much of any religion remains at the tacit level of cultural knowledge. It consists of cultural rules for generating emotional states, for interpreting inner feelings, and for responding to the profound crises of life. As we discuss several ultimate problems and supernatural beliefs, it should be kept in mind that they are not merely questions of a rational nature. As Milton Yinger has said,

They are more appropriately seen as deep-seated emotional needs, springing from the very nature of man as an individual and as a member of society. The questions appear first of all because they are felt—the death of a loved one wrenches our emotions, the failure to achieve that for which we yearn saddens and bewilders us; the hostility between ourselves and those around us infuses our social contacts with tension and prevents the achievement of mutual values. Religion may develop an intellectual system to interpret and deal with these questions, but they express first of all an underlying emotional need, not a group of rationally conceived problems.[2]

Ultimate Problems

1. **The problem of meaning**   In addition to interpreting immediate experience and dealing with day-to-day physical needs, human beings question the source and meaning of life. Where did we come from? Why is life like this? Is there any central meaning to life? What is the purpose of existence? The problem of meaning does not always express itself in stated questions, but we can infer its presence from the universal existence of myths and legends that answer a deep human need. The people of the Gilbert Islands tell a story of Naareau, the elder who lived in a void but, because there was nothing else, decided to create a woman. As the tale progresses, it tells of the creation of men, night and day, and a variety of other worldly features. The Australian Aborigines speak of the Dreaming, a time when everything was created and came to be as it is. Knowledge of the dreaming is so detailed, yet fluid, that Australians can use it to explain their own existence as well as the place of every trail, hill, water hole, and animal. An intellectual living in a secular Israeli kibbutz, despite his dissatisfaction with certain Marxist interpretations of life, says, "I value Marxism very highly. In times like ours when there is no faith and there is no God,

---

[1]This definition draws on the work of Milton Yinger, *Religion, Society, and the Individual: An Introduction to the Sociology of Religion*, New York: Macmillan, 1957.

[2]Ibid., p. 9.

Death is a fundamental human problem requiring explanation and the ritual management of grief. Death practices require special care of the corpse, as in New Guinea, where a body is seen here being carried on a litter.

Marxism does provide you with a *Weltanschauung*; it does fit every theory and every science into a scheme and, thus, it brings order out of chaos."[3]

2. **The problem of death**   Every person faces the biological certainty of death, and every culture must deal with the questions that surround death. Is death the end of existence? What happens after death? When will I die? In addition to such individual questions, each death is a problem for society and often requires major changes in status for the living. The cultural knowledge for responding to death, for interpreting it correctly, and for mourning the deaths of others constitutes part of every religion.

3. **The problem of evil**   In every society certain forces that are beyond their control impinge on people. Social structures and political decisions result in inequality. Illness and misfortune raise persistent questions. Somehow the forces of evil do not strike uniformly in society. Why was that child and not another killed by a drunken driver? Why did the tornado strike my home and not some other? Why are those people so wealthy while I am poor? Cultural rules create inequality and can result in further questions that religion must handle.

4. **The problem of transcendent values**   In every society some individual interests and desires conflict with the values of the group. Hostilities are aroused by conflicting in-

terests, and individuals must handle these aggressive feelings. This is more than a personal problem; it raises the question of the very existence of society. Religions seem to provide a set of transcendent values, sometimes supernaturally legitimized, sometimes not, that enable people to give allegiance to a way of life on which their very survival depends. One of the main functions of religion is to provide a set of transcendent values that are given supernatural sanctions for the members of a society.

The Supernatural

The knowledge for coping with the ultimate questions of human existence is most often based on ideas of the supernatural. The supernatural refers to a realm that is beyond ordinary experience, but open or accessible to people. It usually involves powers and beings and ways to communicate with them. However, even in societies that deny the supernatural, there are ideologically structured parts of culture that can be called religious. In this chapter we will deal primarily with those that are religious in the sense of dealing with the supernatural.

For many educated people in our own society, religion and the supernatural tend to be treated in a highly intellectual and rational manner. But in most societies, religion is neither an abstract cultural system nor a highly rationalistic one. It involves people performing rituals, fearing ghosts and ancestors, praying for help in the time of crisis, and explaining unanticipated events. Religion is a personal and often very emotional area of cultural experience. As we discuss the concepts that anthropologists have developed for describing and understanding religion, we will do so in the context of two extended cases. In this way we hope to show how religions in widely different cultural settings are used by people to cope with the ultimate problems faced by all human beings.

Illness Among the Azande[4]

The morning was especially hot in the southern Sudan as Bazugba, a dark, strongly built Azande man in his early forties, walked through the tall grass and brush toward a small secluded clearing. He moved vigorously, the effort causing beads of perspiration to form on his brow. On his left he caught sight of a line of tall trees that announced the presence of a stream whose waters he knew well. He had lived in a homestead on the banks of that stream when he was a boy, but had been moved with his family to a more compact government settlement by British officials. The British explained that tsetse flies lived in the shadows by the water and that these small insects were the cause of sleeping sickness. As he walked along Bazugba wondered, as had other people at the time, what real purpose the officials had had in mind. No fly could cause a disease.

Nearing the clearing, Bazugba recalled the events that had brought him on his day's journey. A month earlier he had awakened to the usual noises and sights of his bustling homestead. He could hear the sharp words of his first wife, the ill-tempered Namarusu, as she chided her children about their lack of cooperation in

[4]Material for the Azande case is drawn from E. E. Evans-Pritchard, *Witchcraft, Oracles and Magic Among the Azande*, Oxford: Clarendon Press, 1937.

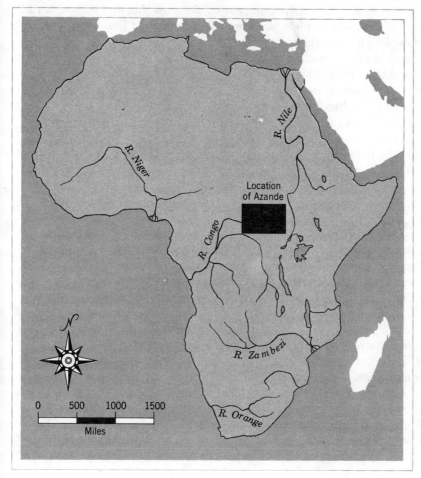

The Azande live on the high ground between the headwaters of the Nile and Congo Rivers. Although located quite near the Karimojong discussed in Chapters 6 and 7, the Azande are horticulturalists rather than pastoralists.

her morning's work. As he walked into the sunlight of the new day, he caught sight of his youngest wife, Mamenzi, straining awkwardly under the weight of a head load of firewood. She carried quite a burden, he thought, for a woman 8 months pregnant. His thoughts were disturbed, however, by the urgent call of a small boy, the son of his second wife, Nabani. "Father, Father," exclaimed the little figure. "Come to our hut. Mother has just become very ill."

Bazugba hurried after the lad, and the sight that met his eyes was most distressing. Nabani, his favorite wife, the most cheerful, helpful, and hardworking person in the compound, lay doubled up in pain. He felt her body, and, as he feared, it was hot with fever. At his touch, Nabani recognized his presence and managed to tell him about the sudden attack of pain in her stomach, arms, legs, and head. "I am dead," she moaned. "I am surely dead."

However, Nabani, Bazugba recalled, had survived the onset of her illness and some of her pain subsided. Yet over the next few weeks she did not regain the full vigor of her former health. Instead, failing to eat, she grew thin and listless, hardly able to move about and complete her work. Bazugba feared that she might die and on this morning, he thought as he walked along the dusty path, he would discover the cause of her illness and do something about it.

Bazugba knew of no physical causes for sudden or long-term illness. As he said, "Flies cannot cause disease," nor are people, by themselves, able to make others ill. Clearly Nabani's problem was caused by witchcraft, for although her illness had struck suddenly, an indication of sorcerers, it had lingered on for some time, a sign that could only mean witchcraft. He would have to discover the identity of the witch and take the proper magical countermeasures to protect his ailing wife from the force that was trying to devour her.

Misfortune in Chicago[5]

Mary Jean Getz stood on the sidewalk in front of the old apartment building in which she and her husband Bob rented a flat. Moments earlier a neighbor had called to inform her that her car was damaged; she now surveyed the vehicle. The rear tires of the aging Buick LeSabre were flat, slashed by the knife of some unknown assailant. A window on the passenger's side was cracked by the effects of a jimmy with which someone had tried to unlock the door. On the other side of the car a deep gouge marred the paint from the rear wheel well to the front door handle. With tears in her eyes Mary Jean muttered, "Damn these people around here!" and ran upstairs.

Mary Jean and her husband had grown up in the small rural town of Ham Lake, Indiana. They had dated each other through high school and married 2 days after their graduation. Although he had asked everyone, Bob had not been able to find work in Ham Lake and, like so many other young people from the town and surrounding farms, he and Mary Jean decided to look for a better life in Chicago.

Unfortunately, thought Mary Jean, Chicago did not turn out to be the promised land. Both she and Bob had found jobs, although their lack of skills and education kept them from doing anything that paid especially well. Mary Jean worked as a sales clerk at Sunny Side Store, a local discount house, and Bob found a job as night man, pumping gas at a filling station. The arrangement was distressing to Mary Jean because she was alone at night and only managed to see Bob for any length of time on Mondays, when they both had a day off. But worse, her discomfort was compounded by life in the city itself. The vandalism to the car was only the last in a series of events that made urban existence so unpleasant for her. Adolescent boys leered at her when she walked to the corner grocery store, and one of her neighbors had actually been robbed of her purse only a few days before by a gang of young toughs. Mary Jean and Bob experienced similar trouble when, returning from a movie one Monday evening, they discovered that someone had en-

[5]Material for the Jehovah's Witnesses example came from interviews conducted by one of the authors and from several books published by the Watch Tower Bible and Tract Society of New York. These include *The Truth That Leads to Eternal Life*, 1968; *Did Man Get Here by Evolution or by Creation?* 1967; and *Things in Which It Is Impossible for God to Lie*, 1965.

tered their apartment, overturning the furniture and throwing their belongings on the floor. There was little the thief could take, so they had not lost much, but the experience, like the damage to the car, was just another sign of the hostility of the city. Why were people so evil here anyway?

As she walked back into her apartment house, Mrs. Roberts, the neighbor who had alerted her about the damaged car, stopped her in the hall and suggested she drop by for a cup of coffee. She accepted gladly, and entered Mrs. Roberts' clean, immaculately tidy but simply furnished apartment. As Mary sat in the kitchen, she expressed her despair over the car and life in the city. Listening patiently, Mrs. Roberts asked her if she ever wondered why things like this happened. "Have you ever noticed," she said, "that crime is getting out of hand all over the country? Perhaps it is part of a greater plan?"

Mary Jean asked her what she meant, and Mrs. Roberts replied, saying that God Jehovah had made this world and the people in it, but he had not made evil. It was the devil and his agents who were responsible for trouble, and lately the devil had been more active. That is why the crime rate was soaring all over the country. Mary Jean wondered about this explanation. She and Bob had been brought up in a fundamentalist church in Ham Lake, and she knew that the devil could possess people.

Mrs. Roberts went into her bedroom and came back with a small book entitled *The Truth That Leads to Eternal Life.* "This book is published by the Jehovah's Witnesses," she said. "If you read it, it will open your eyes about a lot of things that are going on in the world these days." When Mary left the apartment, she carried the book with her and decided to read it.

As we have just seen, both Bazugba and Mary Jean's neighbor, Mrs. Roberts, use their religion to explain adversity. But how does the supernatural affect human affairs? The answer lies in the concept of supernatural power, for Bazugba and Mrs. Roberts both believe that trouble is the result of its malevolent application.

SUPERNATURAL POWER

Supernatural power refers to the ability of the supernatural to act. When one sees the elements of an electric stove glow red and feels their warmth, he or she knows that the electrical power is on. All of us learn about the effects of electricity and the rules for its control. When Bazugba witnessed the slow, wasting disease that afflicted Nabani, he, too, knew that a power was present. But instead of a physical power generated in an electrical plant, Nabani was affected by a supernatural power emanating from a witch. Every religion contains conceptions of supernatural power and strategies for controlling and dealing with supernatural force. While the variety of these beliefs is astonishingly wide, we may classify supernatural power into two broad categories, the *personified force* of supernatural beings and the *impersonal force* at large in many things and places in the world.

Supernatural Beings

In addition to physical forces such as electricity, human beings also experience the effects of *personal forces* as they conduct their social lives. A bank teller, for exam-

Supernatural beings take many forms, from remote and powerful deities to personal guardian spirits. This Guere dancer from Africa is dressed as an ancestral spirit.

ple, knows that he is subject to the authority of the bank president and other managers. The president can hire and fire employees like the teller, decide whether or not to grant loans, and raise or lower interest rates. He possesses the power to cause others to act. The supernatural realm also contains personified force associated with <u>supernatural beings</u>. Such beings have the power to affect human events and to control human destinies. In India, for example, there is a malevolent goddess known as Sitala Mata. Much of the time she is quiet, pleased with the attention people pay her when they worship at her shrines. However, she has the power to harm people by afflicting them with smallpox, and this she does from time to time in a capricious way. Her force is personified in the sense that it is associated with her identity, just as the bank president holds power because of who he is.

The nature of supernatural force varies with the personalities of the beings with whom it is associated, and such beings are often thought to resemble real people in their habits and temperament. Some, like Sitala Mata, are evil. They employ their power to hurt their victims and destroy human fortune. Some are kindly and helpful; they can be trusted to exert power in support of those who need it. Still others are stern and authoritarian, fair and helpful when treated properly, but quick to take retribution on those who fail to care for them properly.

Some supernatural beings are thought to be so similar to human beings that they can be treated almost like normal people. For example, on Taiwan most rural Chinese families keep an altar in the central room of their houses. There rest the tablets of the family's ancestors. This altar, however, is not simply a memorial to the dead, it is their residence. They are treated by their descendants as though they were actually present in the room, queried when family decisions are to be made, addressed when people talk, eat, drink, and play, and included in family ritual. Although they cannot be seen, their presence is felt as part of the normal rhythm of family life.

The intensity and extent of power wielded by supernatural beings also vary. People in many societies conceive of high, remote gods and goddesses whose power is both intense and widely felt. It is these beings who created the world and the people, animals, landforms, and other spirit beings that are found in it. Such deities, however, tend to be remote and too important to bother themselves with the daily life of mortals. That job is reserved for other gods, godlings, spirits, ancestors, and ghosts that have power over most happenings in people's lives, and who reside nearer those whom they affect. Finally, there are many lesser beings who possess limited power and whose activities can be countered by higher supernatural beings.

Mrs. Roberts and other Jehovah's Witnesses divide supernatural beings and their associated powers into categories somewhat similar to those already mentioned. First, there is the high deity, Jehovah God, who created the world. As the Bible help entitled *The Truth That Leads to Eternal Life* points out, Jehovah God created the heavens and the earth, all living creatures and creeping things, other spirit creatures, and human kind. He also created Jesus and a host of angels, including Satan and others who later became demons (see Figure 13-1).

As Mary Jean read the Bible help and spent additional hours talking with Mrs. Roberts in Bible study, she was impressed by the Bible explanation for the origin of troubles on earth. The answer given there involved a conflict for power among the many supernatural beings, including Jehovah God himself. The struggle over power came about almost at the very beginning. Jehovah had created Adam, and from Adam he made Eve and placed them in a paradise, the garden of Eden. There they lived according to His wishes in a state of perfection. Jehovah, however, had also created many angels and had given them free will. One of these, Satan, exercised his free will and decided to be disobedient, challenging Jehovah God's authority in the newly created world. In the form of a snake he tempted Eve, who had also been granted free will by Jehovah, and she and Adam deviated from God's perfect knowledge.

Instead of destroying the world and its disobedient beings as he had the power to do, Jehovah permitted Adam and Eve's descendants to continue living with the opportunity of returning to his flock. He also permitted the devil to persist in his

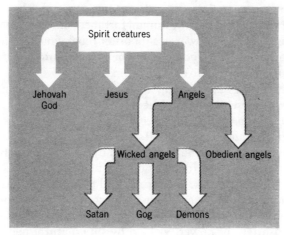

FIGURE 13-1
Spirit creatures.

quest for power. When the evil work of Satan became too much for him, however, he sent the flood to eliminate almost every human being and animal from the face of the earth, but the devil resumed his conflict with Jehovah when the earth was repopulated. To counteract Satan's efforts, Jehovah changed Jesus, who was king of God's heavenly kingdom, into a human being to work among people and lead them back to His perfect way. But Satan managed to kill Jesus, and 3 days after his death, God turned Jesus back into a spirit. From that time to 1914 Satan ruled both heaven and earth, and it was not until 1914 that God cast the evil one out of heaven. Deposed, Satan now roams the earth causing trouble and working to thwart Jehovah God's plans.

Mary Jean was clearly affected by this view of supernatural beings and their power. It explained why life in the city was so difficult, why there had been so many earthquakes, famines, and wars in the world, and why these events were occurring with increased regularity. The devil and his demons were now loose in the world, turning one person against another and causing disease and destruction. She decided to spend more time with the Jehovah's Witnesses, and she began to interest Bob in what she had learned.

Impersonal Supernatural Force

Bazugba had a different view of supernatural power. He attributed human troubles to the activity of an impersonal supernatural force controlled by malevolent people. Force of this sort has usually been called *mana* by anthropologists. From 1863 to 1887 a missionary named Bishop Codrington lived and worked in Melanesia. During his long stay there, he discovered that the inhabitants of the islands conceived of an impersonal supernatural force called *mana* that could reside in people and unusual objects. As he described it, *mana* worked more like the electric power that we spoke of earlier. It was not force associated with a particular person or deity, although people and spirits could control and use it. It was free in the environment where, if people and spirits knew the proper strategies, it could be captured and controlled.

Codrington tells of a Melanesian who, on seeing a peculiarly shaped stone, suspected that it might contain *mana*. He picked it up and placed it in his garden, where he was rewarded by a higher yield of yams. After a few years the yield decreased, and he surmised that the rock had lost its *mana* and ceased to be an asset. The Melanesian concept of *mana* has been extended by anthropologists to label any form of impersonal supernatural power.

The concept of *mana* also exists in Polynesia, but there it has much more dangerous characteristics. Like electricity, in large amounts, it can harm people who encounter it. Chiefs were thought to possess high levels of *mana* and thus were dangerous to the average Polynesian. This is why on some Polynesian islands there were special talking chiefs who had enough *mana* to be secure in the presence of a highly charged personage, but not so much that they would harm commoners with whom they wished to communicate. In addition, *mana* in this dangerous form could be placed in things, making them dangerous to the touch. Such things were said to be *tabu*, and like *mana*, anthropologists have adopted this term (taboo) to label rules that proscribe things or activities.

Influencing Supernatural Power

Just as all of us can throw a switch to regulate the flow of electrical power, thus gaining some control over its operation, so can people influence supernatural power so that it will act in ways that are beneficial or desirable. As in the case of supernatural power, strategies to influence the supernatural vary markedly from one society to the next. There are several forms of influence, however, that occur widely and bear discussing.

Prayer

Prayer is a petition directed at supernatural beings. Prayer stresses the supplicant's needs and weaknesses and is a request for help. It may also be a statement of faith, a testimony to the supplicant's obedience to the higher power.

It was with such testimony in mind that Mary Jean and Mrs. Roberts frequently prayed to Jehovah God. Not that prayer would help at once, for Witnesses were not usually blessed with immediate results. However, prayer, along with righteous living, demonstrated to Jehovah and Jesus that people were leading their lives according to God's original plan. Righteous living would lead any year now to everlasting life in a paradise on earth. For the world as it is now would soon come to an end, destroyed by Jehovah within a generation of Jesus' return to heaven. Those who deviated from righteous living, who were not part of Jehovah's flock, would be swallowed up in the holocaust along with Satan and his demons. Only some chosen ones who would live in God's heavenly kingdom, and other members of Jehovah's flock who would inherit a paradise on earth, would survive total destruction.

Thus as Mary Jean prayed she felt a growing feeling of confidence. Things were bad now to be sure, but by praying and following other rules laid down in the Bible, she could attain everlasting life in an unbelievably rich and tranquil paradise.

Sacrifice

Sacrifice represents the act of giving up something of value to influence supernatural beings. Like prayer, however, sacrifice may have two motives. In some cases, it represents a gift or bribe designed to obligate a supernatural being to use its power in some desired way. In other instances sacrifice is a means for the supplicant to demonstrate his or her faith. In either case sacrifice is a way to influence supernatural power.

Witchcraft

Witchcraft labels the activity of people who possess supernatural force and use it for evil purposes. Bazugba, as we have already seen, recognizes the existence of witchcraft, which he calls *mangu*. *Mangu* is a black substance found in the bowels of a witch. Witches inherit this substance, boys from their fathers and girls from their mothers. However, it is not the witchcraft substance itself that attacks people, but its force or essence. Through this source of impersonal supernatural power the witch, who is a jealous person of ill will, can cause harm to other people and things by eating or stealing their vitals. When this occurs, the victim, such as Bazugba's wife Nabani, dies slowly.

The scope of Azande witchcraft, and consequently the events it explains, however, is far greater than illness. It causes many unusual events, as Evans-Pritchard points out.

Food, animals, or even human beings may be offered in sacrifice. The goat pictured here will be killed as a sacrificial offering during the investiture of an African curing specialist.

If blight seizes the ground-nut crop it is witchcraft; if the bush is vainly scoured for game it is witchcraft; if women laboriously bail water out of a pool and are rewarded by but a few small fish it is witchcraft; if termites do not rise-when their swarming is due and a cold useless night is spent in waiting for their flight it is witchcraft; if a prince is cold and distant with his subject it is witchcraft; if a magical rite fails to achieve its purpose it is witchcraft; if, in fact, any failure or misfortune falls upon anyone at any time and in relation to any of the manifold activities of life it may be due to witchcraft.[6]

Many might think that the Azande must live in constant fear of witches. Actually Bazugba would be anxious without his knowledge of witches and their activities. With such knowledge he can identify and treat troubles. Once witchcraft is discovered or, even if it is only suspected, he may attempt to hide its victim, for witchcraft cannot see well. Most Azande, including Bazugba, carry on ritual by hiding in the bush because of this threat, and they are vague about where they will be and whether or not they intend to visit another village or attend a feast. They may also counter witchcraft by the use of magic.

Magic

Magic refers to strategies that people use to control supernatural powers. Magicians have clear ends in mind when they perform magic, and they use a set of well-defined procedures to control and manipulate supernatural force to gain that end. In his classic work, *The Golden Bough*, Sir James Frazer divided magic into two types, imitative and contagious.[7] Imitative magic consists of formulas that imitate the ends sought by the magician. For example, the Bhils of Ratakote, India, perform a magical ritual to cure some kinds of stomach disorders. If a person has abdominal pain and other difficulties such as diarrhea, the cause is often attributed to a misplaced *gola*, a ball-like lump that normally resides in the abdomen just above the navel. Troubles occur when the ball becomes misplaced. If a curer decides that the *gola* is causing the difficulty, he will initiate a ritual designed to bring it back in place. He takes a knife and draws a circle on the ground, places a dot at the center, and draws seven spokes from center to circumference to make spokes. Then, with an assistant placing a hand on the patient's stomach to act as a conductor for the force, the curer puts the tip of the knife at the center of the wheel diagram and intones a powerful saying. The saying unlocks impersonal supernatural power, and this in turn works to pull the patient's *gola* back into place. The diagram with its centered dot imitates the proper location of the *gola* and with the infusion of power, pulls the ball back into its proper position.

Contagious magic is built on the belief that what happens to one thing will happen to another if the two are closely associated. For example, in some societies, a magician attempts to procure something—hair or nail clippings, feces, an item of clothing—belonging to someone else, and by treating these with incantations or

[6]E. E. Evans-Pritchard, *Witchcraft, Oracles and Magic Among the Azande*, Oxford: Clarendon Press, 1937, pp. 63–64.

[7]See James George Frazier, *The Golden Bough: A Study in Magic and Religion*, 12 volumes, 3d ed., revised and enlarged, London: Macmillan, 1911–1915, Vol. 1, pp. 52–219.

- To prevent rain
- To increase the peanut crop
- To prevent wounded animals from escaping
- For hunting dangerous beasts
- To direct the aim of the bowman
- To kill fish
- To insure successful iron working
- To insure good singing
- To protect against witches and sorcerers
- To produce true revelations in dreams
- To attract followers
- To insure successful exchange at feasts
- To gain sexual potency

FIGURE 13-2
Some uses of magic among the Zande.

other magical procedures, hopes to affect the person. In societies where contagious magic is used to harm others, people are particularly careful to guard their personal belongings, going so far as to keep nail and hair clippings in a pouch or in some hidden place.

Sorcery

Sorcery refers to the malevolent practice of magic. Sorcerers use medicines and spells to control supernatural force for evil ends. Unlike witches, who normally inherit their ability to control evil power and who can harm others without the use of magic, sorcerers must employ magical ritual to cause harm to their victims. Like witchcraft, however, sorcery is difficult to discover. In most societies where it is found, few, if any, sorcerers practice openly and may actually not exist at all. But because individuals believe in its existence, sorcery continues as an explanation of adversity and permits victims to take counteraction.

Azande Magic and Sorcery

When Nabani was first stricken with pain and fever, Bazugba thought she was the victim of a sorcerer. Evil magic (*kitikiti ngua*) strikes suddenly, causing those toward whom it is directed intense pain that is often fatal. One remedy for sorcery, or for an attack of witchcraft, is the use of magic. Azande magic typically involves the use of medicines (*ngua*) and is employed in a variety of ways (see Figure 13-2).

If someone who is attacked by a witch dies, the Azande commonly retaliate with vengeance magic (*bagbuduma*). Such a thing had happened when Bazugba was a boy. His father's brother had died, the victim of a witch, and his father had sent vengeance magic to kill the culprit. He prepared the vengeance medicine and addressed it with these special instructions.

An Azande stirs and addresses bingiya *medicine*, which he will use to draw wild game into his hunting net.

A bundle of medicine hangs beneath the roof of the small shelter near the door of this Azande house. It has been placed there to protect household items against theft.

Medicine of vengeance are you here? Seek out the killer. May misfortune come upon him, thunder roar, seize him, and kill him. May a snake bite him so that he will die. May death come upon him from ulcers. May he die if he drink water. May every kind of sickness trouble him. May the magic hand him over to the Europeans so that they will imprison him and he will perish in their prison. May he not survive this year. May every kind of trouble fall upon him. If he eat cooked

(Left-hand picture) Magic may be used in many settings, even those that seem commonplace to the western observer. Here an Azande has driven an axe-head into the ground amid magic plants to prevent rain from falling during a feast.
(Right-hand picture) The medicines hanging below this Azande granary are thought to ensure a prosperous and peaceful feast.

foods may he die. When he stands in the center of the net, hunting animals, may his friend spear him by mistake.[8]

By intoning these words and by using his special medicine, Bazugba's father felt he was doing something about his brother's death. This magic, like magic everywhere, permitted him a degree of confidence in a stressful situation.

A knowledge of supernatural power is crucial if people are to understand their experiences, but such power also underlies human action. Let us now look at the way people communicate with the supernatural to control or influence it.

COMMUNICATION WITH THE SUPERNATURAL

The existence of personified and impersonal supernatural power implies the need for communication. Their efforts may involve revelation through the interpretation of myth, divination, spirit possession, and the offices of religious specialists.

[8]Adapted from E. E. Evans-Pritchard, *Witchcraft, Oracles and Magic Among the Azande*, Oxford: Clarendon Press, 1937, pp. 289–290.

Divine Revelation

Religious knowledge about people and their place in the world is often contained in myths. Myths are stories, usually involving supernatural beings, that speak of how things have come to be. In some cases myths seem orderly and precise to the Western reader, but in many societies, they appear to be loosely structured. In either case myths are a means of communication because they reveal religious knowledge. People can use them to explain the nature of the world and the reasons that people behave as they do.

Revelation of this sort may also predict future events. Mary Jean's neighbor, Mrs. Roberts, as well as other Jehovah's Witnesses, believes the Bible foretells things to come. Before Jesus Christ died he foretold the signs of His return, when He would come back not in human form, but as the ruler in heaven. He stated that "Nation will rise against nation and kingdom against kingdom, and there will be food shortages and earthquakes in one place and another."[9] This prediction came to pass in 1914, Mrs. Roberts believes, with the start of World War I. Never before had so many countries arisen in arms against one another. Soldiers died by the millions as nation fought nation.

From that point on, the world has been a place of strife, famine, earthquakes, floods, pestilence, and crime. The devil, cast out of heaven by Jesus in 1914, would trouble earth for one full generation. Then, she claimed, the Bible foretold that God would put an end to "this system of things" at Armageddon. Bible prophecy also indicated that Jehovah God would create a new earthly paradise, as we have seen, one free of wicked humans and demons, one in which people would learn righteousness, one where "the earth will certainly be filled with the knowledge of Jehovah as the waters are covering the very sea."[10]

Spirit Possession

One of the most common forms of ritual communication is spirit possession, in which a supernatural being enters and controls the behavior of a human being. A possessing spirit may actually talk to people or in some other manner communicate messages or its presence. Neither Bazugba nor Mary Jean employs this means of communication to discover answers to their questions, although there is one kind of ritual specialist among the Azande who dances wildly about at public seances and, in a trancelike state, identifies witches. However, many other people in the world are well acquainted with possession and use it regularly to communicate with supernatural beings.

Kanji Katara, the Bhil from India described in Chapter 5, is one such individual. In Kanji's village there are ritual specialists called *bhopas* who are regularly possessed by several local deities. They begin by alerting the deity that his presence is needed. When the spirit appears, it causes the body of the medium to shake violently and breathe in a peculiar and stylized manner. Then the spirit speaks through its mortal vehicle, informing people who are there of things they wish to

[9]Matthew 24:7.

[10]See Isaiah 26:9, 11:9; Acts 17:31.

A Bhil bhopa (shaman) possessed by the hill god Mangrababa. The god, speaking through the shaman, questions a man suffering from a stomach disorder about his ailment, and promises help.

know, answering questions, and blessing the infirm. There is no more direct or dramatic means of communication than possession, and no greater proof of the existence of supernatural beings to those who communicate with spirits in this scene.

Divination

Divination is as common to the Azande as spirit possession is rare. Since life is under constant threat of attack by witches, sorcerers, and ghosts, the outcome of almost every venture is in doubt. It pays to discover beforehand if such an attack might occur so that it can be avoided or precautions taken to lessen the harm caused by the attack. For this reason, Bazugba and his fellow tribesmen employ several means of <u>divination</u>, the use of supernatural force associated with material objects to provide answers to particular questions. Bazugba owns a rubbing board oracle (*iwa*) that when prepared and addressed properly, indicates the answers to questions by causing pieces of wood to stick as one is drawn over the other. Or he can employ the three-sticks oracle (*mapingo*), by placing three small sticks in a pyramid outside his house at night and interpreting its answer by whether or not the sticks remain in their original position. He may also use the termite oracle (*dakpa*) by placing two small branches of different kinds of wood into a hole in a termite nest and reading the answer by observing which of the sticks, if any, is eaten the next day.

The most important form of divination, however, the one that always answers truthfully, is *benge*, the poison oracle. In fact, when we first met Bazugba, he was walking to the secluded place where he and his friend Bafuka could consult this oracle. Knowing by the long-term nature of her disease that Nabani had been attacked by a witch, and having in mind the name of a particular person, Kisanga, because of the answers given him by the rubbing board oracle, Bazugba intended to divine the name of the culprit by the surest method possible. Bafuka had preceded him, carrying a basket filled with half-grown chickens and a bundle containing *benge*, the powdered substance made from a creeper that, when fed to chickens, answered the questions put to it. As Bazugba approached the clearing, he could see Bafuka already seated on the ground. Before his friend were the basket of chickens and a shallow leaf-lined hole in which he had mixed some of the *benge* powder with water to make a paste. Each man greeted the other, and Bazugba sat down saying, "Let us begin."

Bafuka opened the basket and took out a small pullet, pinning the bird by her wings to the ground beneath his feet. Next, he picked up a small bundle of grass that he had fashioned into a brush, and twirled it round and round in the *benge* paste. Then he selected a special leaf he had gathered to make a filter and, using it to roll up the little paste-laden brush, placed it inside the bird's beak, squeezing the liquid from the paste into the bird's throat as he did so. Bazugba now addressed the *benge*:

Benge, benge, *you are in the throat of the fowl. Is Nabani's illness due to Kisanga? Oh*, benge, *hear it, kill the fowl.*

Over and over again Bazugba addressed the *benge* in this fashion, continuing to intone the words as Bafuka administered a second dose of *benge* to the chicken, shook it by the feet, and placed it on the ground. At first the pullet appeared to walk normally, then it faltered as if suddenly paralyzed, and fell, fluttering, on its side. When it was dead, Bafuka cut off one of its wings and threw the body into the brush.

Although the *benge* had identified Nabani's attacker during this first test, Bazugba knew that a second test was necessary to confirm the answer. Bafuka took out another fowl, administered the poison twice, and held it while Bazugba addressed the *benge* a second time. But what he said was different; this time he asked the *benge* to spare the chicken.

Benge, benge, *you are in the throat of the fowl. Is it Kisanga who has attacked Nabani? Oh*, benge, *hear it, spare the fowl.*

Placed on the ground like the first, the second bird staggered for an instant, defecated profusely, then pecked at bits of leaf and wood it spied on the ground as if nothing unusual had happened to it. When he realized this bird would live, Bazugba knew that he had identified the witch and made plans to inform Kisanga of his transgression.

Thus, by unleashing the supernatural force locked in the *benge*, Bazugba was able to find an answer to a puzzling question. With the wing of the dead fowl in hand he would approach Kisanga and ask him to "cool" his witchcraft. Kisanga would apologize for his witchcraft, claiming that he was not aware of what it was doing, and blow a mouth full of water on the wing as a sign of cooperation. If all went well, Nabani would get better.

Religious Specialists

Although the members of most societies are able to communicate personally with the supernatural, many groups possess people with special religious knowledge who either control supernatural power outright or facilitate others in their attempt to influence it. These specialists are called shamans and priests.

Shamans

Shamans are religious specialists who control supernatural power. They often possess a personal relationship with supernatural beings or know the secret medicines and spells necessary to use supernatural force. They do not head congregations, conducting their rites only when there is need for them. They are frequently associated with curing and are often represented in the popular literature as medicine men and witch doctors. The Bhil *bhopa* mentioned earlier is a shaman. So are older Azande men who know about many different medicines and use them magically.

Priests

Priests are religious specialists who mediate between people and supernatural beings. Unlike shamans, they do not control supernatural power. They usually lead congregations at regular, cyclical rites. They help their congregations petition the supernatural to demonstrate faith and obedience.

The Jehovah's Witnesses are unusual in respect to the presence of priests, for among them, every member of the congregation is considered a religious specialist. As Mrs. Roberts pointed out to Mary Jean in one of their regular Bible study sessions, the road to salvation requires obedience to God's word and the conduct of one's life in a way that will convince Jehovah God that one understands His laws as they are revealed in the Bible. Of paramount importance is studying and learning God's perfect knowledge. Righteous people must live in moderation according to God's will and associate only with God's sheep, that is, with other righteous people who have chosen to obey Jehovah.

To achieve these prescriptions, Jehovah's Witnesses organize themselves into local congregations, each with its own *Kingdom Hall*. These, in turn, are part of *circuits*, *districts*, and larger units that encompass almost every part of the world. Every other week the members of the board of the Watch Tower Bible and Tract Society of Pennsylvania send out copies of *The Watchtower* and *Awake!* Every Sunday morning, congregations all over the world take an hour to study the mes-

Priests are usually full-time specialists who possess the complex knowledge necessary to mediate between people and the supernatural. This Japanese Buddhist priest is seen in meditation, surrounded by ritual items that symbolize his special position.

sages printed that week in *The Watchtower*, messages that teach how the Bible speaks of the world and the need to act righteously now before Armageddon strikes people down. The society also prints various kinds of books, such as Bible helps, for study by its congregations. Local units, such as the East Congregation to which Mrs. Roberts belongs, are organized to distribute, study, and disseminate the information printed in these materials. The congregation has a Congregation Servant and a Bible Study Servant who look after the needs and activities of the members.

But the servants are not the only priests in the congregation; everyone is trained to preach and minister to people. Perhaps the most distinctive and time-consuming activity, one that best communicates to God one's righteous devotion to His perfect knowledge, is the door-to-door ministry, or "publishing," as Witnesses often refer to it. Jehovah God did not mean for his flock to be led by special ministers. Instead, all righteous people are to be ministers of God's perfect knowledge. That is why the congregation has no pastor, but simply members who serve the others in an organizational capacity. And that is also why every adult Witness is expected to carry God's word from door to door, preaching a sermon to any who will listen.

Mary Jean became such a minister or, in our terms, a priest, when she decided, on the basis of her many long talks with Mrs. Roberts and subsequent activities at Kingdom Hall, to accept Jehovah God and join the East Congregation. She remembered well the first time she went out "in service." Almost immediately on joining the East Congregation she began to train in the ministry, learning how to put together a simple but powerful sermon about Bible truth and Bible prophecy. She stood up before the congregation on several occasions and gave sermons, and the others critiqued her delivery and the strength and clarity of her message. But there was no substitute for the real thing, and soon Mary Jean accompanied Mrs. Roberts to a section of a working-class neighborhood in a suburb just west of Chicago. Getting out of their car, Mrs. Roberts and Mary Jean checked their appearance (they dressed neatly when they published from door to door), looked in the briefcase each carried to see that they had copies of *Awake!*, *The Watchtower*, and a pamphlet entitled "Is Time Running Out for Mankind?" and walked up to the first house on the block. Almost at once an older woman answered the door bell, opening the door only wide enough to see what the pair wanted. Mrs. Roberts spoke first. "Good morning," she said. "My name is Mrs. Roberts, and this is Mrs. Getz. We were in your neighborhood this morning and thought you might be interested in what the Bible tells us about the times we live in." Almost before the last words were out of her mouth, the door slammed in Mrs. Roberts' face. Mary Jean looked at her and, addressing the door as though it could hear, quietly exclaimed, "And have a nice day!"

Mrs. Roberts smiled at Mary Jean and told her that people often shut their doors like that, but others would listen, and occasionally someone would show real interest. In the latter instance Mary Jean and Mrs. Roberts would note down the need to make a return visit, or "call back." As they worked their way down the street, one man took a copy of "Is Time Running Out for Mankind?" from them, several people politely said they were not interested, and one woman invited them in for a cup of coffee.

As Mary Jean published from door to door, and as she and Bob came to know the other members of the East Congregation, her sense of confidence in herself and the purpose of her life was restored. To be sure, there was crime and unpleasantness in her neighborhood, but these were good signs, indications of the coming of a new world. Just as Bazugba took appropriate actions of a religious nature to restore his wife to health, so did she behave in a way designed to free her from this unpleasant world.

SUMMARY

Religion is the cultural knowledge of the supernatural that people use to cope with the ultimate problems of human existence. Ultimate problems include those of meaning, death, evil, and transcendent values. An important aspect of religion is the supernatural, or the realm that is beyond ordinary experience. It is through the supernatural that an Azande husband and an urban American wife can solve the problems that afflict them.

Religion involves supernatural power, the ability of the supernatural to act. Supernatural power may be divided into two types, personified power associated with supernatural beings and impersonal power found free in things and people. Supernatural power may be influenced by prayer, a petition directed at such power, sacrifice, the act of giving up something to the supernatural, witchcraft, the activity of people who inherit supernatural force and use it for evil, and magic, the strategies people use to control supernatural power.

The existence of personified and impersonal supernatural power implies the need for communication. One means of communication is divine revelation. This information, often of a predictive sort, is about the nature of the world and present and future events. Direct communication is possible through spirit possession, the habitation of a human being by a spirit so that the human being's actions are thought to be those of the spirit. Through the practice of divination, the supernatural may communicate answers to questions by objective signs in material objects. Finally, communication may be directed or facilitated by shamans and priests. Shamans control supernatural power, have no congregations, and direct rituals only when there is need for them. Priests mediate between people and the supernatural and lead congregations at regularly held cyclical rites.

MAJOR CONCEPTS

RELIGION	PRAYER
ULTIMATE PROBLEMS	SACRIFICE
TRANSCENDENT VALUES	WITCHCRAFT
THE SUPERNATURAL	MAGIC
SUPERNATURAL POWER	SORCERY
PERSONIFIED POWER	DIVINE REVELATION
IMPERSONAL SUPERNATURAL FORCE	SPIRIT POSSESSION
	DIVINATION
SUPERNATURAL BEINGS	SHAMANS
MANA	PRIESTS
TABOO	

SELECTED READINGS

Banton, Michael (editor): *Anthropological Approaches to the Study of Religion*. Association of Social Anthropologists of the Commonwealth, Monograph No. 3, New York: Praeger, 1966.

A collection of five papers, two of which deal with the nature and explanation of religion; the remaining three describe aspects of African religious systems.

Evans-Pritchard, E. E.: *Nuer Religion*, Oxford: Clarendon Press, 1956.

A classic ethnography of religion among the Nuer detailing the nature of Nuer supernatural beings and practices and relating these to other features of Nuer life.

Lessa, William, and Evon Z. Vogt (editors): *Reader in Comparative Religion: An Anthropological Approach*, 3d ed., New York: Harper & Row, 1971.
A broad collection of articles on religion with extensive comment by the editors. The book includes a wide variety of both descriptive and theoretical articles and is an especially important and valuable source on religion.

Middleton, John (editor): *Magic, Witchcraft and Curing*, Garden City, N.Y.: Natural History Press, 1967.
A broad collection of articles on various aspects of the study of religion.

Norbeck, Edward: *Religion in Primitive Society*, New York: Harper & Row, 1961.
This book is an introduction to the anthropological study of religion that takes a functionalist point of view.

Wallace, Anthony F. C.: *Religion: An Anthropological View*, New York: Random House, 1966.
A view of religion that stresses its social and psychological functions. Includes a classification of religious behavior and a discussion of revitalization.

CHAPTER FOURTEEN

World
View and
Values

In the study of any single culture, anthropologists engage in *analysis*. In making cross-cultural comparisons, we should also analyze each culture into parts. We break down social life into basic elements, searching for categories, isolating domains, and identifying rules. We segment and classify social behavior into analytic concepts such as language, social structure, kinship, economics, technology, and religion. This is done because the route to scientific knowledge lies in taking things apart for more careful scrutiny. Literature, art, and music may try to capture the grand design, but science has the primary task of analysis and classification. Yet anthropologists also lay stress on *synthesis*. We examine each part of a culture; we also seek to understand the whole.

PATTERNS OF CULTURE

There are three ways in which anthropologists attempt to deal with the total pattern of a single culture; we focus on the *context* of a single part, the *function* of elements, and the *configuration* of all the parts.

Context

In dealing with cultural subsystems such as kinship, or religion, we have emphasized the importance of context. Context refers to the network of customs that are immediately linked to a particular cultural practice. The social structure was broken down into concepts such as status, role, and group. However, statuses are symbolized in language, roles are enacted in economic and religious events, and groups have specialized communication systems. We examined territorial groups, age sets, men's and women's organizations, caste, and kinship, but each of these interpenetrate the language, politics, and religion of any culture. Tools and technology are used by people as they play assigned roles; exchanges occur between kinsmen and age mates; production and trade almost always involve speech. Religion was separated into magic, taboo, ritual, and supernatural beings, but in everyday life it cannot be so easily compartmentalized. If cultural anthropology says anything about social behavior it proclaims that we must understand the full context of each action, each custom.

Function

The second way in which anthropologists show that the parts of any cultural system are interrelated is to trace their function. Function refers to the consequences of a particular cultural practice. As we have shown, rites of passage have consequences far beyond the rituals themselves. Religion serves a variety of human needs, contributing to the integration of society, whether one is an Azande or a Jehovah's Witness. Rituals often integrate a society or some group within it, reinforcing social values and creating strong bonds among people. Economic systems provide for physical needs, but they also have consequences for political life and a society's ranking system. In tracing the function of any cultural behavior, we examine its consequences on other parts of the wider cultural system.

Configuration

In addition to examining context and function, anthropology aims to describe the overall configuration of each human culture. Configuration refers to the pattern of interrelationships among all the major elements of a culture. Insights do result from a careful analysis of parts, but cultures form integrated wholes and can be treated as such. Although the emphasis on configuration received great impetus from Ruth Benedict's classic book, *Patterns of Culture*, the search for integration and synthesis reaches back into the nineteenth century. The dominant trend in contemporary research is in the direction of more rigorous analysis of smaller cultural elements, but interest in larger patterns remains.

In this chapter we shift our attention from the parts of cultural systems to the patterns that make up the total culture. In order to see how cultures are patterned and integrated, we will discuss a single example, the Mae Enga of Highland New Guinea studied by the anthropologist Mervyn Meggitt.[1] As an ethnographer, your task is to discover the patterns that underlie the surface categories, the rules, and the coded information of this culture. To assist in this project, we will discuss some of the concepts that anthropologists have used to understand the larger configurations of individual cultures. Together we will try to formulate some of the major patterns of Mae Enga world view and values.

THE MAE ENGA

Across the Torres Straits, due north of Australia, lies the enormous island of New Guinea, second in size only to Greenland. Like a giant bird pointing to the north-

[1]This case study is based on the many publications of M. J. Meggitt on the Mae Enga. The most recent source that gives references to many of the earlier publications is his *Blood Is Their Argument*, Palo Alto, Calif.: Mayfield, 1977.

A high valley in Mae Enga territory. Gardens often are located as high as 8500 feet above sea level.

west, this island stretches for 1500 miles. Rugged mountain ranges run down the center of the island, their high valleys drained by fast-flowing rivers with such names as the Sepik, the Lagaipu, the Maramuni, and the Mamberambo. Some mountain peaks reach to more than 15,000 feet in elevation. In the Central Highlands, scattered along the Lai, the Lagaipu, and the Ambumu river valleys, live some 30,000 Mae Enga. European explorers first encountered the Enga people in 1934.

It is not difficult to fly from the coast into Wabag, a small town from which this subdistrict is administered. From there to the Kauwai clan territory you must walk, and you are exhausted on arrival, partly because of the quick change in altitude. By means of an interpreter and your own limited knowledge of pidgin, you finally make it clear to Wakul, the "Big Man" in this clan, that you wish to stay here and would like to hire someone to build a house for you. You had noticed a cluster of several large, thatched houses, some at least 30 feet long. "That must be where these people live," you thought to yourself; perhaps it will be possible to have one built nearby. Wakul laughed in surprise when your interpreter made your suggestion. "Oh, no!" his reply came back. "Those are women's houses, men do not live there!" Here was your first introduction to Mae Enga culture. Wakul and several others agree to build a small house for you near their men's houses, but it will take a week or so to collect the materials and then 4 days to complete. The time passes quickly, and soon you are settled into your new house, eager to commence fieldwork.

You begin to learn the Enga language, improve your pidgin, and fit into the daily round of life. From your house, which is on good garden land, the ground slopes toward the rushing river nearby. For the next year you will live at this 7000-foot elevation, sometimes climbing to gardens and other homesteads located as high as 8500 feet along the sides of the valleys. You will occasionally hunt with the Kauwai men in the pine and hardwood forests that stretch out above these homesteads, eventually running into the scrubby trees above 9500 feet. In this part of Enga territory the valley floors are above 5500 feet and, because of the density and land demands of this population of gardeners, support relatively few trees. In the lower valleys inhabited by other groups of the Enga, however, there are thick rain forests, a haven for malarial mosquitos, where few homesteads are built.

Mae Enga men putting up the frame for a new house. House-building is a major occasion for cooperative activity among the men.

Mae Enga gardens along the steep valley walls above the river.

One day, during your first month among the Mae Enga, you go with Wakul to eat at the house where his wife lives. Like the other men, you sit on one side of the yard, apart from the women. It is difficult to understand what people are saying; you listen, watch, eat. You notice that most of the men are served steamed bananas, taro, sweet potatoes, and some possum meat, whereas some of the older men and all the women are eating house rats that the women have cooked. The women also eat grasshoppers, beetle larvae, and what look like spiders.

When the meal is over, Wakul motions for you to come, and along with his wife you walk toward his sweet potato gardens, which are about half a mile up the slope. As you near the gardens, you notice hanging from a vine stretched around the garden old pieces of women's aprons. Wakul's wife now walks ahead of you, goes underneath the vine, and begins to inspect the sweet potato plants. Wakul stops, but you continue to walk toward the garden. Suddenly, when you are about 10 yards beyond him, Wakul shouts loudly, "No! No!" You look back and see that he is pointing at the aprons hanging from the vine and motioning you back; his manner indicates that this is a serious matter. You take a few more steps toward the garden, and his urgings grow more intense. Now his wife, hearing him call, turns and warns you back with a quick motion of her hands. You still aren't sure why they have stopped you. A few minutes later, when Wakul's wife rejoins you for the walk back to the thatched houses, she seems under no stress, thus leaving you totally confused as to why they should both have been so concerned that you not pass under the aprons. You make note of this brief incident, and as your facility with the language grows, you ask about it. "Yes," they all tell you, "it is dangerous for a man to enter the gardens under such aprons."

Wakul has two wives, and while this doubled his payment of bridewealth, it is one reason people recognize him as a Big Man. His other wife frequently lives for long periods with her own people in the territory of the Kondama clan. One or two Big Men have four wives, and in the Kondama clan there is one who has eight wives. Not many men have even two wives, and it seems to be of considerable importance, something others would like but cannot achieve. Each of his wives has her own house, and both contain 10 stalls inside, between the sleeping area and the living room, for Wakul's pigs. One day Wakul comes to your house. The cassowary quill through his nasal septum gleams in the light as he enters, and his mushroom-shaped wig, decorated with leaves and tattered feathers, looks very impressive. He tells you he has been with his brother to another clan where they discussed bridewealth. His brother's son, Kinala, has been betrothed to a girl there, and they hope he will marry soon. He is nearly 30 years old, and Wakul confides in you that Kinala is putting up considerable resistance to the plan. Not that he doesn't want this particular girl—it is the timing. Kinala wants to wait a few years before settling down to married life; his father wants him to marry now so he will have grandsons soon. A few weeks later a large number of pigs are escorted to the Tereposa people and Kinala's bride-to-be returns with the party. A new house is built for her and, when Kinala's family kills the pigs sent in return for the bridewealth, the marriage is final. It seems strange to you that at this point Kinala disappears from the homestead area and is gone for nearly a month, but no one else seems to notice, least of all his new wife. On his return you ask him about the wedding and where he went. He explains, "My father said it was time to marry and have children. If I did not, his ghost would return to kill me. I've been staying with a married kinsman learning magic." In the months to come you find that Kinala is not the only young bachelor who would like to postpone his marriage but goes ahead with it for fear of ghostly retaliation from his father at some future time.

Pigs are everywhere in this high valley. When among trusted friends or relatives the men talk constantly of their herds, of exchanges, of new pigs they have received, and each new litter causes considerable excitement. Whenever you are at the women's houses it is not uncommon for pigs and piglets to be underfoot everywhere. They often run loose inside the house, they eat leftover food from meals, and everyone pays special attention to them. You have seen Wakul's wife, as well as other women, holding young piglets to their breasts to nurse. Orphan pigs especially are suckled along with children. Pigs are not eaten at regular meals, but there have been times when they have been killed, cooked, distributed to many people, and eaten.

Early one morning you are awakened by a commotion outside your house and find a group of men are arguing noisily in front of the men's house. Pulling on your clothes you join them and try to make out what has happened. It soon becomes clear. One of Wakul's boars, a large one with a deformed stomach, has destroyed half an acre of another man's garden. Everyone knows that Wakul will have to repay the man and that he will probably cut off his youngest son's earlobe, cook it, and make him eat it so he will pay attention when herding the swine in the future. But this is not what concerns the men. They discuss in low tones a much more serious matter—why this boar destroyed the garden; it seems to have something to do with a ghost. Within the hour the men are heating rocks for the oven in front of Wakul's wife's house, all except for Wakul, who cannot handle these stones because, he tells you, he had sexual intercourse with his wife this morning. Two pigs are slain, but not the large boar that did the damage. Wakul carefully cuts off the penis of each pig and fashions them into bracelets for his daughter to wear. Weeks later they will rot and drop unnoticed, but until then people will comment on their attractiveness and on his wealth. When the pigs are roasted, a small ceremony is enacted before the meat is distributed and eaten.

By the time you have been with the Kauwai clan for 6 months you will have observed many more events like these, inquired about the rules for behavior, and compiled a long list of cultural categories. From these three incidents alone and your careful inquiry about their meaning you can formulate the following cultural rules.

1. Men should not enter gardens when women's aprons are hanging from the vines around them.
2. Married men would like to have two wives.
3. Big Men often have more than one wife.
4. Young men resist getting married.
5. Young men marry out of fear of their fathers' ghosts.
6. Men and women must live in separate houses.
7. Pigs are killed in connection with ghosts.
8. Men cannot touch cooking stones on a day they have had sexual intercourse with their wives.

Most of these rules pertain to the men's culture on which you are gathering most of your information. These and many other bits of interesting information are beginning to fill your field notes about Mae Enga culture. You have names for the lineages, clans, and phratries to which the 30,000 Mae Enga belong. You have collected the names for 31 varieties of sweet potato, more than 10 different kinds of frogs, and many names for other plants and animals. You realize that your lists of cultural categories and rules could be extended indefinitely and that each might be classified into larger categories such as language, economics, and religion.

You also know, however, that an adequate description of Mae Enga culture must contain more than a random list of cultural rules. These are only a beginning, the first faltering steps toward discovering the larger patterns of this culture. Like an iceberg, much of Mae Enga culture is beneath the surface of social life, an unconscious patterning that gives the overall configuration its meaning to the Mae Enga. Your search will be better informed by an understanding of the concept of *world view*.

WORLD VIEW

Every culture involves a way of viewing the world, a perspective for interpreting the universe of human experience. World view is the way a people characteristically looks out on the universe. It consists of the most general and comprehensive concepts and unstated assumptions about life. World view, in part, helps to integrate the bits and pieces of culture, the customs that seem unrelated or contradictory; world view permeates the hundreds of named categories and domains. A particular world view cannot usually be stated or formulated with precision by the people. You will have to discover Mae Enga world view by searching for the unstated ways of looking at life, by putting together the pieces of this puzzle and making inferences about the perspective that gives it overall meaning.

Universal
Features of World View

Robert Redfield maintained that the ground plan for every world view is similar. Each human culture, he argued, is like a stage set; it provides people at the center of the stage with a view, a perspective. Every such stage set includes very general conceptions of the following.

1. The self as a kind of actor on the stage.
2. Others as generalized kinds of people.
3. Groups of people.
4. Ways in which men and women differ.
5. A distinction between "we" and "they," between one's own people and other people.
6. A distinction between that which is human and that which is nonhuman.
7. Invisible beings, forces, or principles.
8. Animals.
9. Concepts of human nature.
10. A spatial orientation.
11. A temporal orientation.
12. Ideas about birth and death.

Although this list may be helpful, it is only a start, and these conceptions cannot be easily separated among the Mae Enga. As you participate in the daily round of life, visiting gardens, sitting for long hours at night in the men's houses, talking with Wakul, Kinala, and others, traveling to nearby lineages to distribute pork or search for lost pigs, sitting in the yards outside one or another woman's house, you begin to gain an understanding of Mae Enga world view.

The Nature of
Male and Female

Human nature, for example, is a complex matter. The Enga believe that during sexual intercourse semen and menstrual blood combine to form the new life; 4 months later it receives a spirit and personality. Although each person is formed by the collective spirits of his maternal and paternal kinsmen, their roles are dif-

Young children, whether male or female, are part of the women's world. Only after a boy grows older will he begin to leave the house of his mother to live in the men's house.

ferent. Wakul explains it to you: "When people die, their spirits go to live with the clan spirits. The spirits of all my father's clan members, the Kauwai people, these spirits made my spirit and my children's spirits. My body was made by the blood and vitality of my mother and her kinsmen, the people of the Yumanda clan. All people have two parts, spirit and flesh." You also discover that men and women are made differently. Females have flesh that is laid vertically along their bones, male flesh follows a horizontal pattern. Females mature much earlier than males, a reason that young men must use magic to hasten their own physical development. Young girls are ready to marry when they are 15 or 16, but no man would think of marriage until he is in his mid-twenties, and many postpone it until after 30. Women can tend pigs, but only men can kill them and cook their meat. The Mae Enga view of human nature and the differences between men and women seems very important.

In fact, you find that male and female are two principles that organize much of Mae Enga experience. Flesh and blood are female, spirit is male, pigs are part of the female world, game is male; the moon is female, the sun is male. Even the immediate spirit world is divided on the basis of male and female: ghosts of one's mother's clan and ghosts of one's father's clan. The left hand is considered female and the right hand male, as you are soon to discover.

Ancestral Ghosts

One afternoon Wakul returned to the men's house deeply troubled. Mapu, his eldest son of 14 years, had suddenly become ill. You visit him, lying on a low bed in the men's house, and his symptoms suggest pneumonia. There is little you can do. Wakul tells you, "It is my mother's ghost. She has bitten Mapu." Later that afternoon he kills two fowls and a pig and offers them to his mother's ghost. As men sit around and eat the meat, this "shadow pork" offered to Wakul's mother, there is a somber appearance on their faces. Everyone wonders whether the ghost will end her attack. Wakul returns to sit beside Mapu, to watch for signs that the gift of pork has convinced her to stop eating his son.

You wonder how Wakul knew it was his mother's ghost, since he did not call a diviner. The next day you find out from other men. Several years before his parents died, Wakul received an enormous pig in a ceremonial distribution. His mother and father each wanted the animal and urged him not to give it away to other people, to give it to them. Sometimes old women can "own" a pig, and his mother wanted this one for herself. Wakul eventually, however, gave it to his father and greatly angered Wane, his old and domineering mother. She berated him in public for his meanness and told everyone again what an ungrateful son she had borne when, a year later, Wakul's father gave the pig away in a distribution. Now it became clear why Wakul's large boar with the deformed stomach had destroyed another man's garden. Everyone knew when it was born with a deformity that Wakul's mother's ghost was still angry. Some said he should kill this pig immediately and give it to his mother's ghost, but he refused, and it grew into an enormous boar. When it rooted up the garden, everyone was sure that it was his mother's ghost at work, that she wanted pork, and that this boar should be quickly killed and offered to her. Instead, Wakul gave it to another clan in a distribution of wealth, and now his mother had retaliated and attacked his eldest son. A few days later Mapu died.

Wakul was grief stricken, yet the mourning period was hardly over before he had to send 10 pigs to his wife's clan as payment for the injury to Mapu's maternally derived flesh. Wakul knew that his mother would only kill once; she would now merge with the ancestral spirits of the clan, driven away by her victim, the ghost of Mapu. But now Wakul had a new worry. It was not long before he began to dream that Mapu appeared to him with an angry reproachment: "If you had not sent that deformed boar to another clan to feed a stranger's ghost, your mother's ghost would not have bitten me." As soon as a diviner helped Wakul to interpret the dream, he sacrificed a pig to feed "shadow pork" to Mapu's ghost. It would only be a matter of time before he would attack someone dear to Wakul.

Hardly a day goes by that you do not hear someone talking about the activities of one or another ghost. Sometimes events among the Mae Enga are not so clear as to indicate which ghost has killed someone. Whenever illness comes quickly, someone has an accident, or there is a sudden death, everyone knows it means a ghost has bitten someone. In the case of death an autopsy reveals whether the ghost is from your mother's kinsmen or from your father's kinsmen. You have heard other men discussing such autopsies. "There were black marks on the right side of his lungs," someone reports. "His paternal kinsmen killed him." If the marks are on the left side, in the heart or lungs, it is the maternal ghosts. Since the maternal ghosts make the body, if they also cause the death, no payment is required. But in the case of Mapu the ghost that killed him was considered part of his father's clan, so pigs had to be sent to Mapu's mother's relatives.

Each day leads to new events among the Mae Enga, events that furnish you with new questions and more clues to decoding this complex culture. Even as you investigate their social system, language, kinship system, animal husbandry, and gardening practices, you continue to gain insight into the broader features of this culture, the Mae Enga world view. The pervasive distinction between male and female and the constant fear of ghostly attack seem to be two fundamental principles of Mae Enga world view.

The concept of world view lacks the precision of many anthropological concepts, partly because its function is to call attention to very general features of the cultural landscape, not to the details of every rock or blade of grass. Anthropologists have used many other concepts in this same way, all in an effort to clarify the overall pattern of a culture. Some have looked for *themes* that run through the content of a culture, like the major ideas of a novel. Others have emphasized *basic personality* or *national character*, seeking to describe the kinds of persons molded by a particular culture. Still others have tried to fit together the pieces of a cultural puzzle with the concept of *ethos*, the dominant emotional tone. We think that one of the most useful concepts to clarify and further our understanding of the underlying ideology of a culture is the notion of *values*. In the rest of this chapter we will leave our partial analysis of world view and turn to an examination of the core values of Mae Enga culture. In so doing, we will extend our understanding of their world view and the overall pattern of this culture.

VALUES

A value is any concept referring to a desirable or undesirable state of affairs. In your research you have already identified many Mae Enga values. "Husbands and wives should not sleep in the same house," Wakul tells you, "nor should a woman enter the men's house." These are undesirable states of affairs. It is, on the other hand, a good thing for a man to have more than one wife, especially if he has a large pig herd. Young men hope their complexions will be clear and unblemished, a desirable state of affairs for Mae Enga males. Our own culture is also constructed largely out of value concepts. Most Americans believe it is desirable that a man have only one wife at a time. If your car suddenly gets a flat tire while you drive along a lonely highway at night, you probably consider it to be an undesirable occurrence. On the other hand, a high grade on a final examination is a desirable event. The financial investor hopes his stock dividends will go up; the sixth-grade boy saves his money to purchase a bicycle; the teen-aged girl likes to know that she has many friends; the middle-aged executive hopes his yearly physical examination will reveal that he is healthy. These are all objects or states of affairs considered to be desirable. Thus values permeate every culture and become attached to most cultural categories, even those that seem neutral.

Values as Concepts

Like all our cultural knowledge, values are mental conceptions. They are also heavily weighted with emotional feelings. Although it is not possible to observe values directly, there are three routes to learning the values of a people. First of all, it is frequently possible to infer values from observable behavior. For example, from the way men and women act toward their pigs you can infer that it is quite important to take care of these animals properly. They live inside a woman's house, each with an individual pen. At night a fire is kindled in the passageway between the pens in order to protect the pigs from the cold that comes to these high valleys. A second, very rich setting for discovering values occurs when parents are teaching their children proper behavior. You saw, for instance, how angry Wakul was when his son was not careful, and the boar wandered into another man's garden. But when he cut off his son's earlobe and made him eat it to teach him to take better care of his pigs, this was not an impulsive act; it was a customary way to teach an important value. You have seen other Mae Enga men reprimanding their sons for carelessness when herding pigs. On occasion they have cut off their sons' earlobes, and several months ago two men took an axe and cut off the first joint of their sons' fingers when several pigs were lost. One father even tied his son securely and hung him over the fire for several hours, berating him for his negligence and telling him how important it was to give his full attention to caring for the pigs. These actions are generated, in part, by the value concept, "It is desirable to take special care of pigs." Third, many cultural values are expressed verbally. When you talk to the men at night in their house, they will often explain to you, "Pigs are our hearts."

As concepts, values are not merely bits of cognitive information. They are deeply held notions that have strong feelings attached to them. The cognitive maps that make up a culture, including the values that are part of those maps, always have an affective (emotional) dimension. Mae Enga women and men not only believe pigs are important, they feel it deeply. When a father punishes his son by hanging him over the fire for negligence in caring for pigs, he acts out of deep concern for pigs and for teaching his children their importance.

Desirable or Undesirable

Before we go further, it is important to distinguish between two kinds of cultural concepts: (1) states of affairs and (2) desirable or undesirable states of affairs. The former refers to what *is*, the latter to values, or what *ought to be*. There is a difference between a state of affairs, such as "Men and women sleep in separate

Pigs are one of the most important symbols of wealth in the central highlands of New Guinea. Orphaned piglets are often cared for along with young children. The net bag hanging down a woman's back and supported by the head is a customary feature of female attire.

houses," and a value, "Men and women *should* sleep in separate houses." If something is merely a state of affairs, no one will be concerned if someone fails to maintain it. On the other hand, when values are violated, it seldom goes unnoticed. Among the Mae Enga, for example, some men occasionally do sleep in the house of their wives, mothers, or sisters, but people tell you it is only because they are old and poor. The other men and women talk about them in a disparaging manner, pointing out to you that they are eccentric.

Every culture contains concepts that refer to states of affairs. Someone says, "It is raining outside," "That is a sweet potato," or "Those trees are in bloom." Although it may appear that concepts that refer to states of affairs do not involve values, they are always based on *underlying values*. The very premises we employ in order to know that something exists involve values. For instance, we only know it is raining outside because we see, hear, or feel the rain. But this means we are trusting our senses to give us reliable information, something we do because we believe it is desirable.

Or take another example. If someone says, "That is a sweet potato," he is employing a cultural category for identifying the tuber of a particular plant. The Mae Enga have at least 31 names for sweet potatoes, differentiating them by skin color, flesh color, leaf conformation, and various maturing times. Implicit in these categories, whether you use one or 31 terms, is the assumption that it is desirable to classify and name things in one way and not another. If we used the Mae Enga categories when shopping for sweet potatoes at the supermarket, other people would think we were foolish or stupid. If a Mae Enga woman adopted a single term for all the different varieties of potatoes recognized by her family and friends, she would be reminded of the proper cultural categories. Failure to use agreed-on concepts for identifying states of affairs does not go unnoticed, pointing to the fact that even a seemingly neutral cultural category such as "sweet potato" involves a value.

But having acknowledged that values are an implicit feature of every cultural category, we find it useful to identify concepts that are *recognized* to refer to desirable states of affairs. Their value content is overt and clear, not hidden and tacit. Take the case of Wakul's large boar with a deformed stomach. His possession of this pig was common knowledge, a socially recognized state of affairs. Furthermore, Mae Enga culture has concepts for identifying the size of pigs, their deformities, and the causes of such physical abnormalities. But these concepts contrast sharply with the widely shared belief that Wakul *ought* to kill this pig and offer its immaterial double, the shadow pork, to his mother's ghost. Furthermore, Wakul's own personal *desire* was in conflict with what even he knew to be a desirable action—killing this pig. In this instance he failed to live up to the cultural value and, from the Mae Enga perspective, suffered the consequences when his eldest son was bitten by his mother's ghost. It is important, then, to distinguish among the following.

1. Things as they are (facts).
2. Things as they ought to be (values).
3. Things as someone wants them to be (desires).

Core Values

Some values refer to specific actions such as taking care of pigs or killing pigs for ghosts. Other values refer to general categories of behavior and cover many specific instances. Core values refer to the most general concepts of desirable and undesirable states of affairs. Every culture contains a limited number of core values. Once we identify the core values of a culture we can begin to understand the overall culture pattern more clearly. We can illustrate the differences between specific values and more general core values by looking at our own culture.

Cleanliness in American Culture

An observer in our own society would quickly notice that many people carefully wash their hands before eating. As families converge at the dinner table, mothers or fathers ask their young children if they have washed their hands. Sometimes a child is asked to produce his clean hands for inspection, and any evidence that dirt remains means another trip to the bathroom with the comment, "And this time use soap." One can easily formulate the following widely held cultural value from instances such as these.

1. It is desirable to wash your hands before eating a meal.

Further observation would undoubtedly lead to a more general value. For instance, our observer would note that people wash frequently, not merely before meals. She would note that if someone did not have an opportunity to bathe every few days, he might commonly report feeling "grubby." Individuals often use chemical substances to cover or hide body odors and people who do not keep themselves clean and free of certain odors are the subject of gossip. Children are reminded to take baths frequently and might be forced to do so even though they protest that their bodies are clean. Such observations lead to the following more general value statement.

2. It is desirable to keep the human body free from dirt and normal odors.

Now if our observer listened to people talk and made further observations, she could identify related values of wider generality. If she visited someone unexpectedly they might make excuses about the lack of order and cleanliness of their living room. At the supermarket she would find large supplies of cleaning agents that men and women purchase regularly. New products that companies claim work more effectively than any others are advertised on television and in the newspaper. People wash their cars and cover them with chemical substances that make them appear clean for longer periods of time. The creation of mythical heroes such as "Mr. Clean" is not out of place in this culture. Our investigator could easily formulate the more general value as follows.

3. It is desirable to keep most material objects clean and orderly.

Her observations would probably be supplemented by numerous proverbs such as "Cleanliness is next to godliness" and "A place for everything and everything in its place." Thus after careful research she would identify the more general value.

4. It is desirable to live an orderly and disciplined life.

These last two general propositions about what is desirable are core values that would enable her to make sense out of a vast range of social behavior. In general core values enable us to interpret many specific actions and to fit them into the larger patterns of the culture.

Mae Enga Core Values

1. *Pigs are wealth, and it is desirable to increase the supply of pigs and of pork.* This is the most obvious core value, and one that you are able to formulate quite early in your fieldwork. It also enables you to understand much of Mae Enga behavior. For example, one day after you have a fair command of the Enga language and the local people have come to take you for granted, you decide to investigate the inside of the women's houses. You have been in their yards often, but because men seldom enter, you have only looked inside the long, thatched houses. You know that the front part is a room where people congregate but the remainder of the house is divided differ-

Stone axes are one medium of exchange among the Mae Enga. The typical wig of the males appears here almost like a large hat.

ently from the men's houses. Wakul's wife seems eager to have you look around. Beyond the living room is a passageway with five pigpens on each side, and in the back is another much smaller room, one in which the women sleep. Your hostess tells you not to go further; men are not allowed in the back room. Even sexual intercourse between married couples occurs away from the houses in the bush. It is midday, and she explains why one pig is still confined in its pen: "Wakul received that one yesterday from a Big Man in another clan, and it would return home if we let it go with the others to feed in the bush. Later it will learn this is its new home and stay."

When you inquire why he received this pig, Wakul's wife tells you, "It was a payment. Wakul has a large boar that he saw mating with a sow in the bush; he traced the sow to its owner and demanded one of the litter. We watched the moon for 4 months, and the sow had her litter right on time." On the front wall of the living room, stuck into the matted stems and leaves of canegrass, you can see literally dozens of pig bones. These bones, you learn, attract new pigs to the herd. Tucked in beside some of the bones and above them in the gable of the house are packets of iris leaves that Wakul has treated with spells from his store of family-owned magic. These also attract more pigs. These means of acquiring pigs are used because no matter how industrious one is in caring for pigs, no matter how shrewd a man might be in increasing his herd through ceremonial exchanges, he cannot control everything that determines the number of pigs he owns. This magic induces his debtors to meet their obligations and makes men from distant places give generously when exchanges take place. Magic leaves are also used to rub pigs or are fed to unsuspecting pigs inside sweet potatoes to increase their growth. A few days later you visit again and find that Wakul's wife has tied a piglet by its hind legs and has it hanging from the rafters inside the front room of her house. You watch as she takes a fire stick from the fireplace and singes off the pig's hair, then rubs the squealing animal with grey clay while saying magic spells. She knows that if her pigs are scrawny, Wakul may beat her, and this magic, like the use of leaves, helps to make the pigs healthy and fat.

Before you leave the Mae Enga you will have discovered dozens of other strategies for increasing pig wealth. Men marry extra wives because they alone can tend sweet potatoes and care for pigs. In order to escape losing one's entire stock by diseases that can strike down hundreds of pigs in a single area, wives sometimes take their husband's pigs to live in different territories with other relatives. Some men farm out a few pigs to their sisters or other relatives in other clan territories, thus reducing the risk of total loss that might occur if they were kept in one place. Men buy pigs, paying a stone ax-blade or a gourd full of tree oil for a knee-high sow. A 10-foot bamboo of tree oil will buy five pigs. When the Europeans came in about 1940, a pig could be purchased for a single steel ax or spade. Ultimately, the amount of pig wealth any person controls is determined by the ghosts of his paternal relatives, which brings us to two more core values in this culture.

2. *A long life, free from serious illness, malignant disease, and fatal accidents, is desirable.* Because most illnesses and accidents are the direct result of being bitten by a ghost, and because almost all deaths are due to ghostly attack, this value is closely linked to the next.

3. *It is important to be on good terms with ghosts, especially the ghosts of your clan, lineage, and family.* Because ghosts are considered malevolent, the Mae Enga do not

expect them to bestow gifts, protection, or other benefits. Somewhat like people, ghosts are dominated by evil intentions. The goal is to keep them placated, to keep their anger from boiling over into malicious action. Whenever a pig is killed for any reason, the owner dedicates the pig to a ghost or group of ghosts as a form of insurance. Just as social relationships with men are enhanced by gifts of pork and by eating together, so the offer of shadow pork to a ghost helps to keep the relationship in balance. However, ghosts also sometimes demand pork, and a pig must be killed for this purpose alone. Most men readily admit, however, that there is no totally effective means for stopping the malicious activity of ghosts. When you discuss ghost attacks with Mae Enga men, they often say, "The ghost of my father's father killed my father, and my father's ghost will kill me." Giving pigs to ghosts has its counterpart in another core value involving the exchange of pigs among humans.

4. *A man ought to meet his social commitments to distribute pigs.* Although a man's pigs are his own, what he does with his pigs depends on the plans of his kinsmen. One day not long after Mapu's death, you find Wakul in a rage over the behavior of his brother's son, a bachelor in his late twenties. A heated discussion is in progress when you enter the men's house. "You knew we were to send pigs to the Tereposa people," Wakul shouts as he paces back and forth, his displeasure evident for everyone to see. He continues to berate his nephew, and even the boy's father joins in to condemn his son's actions. It will be some time before things have cooled down enough for you to get the details of the dispute. As the group breaks up, Wakul makes one last parting remark to his nephew: "If you keep acting in this way you are going to turn out to be nothing but a Rubbish Man!"

Weeks later you reconstruct the situation. When Mapu was killed by the attack of Wane's ghost, everyone in the subclan knew that a funeral distribution was required. It would take many more pigs than Wakul could muster, and everyone would pitch in, keeping careful track of their contribution. In the future when bridewealth came to the Kauwai people, or another clan sent pigs for a death caused by their ghosts, each person would receive animals according to his rightful share. "But," Wakul tells you, "my brother's son quickly gave his pigs away in private exchanges so he would not have to contribute to the funeral. It made it difficult for us to get together enough pigs to send to my wife's clan."

Mae Enga men do not measure their pig wealth in the size of their immediate herd. Instead, they calculate their pig credits and pig debts as well as the size of their present herd. No one wants others to know how many pigs he has on hand. If he has too large a herd, creditors will descend on him demanding that he give what he owes; if his herd is too small, others will sneer because he is such a poor man. On a single day a man may have a dozen pigs, and if an exchange occurs he might have only two or three the next day. A man's wealth in pigs is estimated also by how many *te* partners he has in other clans. The *te* is a cycle of distributions, involving at least 12,000 men, that occurs periodically. A Big Man may have more than 100 *te* exchange partners in numerous clans, whereas most individuals have less than 25. When the *te* cycle is in full process, more than 30,000 pigs can be moving up and down the valleys, passing from one man to another. At the end of a particular cycle of exchange, each man must repay his partners with a half side of pork for each pig received. Thousands of pigs are killed, and tons of pork, some of it rotten and stink-

A group of men preparing pigs for a ritual feast. Although pigs are eaten, they are usually only killed to appease ghosts or on some ritual occasion such as the trading cycle.

ing, move back along the valleys from one clan area to another. Everyone comes to know the men who give and receive the most pigs. Before your fieldwork is over you will learn of about six cases of homicide in which kinsmen will have to be compensated for the death. There will be 325 pigs given in these six cases, but not all of the 108 men involved make equal contributions. More than half of these pigs will be donated by only 21 Big Men.

Men can advertise their wealth without actually letting on how many pigs they control. After eating a meal of pork you have noticed that men take a bone and slip it over a twig in a high tree. The trees around Wakul's wife's house look as if they are sprouting pig bones. And whenever someone visits Wakul, he points out these bones casually, hinting that he eats pork nearly every day. On every important occasion Wakul wears a net apron to which he, like other men, has attached pigs' tails. More than 80 tails hang from the fringes of his apron, and you have heard of other men who display nearly 100 tails in this manner. Another way men advertise their wealth is by making bracelets from the penis or testes of each pig they kill and giving it to a daughter, niece, or sister, or to some other female relative to display. Each man thus builds a reputation, and people generally know if you are a wealthy Big Man, or poor Rubbish Man, or somewhere in between.

There are several other core values that organize and integrate the cultural knowledge and behavior of the Mae Enga. Although it is not possible to examine all of them here, one is so important to daily life among these people that it must be discussed.

5. *It is desirable. to have a strong body, a beautiful complexion, a high level of self-confidence, and mental well-being.* This concept is shared by men and women, but the concern of men to achieve this core value is much stronger. Girls learn magic spells from their mothers and sisters to increase their beauty, self-confidence, and mental health; boys and men, however, in addition to magic spells, participate in elaborate group rituals and practice many other customs to promote their personal vigor and beauty. In order to understand the way men achieve this value, we must understand more clearly how values function in social life.

Cultural Selection

The most striking feature of human social behavior, in contrast to the behavior of other animals, is the immense range of possibilities available to humankind. Ruth Benedict referred to this as the "arc of possible behavior." All animals engage in behavior directed toward survival, but for most species the range of behavior that will achieve this end is relatively narrow and largely fixed by heredity. Thus what a bee, a dolphin, or a pig *must do* for survival and what each of these creatures *can do* are quite similar. The arc of possible behavior for each of these species is quite restricted. Although people must also perform certain actions in order to survive, what we *must do* as a species and what we *can do* are radically different. Mating must occur for the continuation of the species, but the many ways in which men and women can mate are extremely varied. The young of our species must be taught to cope with danger, but the ways people have devised for dealing with threatening situations vary from attributing them to ghosts to conducting scientific experiments.

The arc of possible behavior is large for humanity. Cultural selection refers to the fact that each culture utilizes only a limited segment of this arc. No society that allowed every possible form of human behavior, that allowed extremely contradictory patterns could survive for long. A society in which people are allowed to murder indiscriminately or one in which all property is owned by individuals and at the same time by all members collectively would be unworkable. Every social order is also a moral order that, based on the society's cultural values, accepts some acts and rejects others. One of the major functions that values serve, then, is to influence the selection of behavior patterns from among the total range of possible alternatives.

If we go back to some of the bits and pieces of Mae Enga culture noted at the beginning of this chapter and restate two of them as specific values, we can then see how such values involve a selection from the arc of possible behavior.

The Mae Enga believe it is desirable for:

1. Young men to postpone marriage as long as possible.
2. Men and women to live in separate houses.

The importance of these values can only be seen if we realize the alternatives they rule out.

The age at which it is *possible* for men and women to marry includes a large segment of the life cycle: child brides as young as 6 years are known among the Nayar of India, and in our own society there are cases where individuals have married after reaching the age of 80 or 90. But not all ages are equally desirable as marriage ages in each society; cultural values function to select some period of time as the one when people should marry. For Mae Enga males the age to marry is during the late twenties or early thirties; for females it is at 15 or 16. Under paternal pressure and fear of ghosts some men marry earlier than others, but none of them marry earlier than girls.

The possible arrangement for domestic living in any society also offers numerous alternatives. Kinsmen can live together by age: children in one house or encampment, young adults in another, elderly in another, and so on. Groups of brothers and sisters could live together in one residence, while spouses live elsewhere, an alternative that exists among the Nayar. Husbands and wives and their immediate children could live in one house or dwelling, while other family members live in other places. Numerous other possibilities could be listed. Mae Enga values influence the alternative selected by most individuals in this mountain valley: men and boys over 5 or 6 years live in a men's house, while wives, daughters, sisters, and small boys live in a house for women. Like all values, these two influence the selection from among alternatives.

Cultural Integration

The rules and values of every culture sometimes conflict. Cultural integration refers to the way conflicting cultural elements are organized so as to minimize contradictions. These clashes are partially resolved by ranking the values themselves. For example, Mae Enga men value both the possession of pigs and the health of their wives and children. Thus the rule that requires a man to kill some pigs if a wife or child is bitten by a ghost presents a conflict of values. The problem can be solved because the Mae Enga value good health more than the possession of pigs. Conflict among specific values can also be resolved by appealing to more general, core values. Although no culture is without internal contradictions, all cultures have some degree of integration; the patterns of behavior selected from the "arc of possible behavior" are not random. Core values function to integrate the categories, rules, and specific values of each culture.

The Sanggai Ritual

As stated earlier, the Mae Enga believe it is desirable for men to have strong, sleek bodies, beautiful complexions, self-confidence, and alert minds. This value integrates many specific cultural beliefs and rules. You have been among the Mae

Enga for more than 9 months when Wakul tells you, "Next month my youngest son will join the bachelors. It is time for the *sanggai*." Wakul seems obviously pleased that his son is to participate in this ritual seclusion of bachelors that occurs about once each year or year and a half. When you inquire about it further he merely says, "It is time that he became a bachelor, for he is no longer a young boy, and he has no magic. The *sanggai* will keep his skin beautiful." You have calculated that his son is about 15 years old, the time when most young men join the bachelors. From now until his marriage, each time the *sanggai* is performed, Wakul's son will participate in the rituals. And then he will no longer need the protection of the *sanggai* because, as Wakul tells you, "He will have his own magic for protection."

It is early April, and the ritual seclusion of bachelors will begin right after the first of May. Since everyone is talking about what will occur, you are able to inquire into the meaning of both these rituals and many of the beliefs underlying them. You have already begun to understand some of the ways the Mae Enga men achieve sleek skins, self-confidence, and strong mind and body, and now it is easy to fill in many of the details. At night the married men are full of talk about their own initiation into the bachelors many years before. But for these months it is the bachelors themselves who hold the center stage in Mae Enga social life.

The Theory of Vital Juices

A man's mental vigor, strength, and complexion, you learn, are directly affected by his own "vital juices." These substances lie just under the skin and are thought to be directly responsible for achieving this condition that all men consider desirable. The most important way that a man's vital juices manifest themselves is as semen. Semen is only one kind of "vital juice" present in the world. The others are shown in the following taxonomy.

Vital Juices	
	Semen
	Milk
	Vaginal secretions
	Sap
	Rendered fat
	Soil grease

Taxonomy of vital juices.

Each time a man ejaculates semen, he loses some of his vital juices, and this loss can lead to enervation, dullness of mind, and skin deterioration. Bachelors derive their protection from the *sanggai*. During the seclusion of 4 or 5 days they will purify their thoughts, rub their bodies with magic iris leaves, and abstain from any reference to sexual or natural functions. They may not see each other's hair, armpits, penises, buttocks, thighs, or soles of the feet. They will not eat pork because women take care of the pigs. During the days of seclusion they will sit around a fire in a special house in the forest, silently meditating on their physical and mental well-being. If a bachelor wishes to go outside for any reason he warns the others to close their eyes, since he might uncover his private parts as he gets up. The ritual period lasts for several weeks; but if any bachelor should violate the taboo on sexual intercourse even after this time it will still affect the health of all the others. In the rare cases where this happens, the culprit must sacrifice a pig, which is ritually consumed by all the bachelors to gain protection. In part, this ritual protects bachelors from uncontrollable loss of their own vital juices and thus contributes to their beauty and well-being.

Once a man marries he is excluded from these periods of ritual seclusion and must depend on his magic to protect himself from uncontrollable losses and to minimize the effects of semen depletion that occur during sexual intercourse. In fact, you now realize why Kinala disappeared right after he was married. Prior to a man's marriage, he seeks out a male relative who has powerful magic, something that can be determined by finding someone with sleek, clear skin. For a bag of pig guts and a few other objects the groom purchases the magic spells this man has used to such good advantage. Then, as soon as he is married, he learns from this man how to practice these spells and to prepare himself for settling down to married life. For at least the first year or two after marriage each man will perform his magic before sexual intercourse in order to conserve his semen.

Female Avoidance

But conservation of one's vital juices is only one way by which men maintain their handsome complexions. Even more important is to avoid contact with women. You had known for a long time that men and women are made differently, that they mature at different rates, and that many taboos surround a woman during her menstrual period. Now you discover the more fundamental reason for many of the customs involving men and women. Wakul explains it to you. "The blood that a woman has each month is very dangerous. It can corrupt your vital juices. If it touches you it will make you sick, you will vomit without being able to stop. It makes your skin grow dark and wrinkled, causing ulcerous sores. A pig can die if it eats the moss that a woman has used; that is why they must bury their moss each month. If a woman steps over your spear, it will weaken its power to kill the enemy. Eventually, if a man comes into contact with this blood, it will dull his mind, cause his blood to turn black, and he may die. This is why the bachelors go into the forest for their *sanggai*. It protects them from the danger of our women."

It now becomes clear to you why there are so many taboos surrounding contact between men and women. The old aprons that hang around gardens are dangerous to men because they have been in contact with women, and menstrual blood may have stained them. They are placed around the garden, you learn, to keep thieves from stealing the sweet potatoes: no man in his right mind would dare walk beneath these pieces of women's clothing. Each month when a woman has her menstrual period, she must be secluded in the back room of her house for 4 days, a place where men never go. Men refer to her as "she with the evil eyes." She must prepare her own food and stay out of the sight of men because, if they look at her, it may damage their skins. When she collects food it must be at night, and she can only take mature "female" crops. If she were to walk over a "male" plant that was later eaten by a man he would sicken and waste away.

Enga males dressed in their ceremonial attire.

Mae Enga men, you have noticed, seem somewhat prudish from your own cultural perspective. Now it is clear why they avoid talking about sexual topics, menstruation, childbirth, or other related matters. Their use of obscenities related to sex is also quite limited. Only once or twice in the most serious quarrels have you heard men call others such things as "eater-of-your-sister's-menstrual-blood," "mother-copulator," or "feces-eater." And on these occasions you could tell that such terms are considered extreme by the other men. You have heard men and women refer to sexual matters, but these references were highly ritualized and on public occasions. For instance, one day a group of men were working together on a bridge. As they attempted to haul a log to the bridge site, young women sang an insulting song at them in which the refrain said, "No wonder that log defies your efforts—you cannot even raise your own tiny penises!" The men replied with their own song. "Stand aside or close your legs lest our huge logs burst your dragging vulvas!" But on such occasions it is usually the women who taunt the men, and the men show considerable embarrassment over any discussion of sexual topics. Moreover, most of the men were bachelors, and everyone knows that they must avoid sexual intercourse entirely, both to conserve their vital juices and to avoid contact with menstrual blood. It will be years before they acquire powerful magic and only then, as married men, will they dare to have such intimate and dangerous contact with women.

These are not the only ways men achieve their goal of good skins and positive health, but they illustrate how this core value and the precautions necessary for its achievement integrate many different cultural practices. We can now understand why men postpone marriage, live in separate houses, avoid gardens where women have hung old aprons, go away after their weddings to learn magic, and refrain from touching the cooking stones after sexual intercourse with their wives (to avoid contaminating the food). This core value, then, like all the core values of a culture, serves to integrate a great many customs that otherwise appear as strange bits and pieces of cultural behavior.

Binary Opposition

At a deeper level of Mae Enga culture there appears to be a classification of concepts into two general categories, of which the opposition between male and female is only one expression. This overall binary opposition is not something Mae Enga individuals formulate consciously, although they recognize the kinds of distinctions that underlie the list of opposing concepts shown in Figure 14-1. This opposition is expressed in numerous core values of their culture and seems to be a fundamental feature of Mae Enga world view.

Values and the Social Structure

The male core value of maintaining physical and mental health, as well as the ways in which Mae Enga men take precautions to achieve it, has a profound influence on the social structure. We can diagram this organization as follows.

Mae Enga social organization.

The basic division by sex is one consequence of this core value, but it also has the effect of actually separating the sexes in many instances. Infants and young children live in the women's houses, but by the time a boy is 5 or 6 years old, his father and brothers begin to warn him of the dangers inherent in such close association with women. He is told that soon he must move out of the women's house and live

Inferiority	Superiority
Nonentity ("rubbish man")	Leader ("big man")
Neighbors/affines	Clansmen
Matrilateral kin	Patrilateral kin
Mother's agnates	Father's agnates
Mother	Father
Female	Male
"Vertical" flesh	"Horizontal" flesh
Flesh and blood	Spirit
Milk	Semen
Sexuality	Chastity
Pollution	Purity
Married man	Bachelor
Domestic life	Ritual seclusion
"Female" crops	"Male" crops
Pigs	Game
Secular dwelling house	Ancestral cult house
Woman's (= mother's) house	Man's (= father's) house
Woman's side of house and yard	Man's (= oven) side of house and yard
Left hand	Right hand
Matrilateral ghost or sorcery	Patrilateral ghost or sorcery
Left side of thorax	Right side of thorax
Moon	Sun
Earth dwellers	Sky dwellers
Dark (brown) skin	Light (red) skin
Mortals	Immortals
Forest (= demons)	Settlement (= kinsmen)
Danger	Security

FIGURE 14-1

Symbolic classification among the Mae Enga. [Source, From M. J. Meggitt, "Male-Female Relationships in the Highlands of Australian New Guinea," J. B. Watson (editor), American Anthropologist, Special Issue: New Guinea, the Central Highlands, 66(4), Part 2, 1964, p. 219.]

with men. If he refuses, his father may beat him to convince him of the desirability of making this residential change. From the age of 6 until he is an old man, and for most men even then, males will avoid close association with women. They will live in separate houses and often eat their meals apart from wives or sisters. Some old men may actually live with their wives, but everyone knows it is because they are too old for the contact to cause great damage, and they will soon die anyway. The bachelors, as an organized group, have no counterpart among the women.

Enga males exhibit a great interest in bodily ornaments, wigs and hair decorations, and the quality of their skin complexion. This picture provides an excellent view of the enormous wigs worn by men, fully decorated in ceremonial fashion.

After the first few years of childhood, a female among the Mae Enga is either a girl or a married woman. One function, then, of this core value is that it results in a particular organization of society.

Core values, as we have seen, are especially important for the selection of cultural behavior from among alternatives, for the integration of a cultural system, and for the way a society is organized. There are numerous other consequences of any particular set of core values that the ethnographer will seek to discover. For example, the values and beliefs associated with vital juices and the contaminating influence of women creates a certain tension between men and women. Men have considerable anxiety about engaging in sexual intercourse, yet they also desire to have children and know that if they do not, their father's ghost may attack. While these may be negative consequences of such beliefs, this core value also offers to each individual an important explanation for misfortune. Skin diseases are a frequent occurrence among the Mae Enga, but they do not affect all men. Some men fail in combat with other clans or their pig wealth declines. In addition to knowing that some ghost may be at work, a person also knows that a woman may have stepped over his spear or his magic may not have protected him from intimate physical contact with his wife. Whatever this misfortune, this core value provides an explanation that makes sense in terms of the world view and values of Mae Enga culture.

SUMMARY

There are three main ways anthropologists deal with the total pattern of a single culture. They examine the context of particular cultural practices, the function of these practices, and the configuration of all the major elements of a culture. Context refers to the network of customs that are immediately linked to a particular cultural element. Function refers to the consequences of cultural beliefs and behavior. Configuration refers to the pattern of interrelations among all the major elements of a culture.

The configuration of a culture can be partially understood by the concept of world view, which refers to the way a people characteristically look out on the universe. There are several universal features of world view such as ideas about the self, groups of people, male and female, and concepts of space and time.

A significant feature of every culture is the values that organize behavior. A value is any concept referring to a desirable or undesirable state of affairs. Cultural values vary in their degree of specificity and generality. Core values refer to the most general concepts of desirable and undesirable states of affairs. We examined five Mae Enga core values.

1. Pigs are wealth, and it is desirable to increase the supply of pigs and of pork.
2. A long life, free from serious illness, malignant disease, and fatal accidents, is desirable.
3. It is important to be on good terms with ghosts, especially the ghosts of your clan, lineage, and family.
4. A man ought to meet his social commitments to distribute pigs.
5. It is desirable to have a strong body, a beautiful complexion, a high level of self-confidence, and mental well-being.

Values have numerous consequences for any culture. They influence the selection of alternatives and the integration of contradictory elements. Cultural selection refers to the fact that each culture utilizes only a limited segment of the arc of possible behavior. Cultural integration refers to the way conflicting cultural elements are organized so as to minimize contradictions.

MAJOR CONCEPTS

CONTEXT	CORE VALUES
FUNCTION	CULTURAL PREMISES
CONFIGURATION	CULTURAL SELECTION
WORLD VIEW	CULTURAL INTEGRATION
VALUE	

SELECTED READINGS

Benedict, Ruth: *Patterns of Culture*, New York: Houghton Mifflin, 1934.
  The classic analysis of general culture patterns. This book examines the Zuni Indians of New Mexico, the Dobuans of Melanesia, and the Kwakiutl of the Northwest Coast of America. Benedict developed her idea of two major types of culture patterns, the Apollonian and the Dionysian.

Forde, Daryl (editor): *African Worlds: Studies in the Cosmological Ideas and Social Values of African Peoples*, London: Oxford University Press, 1954.
  Descriptive studies of the world views of selected African societies.

Hallowell, A. Irving: *Culture and Experience*, Prospect Heights, IL: Waveland Press, Inc., 1955 (reissued 1988).
  This collection of previously published articles examines many aspects of Ojibwa world view and values. See especially Part II: "World View, Personality Structure, and the Self: The Ojibwa Indians."

Kluckholn, Florence R., and Fred L. Strodtbeck: *Variations in Value Orientations*, Evanston, Ill.: Row Petersen, 1961.
  A study of dominant and variant value orientations in the southwest United States. Contrasts are made among Navaho, Zuni, Mormon, Spanish American, and rural American using a specially developed instrument for assessing value orientations.

Leslie, Charles: *Now We Are Civilized: A Study of the World View of the Zapotec Indians of Mitla, Oaxaca*, Detroit: Wayne State University Press, 1960.
  A well-written study of a changing Zapotec community and the world view of its inhabitants.

Read, Kenneth E.: *The High Valley*, New York: Scribner, 1965.
  A vivid account of the Gahuku living in the highlands of northeastern New Guinea. Read focuses on the lives of several individuals in this highly literary work, and through his descriptions reveals the values and world view of these people.

Redfield, Robert: *The Primitive World and Its Transformations*, Ithaca, N.Y.: Cornell University Press, 1953.
  A discussion of the concept of world view with a comparison between literate and nonliterate societies.

CHAPTER FIFTEEN

Culture Change

Every culture is in a constant state of change. Change may occur rapidly, as with the invasion of American armies in the Pacific Islands during World War II. Culture change may take place slowly, especially when a society is isolated from others. The Australian Aborigines remained isolated for hundreds of years, and their cultures changed gradually. Whether rapid or slow, culture change appears to follow certain principles, which we will examine in this chapter.

Culture change can be defined as the process by which some members of a society revise their cultural knowledge and use it to generate and interpret new forms of social behavior. At the heart of all culture change are new patterns of thinking, new ideas, and new cognitive maps for behavior. In order for culture change to occur, someone must revise his or her cultural knowledge and create new ways of understanding experience.

It is often the case that people revise their cultural knowledge because of some major traumatic event. Earthquakes, volcanic eruptions, wars, famine, disease epidemics, population increase, and contact with alien peoples all stimulate culture change. However, in the absence of such events, small revisions in culture are made in a continuous process. Someone makes a small change in a fish trap and the change is adopted by others. A child receives a name created by combining parts of previously used names. The author of a comic strip designs an imaginary creature and calls it a "schmoo"; the name is adopted by others and applied to people who seem to resemble the characteristics of this creature. It is easy for us to recognize the landmarks of cultural change, such as the invention of the telephone, but we may overlook the continuous flow of minor alterations that can be cumulatively more important.

A Culture Change Case Study: The Kwakiutl

The most important precipitating event to bring about widespread culture change among the Kwakiutl of British Columbia was the arrival of Europeans. The first major contacts occurred in the early 1800s. The Europeans brought measles and other strange diseases and between 1835 and 1900 there was a 70 percent drop in population caused by epidemics. This led to vast changes in the social organization and economic system, but mere *contact* with Europeans who lived by a different culture did not bring about culture change. In order for this to happen, individual Kwakiutl Indians had to revise their cultural knowledge and use the new ideas to interpret experience and generate behavior.

Also, a forced change in social behavior does not necessarily involve culture change. In 1921 a law was passed by the government of Canada outlawing the *potlatch*, an important ceremony among the Kwakiutl. Although this made it difficult to put on potlatches, the entire set of cultural ideas related to the potlatch continued as part of Kwakiutl culture. James Sewid, a contemporary Kwakiutl chief was 9 years old when the Royal Canadian Mounted Police started to enforce the "potlatch law."[1]

That eventful day began as usual for young James, who was living with his grandmother in a little shack on the beach at Alert Bay.[2] After gathering firewood, he left for the Indian day school. George Luther, an Indian teacher, started class with a special announcement: "For some time now the mounted police have been here in Alert Bay and going to the other villages with the Indian agent to enforce the old potlatch law. They need to use our school for a courtroom, so there will be no school for a few days." Most of the students did not grasp the full significance of what they heard, but a few of the older ones began asking questions. It was difficult for the teacher to explain why the government had condemned the Indian way of dancing and giving gifts, but George Luther told him, "That is the law, and now everyone has to turn in their masks and regalia." He read the law to them from a notice that had gone out several weeks before.

Every Indian or other person who engages in or assists in celebrating or encourages either directly or indirectly to celebrate any Indian festival, dance, or other ceremony of which the giving away or paying or giving back of money, goods, or articles of any sort forms a part or is a feature, before, at, or after the celebration of the same . . . is guilty of an offense and is liable on summary conviction for a term not exceeding 6 months and not less than 2 months.

It seemed a strange thing to James, and he felt afraid and confused at the same time. His thoughts ran back several years to the large ceremonies he had seen at Village Island when he lived in one corner of the big community house with his mother. Each winter people would come from other villages, and they would sing and dance for days on end, giving away all kinds of things after each dance. And at night the old people would tell him stories about important potlatches given by his grandfather many years before. He thought about the time he had first come to Alert Bay from Village Island to go to school. The other kids had called him

---

[1]This period in the lives of the Kwakiutl is documented in an excellent film entitled, *The Law that Bids Us Dance.*

[2]This event is recorded in James P. Spradley, *Guests Never Leave Hungry: The Autobiography of James Sewid, a Kwakiutl Indian,* New Haven: Yale University Press, 1969, pp. 54–55.

James Sewid held by his grandmother Lucy Sewid at Alert Bay in about 1918.
At about the age of 5 James Sewid began to participate in the native dances.

names, a fight had ensued and, before the day was over, his grandmother and other relatives knew about the incident. Because James had inherited high-ranking positions, it was a serious disgrace to have fought with other boys, and the next day his mother's people from Village Island came to Alert Bay. They called all the people together and gave away many things to make up for the fight the day before. He could still remember the long lecture he received and how bad he felt that his fighting had cost his relatives so much. But now the police were going to enforce the law that made it illegal to have even this kind of face-saving potlatch.[3]

When James Sewid got home from school that day he found that his grandmother already knew about the mounted police. She told him, "A lot of the people have given up their masks, but your relatives, old man Wannock and his wife and old man Herbert Martin, along with some others, they hid their things and refused to give them up. They have to go to the court tomorrow." In the early evening, be-

_____

[3]Ibid., pp. 47–48. The "face-saving potlatch" was only one of numerous kinds of gift-giving ceremonies. For a discussion of the potlatch see Homer G. Barnett, "The Nature of the Potlatch," *American Anthropologist, 40,* 1938, pp. 349–358.

fore it was dark, James went down to the Indian Agent's office and watched the people milling around and listened to them talking. At a little building in back a policeman stood on guard; another boy told James that all the masks, whistles, and other regalia were inside the building and that they were to be taken away. The next night after the trials were over James crept up behind the schoolhouse; his heart was pounding as he looked in the window. There, in the dim light he could see them lying on the floor, the chiefs and their wives, the people who had refused to give up their masks. He knew that some of them were his relatives, and that tomorrow they would be taken off to prison. He thought about tapping on the window when suddenly he heard someone coming from the front of the school. It was one of the mounted policemen on guard. "Hey, you! Go on! Get away from there! There's no school here until next week." That night he lay awake for a long time thinking about what was happening.

By the standards of Kwakiutl culture, the most significant use for material wealth was in gift giving. In a variety of ceremonial settings, referred to as one or

Contemporary Kwakiutl dance group. Flora Sewid, wife of James Sewid, stands at the left end of the front row with a traditional Kwakiutl "talking stick." James Sewid stands in the front row, third from the left. The group is standing inside a recently constructed "long house" built especially to revive the dances, arts, and crafts of the Kwakiutl.

306

another kind of potlatch, the host gave away blankets, large quantities of fish oil, canoes, money, household goods, and other items of value. As we will see, gift giving was the primary means for announcing and validating status. The person who was momentarily poor after a distribution of goods was forever rich in status and prestige. Before long this individual would receive gifts from others seeking to validate their relative positions in the social ranking system. When the Europeans imposed their law and order on the Kwakiutl, this endless round of potlatching seemed strange and even immoral. People needing "better" clothes, housing, education, and food refused to save or use their meager earnings for these "needs." Instead, they gave everything away, a practice that white officials felt must be stopped for the betterment of the Indians themselves.

With the enforcement of the laws against the Indian ceremonies, there were significant changes in the behavior of most Kwakiutl. Many discontinued these customs, others practiced them in secret at remote villages where the Royal Canadian Mounted Police were unlikely to come. Sometimes there would be a ceremony and instead of giving away gifts at that time, the chiefs would go around later from house to house to give money or other articles to those who had attended. However, although the social behavior of the Kwakiutl had changed significantly, it

Mr. and Mrs. Ed Whonnock, shown here, were two of James Sewid's close relatives who were convicted of refusing to abide by the "potlatch law" and give up their ceremonial regalia shown here.

was not a result of revised cultural knowledge. These new forms of behavior were not generated by culture change, but by the threat of imprisonment. Many people retained their cultural knowledge; they used it to interpret past events and, when the law was revised many years later, they again practiced openly some of the customs that they had temporarily discontinued.

A MODEL OF CULTURE CHANGE

Culture change can be understood in terms of four related processes: *innovation, social acceptance, performance,* and *integration.* Generally, there is a sequence of events that follow this order (Figure 15-1). Although variations in the sequence of events occur, we will examine these four stages as they occurred when the Kwakiutl dance performances were revived and changed.

Innovation

The cultural knowledge of every society is constantly modified, enlarged, and changed by new ideas that individuals create. These new ideas are innovations. When Joseph-Armand Bombardier built the first snowmobile, he implemented a novel idea for travel over snow and ice. This innovation later became part of Lapp cultural knowledge. When women of the *Nadar* caste in India began wearing breast cloths, their actions expressed an innovation, the idea that low-caste persons could move upward by adopting the symbols of higher status. When Kwakiutl dancers began in the 1960s to perform for tourists and charged admission, their performance was based on a new set of ideas regarding the meaning and function of ceremonial life. But we must distinguish among such things as snowmobiles, wearing breast cloths, and dancing for tourists and the *ideas* that generate such actions and objects. The substance of every innovation is a cluster of ideas. We will define an innovation as a recombination of concepts from two or more mental configurations into a new pattern that is qualitatively different from existing forms.

Mental Configurations

In Chapter 14 we pointed out that cultures are organized into configurations, the total pattern of all the parts and their relationships. Cultural configurations, in this sense, are formulated by the ethnographer; some informants may vaguely sense such configurations, but only at the most tacit level of cultural awareness. However, an individual's cultural knowledge is not merely a random collection of concepts. It is organized into smaller patterns, mental configurations, that give

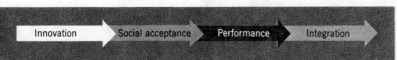

FIGURE 15-1
The culture change process.

meaning to experience. Mental configurations refer to any cluster of concepts that are organized into a unified pattern of experience. Although we perceive and interpret experience in terms of these mental configurations, we become so accustomed to using them that their *organization* is often outside our awareness. We ignore the individual elements of the configuration and treat it as a unitary whole. Even a slight reorganization of some mental configuration can make us aware that we have taken for granted some pattern of our culture.

For example, instead of perceiving a bikini bathing suit as an isolated cultural item, we customarily treat it in terms of a mental configuration. Bikinis cost money, they partially cover the human body, they are exclusively for females, they are worn on special occasions, they have sexual connotations, and they are kept in particular places. These and other concepts form a constellation of ideas that is usually treated as a single entity. It is only when bikinis are worn to college graduation ceremonies, placed on dogs or cats, or otherwise dislocated from their usual associations that we become aware that this cultural configuration is made up of numerous interrelated parts. One spring, for example, two college boys acquired a checked red, white, and blue bikini bathing suit and hoisted it up the flagpole. There were immediate reactions from many different people. One group of students stood nearby, laughing and talking about the feat accomplished by their comrades. Some who passed by saw the humor in the situation; others were disdainful of the prank. The college president looked out his window, smiled to himself, and quickly called the maintenance department to return the flag to its rightful place. Although the cloth that made up the bikini contained the same colors as the flag, the shape and meaning of the bathing suit were quite different. The bikini, as a concept, belonged to a different mental configuration.

When the students first conceived of replacing the American flag with the bikini, they created an innovation, a new mental configuration, although one that did not find the acceptance necessary to become part of the local culture. Like all innovations, this one included a *recombination* of ideas. New relationships were created between the concepts in two widely known cultural configurations. Like all innovations, this one involved three distinct steps. First, the students made an *analysis* of the two configurations. Second, they made an *identification* of elements in the two distinct patterns, treating them as if they were similar. Third, they made a *substitution*, recombining some of the concepts into a new mental configuration. Let us examine each of these steps in an innovation.

Analysis

As we have said, most people take their knowledge for granted and treat configurations as unitary wholes. However, as Homer Barnett has noted, a mental configuration is merely an arbitrary organization of ideas "that can be torn down and reassembled in the wink of an eye."[4] On occasion everyone probably breaks down two or more patterns of ideas into parts and recombines ideas from them into a new configuration. Analysis refers to the process of isolating the constituent parts

---

[4]Homer C. Barnett, *Innovation: The Basis of Culture Change*, New York: McGraw-Hill, 1953, p. 185.

of a configuration. Innovators and highly creative people seem to have the capacity to break down configurations more easily than others. James Sewid created numerous innovations during his lifetime and, even as a young child, he invented toys and constructed mechanical objects by recombining elements from different configurations he had learned. Like all creative individuals he was not locked into a single way of perceiving experience; he could analyze the configurations of his culture as a first step in the process of innovation.

In the simplest case, innovation involves the analysis of two configurations. A prototype configuration refers to the original pattern of ideas that is ultimately reorganized and changed. A stimulus configuration refers to the pattern of ideas that provides a basis for changing the prototype.[5]

Identification

Mental configurations remain distinct and somewhat isolated within a person's repertoire of cultural knowledge. The constellation.of ideas related to bikini bathing suits, for example, is not often brought into association with flags and flagpoles. The cultural ideas associated with women and men in our society tend to be relegated to different configurations and treated as if unrelated. For many people it comes as a novel idea to suggest that women work as truck drivers or that men remain home to care for children while their wives take other employment.

For an innovation to occur, distinct configurations must be treated as if they were partly similar. This occurs by an act of identification, the process of equating concepts from separate configurations. Innovations that lead to a reversal of female and male roles within our own society involve identifying men and women as somehow equivalent kinds of persons. Identification brings two distinct mental configurations into close association.

Substitution

The final step in the innovation process is to create a new configuration from the two related patterns that have been analyzed and identified. Substitution refers to the process of replacing concepts in the prototype configuration with concepts from the stimulus configuration. When the college students identified the "American flag" with a "bikini swimsuit," they could move on to the next step of substituting the swimsuit for the flag. Although this innovative idea probably occurred to them in a flash, it nevertheless involved the innovative process of analysis, identification, and substitution. Humorous situations of many kinds involve this process. We laugh at the man in a skit dressed like a woman or the bikini hoisted up a flagpole, in part, because we know these new ideas will not lead to culture change.

AN INNOVATION FOR THE POTLATCH

After the potlatch law was enforced in 1922, James continued to attend school for a couple of years and spend his summers fishing with one or another relative.

[5]See A. F. C. Wallace, *Culture and Personality*, 2d ed., New York: Random House, 1973, for a discussion of this process and other examples.

When he was 13 his older kinsmen decided he should marry Flora Alfred, a girl from a high-ranking family in Alert Bay. After a time he returned with his wife to the remote community of Village Island where he had lived as a young child. He fished for salmon during the summers, and the rest of the year worked at clamming, logging, and other short-term jobs. Before long he became skipper of a large seine boat with a crew of four or five men. In this remote village, hidden from the surveillance of the mounted police, he took part in many potlatches and went through a long initiation ceremony to become a *hamatsa*, or cannibal. This ceremony and the *hamatsa* dance served as a reminder to the people of the chaos and personal debasement that would result if one let physical passions rule the mind. At the conclusion of this ceremony an unexpected visit from the Royal Canadian Mounted Police caught everyone by surprise. James Sewid recalls what ensued.

Just a couple of days later, before any of the people had returned to their villages, we heard that a sergeant of the mounted police was coming up to Village Island to investigate what was going on. They had heard about our dance there and that a young man had been put through it, which was against the law. That was why they sent this sergeant all the way from Ottawa. All the chiefs of the different villages were still together when this mounted police came in. He told us, "I have been sent from the government to investigate what was going on in this village, and I'd like to see what it is that you are doing." He demanded to see it that night, so we put on a good show for him. The dances we did were all mixed together and not in the right way we had been doing them. I was dancing with a fool's mask on along with a group of masks. The mounted police was standing to one side of the house while the big dance was going on, and one of our people was interpreting to him what it was all about. And he asked him, "What is that dance there?", referring to me. "Well," he said, "he is supposed to be a person who doesn't know anything." Then this mounted police said, "Oh, you people are all wrong. I think he is the smartest dancer in the whole works. He can dance any dance." Well, I was just giving it all I could. I was so strong that I was able to dance with that heavy mask on for over an hour.

When the announcer said that the ceremony was over the mounted police said, "I'd like to see the young man that went through this thing. I'd like to see him dance for me tonight because I was sent here to investigate this young man. I want him to dance with everything he had on, all his masks and everything. I want him to do it just like the way he did it last week." He was referring to me, and the people named my name to him. Well, the chiefs of the village all came and looked for me and found me in the back of the big house and they said, "You have to come out and dance. The mounted police wants you to come and dance for him." So I got all my stuff on and the others who were dancing my dances and came out and started dancing. After I came out my masks came out and danced. At the end he got up and thanked the people and said, "It was a wonderful dance. I really enjoyed it. I can't see anything wrong with it." After that he went back to Ottawa. That was part of my becoming a hamatsa, *and it was a good thing they didn't lock me up."*[6]

[6]James P. Spradley, *Guests Never Leave Hungry: The Autobiography of James Sewid, a Kwakiutl Indian,* New Haven: Yale University Press, 1969, pp. 92–93.

James Sewid at the helm of the Twin Sisters, a large Seine boat used for salmon fishing, named after his twin daughters.

James Sewid lived at Village Island for more than 15 years. Then in 1945 he moved to Alert Bay with his wife and seven children to avail himself of the better health facilities. Within 5 years he had become recognized as a leader of the people in Alert Bay, and in 1950 he became the first elected chief councillor of the Indian Reserve. Soon after the election, he initiated a plan for revising the Kwakiutl dance performances.

James Sewid left his home one warm spring morning in 1951 to go to a committee meeting in the white end of Alert Bay. He walked toward the waterfront, past the large Anglican residential school for Indian children, and turned onto the main street, which ran along the Alert Bay waterfront. As he walked through the Indian end of town, he thought of the problems his people faced and the issues he must deal with as chief councillor. Someday, he hoped, the foreshore property along the water would be returned to his people. He knew that most of the stores in Alert Bay were owned by whites, that the white school was better staffed than the Indian day school, and that his people still could not purchase liquor. He thought about ways to improve conditions for his people and about the recent arguments with the white leaders from Alert Bay who wanted to dump their garbage on the Indian Reserve. He passed Indian children playing in the street and some old ladies returning from the store with groceries. He stopped to talk briefly with old Dan George. On his left the green lawns surrounded a small white building, St. George's Hospital. He turned up the walk, entered the lobby, and went directly to the hospital administrator's office.

For several years the white people in Alert Bay had held an annual benefit program to raise money for the hospital. Two weeks earlier several businessmen had asked James if he would serve on a committee to plan the annual fund-raising project. He agreed, and at their first meeting the others elected him chairman. He asked each member to return this morning with definite suggestions for projects to raise money. He himself had come up with an idea that involved a significant innovation. He decided to discuss it with the other members of the committee.

After some informal talk the meeting got down to business. Several suggestions were discussed, and then James told the others about his idea. "I got to thinking this week," he said, "that it would be a good idea to bring the potlatch custom and the dancing out to the surface again and let the public see it. As you know, it has been outlawed and lost. I had the idea that we wouldn't go and do it the way my people used to do it when they gave people articles like blankets and coppers to come and watch the dancing. The way I figure it could be done would be the other way around, like the theaters, operas, or a good stage program that you put on and the people have to pay money to get in. It would probably draw people from all the little towns in this area like Beaver Cove, Sointula, and Port McNeil." There was more discussion, and then he asked the committee, "Why don't we put on an Indian dance?" There seemed to be a good deal of interest, but one committee member told him, "Well, you would have to be the one to do that." James replied, "Fine, I'll do it if you will pass it in a motion in this committee." It was a unanimous vote.[7]

James Sewid had made a critical analysis of two distinct configurations, a prototype from Kwakiutl culture, a stimulus configuration from Western culture; he then recombined their elements in a new configuration. On the surface this may seem like a rather ordinary idea that did not involve much of a change, but a more careful analysis of these two configurations will show how different they actually were. Both Indians and whites saw these two sets of customs as wholes, as unitary configurations that are not easily analyzed into smaller elements. The various concepts involved (Figure 15-2) show how striking the differences were between the two configurations.

The Kwakiutl ceremonial dances have been discussed more fully in Chapter 4, but we can see here that they involved at least five interrelated elements, all of which were different from Western stage productions. Furthermore, the context in which these two kinds of performances occurred was quite different; one was a sacred activity, the other secular. However, once James Sewid had made this analysis, he was able to go on to make certain identifications and recombine elements from these two configurations to form an entirely new configuration. At

[7]These incidents are drawn from James P. Spradley, ibid., pp. 158-159.

	Cultural Configurations	
	Prototype	Stimulus
Configuration elements	Kwakiutl dance ceremonials	Western stage programs
Identities	Kwakiutl dancers	White performers
Nature of the performance	Ceremonial dances	Various kinds of musical and dramatic productions
Material goods and wealth	Special potlatch goods such as blankets and coppers	Money
Direction of wealth exchange	From the performers to the audience	From the audience to the performers
Purpose and function	To validate inherited rank and status	To earn money

FIGURE 15-2
Analysis of dramatic performance configurations.

least two very difficult equations had to be made between concepts in these two cultural configurations.

1. Kwakiutl dancers = white performers.
2. Ceremonial dances = Western dramatic productions.

Once these identifications had been made, James Sewid could recombine the concepts, making important substitutions to create the following new mental configuration.

Kwakiutl dancers could perform their ceremonial dances in order to earn money that the audience would pay to the performers.

This substitution created a new and significant relationship regarding the exchange of goods between the audience and the performers. Kwakiutl dancers traditionally gave their wealth away to the people who came to watch them dance. This distribution was a necessary part of any claim to status and, if a person danced without making such a distribution, he would be severely criticized. Families would often save their resources for several years, postponing a public performance until they had sufficient resources to make a respectable distribution of gifts. James Sewid's innovation, diagrammed in Figure 15-3, involved "doing it the other way around"; the reversal meant the audience would pay the dancers. As we examine the process of social acceptance, we will see how other Indians perceived this innovation to be a radical departure from appropriate behavior.

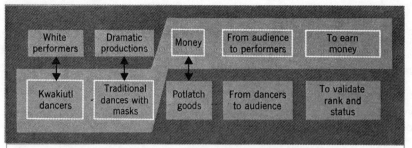

Each box represents the elements in the two configurations that James Sewid analyzed. The arrows show at least some of the ones that were identified as similar. The identification paved the way for a substitution of concepts and a recombination of them into a new configuration. The shaded concepts show the recombination.

FIGURE 15-3
James Sewid's Innovation for the Hospital Benefit.

Social Acceptance

James Sewid walked out of St. George's Hospital that morning in 1951 feeling pleased that his idea had been passed by the committee. However, their vote of approval did not mean social acceptance of an innovation for a very simple reason: *for the white committee members it was not an innovation.* The crucial test of acceptance would come in several weeks when other Indians learned about his idea. For them it would mean a fundamental culture change. James Sewid could only hope that they would accept the innovation.

Social acceptance of an innovation involves three steps: (1) *learning about an innovation;* (2) *accepting an innovation as valid;* and (3) *revising one's cultural knowledge to include the innovation.* Almost daily we learn about innovations of one kind or another. Someone advocates a new diet of spinach and boiled eggs; a religious leader declares that the end of the world is at hand and that everyone should abandon their worldly goods and wait for the cataclysmic event; a woman sets out to live for 100 days perched on top of a flagpole; a protester declares that everyone should fast until all federal prisons become coeducational. Although many people *learn about* such innovations, social acceptance seldom occurs because few accept them as valid and true for themselves.

Recombination and Adopting Innovations

In order to accept a new idea as valid and revise your cultural knowledge to include the innovation, you have to go through the mental process of recombination. Innovators must recombine concepts to *create* a new idea; adopters must make a similar recombination if they are to *accept* a new idea as valid. Otherwise the innovation will appear stupid and ridiculous. But although both innovation and social acceptance require the recombination of concepts, there is an important difference. The innovator creates the recombination; the adopter goes through the steps of recombining configurations by means of a simple learning process. In order to be highly innovative like James Sewid, one must have an openness to experience combined with a high level of self-esteem. These characteristics enable a person to rearrange cultural categories into novel configurations without feelings of anxiety and threat. Sometimes individuals who resist change and refuse to accept most innovations do so because relinquishing the familiar patterns of thinking and acting arouses painful anxiety. But a certain kind of rigidity in thinking is not the only factor that influences how innovations are received.

Some new ideas—such as a mechanical support to hold a smoker's cigar and allow him to use his hands for other things, a self-propelled electric iron, an electrically heated toilet seat, and an inflated rubber bicycle seat—are rejected because people do not perceive a need for them. Sometimes innovations are rejected because they require far-reaching changes in other aspects of cultural behavior. For example, we could dispense with automobiles in our society and thus reduce atmospheric pollution. But even suggestions to limit their use have been rejected because such an innovation would affect so many other areas of social life and require hundreds of other changes. These are only a few of the factors that can influence the adoption or rejection of innovations. Anything that affects the process of learning new information and accepting it as valid can facilitate or hinder the adoption of an innovation. As we follow the fate of James Sewid's idea for using the ceremonial dances, we can examine some of the things that influence social acceptance.

Principles That Facilitate Social Acceptance

A few days after the committee meeting, James Sewid visited Chief Bill Scow, an older man who had moved to Alert Bay from the village at Guilford Island, where he held a position of high status. He was respected by other high-ranking Kwakiutl and was also a progressive individual who had worked hard to improve local conditions. They discussed the idea together, and Bill Scow gave his full support to the plan. Together they wrote a letter to each of the chiefs living in the outlying Kwakiutl villages and invited them to come to Alert Bay with their masks and dance regalia for what had come to be called a "big do," or potlatch. Many of the old people who had participated in potlatches and winter dances before the government made these customs illegal were still alive. James Sewid felt that he must gain their cooperation in order to have enough dancers to stage a performance that would be a financial success for the hospital. The date for the "big do" was set for several weeks later in the spring before the fishing began, on May 24.

This first step in his attempt to gain social acceptance for the project utilized two important principles. First, one should *work through the existing authority structure and gain the support of individuals who can influence others.* Many innovations fail because the individuals who first adopt them have low prestige or cannot influence others to any great extent. Persons with power and prestige may actually reject a new idea merely because it becomes associated with those of lower status. The second principle for gaining social acceptance is to *introduce an innovation at a time that is appropriate to the local culture.* At the beginning of each summer, most of the men and some of the women leave their villages and go out salmon fishing. The fisheries department of Canada controls the amount of fish caught by restricting the season to a limited period of time. When the season is open, everyone spends as much time as possible fishing. If James Sewid had invited the other chiefs to come during the summer, it is unlikely that they could have participated.

The days passed, and word came back from New Vancouver, Kingcome Inlet, Fort Rupert, Cape Mudge, and other villages that many of the people planned to come to Alert Bay in response to the invitation. For several days before the scheduled performance one could see seine boats and gill-netters unloading passengers or docking inside the breakwater at the Kwakiutl end of town. There was an air of excitement as relatives and friends who had not seen each other for many weeks laughed and talked together. James Sewid's home was crowded with guests from other villages, as were most Indian homes. He sent out word that a special meeting would take place for all the chiefs and leading people; more than 200 people crowded into the community hall.[8] James Sewid and Bill Scow sat at a table at the front and, after everyone had drifted in, James got up and welcomed everyone, thanking them for coming. He then explained his idea and ended by saying: "The reason I invited all you people here, and I hope you brought your masks and stuff, is because we would like to put on a big do. We would like to put on a big Indian dance. I feel that you chiefs all did your duty and gave big potlatches in your days, but now that is gone. But you are still the rightful owners of all your masks and things. I think it is a worthy cause to bring you here, and we can all support St. George's Hospital because we all use it. It will be good for the whole district if we can make some money and contribute to the hospital."

When he finished speaking and sat down, the hall seemed filled with a stony silence. A little boy moved about restlessly, looking for his mother; no one spoke for several minutes. Then an old man from Fort Rupert, a chief whom everyone knew and respected, rose to his feet. His words came slowly, but with a firmness that bordered on defiance. "We know you are the new elected chief here, and we came because you invited us. Now that we are all here you think you are going to use all our stuff just like that! It cost us money to show it because we always gave away lots of things when we performed with our masks and other regalia. We have spent all kinds of money to show our stuff before in the Indian way, and you aren't going to just bring us here and ask us to show it in this new way." After that a man from Kingcome spoke and agreed that he was against this new way of putting on the dances. Then others added their opinions until many of the chiefs had spoken out against the idea; not a single person had supported it.

Inside, James Sewid's anger was rising. He wondered if it was because he was young that the older chiefs were against him. Perhaps they felt he was a leader in the new ways, but not in the ways of his grandfather, Aul Sewid. While one after another stood up and criticized the new kind of dance ceremony, he thought to himself how he could gain their respect: "I have some masks and other regalia, and I've taken part in the small potlatches at Village Island, but I've never given a potlatch to show my masks and dances. They know I own these things, but now I'm going to bring them out to the public and show them." Sitting in front of the group he felt betrayed and his anger grew more intense. He wondered how he would respond to all these men whose influence seemed so strong.

---

[8]The events discussed here are recorded in James P. Spradley, ibid., pp. 159–162.

When the last critic had finished talking, James stood up again; he no longer tried to hide his feelings. "Thank you very much!" he said, speaking in his native language. "Thank you very much! You have come at your own expense to Alert Bay as I stated when I first welcomed you. You have come for a good cause to support our hospital. I don't want you to forget this. I'm not a prophet, but I'm going to tell you something. Every one of you are going to go into that hospital before you die. The reason why I brought you here was because I know that the hospital is good for you. It is not just for the Nimpkish Kwakiutl at Alert Bay, but for all the other people as well. I have been working for the hospital and raising money for the hospital and none of you have put one cent in there. This was the only time that you could have put something toward this hospital. Now, I have my boats ready and you can all go home. I'm going to take you back to where you came from and I'm going to pay for your expenses. You might as well get out of here. That is all I can say. I want you to go."

Although James Sewid's age and the traditional rivalries between the Kwakiutl tribes probably accounted for part of the resistance to this innovation, we must not underestimate the profound change it represented for these men who spoke against it. In years gone by they had willingly danced and shown their masks so that they could give away their wealth. This gift-giving part of nearly every Kwakiutl ceremony was the primary means for achieving prestige and validating status. And now it was as if James Sewid wanted them to degrade themselves publicly.

Perhaps we can gain a partial feeling for the radical nature of this change if we examine a different innovation. Let us go back to the hospital committee where James Sewid met with the white leaders of Alert Bay. These men were not unacquainted with occasions where gift giving was appropriate, such as birthdays and Christmas. They also knew of Kwakiutl potlatch customs. Suppose one of them had been a highly gifted innovator who offered the following suggestions: "I've been thinking about how to raise money for the hospital, and this is my idea. In order to get each of the leading businessmen in Alert Bay to contribute to the hospital, we can ask them to take part in a play based on our local history. It would be something that would interest everyone from the towns and villages all over this area. We could invite hundreds of people to come, but we would not charge anyone admission. After the play, each of us who has had any part in this performance would come out on stage and give away money to everyone in the audience. We would announce that all this money would then be donated to the hospital. We know that in the past some of the important Kwakiutl chiefs have given away hundreds and even thousands of dollars in their ceremonies, and we would be able to earn an enormous sum of money for the hospital in this way." The reaction to such an innovation would have been instantaneous and overwhelming. In fact, the other white members of the committee could not have been convinced that their colleague was even serious. Yet James Sewid was asking his people to participate in an event that was equally radical in nature from their cultural perspective.

But the meeting was not over yet, and years later James Sewid would recall what happened after he offered to take everyone back to their villages at his own expense.

You could have heard a dime drop in there. It was real quiet for a minute, maybe 5 minutes. Everybody was just stopped. I was quite young too and I didn't want to get up again. I was sitting there thinking that if Jim Bell was alive that he could come in there and squash those people to pieces. He was that kind of man and he wouldn't want anybody to talk to me like that. Well, I knew I had some friends there somewhere. I had a lot of uncles, and I would say that I was a lucky man. Spruce Martin was still alive and Mungo Martin was alive and Chief Tom Johnson and Ed Whanock were there. Billy Matilpi of the Matilpi people was there, and I think from the Scows at Guilford Island and with Toby Willey and his brothers from Kingcome I had about 10 uncles. Henry Bell was there from Village Island as well as Tom Dawson. So Ed Whanock got up, and I guess he knew that I was mad because I was really shouting at the top of my voice. "Well, Jimmy," he said, "put me on your list. I've got quite a few masks and I'm going to perform to-morrow night. I've got nothing to be ashamed of. I've been showing all my masks for many, many years and I've given away a lot of money and I will do it for nothing so that I can help this worthy cause of saving people." Oh, that was it! He really hit those chiefs when he said, "I've got nothing to be ashamed of." I just held my head down and was waiting. Billy Matilpi got up next. He was from the Matilpi people and related to me through my grandmother, Lucy Sewid. "Jimmy," he said, "Put me on because I'm coming." Then there was Mungo Martin and Spruce Martin. Pretty soon all of them got up one by one and said, "Put me on," and they were just pleading! [9]

In this entire sequence of events we can see three additional principles operating that affect the social acceptance of innovations. First, *adoption is more likely to occur if an innovation meets a felt need.* It seems likely that the men who opposed James Sewid's idea did not feel strongly that the hospital needed their support. Many had never used it, and most knew it was a long distance from their villages. Furthermore, white people owned and operated the hospital, and many Indians assumed that whites were very wealthy and could easily support it. Second, *adoption of an innovation may be facilitated by appealing to prestige motivations.* James Sewid's offer to take people home at *his* expense and his uncle's claim that he would not be ashamed to dance in this new way both appealed to prestige motives. James Sewid's statements implied that the visiting chiefs were too poor to pay their own expenses home, his uncle's that they really did not have the wealth to distribute even if it were allowed. Although neither of these implications may have been true, no self-respecting Kwakiutl chief could let them pass unnoticed.

Third, *adoption of an innovation is more likely if some continuity with traditional customs can be established.* James Sewid carefully pointed out to the assembled chiefs that they had all done their duty in the past giving potlatches. He recognized them as the rightful owners of their masks, songs, and dances. Even his invitation to come to Alert Bay for the occasion was a familiar cultural practice. As host he welcomed them in a manner that recalled the earlier days of potlatches and winter ceremonials. Also, as we will see, other elements of the traditional

[9]Ibid., p. 161.

dance ceremonies were preserved while the innovation of dancing to raise money for the hospital was performed.

Undoubtedly one of the most important factors in the final acceptance of the innovations was the manner in which James Sewid's kinsmen came to his support. He began by using the traditional authority system and working through people who could influence others. In the final showdown it was when his kinsmen came to his aid that the others were convinced to go along with putting on the dance.

Performance

As the meeting ended, it was agreed that the dances would be performed the following night. This did not mean, however, that social acceptance of James Sewid's innovation was total and complete; it takes time to assimilate new ideas. Partial acceptance may be enough to initiate a change, and acting in terms of a new idea facilitates a person's ability to adopt it fully. In the events that followed the decision of the Kwakiutl to go ahead with the dances, people continued to learn and accept the full significance of the innovation. That night they talked together, discussing the merits and problems of changing their customs to help St. George's Hospital. Some continued to criticize the project, and although most of the leading men danced on the following night, some with less status declined participation.

Not every innovation can lead to overt behavior or to the creation of some tangible object. New philosophies, myths, or religious ideas, while being used to interpret experience, cannot be translated into behavior or objects. But, in order for an innovation to result in culture change, it must influence behavior in some way. Performance occurs when an innovation is used by some members of a society to interpret experience and/or generate behavior. A new religious idea leads to a new feeling of awe or appreciation for nature; a political innovation gives people a new way to interpret traditional behavior; an innovation in a myth or folktale influences behavior in that people recount the story involved and draw meaning from what is told. When the dances were performed to raise money for St. George's Hospital, a performance of an innovation occurred. Some people began acting on the basis of this new idea even before the dance was held; others found their acceptance of the innovation growing more complete during the events that followed the meeting.

People were beginning to leave the community hall when someone from Kingcome Inlet said to James Sewid, "I didn't bring my masks and other stuff and neither did the others from our village. How are we going to dance tomorrow?" It soon became clear that others had also left their ceremonial regalia behind. Everyone knew that the slow-moving fishing boats owned by some of the men could never make the roundtrip to the villages in time for the dance on the following night. James Sewid talked with some of the people about it for a few minutes and then said, "There is a water taxi service here in Alert Bay with speedboats. It will cost $15 or $20 for each boat, but I'll pay the expenses for them to take one or two men back to each village to get all the masks and things." After midnight the noise of high-powered speedboats racing across the cold waters of the harbor at Alert Bay could be heard. The night was calm, so they could make good time, but it would still be 4 or 5 hours before the last one would return from Kingcome Inlet loaded with raven masks, crooked-beak masks, hamatsa masks, cedar bark head-dresses, and other ritual objects for the dances.

All afternoon the next day dancers practiced. Nearly an hour before the performance was to begin the community hall began to fill up. Whites from Alert Bay and other communities in the area joined with Indians, paid their admission, and found their places to watch and listen. James Sewid started the evening with a short speech. Without realizing it, he again called attention to the crucial elements in the innovation that were the basis for the evening's activities. "I want to welcome all you people from the white communities who have come tonight," he said, "and I want to welcome all of my people who are going to put on this performance. In the early days when the Indian people used to put on this kind of dance, the chiefs used to call the people together to come and watch their dance and they paid them to come and watch. *Tonight we are going to reverse it.* You people that are here tonight have paid to come in to watch this wonderful performance that is going to be put on for you tonight by my people. I'm sure you are going to enjoy it, and it is for a good cause." Then Chief Bill Scow, who had been appointed as Master of Ceremonies for the performance, announced the start of the dances. Then the dancers began coming out, and he interpreted the meaning of each dance to the audience. For more than 5 hours the dances went on. The man beating the boards behind the dancers grew tired, but no one suggested they stop. High-ranking chiefs from all the Kwakiutl villages danced that night and before the evening was over, James Sewid brought out some of the masks he had inherited from his grandfather and showed them for the first time since that night many years earlier at Village Island when he had become a *hamatsa*.

Integration

Innovations that are accepted and performed do not remain isolated islands of custom. Each new configuration touches other areas of culture, and people must adjust to the consequences of the change. Integration refers to the process of adjustments that occur as a consequence of adopting an innovation. These adjustments may or may not involve additional innovations. The introduction of television in our society altered the frequency and intensity of family interaction and reduced attendance at theaters. It also led to innovations such as TV dinners and concepts such as "Movie of the Week." New ideas in science led to revised textbooks and encyclopedias. The introduction of snow tires with small steel spikes reduced the number of winter auto accidents, but they damaged road surfaces, requiring more frequent resurfacing of streets. New kinds of appliances that operate with electrical current led to building new and larger generating plants, which in turn affect the environment by changing the temperature of water in streams and lakes. The adjustments that follow an innovation may go on for many years. No culture is ever perfectly integrated nor is any custom perfectly adjusted to the rest of a culture. The process of integration is continuous and almost always results in further modifications of the innovation itself.

*Elaborately etched "coppers" were used by the Kwa-
kiutl as a symbol of wealth. They were often given away
during potlatches or broken to show how a man dis-
dained the wealth he possessed. In a recent potlatch
James Sewid talks about the history of this copper to
those assembled.*

Even as James Sewid and the other dancers were practicing for the hospital
benefit performance, the process of integration had begun. The series of adjustments have continued right up until the present and will undoubtedly go on for
many years. Bill Scow took charge of writing down the names of dancers and

322

sketching out a program for the evening dances. Together with James Sewid, they began to organize the practice session and make some decisions about which dances should come first and how many dancers they would need. In James Sewid's mind the change had been complete: *the dances would now be used to raise money, not to raise the prestige or validate the status of any single dancer.* They would reverse the way money was used in connection with ceremonial dances. But the Kwakiutl employed another effective device to symbolize differences in status and rank: *the order of events.* It was not merely the order in which gifts were given that announced a man's rank, it was also the order in which he danced. Furthermore, status and prestige were not merely individual matters; the various tribes of the Kwakiutl were also ranked.

Years later James Sewid recalled the adjustments that had to be made that afternoon in order to put on the dances in the new way he had conceived.

The next day we all got together to practice, and then all those people started fighting among themselves about who was going to be first and who was going to be next. The tribes of the Kwakiutl nation are all in order; the Fort Rupert Kwakiutl are first, then the Mamalilikulla, then the Nimpkish, and so on, and everybody wanted to be in the right order. For instance, there were four or five people who wanted to put on a dance from the Kwakiutl people at Fort Rupert and they wanted to be in order as well, so we had to be very careful. I whispered to Bill Scow, who was writing down what our program was going to be, to just go along with them, because we didn't want any more trouble in our family. I wanted to do this thing right because it was like a test case and was going to be the first one and it was going to be a big one. So we put everybody in order and they practiced all day. As they came in according to the rank of their tribe we gave each one so many minutes to do their dance and then we cut it off.[10]

A complete inventory of the consequences of this one innovation would require a lengthy discussion of recent changes in Kwakiutl life. As the dances were used in the future for other economic purposes, the length of time for an evening performance became shorter to conform with widely held ideas about entertainment functions. When the Indian Act was revised, allowing Indians to again distribute gifts at potlatches and other ceremonies, Kwakiutl dances were used for both ceremonial and economic purposes. This dual function increased the need for a more appropriate setting in which to perform, and in the early 1960s James Sewid and other Indians designed and built a traditional Kwakiutl community house. In recent years this house has been used for various potlatches and dances carried out in the traditional way, with men and women like James and Flora Sewid giving away hundreds of dollars' worth of money and other gifts. It is here also that tourists come each summer and contribute to the local Kwakiutl economy by attending the dance performances and purchasing arts and crafts made by the Indians. Other ideas have entered the stream of Kwakiutl culture through innovations such as the one we have considered in this chapter. And, like culture change everywhere, as these innovations have found social acceptance and influenced social

[10]James P. Spradley, *Guests Never Leave Hungry: The Autobiography of James Sewid, a Kwakiutl Indian*, New Haven: Yale University Press, 1969, pp. 161–162.

These Kwakiutl in traditional ceremonial regalia are close relatives of James Sewid. From left to right are his mother, Emma Sewid, his uncle, Henry Bell, and his father, James Sewid. The large wooden bowls in the foreground were used during feasts.

behavior, they have begun to be integrated into the body of knowledge that the Kwakiutl use to give meaning to their lives.

SUMMARY

Culture change is an inherent feature of every culture. It is the process by which some members of a society revise their cultural knowledge and use it to generate and interpret new forms of social behavior. Culture change is continuous in all societies. It means a revision of the knowledge used to generate social behavior, not merely a change in social behavior. Coercion can be used to force people to change behavior without culture change. But culture change also involves more than new information; it must lead to new ways of interpreting experience or new forms of social behavior.

Culture change can be understood in terms of four related processes: innovation, social acceptance, performance, and integration. Innovation is a recombination of concepts from two or more mental configurations into a new pattern that is qualitatively different from existing forms. A mental configuration is any cluster of concepts organized into a unified pattern of experience. There are three steps in the process of innovation: analysis, identification, and substitution. Analysis refers to the process of isolating the constituent parts of a configuration. This must be done for both prototype configurations and stimulus configurations. Identification, the process of equating concepts from separate configurations, follows as the second step. Finally, substitution occurs in which concepts in the prototype configuration are replaced with concepts from the stimulus configuration.

Social acceptance means that people must learn about an innovation, accept it as valid, and then revise their cultural knowledge to include the new configuration. Several principles that facilitate the acceptance of innovations were discussed in light of the new purpose for the Kwakiutl dances: (1) work through existing authority structure and gain the support of individuals who can influence others; (2) introduce an innovation at a time that is appropriate to the local culture; (3) adoption is more likely to occur if an innovation meets a felt need; (4) adoption of an innovation may be facilitated by appealing to prestige motivations; and (5) adoption of an innovation is more likely if some continuity with traditional customs can be established.

The next stage in the process of culture change is performance. This occurs when an innovation is used by some members of a society to interpret experience and/or to generate behavior. Finally, innovations that are accepted lead to numerous adjustments as they are integrated into the existing culture pattern.

MAJOR CONCEPTS

CULTURE CHANGE	PROTOTYPE CONFIGURATION
INNOVATION	STIMULUS CONFIGURATION
MENTAL CONFIGURATION	SOCIAL ACCEPTANCE
ANALYSIS	PERFORMANCE
IDENTIFICATION	INTEGRATION
SUBSTITUTION	

SELECTED READINGS

Barnett, Homer C.: *Innovation: The Basis of Culture Change*, New York: McGraw-Hill, 1953.
An extensive analysis of the innovative process showing how all innovations involve a recombination of configurations. Factors involved in acceptance and rejection are covered in depth. This book continues to be one of the best treatises on culture change from an anthropological perspective.

Bohannan, Paul, and Fred Plog (editors): *Beyond the Frontier: Social Process and Cultural Change*, Garden City, N.Y.: Natural History Press, 1967.
A sourcebook on culture change containing many of the classic articles in anthropology.

Erasmus, C. J.: *Man Takes Control: Cultural Development and American Aid*, Minneapolis: University of Minnesota Press, 1961.
This book presents a general theory of culture change especially suited for understanding the development process. An extended case of development in Mexico is used as an example of the theoretical discussion.

Niehoff, Arthur H. (editor): *A Casebook of Social Change*, Chicago: Aldine, 1966.
A series of articles that describe attempts at planned change in a variety of societies around the world.

Steward, Julian: *Theory of Culture Change: The Methodology of Multilinear Evolution*, Urbana: University of Illinois Press, 1963. First published in 1955.
A classic study of cultural evolution that develops the concept of levels of sociocultural integration. Steward proposes several methods for studying evolutionary levels and then applies these to various societies from the family level to complex contemporary societies.

Wallace, Anthony F. C.: "The Psychology of Culture Change," Chapter 5 in *Culture and Personality*, 2d ed., New York: Random House, 1973.
An insightful discussion of innovation, microtemporal processes of change, and psychological factors in acceptance and rejection of innovations. Probably the best analysis of revitalization processes.

Worseley, Peter: *The Trumpet Shall Sound: A Study of "Cargo" Cults in Melanesia*, second augmented edition, New York: Schocken Books, 1968. First published in 1957 by MacGibbon and Kee, London.
A description and analysis of this specialized form of revitalization movement in the South Pacific.

CHAPTER SIXTEEN

The
Uses of
Anthropology

As the cool breeze from Puget Sound meets the Seattle waterfront, it begins to ascend, climbing up the steep hills of the city. Washed frequently by soft rains, the air seems especially clean tonight as you walk down First Avenue, only one street back from the waterfront with its docks, curio shops, specialty restaurants, and ferry landings. You pass an all-night theater, the bright marquee announces the double feature for 50 cents. Pawn shops, closed for the night, stare back at you in silence, their windows crowded with tools, typewriters, radios, binoculars, and other valuables waiting to be purchased or redeemed. You pass penny arcades, the barber school, old hotels, and the numerous bars that form the basis of Seattle's skid row; all are shoddy, dilapidated, and in need of paint. The sun has already set behind the Olympic Mountains, but darkness will not descend until nearly 10:00 P.M.

Oblivious to your presence, a young couple walk past arm in arm. Two ladies stand outside a penny arcade; shiny knee-high boots, heavy makeup, and long blond wigs all seem to announce their intentions. Two couples, the women in long evening gowns, their escorts dressed in dark suits, pass you on their way to dinner at the Polynesian restaurant. Across University Avenue you see a man coming toward you. His course down the sidewalk is unsteady and, as he draws nearer, you can see that he is unshaven. As others pass him their paths change slightly as if to circumvent an invisible sphere that envelops him, transforming social distance into a physical one. He is only a few steps away when you are assaulted by the odor of cheap wine. But he does not avert his eyes, a custom most strangers respect when they pass on the street. His gaze is fastened on yours, his open hand holds a few coins that seem to cry out silently for your attention. And before you can avoid him, he asks, "Can you spare something so I can catch a bus home to Ballard?"

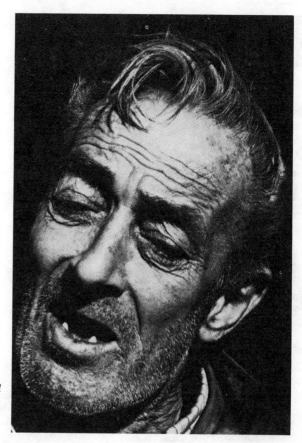

Tramps such as this man are easily seen as derelicts by the outsider. To the ethnographer, such men are viewed as one or another kind of tramp such as a bindle stiff, mission stiff, home guard tramp, *or the other kinds discussed in Chapter 1.*

Eight months ago when you began an ethnographic investigation of skid row in Seattle, you had some difficulty comprehending the lives of men like this.[1] At first they made you feel uncomfortable; you resisted the idea of repeated handouts to the irresponsible. Like most people you had your categories for labeling and understanding these men: bums to be pitied; skid row alcoholics in need of treatment; homeless men who might be rehabilitated; perhaps even vagrants who would sooner or later be arrested by the police. The first time you encountered a man such as the one before you now you felt sure he was down on his luck, out of resources, a person to be pitied. Like a rudderless ship, he seemed adrift at the bottom of society, cut off from a life-style ordered by cultural rules. He might have made an excellent subject for the psychologist investigating abnormal behav-

[1]The major example in this chapter is based on the field experiences of James P. Spradley. Although most of the information is drawn from unpublished field notes, some is from *You Owe Yourself a Drunk: An Ethnography of Urban Nomads*, Boston: Little, Brown, 1971. See Chapter 1, pp. 14–15, for additional sources on tramp culture.

Seattle street scene in an area on the edge of skid row. During the day such areas are filled with people from other walks of life while at night they are left mostly to tramps.

ior, but how could anyone consider him a useful informant for the anthropologist in search of culture? After all, the very concept of culture implies recurrent patterns of behavior, organized activities, plans for accomplishing purposes, and successful adaptation to one's physical and social environment.

However, that was many months ago, before you had listened to scores of men like this, before you had searched for the underlying cultural code these men use to organize their behavior. That was before you discovered they identified themselves as *tramps* and used numerous strategies for survival, a cultural domain they called *ways to make it*. Instead of seeing them as "skid row alcoholics," you discovered their view of drinking and the meaning of alcohol for their social life. Instead of treating them as "homeless men," you listened to find out their definitions of human dwellings and discovered that they employ more than 100 categories of places to sleep, a cultural domain called *flops*. Instead of condemning them as "bums," you charted their goals and work priorities, their encounters with police, and their strategies for survival in a hostile social environment.

As your research progressed, you discovered that these men operate with several different statuses, depending on the social situation. In jail they are *drunks, lock-ups,* and *trustees,* of which there are more than 40 different kinds. On the street they recognize themselves and others of their culture, not as derelicts, vagrants, or alcoholics, but as *bindle stiffs, box car tramps, mission stiffs,* or some other kind of tramp. Although there are numerous cultural domains left to investigate, you had by this time established the outlines of their cultural knowledge and had examined in detail several aspects of that culture.

So tonight you see this man before you in a different light, from a different perspective than you would have taken less than a year before. As you reach into your pocket and place all your loose change in his hand, you scrutinize his face and wonder how many times you have seen him in court. On down First Avenue you cross James Street and, in your thoughts, you climb up the steep hill to Fifth Street where the Public Safety Building stands across the street from the City Hall. There, in the Municipal Criminal Court, on the seventh floor of the Public Safety Building, you spent many hours watching and listening as nearly 60 men each morning faced the judge who decided their fate. Those who were sentenced for public drunkenness would return slowly back into the jail to serve their time.

This protected place for sleeping at the back of a building in the skid row district is one kind of flop *for tramps.*

A doorway is a good flop because it provides protection from the wind and cold air at night. The heat from inside a building seeps out of the doorways and window wells, warming the air in the immediate vicinity.

You move on down the street, across Yesler Avenue, which borders one side of a small triangle of grass; Pioneer Square, it is called. Tonight men lounge on the grass and sit on the benches that line the edges of this historical landmark. Yesler Avenue becomes a steep hill after it leaves Pioneer Square, a hill where early settlers skidded logs down to the water of Puget Sound to be towed away to hungry sawmills. Here, more than 100 years ago, the first bars and cheap hotels sprang up to accommodate the loggers and fishermen who came to town, and forever after the term "skid road" has been associated with single men, excessive drinking, and a raucous style of life. As this name was applied to the deteriorating sections of cities across the country, it changed to "skid row" and lost some of its original meaning.

THE USES OF ANTHROPOLOGY

For months now your primary question has been, "What is the cultural code that underlies the behavior of tramps?" Tonight, as you walk past Pioneer Square and on down First Avenue to Washington Street, the center of Seattle's skid row, another question runs through your mind: "How can an anthropological study of tramp culture be most useful?" Certainly it is interesting to know the social system tramps follow when they form personal relationships, but what good is this knowledge to an outsider like yourself? You know much about the economic exchange systems of this culture, everything from *taking a rake-off* (trading contraband in the city jail) to *selling blood* at the local blood bank. But, you wonder, what good is this knowledge outside of understanding another cultural system and making comparisons with the economic systems of other societies? You know the identity systems and strategies for gaining a shorter sentence when arrested, important cultural domains to tramps, but how can you use this information of tramp cultural rules?

Questions such as these have probably gone through the mind of every cultural anthropologist, every ethnographer who seeks to describe an alien culture. Some dismiss these questions as irrelevant to the aims of pure science; they claim that if we allow these questions to intrude, our research will not be "value free." However, values affect the ethnographer at every stage of research from selecting a research problem, selecting a population to study, and selecting informants, to analyzing and publishing results. Today most anthropologists recognize that no one can afford the luxury of ignoring the *uses* of anthropological knowledge. Even if the anthropologist who describes a culture wishes to use his or her information exclusively for scientific purposes, other people will have access to the published reports, and they can use the ethnographic description in a variety of ways. You began to realize this fact, especially when you mapped the cultural categories tramps referred to as *flops*, or places to sleep. Informants reported to you that they were often arrested when sleeping in an alley or a doorway to a building, so you realized that the local police in Seattle knew some of the places where tramps slept. However, you wondered, did they know the more than 100 different kinds of flops? Some were ingenious, such as the one located at the end of University Avenue near the waterfront. Here, underneath the street, was a large cavernlike area where steam pipes ran between buildings on each side of the street. During cold weather this flop was actually heated by these pipes and attracted numerous tramps. As one informant said:

You can get under there and adjust your room temperature by moving away from them or getting closer to them. You might be the first there in the night and when you wake up in the morning it's like a bunch of snakes all coiled up, stacked close together, trying to get to that heat 'cause it's pretty cold.

However, you wondered, did the police know of this flop? Did they know of the sand houses, brick kilns, stairwells, used-car lots, and mortar boxes where tramps slept? You are aware that the police could make use of your cultural description to locate men and arrest them for vagrancy or public drunkenness.

Every cultural description has a multitude of potential uses, some for the benefit of those who employ the knowledge to organize their behavior, some to their detriment. What anthropologists do with their collected data can have serious consequences for the people studied as well as for other groups. For this reason anthropologists have given increasing attention to the matter of professional ethics. The American Anthropological Association has adopted a set of principles to guide its members in gaining financial support for their research, in working with informants, in publishing their findings, and in teaching students. In this chapter we will examine some of the uses of anthropological knowledge in the context of tramp culture. Our discussion will also involve some of the ethical issues of anthropology. A detailed examination of this single case should help to throw light on the general problem of using anthropological knowledge in the context of any culture in the world.

Adaptation

Cultural systems are not mere ornaments attached to human societies by the process of evolution; they are complex bodies of knowledge necessary for human survival. People everywhere use their cultural knowledge to interpret their experience and to generate action. The first and most important use of any body of cultural knowledge is *human adaptation*. Consider for a moment a few of the cultures we have discussed in previous chapters. The Kwakiutl employ their cultural knowledge to fish, build houses, and perform rituals that enhance social relationships. The social and physical world of each individual Kwakiutl becomes manageable by means of the culture they learn. The Bhils use their knowledge to communicate, to maintain relationships among kinsmen, and to adapt to the requirements for living together in communities. Without a cultural code they could not maintain their biological and social existence. The Karimojong use their cultural knowledge to herd cattle, maintain order, transfer political authority from one generation to the next, and exploit the arid environment of northern Uganda. The Mae Enga use their knowledge to survive in the high valleys of central New Guinea, to maintain relationships between clans, to adapt to the world as they define it. Tramps use their cultural knowledge to earn money, to acquire alcoholic beverages, to find places to sleep, and to locate and maintain human companionship. Their cultural code enables them to deal with the police, judges, jail guards, bartenders, and social scientists. Every culture has a variety of uses, but the most basic one is adaptation to a particular social and physical environment.

The cultural knowledge of anthropology can also be used for adaptation. Individual anthropologists teach, write, and conduct research, in part, to acquire the goods and services necessary for life. Anthropologists share a culture, a body of systematic knowledge to guide their behavior; few of us can afford the luxury of participating in the social world of anthropology merely for the pursuit of scientific truth or to gain an understanding of human behavior. We use the culture of our discipline for such mundane purposes as acquiring clothing, shelter, food, and other basic necessities. In learning this complex culture, we also acquire one or more identities that enable us to relate in meaningful ways to others, be they our students, a college dean, or the head of a foundation that gives money for scientific research. No one has yet undertaken a thorough ethnographic study of anthropologists' culture, but it is clear that one of its primary uses is for adaptation in the contemporary world.

The Culture of Anthropology: A Taxonomy of Uses

Anthropological knowledge is used for a variety of other purposes. We cannot discuss them all, but we will examine some of the more important ones. Two broad categories of usage can be identified: *academic anthropology* and *applied anthro-*

Uses of Anthropology	Academic anthropology	Research
		Teaching
		Writing
		Filmmaking
	Applied anthropology	Adjustment anthropology
		Administrative anthropology
		Action anthropology
		Advocate anthropology

FIGURE 16-1

A taxonomy of uses of anthropology.

pology. Each of these major categories contains at least four subtypes or more specific uses (see Figure 16–1).

Academic anthropology includes any use of anthropological knowledge to inform, enlighten, or increase the understanding of some individual or group. The majority of anthropologists use anthropology academically. On a typical day, John Anderson, Assistant Professor of Anthropology at Brandon College, makes numerous academic uses of anthropology. At 9:15 A.M. he arrives at his office and opens his mail. A book has arrived, *Adoption in Eastern Oceania*, edited by Verne Carroll. He takes a few minutes to scan a chapter by Ruth Goodenough about adoption of children on the Truk island of Romonum. He has read other published work on Trukese culture, and this chapter adds to his own knowledge. In the first chapter of the book he finds a discussion of the meaning of "adoption" by Verne Carroll and makes a mental note to study the discussion carefully at some later time. It will be of value in comparing the practices on Romonum Island with those he had observed during his field work in the Gilbert Islands.

At 10:00 A.M. Professor Anderson briefly reviews his lecture notes for his first class, "Peoples and Cultures of the Pacific," which he must teach at 10:30. Then he is off to class where, for 50 minutes, he instructs and informs more than 70 students, contrasting the differences among the political systems in Polynesia, Micronesia, and Melanesia. At the end of his lecture three or four students wait around to ask some specific questions about the Big Men in Melanesian societies, and Professor Anderson participates in an informal discussion with them for 15 or 20 minutes. After lunch he plans to work on an article that is nearing completion, a cross-cultural study of divorce. In the middle of the afternoon a long-distance phone call interrupts his work. It is from another anthropologist with whom Professor Anderson has been working to make a film on Gilbertese family life. They discuss some of the scenes and make a decision to meet later in the month for an intensive film-editing session.

In each of these activities Professor Anderson is making academic use of anthropology. He is taking the cultural knowledge of anthropology and using it to inform himself, his students, his colleagues, or the general public. However, academic anthropology cannot always be easily separated from applied anthropology. Tonight Professor Anderson will lecture to a group of Peace Corps volunteers to help prepare them for their adjustment for working in Micronesia. After the meeting he will return home and proofread the galley pages for an article for *Human Organization; Journal of the Society for Applied Anthropology.* This article, to be published in the next issue, is a detailed report on his own participation in a community action program in the Gilbert Islands. Academic and applied anthropology almost always occur together, research informing action and vice versa.

APPLIED ANTHROPOLOGY

Applied anthropology includes any use of anthropological knowledge to influence social interaction, to maintain or change social institutions, or to direct the course of cultural change. These uses may be as limited as using the knowledge about another culture to close a business deal, purchase a house, or greet someone in an appropriate manner. They may be as complex as removing the Bikinians from their native island, settling them in another place while an atom bomb is tested on their homeland, and years later taking them back to resettle on their island. Because all human beings are guided by their cultural knowledge as they engage in social behavior, any attempt to control, change, or direct human interaction must take into account the specific cultures as well as the general principles of cultural processes. Let us return to the culture of tramps to see how anthropology might be applied at different levels and in different ways within this urban culture.

Adjustment Anthropology

The first major use of applied anthropology is more concerned with individuals than with the community as a social unit. Adjustment anthropology involves any use of anthropological knowledge that makes social interaction more predictable among persons who operate with different cultural codes. The missionary, soldier, or businessperson may use anthropology when he or she travels to distant lands to work and live among people with another culture.[2] The teacher in an inner-city school may use anthropology to understand and communicate better with the students. An exchange student will find it useful to learn something of the cultural rules followed in the host country. In our own society where rapid social change occurs, anthropology is useful in understanding the behavior of parents and grandparents who sometimes live by a different set of cultural precepts.

The tramps you meet in the skid row district of Seattle do not live in isolation. If you followed them through a few typical days you would see them talk to tourists on the streets, interact with the laboratory technician at the local blood bank, listen to the judge in the criminal court, follow the orders of the policeman who is searching them at a police call box, purchase liquor from the clerk in the state liquor store, and encounter other people from many walks of life. Some individuals, through long years of association, have a genuine appreciation for the culture of tramps. The vast majority, however, employ one or another stereotype to account for their behavior. Many see them as irresponsible bums and often turn away in disgust or fear when approached by a tramp.

[2]For a journal on applied anthropology specifically geared to missionaries see *Practical Anthropology.*

However, an understanding of the cultural code of tramps would enable almost any outsider to anticipate their behavior and understand many of their intentions. For example, on a typical Monday morning, Mr. Brenton, a businessman, heads for his office on the third floor of an old building at Washington and First Avenue, near the heart of skid row. As he walks from the parking garage, he meets a tramp who seeks to panhandle from him. Instead of reacting with disgust because he suspects that this man will take anything given and purchase some cheap wine, he could recognize that this is one strategy the tramp has for survival. He may contribute to his needs with the realization that the tramp views a bottle of wine as a kind of medicine, not much different from the aspirin Mr. Brenton will take before this hectic day is over. If he chooses not to assist this man today, he need not proceed to his office feeling guilty or condemning the man for begging; he can rest assured that tramps have numerous other strategies for survival.

As he enters the doorway of his office building, Mr. Brenton sees another tramp sleeping in a corner. His anger rises when he thinks that all his employees must enter this same doorway; he takes the elevator up to the third floor and calls the police: "There's a drunk passed out in the doorway at 101 Washington Street. Could you come and get him?" Without realizing it, he has set in motion the legal procedures that will mean that the tramp he passed a few minutes before will spend 60 days in jail, merely for choosing the wrong "flop" on a warm summer night. Had Mr. Brenton understood the cultural code of tramps he would have understood that this was a sheltered place to sleep, that the sleeping man was not causing any harm, that in a few hours he would waken and be on his way looking for a spot job or catching a freight to Portland. The tramp's behavior would not seem any more strange than that of middle-class families who sleep on beaches and parks when camping throughout the state of Washington.

As you continue your research on tramp culture, it becomes clear that many people consider them to be unpredictable, and therefore they interfere with their style of life. One tramp expresses his frustration to you.

Isn't it a man's personal business to live the way he wants? He's got a right to live and enjoy life like that—that should be his privilege as an American to live that way. Who the hell is the law to tell you that you can't drink—after all, the bars are open! Those bartenders and waitresses will tell you to get the hell out of there—to stay awake and order something or they may pretend they are going to call the cops. They might call a bull and grab you by the neck and pull you out— even drag you out the door. And the bulls, they'll come in the taverns and stuff, maybe a guy's been there only an hour, maybe he's been in there half a day. He's been drinking and he's still able to be served a drink, but yet they'll come in and get you and drag you off the stool and arrest you for being drunk in public or drinking in public. And every son-of-a-bitch in there is drinking. I don't see the law—when they can get you for being drunk in public, and what the hell does people go in the tavern for if they ain't gonna drink beer or something?[3]

---

[3]James P. Spradley, *You Owe Yourself a Drunk: An Ethnography of Urban Nomads*, Boston: Little, Brown, 1971, p. 119.

Even when they are outside the large urban centers, other people seem to view tramps as unpredictable and take coercive action against them. One of your informants recalled his experience outside of a small town in eastern Washington.

There was four of us and we had a job over in eastern Washington—near Entiat. We got about $75, maybe $100 worth of groceries and asked the guy at the harvest when we gonna go to work. This guy said, "Well, I'll have my cabins cleaned up in the morning." We carried everything across the railroad tracks, you know by the big creek, and here I'm comin' across the tracks, there's the highway patrolman standing right in the middle of the railroad tracks. "Hey, there," he says, "What you got?" "I got three quarts of milk, a gallon jug of water, and a pound of hamburger." Well, he busted me for vag. I had money, all those groceries, had just quit one job and was going to work the next day! That didn't make no difference. They went across and got the other guys then. Here's all of our meat and everything—looked like they had drug it through the dirt, rocks and everything on our eggs. They took all four of us to the jail. Oh, we had wine and beer and if we had been drinking they put a drunk charge on us, if we hadn't been drinking they would put a vagrancy charge on us. We had enough money to bail out, but they wouldn't let us bail. They put us in jail there for three nights and there was no place even to get a drink of water in that drunk tank. All there was in there was a Prince Albert can to get the water comin' into the toilet if we wanted a drink. And that's where we spent our time. . . . [4]

In the case of tramps, few outsiders are interested in learning their culture. Even those social workers, physicians, nurses, and law enforcement officials who could gain much from such an understanding often seem uninterested. In most cross-cultural situations, however, one or more parties have a vested interest in learning the cultural code of the other in order to facilitate social interaction.

How does adjustment anthropology work? Underlying this use of applied anthropology is the basic notion that a major function of any culture is that *it makes behavior predictable.* When two people share a cultural code, they can anticipate each other's actions. They can understand the meaning of what the other does because each shares the same implicit assumptions about the world. The person who knows about the nature of culture and has learned about a specific culture is better prepared for culture shock. Much of the discussion in Chapter 2 on doing fieldwork was based on using anthropological knowledge for personal adjustment.

Whereas adjustment anthropology is useful primarily at the level of interpersonal relationships, the other kinds of applied anthropology—administrative, action, and advocate—involve groups of people or communities. Furthermore, they frequently involve attempts to initiate and direct the course of culture change. When a Peace Corps volunteer, for example, attempts to introduce a new variety of high-yield corn to farmers in Peru, she is working to bring about culture change. When a public health physician asks people to boil water before drinking it, he is attempting to introduce a new cultural practice. When someone seeks to organize the poor into a tenants union for collective action against their landlords, she is initiating culture change. Before we discuss how each kind of applied an-

[4]Ibid., pp. 120–121.

thropology can be used in such situations, we will present a model for planning and implementing culture change. As we isolate the major elements in the process of planned change, we can then contrast the three types of applied anthropology.

A Model for Planned Change

In the last chapter we saw that culture change involved four major steps: innovation, social acceptance, performance, and integration. The applied anthropologist seeks to make use of our knowledge about culture change in order to control and influence specific changes. Our model of planned change involves five elements (see Figure 16-2).

1. Existing conditions.
2. The goal (what someone *wants* the conditions to be).
3. Research (to discover what is *needed* to achieve the goal).
4. The innovation blueprint (statement of what is needed and how to achieve it).
5. Implementation.

Using this model, the applied anthropologist can be likened to an architect. Someone wants a particular kind of structure, say an office building (the goal), and asks the architect to find out what is needed to construct the building in a particular place (research). The architect must become familiar with the site, whether it is marshy or sandy, how it may be affected by earthquakes, and much other information (existing conditions). On the basis of this knowledge and the goal, he draws up a blueprint or plan for the office building (the innovation blueprint). Finally, someone must set to work and construct the building on the basis of the plan (implementation). A similar process is involved in using anthropological knowledge to plan for change, as we will see in the following example.

Hausa Sleeping Sickness[5]

In 1903 the conquest of northern Nigeria was completed and the British Colonial Government established peace among various warring groups. One consequence of peace was the increase of mobility among people in this area, bringing about more frequent contact with the tsetse fly, which led to the spread of a disease

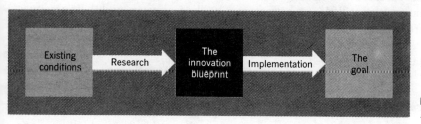

FIGURE 16-2
A Model of Planned Change.

[5]This case is based on Horace Miner, "Culture Change Under Pressure: A Hausa Case," *Human Organization, 19,* 1960, pp. 164–167.

known as sleeping sickness. This disease produces sporadic fever, headache, general weakness, and eventually affects the central nervous system, bringing about drowsiness and mental disorder. By 1928 sleeping sickness had reached epidemic proportions among the Hausa of this area, and the colonial administration took steps to deal with the problem. In doing so, they utilized their knowledge of the native social structure and authority system to bring about extensive changes that would reduce the spread of the disease.

Given these *existing conditions* and their *goal* of eliminating the disease, the British set about to do *research* on the problem. Dr. Nash, a staff entomologist, knew the illness was spread by the tsetse fly and, by studying its life cycle and living conditions, discovered that it could only live in a relatively cool environment. The flies were found exclusively along shaded stream banks and near water holes, places where humans were bitten and infected. A plan was drawn up known as the Anchau Scheme. This *innovation blueprint* was aimed at clearing nearly 700 square miles of brush along the stream banks in the vicinity of Hausa villages. Some resettlement of people would be required so they could work at the yearly clearing operation. The first year of work would be carried out by paying native labor; after that the colonial administrator would issue orders to the village headmen to organize their people and have them clear the stream banks in their vicinity. A knowledge of Hausa political systems and authority structures would be used to gain cooperation of the people.

The Hausa leaders were told that the clearing project was necessary to eliminate the tsetse fly, which bit humans and caused little "fishlike animals" to enter the body and bring about sleeping sickness. *Implementation* of the planned change was carried out successfully, in part because the administrators worked indirectly through native leaders, allowing them to organize work groups along customary Hausa lines. All went well for the first year when natives were paid to clear the stream banks, but when the time came for second-year clearing operations, passive resistance occurred. Almost no one showed up for the work, and the British supervisors took drastic action. They removed headmen from their positions, fined others for not cooperating, and put increasing pressure on the Hausa to carry out the slashing operation. These strong sanctions were effective, and from then on each year the orders were carried out as planned. Within a few years medical tests revealed the virtual elimination of sleeping sickness. Twenty years later the Hausa were still clearing the stream banks each year, and their area was relatively free of the tsetse fly. The goal of this applied anthropology project had been successfully achieved. We may diagram the elements using our model of planned change in Figure 16-3.

Administrative Anthropology

It is probably impossible to formulate a plan for culture change in which everyone involved accepts the *goal* and the *innovation blueprint* as the most desirable. Disagreements occurred between the British and the Hausa over the plan to resettle some groups and to clear the brush each year from stream banks. When an architect draws up a blueprint, the person who will pay for his services and construc-

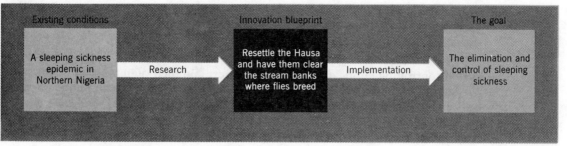

FIGURE 16-3
Planned Change to Eliminate Sleeping Sickness.

tion work has the power to decide on the type of building and to select or reject the planned structure. No such easy purchase can be made of human behavior. There are always alternative goals and alternative ways to achieve those goals. The most important question in applied anthropology is, "Who has the power to decide on the best goal, to select and design the wisest innovation, and to implement these plans?" The distinction between *administrative, action,* and *advocate* anthropology hinges on who has this power to select from among the known alternatives.

Administrative anthropology involves the use of anthropological knowledge for planned change by those who are external to the local cultural group. The Hausa case is clearly one of administrative anthropology, one in which the British held political power and could choose among the alternatives. They used their knowledge of Hausa culture to bring about changes of their choosing. But there are other kinds of power, such as economic and technological, that can be used to retain the right to select alternatives in any situation of planned change. *One of the most important kinds of power involves knowledge itself.* Merely by knowing more than others, one achieves the power to influence the course of change, and it is this fact that places the anthropologist in a serious ethical dilemma. Anthropological research, even if one is not committed to the goals of external power holders, provides the anthropologist with an important source of power. He can choose who will have access to this knowledge, and can decide, in part, how this power will be used.

Applied Anthropology on Skid Row

Let us go back to the ethnographic study of skid row in Seattle. In your research you meet many different professionals who are concerned about the needs of tramps, although they usually refer to them as "alcoholics." You have talked with social workers, court officials, and the staff of the county alcoholism treatment center. These people all share a common goal: *to change the drinking behavior of tramps.* Each year in Seattle the police make more than 12,000 arrests for public intoxication, mostly of tramps. After a few days or many months in jail, depending on the individual sentence, the convicted man returns to the streets where many are arrested again in a short time. The "revolving door" of the jailhouse has seemed ineffective to many people in changing the behavior of this population. It does control their drinking while they are incarcerated, but seems to influence them little after their release.

You learn that some people believe there are alternative ways to achieve the goal of controlling public drunkenness. They explain their plan to set up a special alcoholism treatment center for some of the men sentenced to jail for public intoxication. Sufficient funding has been secured from the city, county, and state governments to construct a new facility near Seattle. At this center the tramps will be reeducated, treated for their physical ailments, provided with special forms of therapy to help them stop drinking, and given job skills training. Underlying this plan is the belief that these men have a disease called *alcoholism*, which can be cured or arrested with the proper treatment. The treatment center will also be more humanitarian than the jail. The professionals involved in this project recognize that the culture of tramps will influence any attempt to change their drinking patterns. They would like you to carry out research to assist them in the design and operation of the treatment center. It seems like an important contribution, so you agree to conduct research that may help to achieve this goal. You believe the information will also be useful as other treatment centers are developed across the country.

Pine Valley Alcoholism Treatment Center, located about 25 miles from Seattle, was ready to admit men several months after you started your investigation of tramp culture. You accompanied the Staff Counselor as he selected patients from the drunk lineup in court. The court docket is a large room with steel benches where more than 25 men are waiting to be arraigned before the judge. The staff counselor tells them about the treatment center.

Good morning, men. I'm Fred Chase, counselor for Pine Valley Alcoholic Treatment Center. Do you want to do anything about your drinking problem? Pine Valley Alcoholic Treatment Center is a new center for men like you. If you are sick and tired of being sick and tired, you could be a candidate for Pine Valley, and you could make this your last arrest. If you want to go, tell the judge before he sentences you and he will hold you over. You will be interviewed by me, and we'll give you a physical and then the Seattle Police Department will decide, together we will decide if you are eligible to come out to Pine Valley. We'll take you out. The sentence is 180 days, but that is a rare case who stays there that long. If you are receptive and you've been trying, you can get out earlier than 180 days.[6]

You return to the courtroom with Mr. Chase and watch as the men file in, plead guilty, and accept their sentence. Four men tell the judge this morning that they would like to go to the treatment center and the judge holds them over without giving a sentence at this time. Later they will be interviewed and returned to court where the judge will sentence them to 6 months at Pine Valley Alcoholism Treatment Center.

You began visiting the treatment center several times each week to participate in the activities there. You explain your role to both staff and patients, but it is some time before patients believe you are not a "bull," or police officer in disguise.

[6]This quote is from James P. Spradley, unpublished field notes.

At first there are less than 20 patients at Pine Valley but, as the months go by, the population grows to more than 100. You eat with the patients, sit in on lectures and therapy classes, play cards in the dormitories, attend staff meetings, and in other ways assume the role of participant observer. All the time you are making field notes about the culture of this institution and how the tramp culture affects the operation of the center.

It is not long before you find ways that the treatment program could be made more effective. For instance, one of the major themes you have discovered in tramp culture is *mobility*. A major feature in the identity of a tramp is traveling from one place to another, and most men are not accustomed to staying in one location very long, at least, not by choice. They know that if they go to jail for public drunkenness, they will receive sentences of 30 to 60 days, although the maximum of 6 months is always a possibility. When they choose the treatment center instead of the jail, they are sentenced to 6 months and, although the conditions are more humanitarian, no one is allowed to leave the confines of the treatment institution. Within a few months after opening, the length of sentence becomes a major complaint by patients, causing them considerable anxiety and detracting from the effectiveness of the therapy programs. Because it is a minimum security institution and there are no fences around Pine Valley Alcoholism Treatment Center, several men decide to run away, or "rabbit," as tramps refer to it. It seems apparent that a change in the length of commitment or eliminating the sentence altogether would contribute to the success of treatment. Using the model of planned change, we can formulate the anthropologist's role in this setting (see Figure 16-4).

Although you have many suggestions like this that might be of value to the success of the program, you decide to wait until after your research is over before making most of them known. That way it will be possible to minimize your influ-

FIGURE 16-4

Administrative Anthropology in the Treatment of Skid Row Alcoholics.

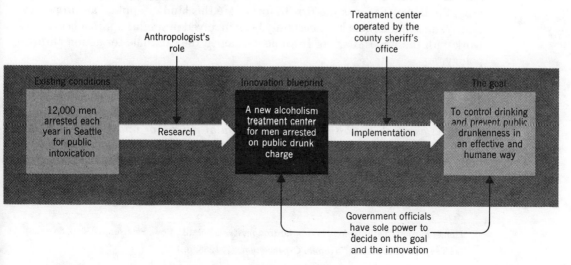

ence on the course of development and change. At the same time it is clear that your work is based on the goals set by the staff of the treatment center. You are participating in a program of administrative anthropology. What Homer Barnett has said regarding the role of anthropologists assisting the government in Micronesia is also true of your role in this project. The anthropologists are experts on

attitudes and behaviors, they are expected to devise and recommend techniques to accomplish the objectives settled upon by the administration. In short, they are responsible for means, not ends.[7]

Action Anthropology

But incarceration and treatment are not the only alternatives available to reduce public drunkenness and treat tramps more humanely. Early in your research you learn that it is important to distinguish between *drunkenness* and *public drunkenness*. It is primarily the latter that concerns the law enforcement officials in Seattle. If tramps lived in homes and stayed out of sight when drinking or while intoxicated, it would be a different matter. One of the local ordinances in Seattle makes it a crime to drink in public, and in one group of 100 tramps you find that nearly three-fourths of them had been arrested for merely drinking wine or other liquor in an alley, on a street corner, or in some other public place. Now it would be possible to provide enclosed shelters where tramps could congregate, eat, sleep, and drink in private. The cost would undoubtedly be less than the expense of arrest, arraignment, and incarceration. This plan would be an innovation, to say the least, and one that some tramps might find more desirable than going to jail or to the treatment center. Undoubtedly there are other alternatives that could be followed to reduce the incidence of *public* drunkenness.

Action anthropology operates on the principle that there are always alternative goals and innovation blueprints and that the right to choose from these alternatives should be left to the people involved. We can define action anthropology as any use of anthropological knowledge for planned change by the local cultural group itself. Sol Tax was the first to formulate this kind of applied anthropology clearly, although others have certainly been involved in similar approaches. In his work with the Fox Indians of Iowa he developed the rationale for action anthropology.

All we want in our action programs is to provide, if we can, genuine alternatives from which the people involved can freely choose—and to be ourselves as little restrictive as is humanly possible. . . . Such a program requires that we remove ourselves as much as possible from a position of power, or undue influence. We know that knowledge is power, and we try hard to reject the power that knowledge gives us. . . . We realize that we have knowledge that our Indian friends do not have, and we hope to use it for their good.[8]

[7]Homer Barnett, *Anthropology in Administration*, Evanston, Ill.: Row, Peterson, 1956, p. 88.
[8]Sol Tax, "The Fox Project," *Human Organization, 17,* 1958. p. 18.

It is important to recognize that in any situation of applied anthropology there are always alternative means and ends. As we have said, the most important ethical question in applied anthropology is *who* will choose the means and the ends. Consider the Hausa sleeping sickness problem again. The goal to eliminate the epidemic by controlling tsetse flies was certainly not the only possible innovation blueprint. Drugs were known that effectively treated the disease, and these could have been administered each time someone was infected or reinfected. Although this method of control might have been more inconvenient and less desirable from a public health standpoint, it would have had certain advantages for the Hausa. They could have remained in locations of their choice and would not have had to clear the stream banks each year. Moreover, some Hausa refused to cut certain areas of growth because they believed supernatural spirits dwelled there; this alternative plan would have preserved such sacred places. But in this case it is clear that the power to select both the goal and the means to that end was not held by the Hausa but by the British.

Even if there had been wide acceptance of the plan to eliminate the tsetse fly, the Anchau Scheme was not the only alternative innovation. The wealth and resources that the British were taking out of Nigeria could have been used to support fully the stream clearance project. Natives could have been hired and paid by the British each year, thus eliminating the need to coerce the Hausa to move and maintain the annual slashing of brush. Even after 20 years of clearing projects, Horace Miner found that every Hausa leader agreed that if they were not ordered to clear the streams they would abandon the work. Many Hausa continued to attribute the disease to supernatural beings, and some believed they were required to clear the streams because the tsetse fly bite was painful or because the clearing was a means to drive out monkeys that destroyed crops.

In contrast to administrative anthropology, action anthropology involves the anthropologist only indirectly in selecting goals and innovations. The action anthropologist acts as a *catalyst*, presenting alternatives to the local people and providing information to assist them in making decisions. He begins his work before an innovation blueprint or a goal has been identified. Action anthropology values the freedom of a local cultural group, even the freedom to make mistakes. Ralph Piddington summarizes this role in relation to the Fox Project mentioned earlier.

The Fox are faced with the need of making decisions relevant to their future. The function of the anthropologist is not to impose his own decisions, much less those of administrators and other whites. His function is to act as a catalyst, to help clarify issues for the Fox and to make available to them possibilities of choice which may not have occurred to them, or which might not have been available to them apart from the programme of action anthropology. In light of such clarification, any decision reached by the Fox is by definition the right decision. Any lines of action, including those which appeal to the action anthropologist, must be rejected if they are not acceptable to the Fox.[9]

---

[9] Ralph Piddington, "Action Anthropology," *Journal of the Polynesian Society,* 69, 1960, p. 205.

In cooperation with the action anthropologists, for example, the Fox organized a small group that used Indian designs in the production of ceramic tiles and greeting cards. This project was a commercial success and contributed to the Indians' awareness that successful economic ventures were not beyond their capability. The action anthropologists assisted at each stage in the development of this innovation.

Requirements for Action Anthropology

In your work with skid row tramps you have thought about action anthropology, an approach that appeals to you more than administrative anthropology. However, the social and political structure of Seattle makes it all but impossible to engage in action anthropology with those who live by the tramp culture. Tramps are powerless, a condition that seriously limits the possibilities of this kind of applied anthropology. There are three necessary requirements for action projects, each of which is absent for the men who are repeatedly arrested for public drunkenness.

First, *action anthropology requires that the community or group concerned have enough independence and power to select among alternative goals and plans*. In this case the county sheriff's office has designed the treatment center and set the goals of this new institution. Tramps were not consulted, and they are powerless to influence the project. The decision to arrest individual men for public intoxication is a power reserved for the Seattle city police. The local judge alone has the power to suspend a 2-day sentence or to commit a tramp to 6 months in jail. In short, tramps are powerless to select either the goals or means for their achievement. Their only recourse is to get out of town in a never-ending attempt to escape those who hold enormous power over their lives.

Second, *action anthropology requires that the cultural group have some legitimate process for making decisions*. Although tramps do have a culture, they have no political structure, no way to make a collective decision that would be binding. Many oppressed groups live under similar conditions and are therefore unable to select among alternative goals and innovations.

Third, *action anthropology requires that the cultural group control the resources necessary for implementing a selected innovation*. Even if tramps were an independent group with legitimate decision-making processes, they are extremely poor and without resources to bring about changes. The factor of resources is very limiting, particularly in the non-Western world. Even when groups have the ability to choose a certain course of action, colonial governments and external political powers have often maintained control over economic resources, leaving the local people impoverished.

The absence of one or more of these prerequisites among the people studied by most anthropologists frequently makes it impossible to engage in action anthropology. But there is an alternative kind of applied anthropology. It is possible to become an advocate for people who are oppressed, whether they are tramps, powerless at the hands of the police, consumers at the mercy of large corporations, urban poor who cannot deal adequately with the welfare system, or native peoples who still live under some form of colonial rule. Let us examine the nature of advocate anthropology and how it was applied in the case of tramps.

345

Advocate Anthropology

Advocate anthropology is any use of anthropological knowledge by the anthropologist to increase the power of self-determination for a particular cultural group. This kind of applied anthropology is based on the conviction that the fundamental issue in planning and implementing culture change is *power*. Instead of focusing on the design of innovations, resistance to change, and the problems of implementing blueprints for change, the advocate anthropologist seeks to discover who holds the power over the lives of informants and how that control can be reallocated to the people. Underlying every specific goal and effort to bring about cultural change is the major goal in advocate anthropology—the democratization of society.

We can contrast the three kinds of applied anthropology that concern groups in terms of how they deal with the power of self-determination. The administrative anthropologist rejects the use of power, believing it is best left in the hands of some external authority.[10] The action anthropologist rejects the use of power and believes that the local cultural group can best make and carry out decisions regarding its future. The advocate anthropologist, on the other hand, seeks to use the power that knowledge gives in order to increase the power of self-determination for the cultural group he investigates. Instead of leaving the value choices up to administrators or the people themselves, the advocate anthropologist takes the responsibility of making ethical choices in selecting goals and desired changes. At the same time, decisions about goals and plans that are in the "public interest" are made in consultation with the people studied. The advocate anthropologist prefers the risk of making a mistake to the danger of inaction. When the American Anthropological Association adopted their Principles of Professional Responsibility in 1971, they emphasized the importance of using anthropology in the public interest.

> *As people who devote their professional lives to understanding man, anthropologists bear a positive responsibility to speak out publicly, both individually and collectively, on what they know and what they believe as a result of their professional expertise gained in the study of human beings. That is, they bear a professional responsibility to contribute to an "adequate definition of reality" upon which public opinion and public policy may be based.*[11]

As your ethnographic investigation of the tramp world progresses you decide to take the role of an advocate for tramps. Let us look at the existing conditions, the innovative blueprint, and the goals.

---

[10] These three types of applied anthropology are ideal types; in actual practice, as in the example from Seattle, the anthropologist becomes involved in each type of applied anthropology. Furthermore, the administrative anthropologist may not necessarily agree with the aims and methods of the government, corporation, or other agency that employs him. Some anthropologists have worked in this capacity because they saw it was the only means to assist the people they studied. By participating as a professional within a government agency or other powerful group, they were able to prevent the implementation of policies that would have been harmful to native peoples.

[11] From the *Principles of Professional Responsibility*, adopted by the Council of the American Anthropological Association, May 1971.

Existing Conditions

Although much of your time is spent listening to tramp informants and observing their behavior in order to formulate a cultural description, you also find opportunities to talk to professionals who come into contact with tramps. These people explain to you that your informants are actually alcoholics, many of whom could be cured if they would only accept treatment. The judge who sentences drunks each morning believes that spending time in jail is often beneficial for tramps, allowing them an opportunity to "dry out." Police officers report that tramps actually like to be in jail, some of them asking to be sentenced so they can escape the debauchery of their street lives.[12] Physicians and public health officials tell you that the jail is actually the best place for these men, a place where they can get food, medical care, and other basic necessities of life. Even some of the treatment center staff believe that jailing drunks is often beneficial because it interrupts their drinking behavior and makes them aware they have "hit bottom," an experience some believe to be necessary for recovery.

These views of what tramps experience contrast sharply with the way tramps themselves view their situation. You can still remember when you first began to learn how they defined the jail experience. The first group of patients had arrived from the city jail to be admitted to Pine Valley Alcoholism Treatment Center. As they stood in line to receive the uniform all patients wore, they talked about the jail and conditions there. One man said, "The bucket is really crowded, men were sleeping on the floor." Much later you would discover that the drunk tank with its cold cement floor, designed for 35 men, would sometimes contain 75 or 80 men, crowded together in close confinement. Harry, an old man from Milwaukee who had been a tramp for nearly 30 years, complained bitterly about the drunk tank.

Well, I've been in there when they stack them up like cordwood. I was in there once on a weekend of the 4th of July when we laid there Friday, Saturday . . . and they bring these guys in there, they throw the son-of-a-bitches with you, bugs running all over them. They feed you like a bunch of cattle in there, why if they did that to a bunch of dogs in the humane society, Christ Almighty, people would scream bloody murder.[13]

Another informant later told you,

That drunk tank is really bad. Whether a person is guilty or innocent when he is picked up he is thrown in that drunk tank. There's no blankets, no beds, there's shit and piss all over the floor. You're thrown in there with guys who are diseased and sick and if you get in there on a Friday you stay in there for two or three days.[14]

---

[12]A sample of 95 tramps who had been repeatedly arrested for public drunkenness were asked, "Have you ever gone up to jail and turned yourself in without being picked up?" Eighty-five responded "No"; 10 responded "Yes." James P. Spradley, *You Owe Yourself a Drunk: An Ethnography of Urban Nomads*, p. 159. (Copyright © 1970 by Little, Brown and Company, Inc.) Reprinted by permission.

[13]Ibid., p. 159.

[14]Ibid., p. 159.

The drunk tank is a bare room in jail without furniture. In the hours immediately following appearance in court the drunk tank may be virtually empty as in this scene. At other times it can be crowded with men.

One man recalled, "I haven't had coffee in 2 weeks because I haven't been able to drink the coffee down at the jail." The food in jail, others will tell you, is always poorly prepared and in short supply. Later you will find that more than one third of the men who go through the jail as drunk arrests feel they are kept on a starvation diet in jail. One young man, a college graduate who had been in the tramp world for several years, tells you,

What is shocking and what the inmates feel in regard to the food situation—especially those who know and who are working in the kitchen—it's really amazing how much meat they have down there, a tremendous amount of meat for the number of people in jail. But we don't see any of it. But the officers, for instance, it makes you kind of mad because you see them get a great big steak like this and the whole works for 35 cents. Everyone else eats so darn well, all this very good food and we get the chowder. The drunk, in general, is not really a criminal type and I don't know why a bank robber should be fed better than he is. Anyone in the county jail eats a lot better than in the city and the drunk is made to feel that he is on the lowest rung of society and he's treated as such.[15]

[15]Ibid., p. 213.

One of the new patients, after turning in his personal belongings for safekeeping, commented that $20 had been stolen from him in jail. Another man added, "I had $22 when I was arrested and they took it away from me at the booking desk. When I left, it was gone and there was no record." In the months that followed you heard dozens of reports of theft and harassment by the police. Reports like the following were commonplace.

In 1967 he shook me down, took my wallet, looked in it, took eleven dollars. Put my wallet back and I said, "Since when do you look for a gun or a knife in a man's wallet?" He split my head and it took four stitches."[16]

You discover that when tramps are arrested they do not receive a property receipt for their personal belongings, although other citizens do. Nearly 40 percent of the men report that they have had things stolen out of their property boxes while they were in jail.

As an advocate anthropologist, you recognize that your informants see things differently than the police, the treatment center staff, judges, and the physicians who deal with tramps. You adopt the most important principle for this kind of applied anthropology: *you allow your informants to define the existing conditions.* Although many of the professional people who deal with tramps do not realize it, they have adopted a common strategy used by people in positions of power. This strategy is to blame the victim for all the problems he or she faces. Instead of seeing the jail as a place of oppression, they blame tramps for drinking too much. Instead of seeing arrest and incarceration as gross inequities based on the different life-style of tramps, they blame tramps for not being willing to seek treatment for alcoholism. Instead of using resources to give tramps the kind of privacy that other members of our society have, they use them to keep tramps in jail. How different is the view from the perspective of your informants. As one insightful tramp told you, "After 30 days in jail, you owe yourself a drunk."

The Goal
In contrast to the goals set for tramps by police, judges, social workers, alcoholism counselors, and others, your informants harbor a different and often unstated want. They never get together as a group and vote to work toward this goal; they have no internal social organization that allows for this kind of action. In their oppressed situation it is often "every man for himself." But as you listen to men talking among themselves, as they begin to trust you and confide in you, their most important desire emerges again and again: they want *freedom from repeated arrest, incarceration, and police harassment for their style of life.* Even the Pine Valley Alcoholism Treatment Center is seen by many men as merely another form of incarceration. Some patients complain bitterly to you that it is merely a "sugar-coated jail," a place that robs them of freedom while offering treatment that is often inadequate and ineffective.

As an advocate anthropologist you take their desires seriously, a goal worth working for. But the problem is enormous. More arrests occur in the United States

---
[16]Ibid., p. 150.

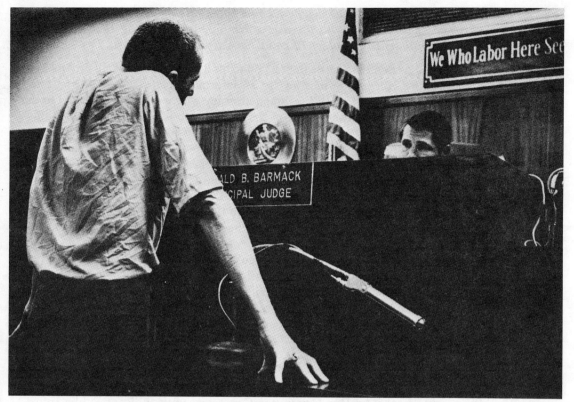

When tramps appear in court they almost always plead guilty because they believe you "can't beat the drunk charge." This man is "making a statement" to the judge in an effort to reduce the severity of the sentence.

for public drunkenness than for any other crime. In 1965, just prior to beginning your research, out of 6 million arrests in the United States, nearly 2 million were for public drunkenness. Every state in the Union has laws that make it a crime to appear drunk in public. Tramps travel from one place to another and, wherever they go, they find oppression at the hands of the local police. Even those men who stay in one place, the "homeguard tramps," find repeated arrest and incarceration becomes a way of life. One of your informants, John Hallman, is a longtime resident of Seattle. You check his police record and discover the startling course of his life.

He was first arrested for public drunkenness in 1947 and two years later declared by the courts to be a "common drunkard"; during the 21 year period, from 1947 to 1968, he was convicted more than 100 times for this crime; he received many suspended sentences and posted $165 in bails which he forfeited; and there were 74 charges of public drunkenness on which he was sentenced to jail during this period. He was given a total of 5,340 days for these convictions, or more than

14 years. *If he had posted $20 bail it would have cost him $1,480. In this man's experience, then, a year of his life was worth only $100! During 1966 he received two six-month sentences which he could have avoided for only $40.*[17]

One night a friend in Seattle invites you to his home, where a small group of politically active citizens are meeting for an informal social hour. At this meeting you are introduced to Tim Hill, a young attorney who was recently elected to the Seattle City Council. In the course of the evening you tell him some of the things you are finding out about the oppression of tramps in Seattle and other places. He expresses an immediate interest in helping these people and offers to make a surprise visit to the city jail early some morning to check on conditions there. He invites you to go along, but you decline and discourage him from taking this course of action. The jail is on the sixth floor of the Public Safety Building, and no one can enter without going up the elevator and through a security gate. Before you could get to the drunk tank the officers in charge would know your intentions and conceal conditions as they actually were. You tell Tim Hill about one young man who was taken from a crowded drunk tank and placed with five other men in a clean, empty drunk tank with a padded floor. Each man was given a blanket and brought in a tray heaped with food. While they were wondering about such favorable and unexpected treatment, a group of visiting dignitaries came through, looked at their conditions, and went on to inspect other parts of the jail where the guards allowed them to go.

Innovation Blueprint

A few months later Tim Hill invites you to become a member of a new committee he is creating, the Ad Hoc Committee Concerned with Indigent Public Intoxicants. During March and April you meet with this committee to plan for an expected change in the laws of the country regarding public drunkenness. You are delighted to discover that the United States Supreme Court has recently heard the case of Mr. Powell, a tramp in Texas who had been arrested dozens of times for public drunkenness. His attorneys had argued before the state courts and eventually before the Supreme Court that Mr. Powell was an alcoholic and that to jail a man for such an illness was cruel and unusual punishment. Everyone expected the Supreme Court to rule in favor of Mr. Powell and across the land every local ordinance that allowed the police to jail drunks would become unconstitutional. The Ad Hoc Committee was formed to plan for this impending culture change and help design some kind of temporary public health facilities where drunks could receive care and detoxification if needed. It appears that the innovation you believe necessary will take place.

The committee works long hours designing a detoxification center and the procedures for using it. Then, during June, the cause for tramps takes a sudden setback. At a meeting of the committee it was announced that the Supreme Court had ruled on the case of *Powell* vs. *Texas* in favor of Texas. The local ordinances in Seattle and other cities will remain in force. The committee, made up of police representatives, public health officials, judges, social workers, and social scien-

---

[17]Ibid., p. 11.

tists, begins to discuss their course of action now that the change in law is no longer impending. Many members of the committee are relieved and feel their work is over.

A physician from the nearby medical school announced, "Well, all things now are provided in the jail, emergency medical treatment and interruption of drinking." A public health physician agreed that the jail was adequate, and since the court did not change the laws, it would be unnecessary to provide new facilities. He told the committee, "Every prisoner is seen at least once per day. The jailer can call the doctor out any time during the night. At 7 A.M. they're lined up and passed before the physician. The only difference in treatment at a center is they are not behind bars."

By now your anger is rising, but Tim Hill, the councilman who is chairman of the committee, takes a firm stand.

Gentlemen, we've got to do something. We expected the court to take a move we consider humanitarian. We felt existing needs, the facilities are not adequate in jail. It's ludicrous to suggest that we would do nothing more. Our efforts should be directed toward a new type of program. The present one is not doing the job.

The discussion continues for the remainder of the meeting. You argue that it is important to remove these men from the jail, to stop the process of having the police arrest them, and to provide them with a more humane facility. The physician from the medical school finally says, "I find it hard put to think that any other facility is going to be able to offer better care, other than the bar bit, than the jail." After the meeting you begin to plan carefully how to use the information you have collected about the tramps' view of arrest and incarceration. It seems evident now that the Ad Hoc Committee faces considerable difficulty in recommending change.

Implementation

The advocate anthropologist does not remain passive after a goal and blueprint have been formulated (see Figure 16-5). Unlike the administrative anthropologist, the advocate realizes that implementing changes that create better conditions for the oppressed does not occur easily. There are numerous vested interests in Seattle who, despite their support of more humane treatment for tramps, do not feel a change is best. Their resistance is based on diverse reasons. The police know that tramps provide a large labor force for the department; those who run the jail hospital believe they are performing an adequate job; some physicians believe that without the practice of jailing tramps, the hospitals would be flooded with such transients. Although there are many ways the anthropologist can become an advocate for informants to facilitate the implementation of plans that will improve their lot, probably the most important one is the *strategic use of information*. The advocate anthropologist has data that can be used to sway public opinion, inform legislators, embarrass those who hold power, and in other ways implement change.

There are at least three strategies for making use of information as an advocate. First, *the advocate anthropologist seeks to write for the layperson*. If research is to

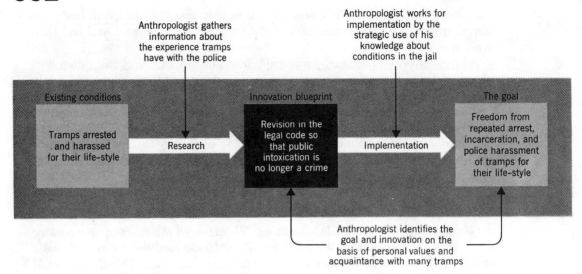

FIGURE 16-5
Advocate Anthropology for Tramps.

benefit informants, the results must be translated into terms that the general public can understand and appreciate. If the anthropologist writes only for other anthropologists, the information will neither be understood nor appreciated by those who have the power to implement change. Second, *the advocate anthropologist seeks to publish his findings in a manner that will give them the widest circulation.* Instead of restricting his writing to professional journals or scholarly books, the advocate anthropologist will call press conferences, release information to the local media, write articles for popular magazines, speak to groups of interested public citizens, and write books for the general public. Third, the advocate anthropologist *tries to release information at the most appropriate time for implementing change.* He may withhold some data from publication until after change has occurred; other findings may be distributed early in order to influence the course of change. In your work with tramps in Seattle you make use of each of these three strategies in order to implement the innovation blueprint.

By now your data about the treatment of tramps in the Seattle City Jail is voluminous, showing in detail the experiences tramps have at the hands of the police and other law enforcement officials. After the meeting with the Ad Hoc Committee, you settle on a plan of action. You will prepare a detailed report about the jail and how alcoholics are treated there. You title the report "The Skid Road Alcoholic's Perception of Law Enforcement in Seattle"[18] and deliver copies to the judge, the city council members, the mayor's office, the police department, and several other professional people. Although some are angered by your report because it is an indictment against the police, within days you begin to receive calls from local

---

[18]James P. Spradley, unpublished manuscript.

papers asking for a copy of the report. One editor of a major city newspaper promises to give your report full coverage if he is given a copy, and you release it to him. The next morning, large headlines on the Seattle *Post Intelligencer* read: "Seattle's Drunk Tank—A Place of Filth, Stench, Human Degradation." And for the next week there is front-page coverage of the report, denials from the mayor and the chief of police about the report's validity, and support from others concerned about the oppression of tramps. City councilmen, under the pressure of the report, make visits to the jail, and some small changes are instituted immediately. The local judge expresses his approval of the report to you and his own concern for more humane treatment of tramps. Within a few months the city council has passed a new ordinance establishing a detoxification program. Although you complete your research and go on to write up your ethnographic description of tramps, you are pleased to learn in the next few years about a statewide change in the laws against public drunkenness in Washington and other states. You hope for the day when the Supreme Court will make a decisive move to protect the rights of men like this, men who have learned the culture of tramps. Perhaps your own research can help these people who are seldom heard.

SUMMARY

Anthropology has many uses in addition to the development of scientific knowledge about the human animal. The primary use of every cultural system is for adapting to the social and physical environment. Cultures are clusters of plans for coping, strategies for personal and collective survival.

The uses of anthropology can be divided into academic anthropology and applied anthropology. Academic anthropology includes research, teaching, writing, and filmmaking; it refers to any use of anthropological knowledge to inform, enlighten, or increase the understanding of some individual or group. Applied anthropology refers to any use of anthropological knowledge to influence social interaction, to maintain or change social institutions, or to direct the course of culture change. Four main types of applied anthropology were identified: adjustment, administrative, action, and advocate.

Adjustment anthropology refers to any use of anthropological knowledge that makes social interaction between persons who operate with different cultural codes more predictable. Adjustment anthropology is useful primarily at the level of interpersonal relationships.

Administrative anthropology involves the use of anthropological knowledge for planned change by those who are external to the local cultural group. Action anthropology refers to any use of anthropological knowledge for planned change by the local cultural group itself. The action anthropologist works as a catalyst. Several conditions are required for this type of applied anthropology: (1) the community or group concerned must have enough independence and power to select among alternative goals and plans; (2) they must have some legitimate process for making decisions; and (3) they must control the resources necessary for implementing a selected innovation.

Advocate anthropology is any use of anthropological knowledge by the anthropologist to increase the power of self-determination for a particular cultural group. This kind of applied anthropology works toward the democratization of society. In consultation with informants the anthropologist identifies goals and innovations and then works to implement the desired changes. In doing so he makes strategic use of the information he has gathered.

MAJOR CONCEPTS

ADAPTATION
ACADEMIC ANTHROPOLOGY
APPLIED ANTHROPOLOGY
ADJUSTMENT ANTHROPOLOGY
ADMINISTRATIVE ANTHROPOLOGY
INNOVATIVE BLUEPRINTS

ACTION ANTHROPOLOGY
REQUIREMENTS FOR ACTION
 ANTHROPOLOGY
ADVOCATE ANTHROPOLOGY
STRATEGIC USES OF INFORMATION

SELECTED READINGS

Arensberg, Conrad M., and Arthur H. Niehoff: *Introducing Social Change: A Manual for Community Development*, 2d ed., Chicago: Aldine, 1971.
After a discussion of the concept of culture, the authors examine the nature of culture change, the motivations for change, and other influences in the guided change process. The book contains a good discussion of American cultural values and field procedures for the change agent.

Clifton, James A. (editor): *Applied Anthropology: Readings in the Uses of the Science of Man*, Boston: Houghton Mifflin, 1970.
This book begins with a brief set of articles that are historical in nature. Part II contains articles on various kinds of applied anthropology. Part III deals with specific cases of applied anthropology in schools, medical settings, technical assistance, and other settings. The last section deals with the ethics of applied anthropology.

Foster, George M.: *Applied Anthropology*, Boston: Little, Brown, 1969.
A basic textbook in applied anthropology that covers the history of this field, the way anthropologists work in applied settings, a model for applied anthropology, and problems in bringing about change.

Goodenough, Ward Hunt: *Cooperation in Change*, New York: Russell Sage, 1963.
An excellent coverage of applied anthropology, this book deals thoroughly with the theory of culture and change. An insightful discussion of the problems faced by change agents and the pitfalls of cultural ignorance.

Hymes, Dell (editor): *Reinventing Anthropology*, New York: Random House, 1969.
Contributions from many authors on the uses of anthropology in the modern world. Many suggestions on new directions for developing an anthropology to serve the needs of humanity.

Niehoff, Arthur H. (editor): *A Casebook of Social Change*, Chicago: Aldine, 1966.
A series of cases is described and critically evaluated. The cases involve attempts to introduce change into various societies in developing areas of the world.

How to Do
a Fieldwork
Project

We believe the best way to learn anthropology is by *doing anthropology*. We consider our field a laboratory science. You can read all the books and articles available, but until you go into the laboratory, become familiar with the research tools, and actually carry out a research project, anthropology seldom comes alive. More and more, students from high school to graduate school are doing anthropological fieldwork projects. In the process their grasp of anthropology gains new dimensions. Admittedly, you cannot become a professional anthropologist in a single semester of fieldwork, nor can you do a project in exactly the same way as Margaret Mead did when she went to Samoa in the 1920s. However, with certain modifications within the structure of a semester course in anthropology, you can carry out an original fieldwork project.

During the last 10 years our students at Macalester College have gone "into the field" and studied hundreds of cultures. They began their projects after only a few weeks into their first course in anthropology. Some have done such excellent research that they have published their papers. From the problems they encountered in the field we began to learn how to adapt the methods of professional anthropology for use by undergraduate students. We have found it is feasible for a student like yourself to do *original* fieldwork, analyze the data you collect, and write up your ethnographic description. You can do it with little training by following the principle of "learning by doing." To that end, we have identified the specific steps you need to follow in order to study any culture. By taking one step at a time, carrying it out, then going on to the next step, you will find it possible to complete a fieldwork project.

How much time do you need? Although anthropologists often spend 1 or 2 years in the field, by scaling down your research goals, you can complete your project in a single term. All you will need are a minimum of 1 or 2 hours a week and a few extra hours at the end of the term for writing up your report. *But you must begin early in the semester and do one step each week*. This is not the kind of project you can leave until the last few weeks of a term. Although you will want to read this entire chapter now to get an overview of the fieldwork project, keep in mind that you will need to return to it again and again during the semester. As you complete one step, reread the instructions for the next step, and so on throughout the project. In order to emphasize this feature of doing fieldwork, we have numbered the steps according to each week of the project.

You are about to embark on an adventure in learning. This adventure will take you out of the classroom, beyond your dormitory, and into the world beyond your campus. In the process you will meet and talk to strangers, observe strange patterns of behavior, and learn how to decipher the cultural codes people are using. Doing ethnographic fieldwork is an exciting learning experience! If you want extra help or if you decide to pursue your project for several semesters, you might like to read one of the following books.

1. *The Cultural Experience: Ethnography in Complex Society*, James P. Spradley and David W. McCurdy (Chicago: Science Research Associates, 1972). This unique book gives specific guidance in doing fieldwork and also includes more than a dozen papers written by undergraduate students.

2. *The Ethnographic Interview*, James P. Spradley (New York: Holt, Rinehart and Winston, 1979). This book gives step-by-step instructions for doing an ethnography project using the technique of interviewing key informants. It will show you how to interview, analyze your data, and write up your ethnographic description.

3. *Participant Observation*, James P. Spradley. (New York: Holt, Rinehart and Winston, 1980). A companion volume to *The Ethnographic Interview*, this book shows you in step-by-step fashion how to do an ethnographic project using the technique of participant observation.

But remember, you do not need to read anything else except this brief appendix to learn everything necessary to carry out your first ethnographic field project. So let us get on with the task of fieldwork!

WEEK ONE/STEP ONE: SELECT A CULTURAL SCENE

In one semester you cannot go to New Guinea or live with a band of Eskimo for 6 months. In the small, non-Western societies anthropologists often study, we can talk about investigating "the culture" of a particular group. But you will not be able to study an entire culture of your town, city, or even a nearby village of one hundred people. The first step in scaling down ethnographic fieldwork to fit the needs of student research involves shifting your attention from studying a "culture" to studying a "cultural scene."

Our society consists of hundreds of different subgroups and social situations. Each has its own rules for behavior. The knowledge people learn and use in particular social situations with a limited group of people constitutes a *cultural scene*. As you move through the day you move from one scene to another, using your cultural knowledge to order your behavior. Riding the bus is such a scene. You need to know where buses stop, how to board, what to pay, how to talk to the driver, how to select a seat or where to stand, and when to get off. During the bus ride you need to know the rules of appropriate bus-riding behavior. Although you will not be able to do an ethnography of the entire town you live in, you could do an ethnography of bus-riding behavior.

The first thing you must do in selecting a cultural scene is to make a lengthy list—at least 50—of possible cultural scenes. Think of potential informants—a bank teller, the garage mechanic, a pet store saleswoman, a judge, a football coach, a garbage collector, even a second-grade student. Each of these informants represents more than one cultural scene, but you can easily identify *which* scene you might discuss with them. Walk around the business district of your city, look through the yellow pages of the telephone book, or ask friends about possible scenes to study. The restaurant down on the corner has several scenes—the customers, the waitresses, the cook in the kitchen, the hostess who seats customers. Each of these people could provide cultural information on a particular scene. You will not have time to study every aspect of that restaurant, but you can do an excellent job of describing one aspect of that institution, one of its many cultural scenes.

Here is a sample list of scenes you might consider.

Dogcatchers	Amusement park behavior
Bank tellers	People waiting in lines
The playground	Policemen
A criminal court	Jeweler
Airport waiting room	Jehovah's Witness
People using Coca-Cola machines	Catholic priest
Mail carriers	Museum guard
Housewives	Potter
Nursery school	Nurse
Savings and loan officer	Antique dealer
Farmer	Jazz musician
Ditch digger	Janitor
Gas station attendant	Kindergarten student
League of Women Voters	Trucker
Hospital orderly	Runner
Sorority sister	Acupuncturist

If these do not look like typical "cultures" studied by anthropologists, do not worry. You are focusing on "cultural scenes" and will do the same kind of research, only in a more restricted way.

Once you have made your list, you are ready to select the one cultural scene you want to study. But how do you decide? Although it is impossible to predict which scene will provide the best learning experience for you, there are some general guidelines for making your decision. Ask yourself several questions. Any scene for which you can answer "yes" on all or most of these questions is a pretty good bet. And even those that meet only half of these criteria can sometimes work out well.

1. Is the cultural scene accessible in that I can enter, make observations, *or* find an informant for interviews?

358

2. Does the informant I would interview have a thorough knowledge from at least 1 or 2 years of experience in this cultural scene?

3. Is this cultural scene unfamiliar to me? (When a scene is too familiar, you already have put on some cultural blinders that make research difficult.)

4. Is this cultural scene one that I can study *now*, or is my potential informant currently involved in it?

5. Will my informant have adequate time or can I gain access to observe for at least several hours each week?

6. Do I need permission to study this scene and, if so, can I gain that permission easily?

7. Is my informant willing and interested to teach me his or her cultural knowledge?

When you make your decision and set up a tentative appointment to interview an informant or visit the scene to make observations, you will have completed the first step of selecting a cultural scene. Do not rush to a quick decision. Consider it from all angles. Try to find a friend or someone you know to put you in touch with a potential informant on the scene. But sooner or later you will have to decide and get started. If it does not work out, you can still make changes up to several weeks from now, but finding a good scene and sticking with it for the semester is better.

WEEK TWO/STEP TWO: ASK DESCRIPTIVE QUESTIONS

In this book we define culture as the knowledge people have learned and use to *generate behavior* and *interpret behavior*. You cannot directly observe cultural knowledge, but you can observe what it produces—behavior. In doing ethnographic research, you will find it helpful to think of this product as falling into three categories.

1. What people do.
2. What people say.
3. What the artifacts are that people make and use.

In your research on any cultural scene, you have behavior, speech, and artifacts with which to work.

Before you can begin to get at the meaning of these cultural products (after all, culture consists of meanings people give to their worlds), you need to describe them in a simple, straightforward manner. This will require that you ask yourself or someone else a series of *descriptive questions*. Descriptive questions ask things like, "What's going on here?", "What do you do all day?", or "Could you describe to me what goes on in this court on a typical day, from the first thing in the morning until it closes at the end of the day?" When you ask descriptive questions, you pretend you are a stranger from the planet Mars without any knowledge of what people do, say, or make. This helps you to keep from overlooking the familiar. And if you have chosen an unfamiliar scene, your task is that much easier.

John's father was in the hospital for a long stay and, since John would have to visit him often, he decided to find a cultural scene in the hospital. Several times a week he rode the elevator to the sixteenth floor, where his father stayed in Room 1641; he decided to study the cultural scene of hospital elevators and base most of his research on participant observation. He asked himself, "Can I describe the process of riding the elevator from the first floor to the sixteenth?" Although this seemed simple, when he took the "Martian perspective," he filled several pages in his field notebook. Here are a few lines to give you an example.

People walk up to the sliding doors that hide the elevator shaft and begin by looking at the lights to see what floor the elevators are on. Then they push the button on the wall, sometimes they push it over and over, then stand back and wait. When the elevator comes, a bell rings and the door opens. Sometimes waiting passengers try to rush in, then have to stand back to let others off. Many different kinds of people get on and off. Once on, everyone pushes a bank of buttons for his or her floor, then they turn facing the door of the elevator and stand quietly. At each floor there are a number of things that can happen. For instance, yesterday, at the third floor, the orderly who was pushing a patient, pushed the "STOP" lever, left the elevator while we all waited, went down the hall, then returned and we were on our way.

Ulrike Linke, a student from Germany, decided to study garbage collectors by using a key informant. In her paper, "Trash to Cash: An Ethnography of the Cultural Scene of Garbage Collectors" (Department of Anthropology, Macalester College), she described her interview. She began by asking descriptive questions, such as "Could you describe a typical day in your work?"

When Mike and I finally "got to work," as he called it, I plugged in my tape recorder and immediately turned it on so as not to miss a single word of what he said. In addition I took notes, which gave Mike the feeling he talked to me and not the small, black machine. So the atmosphere during the interviews was very relaxed.

Ulrike Linke transcribed her interviews and quickly had many pages of field notes—in her informant's own words. We speak of these as "folk terms," because they are the ones informants use normally in the course of their lives. Folk terms hold the key to many cultural meanings, and you want to identify clearly when you use folk terms or others that did not come from your informant. John, in his study of the hospital elevator scene, was filling pages of field notes with his own words. We speak of these as "analytic terms" to distinguish them from what informants say. But John will also collect folk terms whenever he overhears people speaking. Yesterday someone said, "This is the slowest damn elevator I've ever ridden" and, after he got off at the sixteenth floor, John wrote that down in his notes. Participant observation leads to an ethnographic record that is filled with many more analytic terms, but that includes both. Informant interviewing leads to a rich source of folk terms. Indeed, later on, John decided to interview one of the hospital orderlies about the problems he had riding the elevators. In his interview he was able to discover many new folk terms that enriched his final ethnography. Whether your field notes are mostly folk terms or analytic terms, they describe what people do, what they say, and the artifacts they use.

Asking descriptive questions and recording the answers will continue throughout your project. Even as you learn to look for more specific facts, you will want to continue with new descriptive questions. John, for example, will go on to ask, "What are all the ways people dress on the elevator?" and "What do people do with their eyes on the elevator?" Ulrike Linke went on to ask, "Could you describe all the different kinds of trucks used in garbage collecting?" and "Could you describe to me what each route is like?" Once you have 5 to 10 pages of field notes, you are ready to go on to the next step.

WEEK THREE/STEP THREE: IDENTIFY CULTURAL DOMAINS

Cultural knowledge is not a random collection of terms; instead, it is an organized system of knowledge. And the basic unit or organization is called a "cultural domain." A cultural domain is any large category of knowledge that includes smaller categories inside of it. For example, the concept "book" represents a domain in our culture and includes smaller categories such as "paperback book," "textbook," "hardback book," and "best-seller." We say these are all different *kinds of books*.

"Kinds of books" is a *cover term* for a domain. The other terms such as "textbook" and "best-seller" are *included terms*. For your research purposes we will consider all cultural domains to be made up of a single cover term and many included terms. Let us look at examples from the two studies just cited.

In her study of garbage collectors, Ulrike Linke identified the domain "kinds of refuse trucks." It included folk terms like "roll-off," "load lugger," "rear-end," and "front-end." John, in his study of the elevator scene in the hospital, identified a domain he called "kinds of stops." It included things like "emergency stop," "rider stop," "waiting passenger stop," "between floor stop," and "unloading stop."

One way to identify domains in a cultural scene is to locate *cover terms*, the names for large categories. A helpful way to find cover terms is to recognize the semantic relationships that organize a domain. For example, the domain of refuse trucks was organized by the relationship (X) is a kind of (Y), or (a roll-off) is a kind of (refuse truck). Anthropologists and linguists studying many different languages have discovered a limited number of semantic relationships that universally structure cultural domains. In Figure A-1 we have shown eight of the most common semantic relationships you can use in searching for cultural domains. They are illustrated from the study of hospital elevators, but you can easily find examples from your own research for all of those shown.

Searching for cultural domains requires that you read over all your field notes and that you make a separate list of cover terms and included terms. Try to identify as many as possible. Here is an example of a few from Ulrike Linke's study of garbage collectors.

Kinds of accounts (commercial accounts, residential, etc.)
Kinds of refuse trucks (roll-offs, load luggers, etc.)
Kinds of routes (No. 1, No. 102, No. 139, etc.)
Parts of a chassis (frame, cab, rear-end axles, etc.)
Kinds of activities (design routes, update the board, etc.)
Stages in doing a route (pick-up truck, make first stop, etc.)

Semantic Relationships	Statement	Example	Ethnographic question
1. Strict inclusion	X is a kind of Y	A doctor is a kind of passenger.	What are all the kinds of passengers?
2. Part–whole	X is a part of Y	The back wall is part of the elevator.	What are all the parts of the elevator?
3. Cause–effect	X is a result of Y	Stopping the elevator is a result of pushing the stop button.	What are all the results of pushing the stop button?
4. Rationale	X is a reason for doing Y	Playing around is one reason for riding the elevator.	What are all the reasons for riding the elevator?
5. Location for action	X is a place for doing Y	The second floor is a place for stopping	What are all the places for stopping?
6. Purpose	X is used for Y	The elevator is used for transporting patients to surgery.	What are all the other things an elevator is used for?
7. Means–end	X is a way to do Y	Looking down is a way to avoid attention.	What are all the ways to avoid attention?
8. Sequence	X is a step (stage) in Y	Stepping off the elevator is a stage in riding the elevator.	What are all the stages in riding the elevator?

FIGURE A-1
Kinds of semantic relations that organize cultural domains.

You will have completed this step in your ethnographic research when you have made a list of all the domains you can find. But remember, you will be gathering more field notes and need to look for more domains each week. New ones of great importance can emerge even during the last weeks of your investigation. In your final ethnography you will want to include a list of all the domains you have identified, although you cannot describe or analyze each one in detail.

WEEK FOUR/STEP FOUR: DISCOVER TAXONOMIC STRUCTURE

Cultural meaning is based on the way concepts are organized. The internal structure of a domain can be represented by a *taxonomy*. A taxonomy is any set of categories organized on the principle of inclusion. This occurs when a general category like "refuse truck" is used to refer to more specific ones like "roll-off" and "load lugger." But frequently a taxonomy shows that a domain has several levels of inclusion. For example, Ulrike Linke found that her informant classified "refuse" into five basic types and many subtypes. The domain is shown in Figure A-2, a taxonomy of kinds of refuse.

Kinds of refuse																		
Hazardous wastes			Garbage		Trash			Rubbish						Demolition/Construction Material				
Flammable paints	Chemicals		Rotten stuff	Food scraps	Paper products			Rubber	Leaves	Cans	Bottles	Light wood		Concrete	Bricks	Dirt	Heavy Wood	
	Toxic chemicals	Pesticides			Paper	Boxes						Pallets	Crates				Crates	Timber	Trees

FIGURE A-2
A taxonomy of "kinds of refuse."

You can discover the taxonomic structure by asking *structural questions* of yourself or of an informant. For example, in order to find out the taxonomy in Figure A-2, Ulrike Linke had to ask this question over and over again: "What are all the different kinds of refuse?" When it was discovered that "garbage" was one kind of refuse in the perceptual world of the garbage collector, it was important to ask the same structural question, but in a slightly different form: "What are all the different kinds of garbage?" By repeated use of this type of question you can discover all the terms that make up a domain and also discover how they are related.

In doing participant observation, you will have to ask *yourself* structural questions, going through your field notes and searching your memory for the answers. Consider this example from the hospital elevator study. John quickly discovered that in the close quarters of the elevator, people controlled their gaze quite carefully. Looking around at other people, he noticed that almost never did anyone return his gaze. This led to identifying the domain "ways to use your eyes." By asking himself the question, "What are all the ways to use your eyes on the elevator?", it was possible to discover the taxonomy shown in Figure A-3. Most of the terms are analytic; that is, they are labels for recurrent behavior that John used, but those in quotation marks are the ones he discovered through interviewing people who rode the elevator frequently.

Whether you ask structural questions of yourself (and then make observations) or of your informant, you will need to formulate the questions carefully. In Figure A-3, kinds of semantic relationships, we have given eight examples of structural questions. You can use these as a guide to construct your own, but remember, you will have to ask them over and over again to find all the terms for your taxonomy. When you have drawn up a tentative taxonomy, you are ready to go on to the next step.

Ways to use your eyes		
Close eyes		
Shift gaze		
	Look	Look at person talking to
		Read something
		Look at objects
	Stare	Stare at floor
		Stare at person's back
		Stare at door
		Stare at light indicator
		Stare at people
		Middle distance stare

FIGURE A-3
A taxonomy of "ways to use your eyes."

WEEK FIVE/STEP FIVE: SELECT A CONTRAST SET FOR ANALYSIS

Each step takes you into a more narrow focused search for meaning. Instead of skimming the surface of a cultural scene, ethnography seeks to dig deep into the meanings people have learned. In this step you will look over the taxonomies you have discovered and select a single contrast set for in-depth analysis. In order to understand how to do this, we need to look at the nature of "contrast" for the construction of cultural meaning.

The ethnographer continually looks for things informants treat as *similar* and also things they consider as *different*. In riding the elevator, John can see that everyone treats "stops" at each floor as similar. But occasionally there is an "emergency stop" that people treat as quite different from the ones that occur at most floors in the hospital. We want to know which things informants put together and which ones they keep apart. In other words, we want to know how they divide up their world. *Contrast* is a deceptively simple principle of meaning that focuses on the differences among concepts. A contrast set refers to a group of terms in a taxonomy that are all included in a single term at the next higher level. For example, John identified six ways to "stare." They share a feature of meaning tied up in the idea of staring; in this sense these six categories are all similar. However, these six ways of staring are also *different*. The principle of contrast implies that what these terms *do mean* is intimately linked to what each one does *not mean*. In short, we want to ask, "How is the middle distance stare different from staring at the floor?", and so on.

Let us go back to the kinds of refuse that garbage collectors identify. There are several contrast sets in the taxonomy in Figure A-2. Immediately included in "kinds of refuse" are five terms that make up one contrast set. Each of these has several terms included in it, making up at least five more contrast sets. Your task is to look over all the contrast sets and select one or more for intensive analysis. In doing so, you need to ask if you know anything about them, if you have sufficient data to make an analysis. Go back over your field notes and review them for more information.

This week is a good time to catch up on past assignments that may have been only partially completed. Perhaps you need to make more observations with general descriptive questions in mind or to interview your informant with such questions. Perhaps you need to review the section on taxonomies and to search for new included terms. Because each week you are collecting more data, now is a good time to go back over all your new field notes (taken from observations or from interviews) and look for domains. Review the eight basic types of semantic relationships in Figure A-1. See if you have domains that represent each of these types and if you can add to your list all possible domains that you might study in depth.

WEEK SIX/STEP SIX: MAKE A COMPONENTIAL ANALYSIS TO DISCOVER ATTRIBUTES

The attributes of cultural concepts serve to distinguish among members of a contrast set. Once you have discovered the structure of a particular domain and selected a contrast set for analysis, you proceed to search for the attributes associated with each of the categories in the set. This search for attributes is called *componential analysis*. Componential analysis begins by searching through all your field notes to see if you can find any attributes that clearly go with each category.

Let us go back to the hospital elevator. John goes through his field notes and looks for every note he has made about staring behavior. He notices that staring at the floor occurs when the elevator is relatively uncrowded. Closing the eyes does not occur unless the elevator is very crowded. And so he has discovered two attributes: crowdedness and uncrowdedness. He can now go back to make observations and find out if these are associated with any of the other ways of using the eyes.

Ulrike Linke selected the contrast set at the highest level of the taxonomy "kinds of refuse." She can now go back to her field notes and go through every interview to see if any attributes show up for hazardous wastes, garbage, and so on. For example, in reviewing her taped interviews, she might find that her informant said, "Garbage is always wet; it's the worst kind of stuff to pick up." The category "garbage" thus has two attributes: it is wet, and it is evaluated as the "worst" to pick up.

Another way to discover attributes is to ask yourself or your informant "contrast questions." These come in several forms; basically, ask for differences and similarities between the categories you are analyzing. For example, one might ask a garbage collector, "What is the difference between garbage and hazardous waste?" It is also possible to use three categories and ask, "Of these three, which two are alike and which one is different: trash, rubbish, garbage?" Once you have found enough attributes to distinguish all the terms in your contrast set, you are ready to construct a *paradigm*.

As you move forward in your research from week to week, you may want to expand to more than one domain. A final report can sometimes involve a detailed analysis of a single domain and the taxonomy associated with it or can involve several domains. You might want to pick one or more contrast sets from each taxonomy you have analyzed for more research.

WEEK SEVEN/STEP SEVEN: SEARCH FOR EXAMPLES

Ethnographic research, whether you spend 1 year in a village in Ghana or 2 months visiting a nursing home, involves three basic steps: *collecting data*, *analyzing data*, and *writing a cultural description*. These steps do not occur in rigid sequence. Instead, they are like a circle—you collect data, then analyze it, then collect more data, then write up some of your field notes, then analyze some more, and so on. Each week you should make at least one observation or conduct one interview. Although some of the steps focus on analysis (such as the last one in which you did a componential analysis), you will still need to collect new cultural data during that week. Furthermore, it is helpful to begin writing up small parts of your paper in a first draft as you go along. Then, at the end of the semester, when you are preparing your final ethnographic report, you will find it much easier to rewrite what you already have.

Every ethnography has both a skeletal structure and a body of description that hangs on that skeleton. The folk terms, analytic terms, domains, taxonomies, and attributes are all part of the skeleton. Sometimes students think that an ethnographic description consists only of these skeletal features. But this is not the case. Your final report needs to communicate the *feelings*, the *immediate situation*, and the *atmosphere* of the cultural scene you studied. Without that you will have a dry, museum-case picture that is a caricature of the actual situation you have studied. The flesh on the skeleton consists primarily of concrete examples, specific instances, and verbal pictures of the cultural scene. In order to collect these aspects of your data, you can do several specific things.

First, with the domains in mind on which you have selected to focus, read through your field notes and *inventory all examples*. John could take every type of "eye behavior" and see if he has specific instances of persons who used their eyes in each way. If the field notes merely said, "I saw a man staring at the floor," it would be important to go back and observe more detail about that kind of behavior. Describe the *context* so that you have a full-fledged example. Garbage collectors must handle *toxic chemicals*, one kind of refuse. But knowing this single term does not communicate very much. In a final ethnography an example told by an informant about going to a specific pickup point, identifying the kind of chemical, the container, the dangers perceived, and the difficulties in getting it into the truck would be important. In the context of this example, how did the collector feel? What did he think? Once you have gone through your field notes looking for examples, you will have a list of "examples to search for."

Second, with your list in mind, set out to find the examples you need. Now your observations will become quite focused, searching for specific instances of behavior. Your interviews will become quite focused also, asking for specific examples and stories.

Finally, it will help to begin writing up examples in detail as they might go into your final paper. Describe not only the *action* that occurred, but the *actors* and the *setting* as well. File these away for later reference. Such examples can also provide many new attributes for your continuing componential analysis. By the time you have collected new examples and have studied them, you will be ready to go back to finishing your componential analysis by constructing a paradigm.

WEEK EIGHT/STEP EIGHT: CONSTRUCT A PARADIGM

By now you probably have long lists of attributes for the terms in one or more contrast sets. For example, the list for the major kinds of refuse with which garbage collectors deal might look like this.

Hazardous wastes are *nasty slop*.
Garbage comes from a *business account*.
Rubbish is *not smelly*.
Trash is *an easy pickup*.
Hazardous wastes are the *worst pickup*.

You could show all the attributes by simply making lists or by having long descriptive sentences about each term in a contrast set. However, it is useful to represent them graphically by means of a *paradigm*. This kind of chart shows all the terms in the contrast set (which share a single feature of meaning) and how all are different from the others. Figure A-4 shows a paradigm for "kinds of refuse."

A paradigm summarizes a great deal of information. It is part of the "skeleton" of an ethnography. In your final report you must describe and illustrate many of the things summarized in the paradigm. Its function is partly to help you analyze your data, to discover what is missing, and to display a great deal of information in a brief, elegant manner. By examining a paradigm, you can quickly see the similarities and differences among the various members of a contrast set.

WEEK NINE/STEP NINE: DISCOVER CULTURAL THEMES

An ethnography is more than a collection of facts; it is more than a collection of folk terms or analytic terms; it is more than long laundry lists of domains, taxonomies, and paradigms. The goal of an ethnographic description is to communicate the inner meaning and logic of a cultural scene as the "natives" perceive and experience that scene. In the chapter on "World View and Values" we defined and discussed the nature of cultural themes. We saw how they help to integrate and give meaning to a culture. You might like to review that chapter and the kinds of themes that give meaning to the Mae Enga culture in New Guinea before you start your own search for themes.

A cultural theme is a larger idea or premise that appears again and again in the cultural scene you are studying. Often, you can examine a paradigm and it will suggest a cultural theme. A theme that suggests itself from the paradigm on refuse might be stated as, "Garbage collectors face the daily problem of dealing with stuff other people do not want to handle." One theme that emerges from the study

FIGURE A-4
Paradigm of "kinds of refuse".

	Dry	Wet	Compactable	Dangerous	Pick up	Nasty slop	Smelly	Type of account
Hazardous wastes	No	Yes	Yes	Yes	Worst	Yes	Sometimes	Industrial
Garbage	No	Yes	Yes	No	Worst	Yes	Yes	Business
Trash	Yes	A little	Yes	No	Easy	No	No	Business and industrial
Rubbish	Sometimes	Sometimes	Not much	No	Easy	No	No	Industrial Multiple dwellings
Demolition/ construction material	Yes	No	No	No	Easy	No	No	Industrial

of hospital elevators is that "People want to avoid contact with strangers but cannot and have to stand close and often make contact." These two themes then suggest the direction of an ethnographic account. In writing about garbage collectors, you can describe how they deal with the messy things of life that others avoid. In writing about elevator passengers, you could describe how people solve the problem of avoiding contact. In either case, the cultural knowledge people have acquired is a tool for solving human problems. Culture is something we learn and use to cope with recurrent situations of life. The theme often emerges in asking, "What are the people in this situation trying to do? What problems do they perceive and how are they trying to solve them?"

You may discover a theme for organizing your ethnography from what someone said. A tramp commented to one ethnographer, "After you've been in the bucket for 30 days, you owe yourself a drunk!" This became the theme of an entire ethnography (Spradley, 1972). You may find a theme by looking for conflicts between people in the cultural scene. Sometimes people are pulled in several directions and the conflict is in their own mind, thus suggesting another theme. Reading ethnographic descriptions can also be a rich source of themes. Finally, almost any of the chapters in this textbook suggest broad cultural themes that might apply to the scene you are studying.

WEEK TEN/STEP TEN: WRITING THE ETHNOGRAPHY

Every ethnographic report is a translation. You have to take the cultural patterns and their meanings from one scene and *translate* them into a description that outsiders will grasp. If you want to describe the culture of dog shows, your audience will not be dog handlers, dog breeders, or judges at the show. Instead, you will take what these people know already and write for an audience of *uninformed outsiders*. In 10 weeks you will have learned a great deal about the cultural scene you are studying and can easily take for granted that your audience knows about it also! A translation (i.e., an ethnography) cannot take it for granted that the readers already know the culture. If you can keep in mind some single person you know who is ignorant of the culture you studied, your ethnography will succeed in communicating to this "target audience."

With this audience in mind, begin by making a list of all the topics you could include in your report. List domains, themes, setting, taxonomies, and anything else you feel *could be included*. Your goal is to produce a lengthy list of possibilities. In her paper, "Trash to Cash," Ulrike Linke could see the possibility of writing about (1) her research methods, (2) her experience with her informant, (3) her selection of the cultural scene, (4) accounts a collection company has (taxonomy), (5) different systems for picking up refuse (taxonomy and paradigm), (6) various types of trucks and their uses (taxonomy and paradigm), (7) pictures she had collected of trucks, (8) types of containers (taxonomy and paradigm), (9) types of routes (taxonomy), (10) example of a specific route (taxonomy and paradigm), (11) kinds of things a garbage collector does (taxonomy and paradigm), (12) ways to design a route, (13) types of refuse and its meaning (taxonomy and paradigm), (14) introduction, (15) theme of solving problems of picking up messy and dangerous stuff, (16) conclusion, and (17) possibilities for future research.

After you identify all the possible things to include, you will want to *make an outline*. Select things to write about on which you have the most information and arrange them in a logical, but not permanent, order. Outlines are tentative plans for writing, not final arrangements chiseled in granite. As you write, your outline will change to fit the material at hand.

Once a tentative outline has been created, start writing a section of the paper about which you feel most confident. This might be the introduction, or you might find it easier to describe the setting of the cultural scene or even a particular domain you have analyzed in great detail. Many students feel overwhelmed if they have to write a 15- or 20-page paper. But if you redefine your task as writing five or six 3-page papers, it becomes much easier. And when those have been completed, you can write brief transition paragraphs that will "glue" them together into a comprehensive ethnographic report.

Do not forget to include examples, and if you have interviewed an informant, include as many direct quotes as you feel necessary to communicate a firsthand acquaintance with the cultural scene. It is helpful to underline key folk terms that you want to discuss in great detail, especially the first time you introduce them. Consider using a table of contents at the beginning of your paper and a glossary of key terms at the end. Remember to tell your reader how you are using important anthropological concepts such as *culture*, *ethnography*, and *informant*.

These are the steps that will take you through an ethnographic field project. Along the way you will encounter many problems, but most of them you can solve yourself. Sometimes a few students can get together to discuss their problems or a class can break into small "problem-solving sessions" that will help you. Once you have discovered the excitement of discovery, you may want to continue your research. Many students who begin a study of a cultural scene finish with an overwhelming sense that "I have just begun to scratch the surface." Ulrike Linke, for example, continued to study the cultural scene of garbage collectors in the context of many other anthropology courses. Her separate papers became the basis for a comprehensive honors thesis that included comparisons with garbage collection in Europe, studied during a semester abroad. But whether you spend 10 weeks or 4 years in studying one cultural scene, the methods described here can take you a long way. With practice and patience, you can "learn to do ethnography by doing it" and acquire valuable skills in seeing the world from some other groups' point of view. Good luck in the adventure of doing your fieldwork project!

REFERENCES CITED

Aberle, David F. et al., 1950: "The Functional Prerequisites of Society," *Ethics*, *60*, pp. 100–111.

Achebe, Chinua, 1958: *Things Fall Apart*, London: William Heinemann.

_____, 1961: *No Longer at Ease*, Stamford, Conn.: Astor-Honor.

_____, 1966: *A Man of the People*, Garden City, N.Y.: Doubleday.

_____, 1967: *Arrow of God*, New York: John Day.

Alland, Alexander, Jr., 1972: "Is Territoriality Imperative?" *The Human Imperative*, New York: Columbia University Press, Chapter 3.

American Anthropological Association, 1971: "Principles of Professional Responsibility."

Arensberg, Conrad N. and Arthur H. Niehoff, 1971: *Introducing Social Change: A Manual for Community Development*, Second Edition, Chicago: Aldine.

Barnett, Homer C., 1938: "The Nature of the Potlatch," *American Anthropologist*, *40*, pp. 349–358.

_____, 1953: *Innovation: The Basis of Cultural Change*, New York: McGraw-Hill.

_____, 1956: *Anthropology in Administration*, Evanston, Ill.: Row, Petersen.

Basso, Keith, 1967: "Semantic Aspects of Linguistic Acculturation," *American Anthropologist*, *69* (2), pp. 471–477.

_____, 1972: "Ice and Travel Among the Fort Norman Slave: Folk Taxonomies and Cultural Rules," *Language and Society*, *1* (1), pp. 31–49.

Belshaw, C. S., 1965: *Traditional Exchange and Modern Markets*, Englewood Cliffs, N.J.: Prentice-Hall.

Benedict, Ruth, 1934: *Patterns of Culture*, New York: Houghton Mifflin.

Berreman, Gerald D., 1962: *Behind Many Masks: Ethnography and Impression Management in a Himalayan Village*, Ithaca, N.Y.: Society for Applied Anthropology: Monograph No. 4.

Birdwhistle, Ray L., 1970: *Kinesics and Context: Essays on Body Communication*, Philadelphia: University of Pennsylvania Press.

Boas, Franz, 1897: "The Social Organization and the Secret Societies of the Kwakiutl Indians," Report of the U.S. National Museum for 1895, pp. 311–738.

———, 1921: *Ethnology of the Kwakiutl*, 35th Annual Report 1913–1914, Bureau of American Ethnology, Washington, D.C.

———, 1935: *Kwakiutl Culture as Reflected in Mythology*, New York: G. E. Stechert.

———, 1943: "Recent Anthropology," *Science*, 98, pp. 334–337.

———, 1966: *Kwakiutl Ethnography*, Chicago: University of Chicago Press.

Bohannan, Paul J. and George Dalton, 1965: *Markets in Africa: Eight Subsistence Economies in Transition*, Revised Edition, Natural History Library, Garden City, N.Y.: Doubleday/Anchor.

——— and John Middleton (editors), 1968a: *Kinship and Social Organization*, Garden City, N.Y.: Natural History Press.

——— and John Middleton (editors), 1968b: *Marriage, Family, and Residence*, Garden City, N.Y.: Natural History Press.

——— and Fred Plog (editors), 1967: *Beyond the Frontier: Social Process and Culture Change*, Garden City, N.Y.: Natural History Press.

Burling, Robbins, 1970: *Man's Many Voices: Language in Its Cultural Context*, New York: Holt, Rinehart and Winston.

Butler, Philip, 1977: "The Tap Code: Ascribed Meanings in Prisoner of War Communications," *Urban Life: A Journal of Ethnographic Research*, 5, pp. 399–416.

Carey, James T., 1968: *The College Drug Scene*, Englewood Cliffs, N.J.: Prentice-Hall.

Chagnon, Napoleon A., 1968: *Yanomamo: The Fierce People*, New York: Holt, Rinehart and Winston.

Clifton, James A. (editor), 1970: *Applied Anthropology: Readings in the Uses of the Science of Man*, Boston: Houghton Mifflin.

Cohen, Ronald and John Middleton (editors), 1967: *Comparative Political Systems: Studies in the Politics of Preindustrial Societies*, Garden City, N.Y.: Natural History Press.

Cohen, Yehudi (editor), 1974: *Man in Adaptation: The Cultural Present*, Second Edition, Chicago: Aldine.

Coon, Carlton S. (editor), 1948: *A Reader in General Anthropology*, New York: Holt, Rinehart and Winston.

Dalton, George (editor), 1967: *Tribal and Peasant Economies: Readings in Economic Anthropology*, Garden City, N.Y.: Natural History Press.

——— (editor), 1971: *Economic Development and Social Change: The Modernization of Village Communities*, Garden City, N.Y.: Natural History Press.

Devos, George and Hiroshi Wagatsuma, 1966: *Japan's Invisible Race: Caste in Culture and Personality*, Berkeley: University of California Press.

Dyson-Hudson, Neville, 1958: "The Karimojong and the Suk," *Uganda Journal*, 22, pp. 173–180.

———, 1963: "The Karimojong Age System," *Ethnology*, 2, pp. 353–401.

———, 1966: *Karimojong Politics*, Oxford: Clarendon Press.

———, 1972: "Factors Inhibiting Change in an African Society," *Transactions of the New York Academy of Science*, Series 2, 24, pp. 771–801.

——— and Rada Dyson-Hudson, 1957: "The Water Supplies of Southern Karamoja District," map published by Uganda Surveys Department.

Dyson-Hudson, Rada, 1960: "East Coast Fever in Karamoja," *Uganda Journal*, 24, pp. 253–259.

_____, 1960: "Men, Women and Work in a Pastoral Society," *Natural History, 49,* pp. 42–57.

_____, "I Am a Mountain," *The Johns Hopkins Magazine, 21* (3), pp. 28–31.

_____, 1972: "Pastoralism: Self-Image and Behavioral Reality," *Journal of Asian and African Studies, 7* (1 and 2).

_____ and Neville Dyson-Hudson, 1959: Karimojong Settlement and Land Use Patterns, a series of 1/50,000 scale maps, Kampala.

_____ and Neville Dyson-Hudson, 1962: "A Marriage Economy," *Natural History Magazine, 71,* pp. 44–53.

_____ and Neville Dyson-Hudson, 1969: "Subsistence Herding in Uganda," *Scientific American, 220* (2), pp. 76–89.

_____ and Neville Dyson-Hudson, 1970: "The Food Production Systems of a Semi-Nomadic Society: The Karimojong, Uganda," in P. McLoughlin (editor), *African Food Production Systems: Cases and Theory,* Baltimore: Johns Hopkins Press.

Epstein, A. L. (editor), 1967: *The Craft of Social Anthropology,* London: Travistock.

Erasmus, C. J., 1961: *Man Takes Control: Cultural Development and American Aid,* Minneapolis: University of Minnesota Press.

Evans-Pritchard, E. E., 1937: *Witchcraft, Oracles and Magic Among the Azande,* Oxford: Clarendon Press.

_____, 1940: *The Nuer,* Oxford: Clarendon Press.

_____, 1951: *Kinship and Marriage Among the Nuer,* London: Oxford University Press.

Firth, Raymond, 1956: *Elements of Social Organization,* London: Watts.

_____ (editor), 1967: *Themes in Economic Anthropology,* London: Travistock.

Forde, Daryl (editor), 1954: *African Worlds: Studies in the Cosmological Ideas and Social Values of African Peoples,* London: Oxford University Press.

Foster, George M., 1948: *Empire's Children: The People of Tzintzuntzan,* Westport, Conn.: Greenwood.

_____, 1961: "The Dyadic Contract: A Model for the Social Structure of a Mexican Peasant Village," *American Anthropologist, 63,* pp. 1173–1192.

_____, 1967 (reissued with changes 1988): *Tzintzuntzan: Mexican Peasants in a Changing World,* Prospect Heights, IL: Waveland Press, Inc.

_____, 1969: *Applied Anthropology,* Boston: Little, Brown.

Fox, Robin, 1967: *Kinship and Marriage: An Anthropological Perspective,* Baltimore: Penguin.

Frake, Charles O., 1964: "A Structural Description of Subanun 'Religious Behavior,'" in Ward Goodenough (editor), *Explorations in Cultural Anthropology,* New York: McGraw-Hill, pp. 111–130.

Frazer, Sir James George, 1911–1915: *The Golden Bough: A Study in Magic and Religion,* Third Edition, 12 Vols., London: Macmillan.

Freilich, Morris (editor), 1972: *The Meaning of Culture: A Reader in Cultural Anthropology,* Lexington: Xerox College.

Gibbs, James L. Jr., 196: "The Kpelle Moot: A Therapeutic Model for the Informal Settlement of Disputes," *Africa, 33* (1), pp. 1–11.

Gleason, H. A., 1961: *Introduction to Descriptive Linguistics,* New York: Holt, Rinehart and Winston.

Gluckman, Max, 1955: *The Judicial Process Among the Barotse of Northern Rhodesia*, Manchester: Manchester University Press.

———, 1962: "Les Rites de Passage," in *Essays on the Ritual of Social Relations*, Manchester: Manchester University Press.

Goffman, Erving, 1959: *The Presentation of Self in Everyday Life*, New York: Overlook Press.

Golde, P. (editor), 1970: *Women in the Field: Anthropological Experiences*, Chicago: Aldine.

Goodenough, Ward H., 1957: "Cultural Anthropology and Linguistics," Georgetown University Monograph Series on Language and Linguistics, No. 9, pp. 167–173.

———, 1963: *Cooperation in Change*, New York: Russell Sage.

———, 1965: "Rethinking 'Status' and 'Role': Toward a General Model of the Cultural Organization of Social Relationships," in Michael Banton (editor), *The Relevance of Models for Social Anthropology*, New York: Praeger, pp. 1–22.

———, 1970: *Description and Comparison in Cultural Anthropology*, Chicago: Aldine.

Greenberg, Joseph H., 1968: *Anthropological Linguistics: An Introduction*, New York: Random House.

Gumperz, John and Dell Hymes (editors), 1972: *Directions in Sociolinguistics: The Ethnography of Communication*, New York: Holt, Rinehart and Winston.

Hall, Edward T., 1959: *The Silent Language*, New York: Doubleday.

———, 1966: *The Hidden Dimension*, Garden City, N.Y.: Doubleday.

Hallowell, A. Irving, 1955 (reissued 1988): *Culture and Experience,* Prospect Heights, IL: Waveland Press, Inc.

Hardgrave, Robert L., Jr., 1969: *The Nadars of Tamilnad: The Political Culture of a Community in Change*, Berkeley: University of California Press.

Harner, Michael J., 1973: *The Jivaro: People of the Sacred Waterfalls*, Garden City, N.Y.: Doubleday/Anchor.

Harris, Marvin, 1966: "The Cultural Ecology of India's Sacred Cattle," *Current Anthropology*, 7, pp. 51–56.

———, 1968: "Emics, Etics and the New Ethnography," Chapter 20 of *The Rise of Anthropological Theory: A History of Theories of Culture*, New York: Crowell, pp. 568–604.

———, 1974: *Cows, Pigs, Wars & Witches: The Riddles of Culture*, New York: Vintage.

Hoebel, E. Adamson, 1954: *The Law of Primitive Man*, Cambridge: Harvard University Press.

Honigmann, John, 1959: *The World of Man*, New York: Harper.

Hughes, Charles, 1960: *An Eskimo Village in the Modern World*, Ithaca, N.Y.: Cornell University Press.

Hymes, Dell (editor), 1964: *Language in Culture and Society: A Reader in Linguistics and Anthropology*, New York: Harper & Row.

——— (editor), 1969: *Reinventing Anthropology*, New York: Random House.

Jackson, H. A. (editor), 1968: *Social Stratification*, London: Cambridge University Press.

Kimball, Solon and James B. Watson (editors), 1972: *Crossing Cultural Boundaries*, San Francisco: Chandler.

Kluckhohn, Clyde, Florence R. Kluckhohn, and Fred L. Stodtbeck, 1961: *Variations in Value Orientations*, Evanston, Ill.: Row, Peterson.

Kolenda, Pauline, 1978 (reissued 1985): *Caste in Contemporary India: Beyond Organic Solidarity*, Prospect Heights, IL: Waveland Press, Inc.

Kupferer, Harriet J., 1966: "Impotency and Power: A Cross-Cultural Comparison of the Effect of Alien Rule," in Victor W. Turner, Arther Tuden, and Marc J. Swartz (editors), *Political Anthropology*, Chicago: Aldine.

Leach, Edmund R. (editor), 1960: *Aspects of Caste in South India, Ceylon and Northwest Pakistan*, Cambridge: Cambridge University Press.

LeClair, Edward E., Jr. and Harold K. Schneider, 1968: *Economic Anthropology: Readings in Theory and Analysis*, New York: Holt, Rinehart and Winston.

Lee, Richard B. and Irven DeVore (editors), 1968: *Man the Hunter*, Chicago: Aldine.

Lenski, Gerhard, 1966: *Power and Privilege: A Theory of Social Stratification*, New York: McGraw-Hill.

Leslie, Charles, 1960: *Now We Are Civilized: A Study of the World View of the Zapotec Indians of Mitla, Oaxaca*, Detroit: Wayne State University Press.

Lessa, William A. and Evon Z. Vogt (editors), 1972: *Reader in Comparative Religion: An Anthropological Approach*, Third Edition, New York: Harper & Row.

Lewis, Oscar, 1951: *Life in a Mexican Village: Tepoztlan Restudied*, Urbana, Ill.: University of Illinois Press.

_____, 1961: *The Children of Sanchez: Autobiography of a Mexican Family*, New York: Vantage.

_____, 1964: *Pedro Martinez: A Mexican Peasant and His Family*, New York: Vantage.

_____, 1965: *Village Life in Northern India*, New York: Vantage.

_____, 1970: *A Death in the Sanchez Family*, New York: Vantage.

Linton, Ralph, 1933: *The Tanala: A Hill Tribe of Madagascar*, Field Museum of Natural History, Anthropological Series, 22.

_____, 1936: *The Study of Man*, New York: Appleton-Century.

Mair, Lucy, 1962: *Primitive Government*, Harmondsworth, England: Penguin Books.

Martindale, Don (editor), 1965: *Functionalism in the Social Sciences*, American Academy of Political and Social Science, Philadelphia.

McCurdy, David W., 1964: *A Bhil Village of Rajasthan*, Ph.D. Dissertation, Department of Anthropology, Cornell University, Ann Arbor: University Microfilms.

_____, 1971, "Spirit Possession and the Natural Divine World Among the Bhils of Southern Rajasthan," in Mario D. Zamora, J. Michael Mahar, and Henry Orenstein (editors), *Themes in Culture*, Quezon City, Philippines: Kayumanggi Publishers, pp. 119–134.

_____, 1974: "Saving on Loans in Tribal India," in James P. Spradley and David W. McCurdy (editors), *Conformity and Conflict: Readings in Cultural Anthropology*, Boston: Little, Brown, pp. 428–438.

_____ and James P. Spradley (editors), 1979 (reissued 1987): *Issues in Cultural Anthropology: Selected Readings*, Prospect Heights, IL: Waveland Press, Inc.

Meggitt, Mervyn, 1964: "Male-Female Relationships in the Highlands of Australian New Guinea," in James B. Watson (editor), *New Guinea: The Central Highlands*, American Anthropologist, 66 (4), pp. 204–224.

_____, 1977: *Blood Is Their Argument*, Palo Alto, Calif.: Mayfield.

Middleton, John (editor), 1967a: *Magic, Witchcraft and Curing*, Garden City, N.Y.: Natural History Press.

_____ (editor), 1967b: *Gods and Rituals: Readings in Religious Beliefs and Practices*, Garden City, N.Y.: Natural History Press.

_____ (editor), 1967c: *Myth and Cosmos: Readings in Mythology and Symbolism*, Garden City, N.Y.: Natural History Press.

Murdock, George Peter, 1949: *Social Structure*, New York: Macmillan.

Nadel, S. F., 1957: *The Theory of Social Structure*, New York: Free Press.

Nader, Laura (editor), 1965: *The Ethnography of Law*, American Anthropologist, 67 (6), Part 2.

_____ (editor), 1969a: *Law in Culture and Society*, Chicago: Aldine.

_____, 1969b: "Styles of Court Procedure: To Make the Balance," in Laura Nader (editor), *Law in Culture and Society*, Chicago: Aldine.

Nash, Manning, 1966: *Primitive and Peasant Economic Systems*, San Francisco: Chandler.

Niehoff, Arthur H. (editor), 1966: *A Casebook of Social Change*, Chicago: Aldine.

Norbeck, Edward, 1961: *Religion in Primitive Society*, New York: Harper & Row.

Oberg, Kalvero, 1954: "Culture Shock," originally released in mimeograph form. Reprint No. A-329, Bobbs-Merrill Reprint Series in the Social Sciences, Indianapolis: Bobbs-Merrill.

Opler, Morris E., 1941: *An Apache Life-Way: The Economic, Social, and Religious Institutions of the Chiricahua Indians*, Chicago: University of Chicago Press.

Pasternak, Burton, 1976: *Introduction to Kinship and Social Organization*, Englewood Cliffs, N.J.: Prentice-Hall.

Pelto, Pertti J., 1970: *Anthropological Research: The Structure of Inquiry*, New York: Harper & Row.

_____, 1973 (reissued 1987 with changes): *The Snowmobile Revolution: Technology and Social Change in the Arctic,* Prospect Heights, IL: Waveland Press, Inc.

Pfeiffer, John, 1977: *The Emergence of Society: A Prehistory of the Establishment*, New York: McGraw-Hill.

Piddington, Ralph, 1960: "Action Anthropology," *Journal of the Polynesian Society*, 69.

Polanyi, Michael, 1966: *The Tacit Dimension*, Garden City, N.Y.: Doubleday.

Pospisil, Leopold, 1971: *Anthropology of Law*, New York: Harper & Row.

Radcliffe-Brown, A. R. and Meyer Fortes (editors), 1950: *African Systems of Kinship and Marriage*, New York: Oxford University Press.

Read, Kenneth E., 1965: *The High Valley*, New York: Scribner.

Redfield, Robert, 1953: *The Primitive World and Its Transformations*, Ithaca, N.Y.: Cornell University Press.

Rivers, W. H. R., 1910: "The Genealogical Method in Anthropological Inquiry," *Sociological Review*, 3, pp. 1–12.

Roberts, John M., 1965: "Oaths, Autonomic Ordeals, and Power," *American Anthropologist*, 67 (6), Part 2, pp. 186–212.

Sahlins, Marshall, 1964: "Culture and Environment: The Study of Cultural Ecology" in Sol Tax (editor), *Horizons in Anthropology*, Chicago: Aldine, pp. 132–147.

Schiller, R., 1968: "Snowmobiles: The Cats That Conquered Winter," *Reader's Digest*, 90, pp. 49–54.

Schneider, David M. and Kathleen Gough (editors), 1961: *Matrilineal Kinship*, Berkeley: University of California Press.

Schneider, Harold K., 1974 (reissued 1989): *Economic Man: The Anthropology of Economics*, Salem, WI: Sheffield Publishing Co.

Schneider, Louis and Charles Bojean (editors), 1973: *The Idea of Culture in the Social Sciences*, London: Cambridge University Press.

Schusky, Ernest L., 1972: *Manual for Kinship Analysis*, Second Edition, New York: Holt, Rinehart and Winston.

Shapera, I., 1967: *Government and Politics in Tribal Societies*, New York: Schocken.

Spindler, George D. (editor), 1970 (reissued 1986): *Being an Anthropologist: Fieldwork in Eleven Cultures*, Prospect Heights, IL: Waveland Press, Inc.

Spiro, Melford E. (editor), 1965: *Context and Meaning in Cultural Anthropology*, New York: Free Press.

Spradley, James P., 1968: "A Cognitive Analysis of Tramp Behavior," *Proceedings of the 8th International Congress of Anthropological and Ethnological Sciences*, Tokyo: Japan Science Council.

_____, 1969: *Guests Never Leave Hungry: The Autobiography of James Sewid, A Kwakiutl Indian*, New Haven: Yale University Press.

_____, 1970: *You Owe Yourself a Drunk: An Ethnography of Urban Nomads*, Boston: Little, Brown.

_____, 1971: "Beating the Drunk Charge," in James P. Spradley and David W. McCurdy (editors), *Conformity and Conflict: Readings in Cultural Anthropology*, Boston: Little, Brown, pp. 351–358.

_____, 1972a: "Adaptive Strategies of Urban Nomads: The Ethnoscience of Tramp Culture," in Thomas Weaver and Douglas White (editors), *The Anthropological Study of Urban Environments*, Society for Applied Anthropology Monograph 11, pp. 21–38.

_____, 1972b: "Down and Out on Skid Row," in Saul D. Feldman and Gerald D. Thielbar (editors), *Life Styles in America: Diversity in American Society*, Boston: Little, Brown, pp.

_____ (editor), 1972c (reissued 1987): *Culture and Cognition: Rules, Maps, and Plans*, Prospect Heights, IL: Waveland Press, Inc.

_____ and Janice Allen, 1973: "Doing Dope: An Ethnographic Study," unpublished manuscript, Saint Paul, Minn.: Macalester College.

_____ and Brenda Mann, 1975: *The Cocktail Waitress: Woman's Work in a Man's World*, New York: Wiley.

_____ and David W. McCurdy, 1972 (reissued 1988): *The Cultural Experience: Ethnography in Complex Society*, Prospect Heights, IL: Waveland Press, Inc.

_____ and David W. McCurdy, 1974: *Conformity and Conflict: Readings in Cultural Anthropology*, Second Edition, Boston: Little, Brown.

_____ and Mark Phillips, 1972: "Culture and Stress: A Quantitative Analysis," *American Anthropologist*, 74 (3), pp. 518–529.

_____, 1979: *The Ethnographic Interview*, New York: Holt, Rinehart and Winston.

_____, 1980: *Participant Observation*, New York: Holt, Rinehart and Winston.

Swartz, Marc J. (editor), 1968: *Local-Level Politics*, Chicago: Aldine.

_____, Victor W. Turner, and Arther Tuden (editors), 1966: *Political Anthropology*, Chicago: Aldine.

Tax, Sol, 1958: "The Fox Project," *Human Organization*, 17, pp. 17–19.

Uchendu, Victor C., 1965: *The Igbo of Southeast Nigeria*, New York: Holt, Rinehart and Winston.

Van Gennep, Arnold, 1960: *The Rites of Passage*, Chicago: University of Chicago Press.

Vayda, A. P. (editor), 1970: *Environment and Cultural Behavior: Ecological Studies in Cultural Anthropology*, Garden City, N.Y.: Natural History Press.

Wallace, Anthony F. C., 1970: *Culture and Personality*, Second Edition, New York: Random House.

Watch Tower Bible and Tract Society, 1937: *Enemies*, Brooklyn, N.Y.: Watch Tower Bible and Tract Society of New York.

———, 1965: *Things in Which It Is Impossible for God to Lie*, Brooklyn, N.Y.: Watch Tower Bible and Tract Society of New York.

———, 1967: *Did Man Get Here by Evolution or by Creation?* Brooklyn, N.Y.: Watch Tower Bible and Tract Society of New York.

———, 1968: *The Truth That Leads to Eternal Life*, Brooklyn, N.Y.: Watch Tower Bible and Tract Society of New York.

White, Leslie A. and Beth Dillingham, 1973: *The Concept of Culture*, Minneapolis: Burgess.

Wilson, Monica, 1951 (reissued 1987): *Good Company,* Prospect Hgts, IL: Waveland Press.

Wolf, Margery, 1968: *The House of Lim: A Study of a Chinese Farm Family*, New York: Appleton-Century-Crofts.

Worsley, Peter, 1968: *The Trumpet Shall Sound: A Study of "Cargo" Cults in Melanesia*, Second Augmented Edition, New York: Schocken.

Yinger, John M., 1957: *Religion, Society, and the Individual An Introduction to the Sociology of Religion,* New York: Macmillan.

GLOSSARY

A

academic anthropology: any use of anthropological knowledge to inform, enlighten, or increase the understanding of some individual or group.

achieved status: status assigned on the basis of special qualities, often through competition and individual ability.

action anthropology: any use of anthropological knowledge for planned change by the local cultural group itself.

adaptation: the process of coping with a specific physical, biological, and social environment to meet the fundamental requirements for survival.

adjustment anthropology: any use of anthropological knowledge that makes social interaction between persons who operate with different cultural codes more predictable.

administrative anthropology: the use of anthropological knowledge for planned change by those who are external to the local cultural group.

advocate anthropology: any use of anthropological knowledge by the anthropologist to increase the power of self-determination for a particular cultural group.

affinal kin: kin who are related by marriage.

age grades: the cultural categories that identify the stages of biological maturation.

age sets: the organized groups of persons who are in the same or adjacent age grades.

agnatic descent: see patrilineal descent.

agriculture: intensive farming in which fields are regularly cultivated using draft animals, plows, fertilizer, and irrigation.

allocation of resources: the knowledge people use to assign rights to the ownership and use of resources.

analysis: the process of isolating the constituent parts of a configuration.

analytic concept: any concept that is part of the ethnographer's culture and is employed to describe or explain the experiences and social behavior of other people.

Anthropoidia: suborder of primates that includes New and Old World monkeys, apes, and humans.

anthropology: the science of human beings.

applied anthropology: any use of anthropological knowledge to influence social interaction, to maintain or change social institutions, or to direct the course of cultural change.

arranged marriage: marriage arranged by the bride and groom's parents or other designated relatives.

ascribed status: statuses assigned to individuals without reference to their innate differences or abilities.

associations: groups based on common interest, shared purpose, or some attribute such as age or sexual gender.

attributional rank: the social position of individuals or groups based on their association with other ranked items and behavior.

authority: the right to make and enforce public policy.

avunculocal residence: the form of residence in which a married couple goes to live with the groom's maternal uncle.

B

band: the basic local unit of nomads who hunt and gather.

bilateral descent: a rule of descent relating someone to a group of kin through both males and females.

bilateral descent group: any group based on a bilateral (cognatic) rule of descent.

bilocal residence: the form of residence in which a newly married couple goes to live with the parents of the groom or those of the bride.

biological want: any need related to a person's own physical well-being.

C

caste stratification: stratification defined by unequal access to both economic resources and prestige, which is acquired at birth and does not permit individuals to alter their rank.

category: a group of objects or events that are different but treated as if they are equivalent.

clan: a group, normally comprising several lineages, the members of which are related by a unilineal descent rule, but that is too large to enable members to trace actual biological links that tie them to one another.

class stratification: stratification defined by unequal access to both economic resources and prestige, but permitting individuals to alter their rank within the system.

coercion: support that is based on the threat or use of force or other adverse action, or the promise of short-term benefit.

cognatic descent: see bilateral descent.

cognatic descent groups: see bilateral descent groups.

commensality: rules that govern who may dine with whom.

communicative competence: the knowledge that people have acquired that enables them to generate and interpret symbolic messages that are grammatical, meaningful, and appropriate.

community: the largest group of persons who normally reside together in face-to-face association.

configuration: the pattern of interrelationships among all the major elements of a culture.

conflict groups: any groups that contend with each other over the formulation and application of public policy.

consanguine kin: kin who share common ancestry.

contagious magic: formulas applied to something in order to affect something else that is closely related to it.

contest: game of skill in which two parties engage in mental or physical combat according to rules.

context: the network of customs that are immediately linked to a particular cultural practice.

contrast: a principle of meaning in which what something does mean is intimately linked to what it does not mean. Contrast focuses on the differences among concepts.

contrast set: a group of terms in a taxonomy that are all included in a single term at the next higher level.

core value: the most general concepts of desirable and undesirable states of affairs.

court: a formal setting involving designated officials with the authority to settle disputes and enforce decisions.

cover terms: linguistic labels for large categories.

cross-cousins: children of ego's father's sister or ego's mother's brother.

cross-cultural: literally "between cultures," referring to situations where one compares two or more cultures.

Crow terminology: a system of kinship terminology in which ego's parallel cousins are classed with his siblings, his father's sister's daughter is called by the same term as his father's sister, and his father's sister's son is called by the same term as his father's brother.

cultural adaptation: the process of coping culturally with a specific physical, biological, and social environment to meet the fundamental requirements for survival.

cultural ecology: the study of the way people use their culture to adapt to particular environments, the effects they have on their natural surroundings, and the impact of the environment on the shape of culture.

cultural environment: the categories and rules people use to classify and explain their physical environment.

cultural integration: the way conflicting cultural elements are organized to minimize contradictions.

cultural selection: the fact that each culture utilizes only a limited segment of possible behavior.

cultural value: see value.

culture: the acquired knowledge that people use to interpret experience and to generate social behavior.

culture change: the process by which some members of a society revise their cultural knowledge and use it to generate and interpret new forms of social behavior.

culture shock: a form of anxiety that results from an inability to predict the behavior of others or act appropriately in a cross-cultural situation.

D

descent: a cultural rule of relationship that ties together people who may or may not actually be relatives, on the basis of reputed common ancestry.

descent group: any group based on a rule of descent.

detached observation: an approach to scientific inquiry stressing emotional detachment and the construction of categories by the observer in order to classify what is seen.

distribution: the strategies for apportioning goods or services among the members of a group.

divination: the use of supernatural force to provide answers to questions.

division of labor: the rules that govern the assignment of jobs to people.

duolocal residence: the form of residence in which a bride and groom each continue to reside with their own parents after their marriage.

E

ecology: the study of the way organisms interact with each other within an environment.

economic system: the provision of goods

and services to meet biological and social wants.

ecosystem: the plants, animals, and natural features that form an interrelated system within a particular environment.

egalitarian societies: societies that, with the exception of ranked differences between men and women and adults and children, provide all people an equal chance at economic resources and prestige.

endogamy: marriage within a designated social unit.

environmental determinism: the theory claiming that the environment causes particular forms of culture.

environmental possibilism: a theory, expressed by early American anthropologists such as Kroeber, that saw the environment as a limiting, but not determining, factor in shaping culture.

Eskimo terminology: a system of kinship terminology in which lineal relatives are distinguished from collateral relatives.

ethnocentrism: a mixture of belief and feeling that your own way of life is desirable and actually superior to others.

ethnographic present: the description of a culture at one point in time, giving the impression that the account is reliable for any period in the past or future.

ethnography: the task of describing a particular culture.

ethnology: the task of classifying, comparing, and exploring cross-cultural differences and similarities.

ethos: the dominant emotional tone.

exogamy: marriage outside any designated social unit.

explicit culture: the culture about which people discuss, explain, and talk.

extended family: a family that includes two or more married couples.

extralegal dispute: when disputes remain outside the process of law but develop into repeated acts of violence between groups, they become extralegal disputes.

F

faction: a conflict group that exists solely for the purpose of contesting public policy and that represents divisions of existing social groups.

family: a residential group composed of at least one married couple and their children.

feuds: violent extralegal conflicts that occur between subgroups of the same society.

fictive kinship: kinship identities and roles used between persons who are not linked by marriage or descent.

fieldwork: the firsthand experience of studying a culture including all the activities that are necessary when anthropologists go to a new society to discover and describe the cultural knowledge of the people there.

folk concept: any concept that is locally defined by members of a society, thus making up part of their cultural knowledge.

friendship: an informal relationship based on common interests, personal affinity, and mutual obligations.

function: the consequences of a particular cultural practice.

function of law: all the consequences of a particular legal system and the relationships between law and other cultural systems.

G

genealogical method: a method for discovering kin terms and mapping social relationships.

generation set: an organized group of persons who are in the same generation and are usually divided into age sets.

go-between: an individual who arranges agreements and mediates disputes.

government: a political group composed of political specialists and associated with a state.

grammar: the categories and rules for combining vocal symbols.

H

Hawaiian terminology: a type of kin term system that assigns two kin terms to each generation, one for males and one for females.

holistic perspective: understanding something by viewing it within its general context.

horticulture: the process of semi-intensive farming with hand tools such as the digging stick.

hunting and gathering: the process of food getting in which people employ techniques and tools to hunt and collect wild, naturally occurring foods.

I

ideal culture: knowledge about what people ought to do.

identification: the process of equating concepts from separate configurations.

imitative magic: formulas that imitate the ends sought by a magician.

impersonal world view: a view of the world that is based on nonpersonal causative factors, such as the scientific world view.

incest taboo: the cultural rule that prohibits sexual intercourse from occurring between specified classes of relatives.

incorporation: the last stage in a rite of passage.

informants: people who teach their culture to anthropologists.

infralegal disputes: any dispute that is below the level of the legal process.

innovation: a recombination of concepts from two or more mental configurations into a new pattern that is qualitatively different from existing forms.

integration: the process of adjustments that occur as a consequence of adopting an innovation.

interactional rank: the social position of individuals or groups signaled by unequal privilege and by priority in social interaction.

interest group: a conflict group that forms specifically around political issues.

inverted ethnocentrism: an overcommitment to a set of values belonging to another culture.

Iroquois terminology: a system of kin terminology in which parallel cousins are called by different terms from cross-cousins.

K

key informants: individuals whom anthropologists interview regularly and learn most from.

kinship: the complex system of social relationships based on marriage (affinity) and birth (consanguinity).

kinship system: the cultural knowledge for generating and interpreting interaction among kinsmen.

kinship terms: the terms employed to address or refer to different sets of kinsmen.

L

language: the system of cultural knowledge used to generate and interpret speech.

language competence: the possession of rules for encoding and decoding speech messages.

latent function: the unintended and unrecognized consequences of a cultural practice.

law: the cultural knowledge that people use to settle disputes by means of agents who have recognized authority.

leadership: anyone who is able to influence the members of a group to act together is a leader.

legal disputes: those cases that are settled by people or groups with authority.

legal ethnocentrism: the tendency to view the law of other cultures through the concepts and assumptions of Western law.

legal levels: the different levels of authority in a society that have power to settle disputes.

legal principles: a broad conception of some desirable state of affairs that gives rise to many substantive and procedural rules.

legitimacy: support that is derived from people's positive evaluation of public officials and public policy.

levirate: marriage of a man with his dead brother's widow.

life history method: the taking of autobiographical material from an informant.

lineage: a group of kin related to each other by a unilineal descent rule from a common ancestor. Normally the group is small enough for its members to be able to trace their actual relationship with one another.

M

magic: the strategies people use to control supernatural power.

mana: impersonal supernatural force inherent in nature and in people.

manifest function: the function of something recognized by the members of a society themselves.

market exchange: the transfer of goods and services based on price, supply, and demand.

marketless economy: an economy characterized by self-production and use, and reciprocity and redistribution.

marriage: the socially recognized union between a man and a woman that accords legitimate birth status rights to their children.

matrilineal descent: a rule of descent relating ego to a group of consanguine kin on the basis of descent through females only.

matrilocal residence: the residence rule requiring a newly married couple to live with or nearby the parents of the bride.

matri-patrilocal residence: the form of residence in which a married couple lives first with the parents of the bride, then permanently with those of the groom.

maximal territorial group: the largest, most inclusive territory and the people who live there.

men's and women's associations: groups and clubs that restrict their membership to one sex.

mental configuration: any cluster of concepts that are organized into a unified pattern of experience.

military societies: groups whose members have a common interest in warfare or a common experience in combat.

money: a market device designed to facilitate exchange by acting as a medium for it.

monogamy: marriage form in which a person has only one spouse at a time.

moot: community meeting held for the informal hearing of a dispute.

morpheme: the smallest meaningful category in any language.

myth: stories that reveal the religious knowledge of how things have come into being.

N

naïve realism: the notion that reality is much the same for all people everywhere.

natural laboratory: the human communities where people live.

neighborhood: the people and places located adjacent to and nearby a particular person or family.

neolocal residence: the form of residence in which a newly married couple establishes a new residence separate from the parents of either spouse.

nomadism: regular seasonal or cyclical movements of groups from one locale to another.

nuclear family: a family composed of a married couple and their children.

O

Omaha terminology: a system of kinship terminology in which ego's parallel cousins are classed with his siblings, his mother's brother's son is called by the same term as his mother's brother, and his mother's brother's daughter is terminologically classed with his mother's sister.

ordeal: a supernaturally controlled, painful or physically dangerous test, the outcome of which determines a person's guilt or innocence.

P

paradigm: an arrangement of a set of terms that share at least one feature of meaning. The arrangement shows the attributes that distinguish the members of the set and thus reveals similarities and differences.

parallel cousins: children of ego's mother's sister or ego's father's brother.

participant observation: participating in the activities of another society as a technique for cultural discovery.

pastoralism: a form of food getting based on maintenance and utilization of large herds of animals.

patrilineal descent: a rule of descent relating consanguine kin on the basis of descent through males only.

patrilocal residence: the residence rule that stipulates that a newly married couple will go to live with or nearby the parents of the groom.

performance: activities of interpreting experience and generating social behavior. Contrasts with competence.

personal world view: a world view based on the belief that personal beings are a major causative force in the universe.

phenomenal order: events, artifacts, and behavior that can be observed and counted.

phonemes: the minimal categories of speech sounds that signal a difference in meaning.

phonology: the categories and rules for forming vocal symbols.

phratry: groups composed of two or more clans. Members acknowledge unilineal descent from a common ancestor but recognize that their relationship is distant.

physical environment: the world as people experience it with their senses.

policy: any guideline that can lead directly to action.

political process: the events and actions that lead to the formulation and enforcement of public policy.

political system: the process of making and carrying out public policy according to cultural categories and rules.

polyandry: a form of polygamy in which a woman has two or more husbands at one time.

polygamy: marriage form in which a person has two or more spouses at one time.

polygyny: a form of polygamy in which a man has two or more wives at one time.

postmarital residence rules: rules that govern where a couple will live following their marriage.

potlatch: a ritual held by the Kwakiutl and some other Indians of the Northwest Coast of North America, marked by extensive gift giving as a way to validate status.

prayer: a petition directed at a supernatural power.

prestige: an attribute of personal worth measured by the degree of deference someone receives.

priests: religious specialists who intervene between people and the supernatural, often leading congregations at regular cyclical rites.

primata: order of mammals containing the prosimii, Old and New World monkeys, apes, and humans.

primatologists: scientists, many of whom are trained anthropologists, who study primates.

primogeniture: inheritance by the eldest son in the family.

private ownership: individual rights to property that are exclusive and relatively complete.

procedural law: the agreed-on ways to settle a dispute.

productivity: the capacity to comprehend instantly utterances never heard before and to generate novel utterances never heard before.

projective testing: a type of psychological testing that employs unstructured visual pictures, such as inkblot figures, as a stimulus.

prototype configuration: the original pattern of ideas that is ultimately reorganized and changed.

puberty rite: a rite of passage that occurs, in some societies, when youths become adults.

public: the people that a policy will affect.

R

rammage: a cognatic descent group that is localized and holds corporate responsibility.

rank societies: societies stratified on the basis of prestige only.

rapport: the relationship of trust that occurs between an anthropologist and his informant.

real culture: knowledge about what people actually do.

reciprocal exchange: the transfer of goods and services between two people or groups based on their role obligations.

redistribution: the transfer of goods or services between a group of people and a central collecting service based on role obligation.

religion: the cultural knowledge of the supernatural that people use to cope with the ultimate problems of human existence.

rite of passage: the symbolical transition from one position to another, acting as a public announcement that someone is not what he was before the ritual.

ritual pollution and ritual purity: reference to a person's eligibility to approach the gods.

role: the culturally generated behavior associated with particular statuses.

S

sacrifice: the giving of something of value to supernatural beings or forces.

secret societies: groups that restrict their membership and maintain secrecy about their rituals, group practices, and special esoteric knowledge.

self-redress: the actions taken by an individual who has been wronged to settle a dispute.

semantics: the categories and rules for relating vocal symbols to their referents.

separation: the first stage in many rites of passage.

shamans: religious specialists who control supernatural power often to cure people or affect the course of life's events.

shifting agriculture: the form of horticulture in which fields are cleared, often burned over, planted two or three years, then permitted to revert to brush for a long period.

sib: see clan.

social acceptance: a process that involves learning about an innovation, accepting an innovation as valid, and revising one's cultural knowledge to include the innovation.

social groups: the collections of people that are organized by culturally defined rules and categories.

social interaction: systematic behavior that occurs between two or more people.

social mobility: the process of changing status in a system of stratification.

social rank: the estimation that some people and some groups are more important and socially worthwhile than others.

social relationship: a connection between two people that occurs when one acts vis-á-vis the other.

social situation: the categories and rules for arranging and interpreting the settings where social interaction occurs.

social stratification: the ranking of people or groups based on their unequal access to valued economic resources and prestige.

social structure: the part of culture that people use to generate and interpret social interaction.

society: the largest culturally organized group to which an individual belongs.

sociolinguistic rules: rules specifying the nature of the speech community, the particular speech situations within a community, and the speech acts that members use to convey their messages.

sorcery: the malevolent practices of magic.

sororate: marriage of a woman with her dead sister's husband.

soul: the spiritual essence of a person.

speech: the behavior that produces meaningful vocal sounds.

speech acts: the way utterances are used and the rules for this use.

speech community: a community that shares a specific linguistic code and the sociolinguistic rules for using and interpreting the messages generated by that code.

speech situations: a locally recognized unit of social interaction that consists of both verbal and nonverbal events.

spirit possession: the control of a person by a supernatural being in which the person becomes that being.

stateless societies: groups that lack a formal government and clear-cut territory.

states: culturally organized populations that control a specific territory.

status: a culturally defined position associated with a particular social structure.

status passage: the movement of any individual from one position in society to another.

stimulus configuration: the pattern of ideas that provides a basis for changing the prototype. Part of the process of innovation and culture change.

substantive law: the legal statutes that define right and wrong.

substitution: the process of replacing concepts in the prototype configuration with concepts from the stimulus configuration. A process of culture change.

Sudanese terminology: a system of kin terminology in which each cousin is called by a separate term.

supernatural beings: beings that are usually incorporeal and that possess supernatural force.

supernatural power: the ability of the supernatural to act.

support: anything that contributes to adoption of public policy and its enforcement.

symbol: any object or event that has been assigned meaning. It has an arbitrary relationship to its referent.

T

taboo: rules that proscribe things or activities.

tacit culture: the shared knowledge that people usually cannot communicate verbally.

technology: that part of any culture that involves the knowledge that people use to make and use tools and to extract and refine raw materials.

terms: verbal symbols.

territorial group: a group in which the members inhabit a common locality over time and recognize that they share this locality.

theme: a postulate or position, declared or implied, and usually controlling behavior or stimulating activity, which is tacitly approved or openly promoted in a society.

transition: the middle period in a rite of passage.

translation competence: the ability to translate the meanings of one culture into a form that is appropriate to another culture.

tribe: a socially organized unit that includes several local groups, occupies a common territory, shares a common name, and has a tradition of common ancestry.

U

unit of production: the group of people responsible for producing something.

uterine descent: see matrilineal descent.

uxorlocal residence: see matrilocal residence.

V

value: any concept referring to a desirable or undesirable state of affairs.

village: a community that is a political unit within a nation.

virilocal residence: see patrilocal residence.

voluntary associations: groups where membership depends on choice.

W

war: violent extralegal disputes that take place between separate political groups.

ward: a subsection of a village.

witchcraft: the activity of people who inherit the supernatural force and use it for evil purposes.

world view: the way people characteristically look out on the universe.

PHOTO CREDITS

INDEX